PIETRO FORQUET

BRIDGE WITH THE BLUE TEAM

Edited by Ron Klinger

With a Foreword by Hugh Kelsey

LONDON
VICTOR GOLLANCZ LTD
in association with
PETER CRAWLEY
1991

First published in Great Britain 1987
in association with Peter Crawley
by Victor Gollancz Ltd,
14 Henrietta Street, London WC2E 8QJ
Second impression 1991

Original Italian edition published 1971 by U. Mursia editore,
Via Tadino, 29, Milan, Italy

Translated into English by Helen Thompson

British Library Cataloguing in Publication Data
Forquet, Pietro
Bridge with the Blue Team. — (Master
bridge series)
1. Contract bridge — Tournaments
2. Contract bridge — Collections of games
I. Title II. Klinger, Ron III. Gioco
con il Blue Team. *English* IV. Series
795.41′58 GV1282.6

ISBN 0-575-04005-X

Printed in Great Britain by
St Edmundsbury Press Ltd, Bury St Edmunds, Suffolk

INTRODUCTION

This is a translation of the second edition of *Bridge With The Blue Team* in which fifty new deals were added to those of the first edition. Like the first edition, it is divided into three parts:

In the first part over 140 deals are recounted in such a way that the reader is able to compare his play with that of the members of the Blue Team.

In the second part the reader will find a succinct summary of the three bidding systems in use, which will clarify the bidding sequences adopted on the hands. Obviously those wishing to study or learn our systems will understand that these summaries are no substitute for the full original text, which would be indispensable for a complete understanding of the system in question.

In the third part the victories of the Blue Team in World Championships are recorded in chronological order from 1956, the year of the team's first appearance. In addition the results of all the Bermuda Bowl and Olympiads after the Blue Team disbanded are included up to and including 1982.

In choosing the hands I sought to avoid as far as possible repetitive themes. If I happen to appear as declarer or defender more often than some of my teammates, this is not intentional immodesty or selfishness but due solely to the fact that it was often easier for me to remember and reconstruct the play when I was personally involved.

All the hands used arose in actual competition and are faithfully and accurately reported. If on the odd occasion I changed a two to a three, it was done solely out of love for good technique and to clarify the theme involved. I trust you will consider any such instances as cases of poetic licence.

* * *

With the appearance of this work I cannot help recalling with infinite sadness the figures of two friends who passed away just a few days apart, as though linked in a tragic destiny: Eugenio Chiaradia and Carlo Alberto Perroux.

Eugenio Chiaradia was technically the mastermind behind all the aspects that made up the Blue Team. Peerless as a player and in technique, Eugenio came to be considered the founder of modern bridge. As far back as 1948 it was he who understood that the bidding systems hitherto in use were anchored to methods and conventions which were sadly deficient. Thus was born the Neapolitan Club, a system which did not excite merely a few adherents but which in subsequent and diverse versions came to be adopted in every part of the world, even in the United States, the fatherland of the natural approach.

Carlo Alberto Perroux was the creator of the Blue Team. It was he who with boundless patience succeeded in forging out of *six* players *three* pairs and in welding out of *three* pairs *one* team. His wisdom, his psychology and his imperturbable calm were without doubt behind all the successes of the Blue Team.

To two unforgettable friends I dedicate this book.

Pietro Forquet

BRIDGE WITH THE BLUE TEAM

Bridge with the Blue Team sets down the most outstanding hands played by the Blue Team, the astonishingly successful Italian team which achieved a record number of victories in world class championships, a feat unlikely ever to be equalled. The 140 chosen hands are first set out in single dummy form so that the reader may make his own decisions about how he would play the hand before reading the analysis provided. Sections at the end of the book give a summary of the bidding systems employed and a chronological account of the Blue Team's triumphal progress in world championship tournaments.

Pietro Forquet is recognised as one of the most celebrated bridge players of all time and in this book, destined to become a classic of bridge literature, he demonstrates that he would rank similarly as a bridge writer.

FOREWORD

by Hugh Kelsey

The legendary Blue Team of Italy won ten straight Bermuda Bowls and two Olympiad Team titles – a feat likely to stand for all time in the record books. Although the exploits of the players have been documented in the bridge magazines over the years, the only book that brings all the major brilliancies together is this one by Pietro Forquet, first published in Italy as *Gioco con il Blue Team*.

It is a pleasure for me to present this English edition under the banner of the *Master Bridge Series*. When I first read these stories I was quite overwhelmed by the beauty of the hands. The book seemed to me to represent the quintessence of bridge wisdom, distilled through the minds of the greatest players the world has ever seen.

Time has not changed my view. Pietro Forquet shows himself to be as gifted an author as he is a card-player. The style is smooth and flowing, the analysis logical and precise. As one magnificent deal follows another, you will gradually come to appreciate the rare qualities of the individual members of the Blue Team – Eugenio Chiaradia, Guglielmo Siniscalco, Mimmo D'Alelio, Walter Avarelli, Giorgio Belladonna, Pietro Forquet, Benito Garozzo, Camillo Pabis-Ticci, and their peerless captain, Carlo Alberto Perroux.

After reading about the wizardry of these players – the uncanny accuracy in declarer play and defence, the flair, the deceptive style, and the ability to smell out the true position of the enemy cards – you will understand what kept the Blue Team at the top of the tree for so many years. Many of the hands will be completely fresh to English readers, and there are valuable lessons to be learned at all levels. This is a book to savour over and over again, and I shall keep you no longer from your enjoyment.

An 'Impossible' Slam

In 1957 the 'Blue Team' won its first world title by defeating the United States team in New York. The match was very tight from the start and when Eugenio Chiaradia played the following slam, there was next to nothing between the two teams.

♠ Q J 7
♡ A 9 4 3
♢ 9 3 2
♣ 8 6 5

	N	
W		E
	S	

♠ A K 9 8 5
♡ K 8
♢ A Q
♣ K Q 10 2

Both sides vulnerable. The bidding:

SOUTH *Chiaradia*	WEST	NORTH *D'Alelio*	EAST
2♣	Pass	2♡	Pass
2♠	Pass	3♠	Pass
4♢	Pass	4♠	Pass
5♣	Pass	5♠	Pass
6♠	Pass	Pass	Pass

At this time Chiaradia and D'Alelio were using the conventional forcing Two Club opening. The Two Heart response showed the ace of hearts. Two Spades was natural and Three Spades promised support, at least three to a top honour. Four Diamonds and Five Clubs were cue-bids, suggesting a slam, but D'Alelio, with nothing to spare, refused partner's invitation twice.

In that light Chiaradia's final decision appears reckless. To be fair, D'Alelio did hold the absolute minimum possible for his bidding and could have made exactly the same bids with, say, four trumps to the queen or a five-card heart suit or even just the jack of clubs extra.

When Eugenio bid Six Spades, the Bridgerama commentator pointed out that the slam was absolutely unmakable and that even if Chiaradia had passed Five Spades, that contract would have presented problems.

I was a spectator in the Bridgerama auditorium and sitting beside me was our captain, Carlo Alberto Perroux. Those who did not know Perroux cannot begin to imagine what a "delight" it was to be watching a game with him next to you. To his anxious request for a prediction of the outcome of the deal, I had to disclose that the slam could not be made, even if Eugenio had been able to see all the cards. My reply did not go down well. In fact our captain immediately left the room to seek solace in a solitary stroll.

West led the queen of hearts.

How should declarer plan the play?

This was the complete deal:

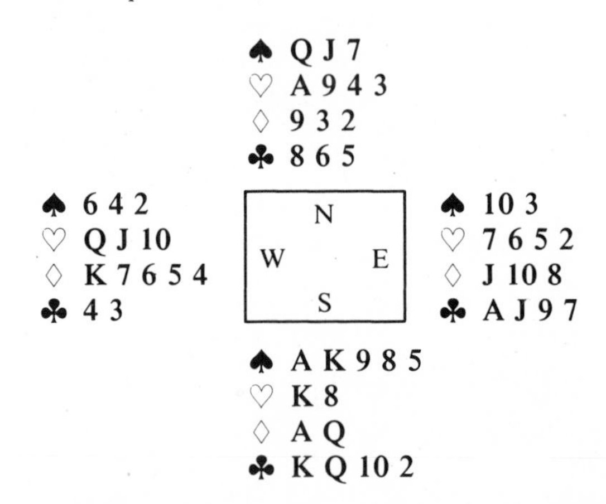

Chiaradia won the lead with the king and continued by playing the *nine* of spades to the queen and a club to the king. He followed this with the *eight* of spades to the jack. This farsighted unblocking received its just reward when the ten of spades dropped doubleton, giving declarer an additional entry to dummy via the seven of trumps.

When Chiaradia led a second club from dummy, East rose with the ace. A club return would have allowed West to ruff, defeating the slam, but as West had followed to the club leads first with the three and then with the four, East assumed his partner had *three* clubs and not *two*.

While East was thinking, Perroux returned to his seat and asked in a resigned tone, "How many down?". I replied that *if* East returned a club, the slam would be down at once, but *if* he returned a diamond, Chiaradia would be able to make his contract *if* he won it with the ace, declining to finesse for the king, *if* he crossed to dummy with the seven of spades and *if* he finessed the ten of clubs: then, *if* he cashed all his winners, he would squeeze West in diamonds and hearts. *If*, on the other hand, East brought back a heart, declarer would have difficulty in finding the winning line in that...

I never finished my analysis because Perroux, dismayed by all my *ifs*, again left his seat and went walkabout.

East did return a diamond and Chiaradia played as though he could see through the cards: ace of diamonds; five of spades to dummy's seven; club to his ten; ace of spades and the queen of clubs. This was the ending:

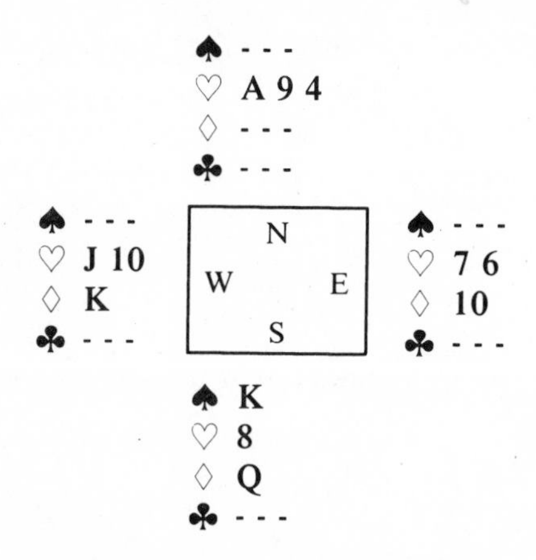

On the king of spades, West was inexorably squeezed in hearts and diamonds and thus Chiaradia had brilliantly made his slam.

Perroux again resumed his seat and, scoresheet in hand, he was serenity personified as he quietly asked, "And what score is Six Spades, vulnerable?"

A Lethal Lead

Another slam that played a decisive part in the 1957 World championship was the following:

♠ A J 9 8 4 3
♡ 5 4
◊ A
♣ K 10 7 5

N
W E
S

♠ 10 6
♡ A 8 7
◊ K Q 9 2
♣ A Q J 8

Neither side vulnerable. The bidding:

NORTH *Siniscalco*	SOUTH *Forquet*
1♠	2♣
2♠	3◊
4♣	4♡
4NT	5NT
6♣	Pass

West led the 7 of spades.

How should South plan the play?

This was the complete deal:

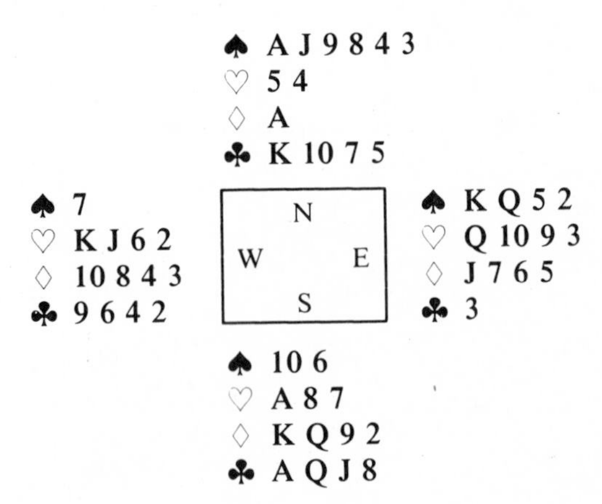

Upon winning the lead with the ace, I continued with a low spade from dummy. East won the king, West discarding the 6 of hearts, and returned the 5 of spades. I ruffed with the ace and followed with the ace of diamonds, ace of hearts, king of diamonds and queen of diamonds, discarding a heart and a spade from dummy.

This was the position:

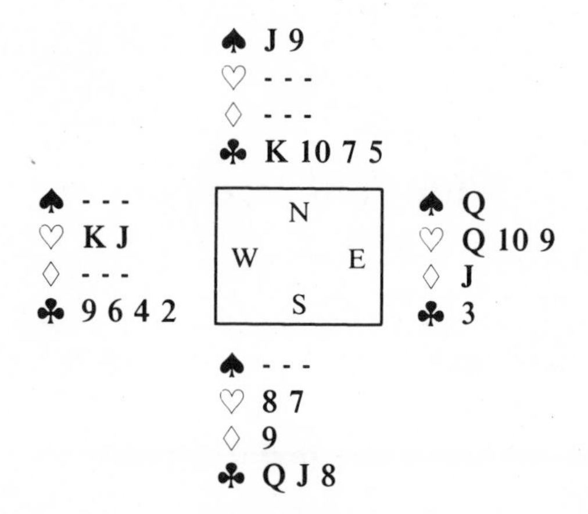

I ruffed a heart in dummy, cashed the king of clubs and continued to cross-ruff the rest of the tricks.

At the other table Giorgio Belladonna found the killing heart lead after which the slam could not be made.

Variations

If, instead of cross-ruffing, I had decided to set up dummy the 4-1 split in trumps would have beaten the contract.

If West had discarded two diamonds on the second and third round of spades and had then ruffed the queen of diamonds, I would still have come home by over-ruffing and continuing with a spade ruffed with the queen of clubs, followed by jack and another club.

Perhaps the best line, after winning with the ace of spades at trick one, would be to cash the ace of diamonds, cross to hand with the ace of hearts and continue with the king and queen of diamonds, discarding a heart and a spade. A spade then sets the stage for the cross-ruff. In this way if West had started with only three diamonds, he would not be able to discard two of them on the second and third round of spades.

At the table I elected to play spades at once in the hope (quite remote, I grant you) that West had not led a singleton (in which case I would have been able to avoid the risk of a ruff by East on the third round of diamonds). On the other hand, if West, together with a singleton spade, had started with only three diamonds, I would still have been able to succeed, provided that West had begun with no more than three trumps.

With Cards Exposed

This contract of Four Hearts, played by Eugenio Chiaradia during the 1959 European Championship at Palermo, can be planned as a double dummy problem:

♠ K 7 2
♡ Q 5 4
◊ A 5 4
♣ J 6 5 4

	N	
W		E
	S	

♠ 4 3
♡ A K 10 9 8 7 6
◊ K J
♣ K 7

Both sides vulnerable. The bidding:

WEST	NORTH	EAST	SOUTH
	Forquet		*Chiaradia*
	Pass	Pass	1♡
Pass	1NT	2♠	3♡
Pass	4♡	All pass	

West led the jack of spades and when this held, he continued with the 5. East won with the queen and returned the ace of spades. Chiaradia's first good decision was to ruff with the ace of hearts, West discarding the 2 of clubs. In view of East's known six-card spade suit, Eugenio continued with the king of hearts to guard against jack-third with West. This was his second good decision, since East discarded a spade on this trick.

On the 10 of hearts West followed low and a third round of trumps to dummy's queen cleared West's last trump.

This was the position:

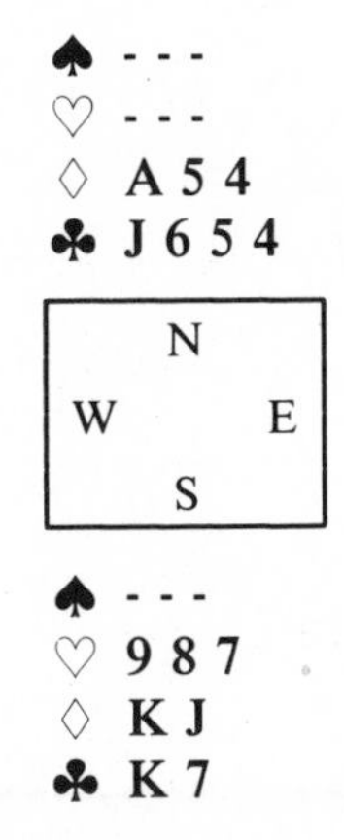

How should declarer continue?

This was the complete deal:

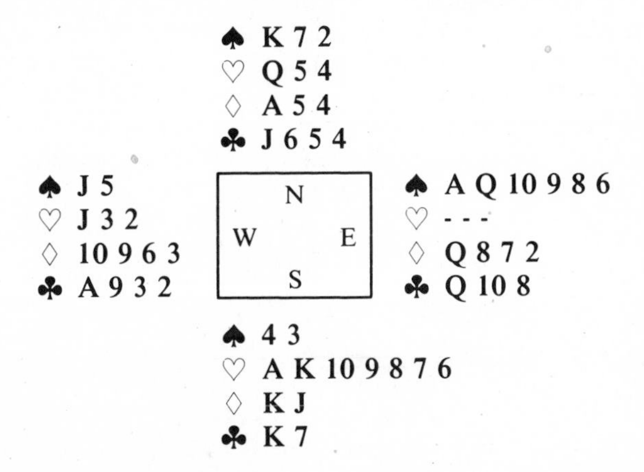

If the ace of clubs were onside the contract would be laydown, but Chiaradia discounted this possibility, since with such an excellent spade suit and the ace of clubs as well. East would no doubt have opened the bidding.

But if West held the ace of clubs, what layout would allow the contract to succeed? Had dummy had an extra entry, declarer could have finessed the jack of diamonds and later used the ace of diamonds for a club discard.

Despite the absence of an additional entry, Chiaradia led a diamond to the jack anyway. Two further rounds of hearts left the following ending:

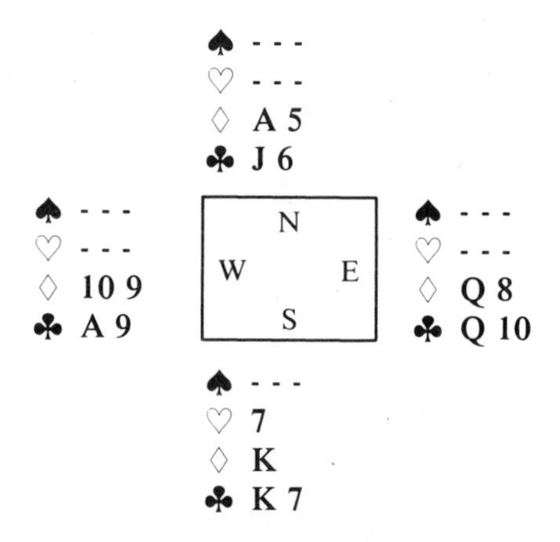

When Eugenio led the last trump West had to discard a diamond in order to keep ace-doubleton in clubs (otherwise declarer could simply lead a low club to set up the king). Dummy let go a club and East, forced to keep control of the diamonds, discarded the 10 of clubs. Chiaradia then cashed the king of diamonds and exited with the 7 of clubs. If East won with the queen, he would have to lead a diamond to dummy, while if West rose with the ace, he would be left with a club to lead to declarer's king.

Variations

If Chiaradia had not taken the diamond finesse, this would have been the ending:

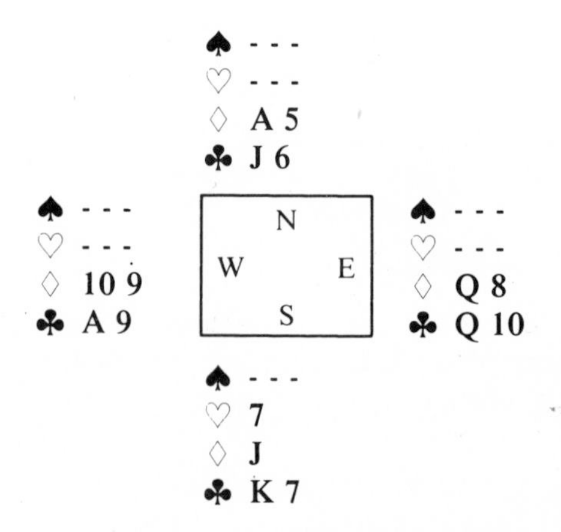

Now, on the 7 of hearts West would have discarded a diamond and North and East would have let go a club. Declarer would have been unable to avoid losing two more tricks, regardless of his line of play.

An Old Ruse But . . .

This 3 NT contract was played by Guglielmo Siniscalco during a European Championship. The theme is not new but my partner was clever enough to recognise the situation immediately and play his cards in normal rhythm so that the opponents did not have the slightest inkling of the trap about to ensnare them.

♠ 6 3 2
♡ J 7
♢ Q J 10 7
♣ K Q 10 8

N
W E
S

♠ A K J
♡ A 9
♢ A 9 8 3
♣ 9 7 6 5

Both sides vulnerable. The bidding:

WEST	NORTH	EAST	SOUTH
	Forquet		*Siniscalco*
1♠	Pass	Pass	1NT
Pass	2NT	Pass	3NT
Pass	Pass	Pass	

West led the 5 of spades and East played the 10.

How should declarer play to maximise his chances of success?

This was the complete deal:

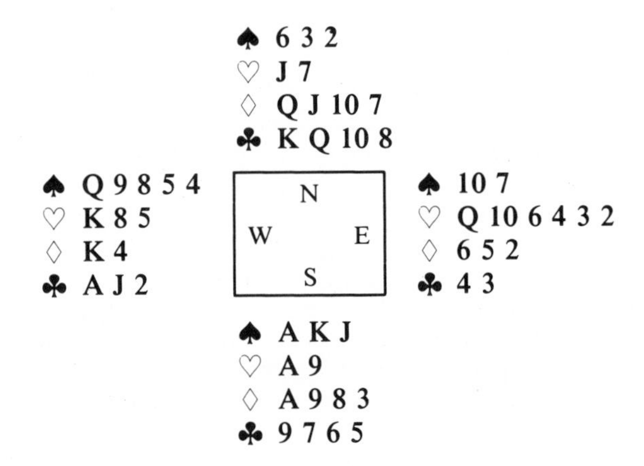

Siniscalco won East's 10 of spades with the *ace* and led a club to the king to take the diamond finesse. West, expecting partner to hold the jack of spades, returned the queen of spades (to prevent declarer ducking if East had the bare jack left). The contract was now easily made with an overtrick (3 spades, 1 heart, 3 diamonds and 3 clubs).

Had Guglielmo taken the opening lead with the jack, the defence would certainly have prevailed. As soon as West gained the lead, he would have found the killing heart switch, since he would have known that declarer had two more stoppers in spades.

Belladonna's Revenge

In 1959 the Blue Team won its third world championship after a touch-and-go match against the United States. The Italian team had a crisis in the fourth session when Giorgio Belladonna lost control of a makeable 3NT contract. This was the deal:

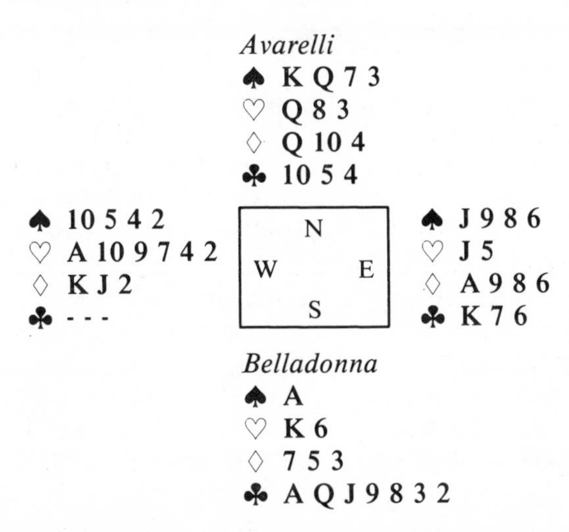

West led the 7 of hearts and Belladonna, winning the king, continued with the ace and queen of clubs (as he had no quick entry to dummy to try for the club finesse). East took the king only on the third round of clubs and returned the 5 of hearts. Giorgio followed with *the 3 of diamonds,* West inserted the 9 of hearts and dummy won the queen.

At this point Belladonna realised that he still had a heart and that he had revoked. The tournament director was called and, law book in hand, he ruled that declarer *must* replace his diamond with a heart, that West *could* change the card played and that *dummy's queen of hearts must still be played.*

Obviously West was quick to replace the 9 of hearts with the ace and poor Giorgio was forced to consign to destruction the queen previously played. The contract was thus beaten by four tricks while at the other table the American North-South made 3NT with an overtrick. Mind you, on this difficult hand Giorgio had played himself into a losing position even without the revoke. If West takes ace of hearts on the second round and returns a spade, declarer is held to 8 tricks. This incident put Belladonna completely off balance so that the session ended in favour of our opponents.

In the next session, the American captain put the same line-up in against Belladonna, but this move backfired when Giorgio, having regained his usual form and composure, was the principal engineer behind our recovery. After he had found a killing double, setting the opposition four tricks, Giorgio found a brilliant and lucky stroke on this deal:

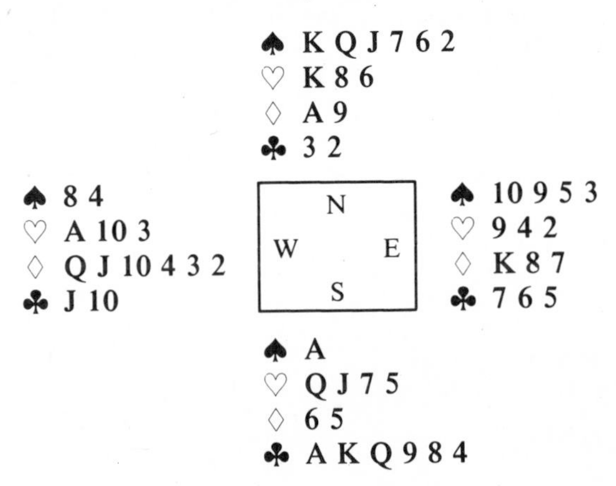

At our table the American North-South stopped in Four Spades and made eleven tricks. I marked this down as a loss since I felt certain that in the closed room Giorgio and Walter would reach the slam, a contract which, whether played in no-trumps, spades or even clubs, was inevitably doomed by the obvious diamond lead.

Contrary to the expected loss, the hand was actually a pickup for us. Belladonna did bid the small slam, did receive the diamond lead but made his contract for the diabolical Giorgio selected as the trump suit . . . *Hearts!*

Winning the lead with the ace of diamonds, Giorgio continued with the ace of spades, ace, king and queen of clubs. West did his best by ruffing with the 10 of hearts, but Belladonna overruffed, discarded a diamond on the king of spades and led the 8 of hearts, letting it run when East played low.

Reciprocal Courtesies

This Four Spade contract arose during an Italian championship:

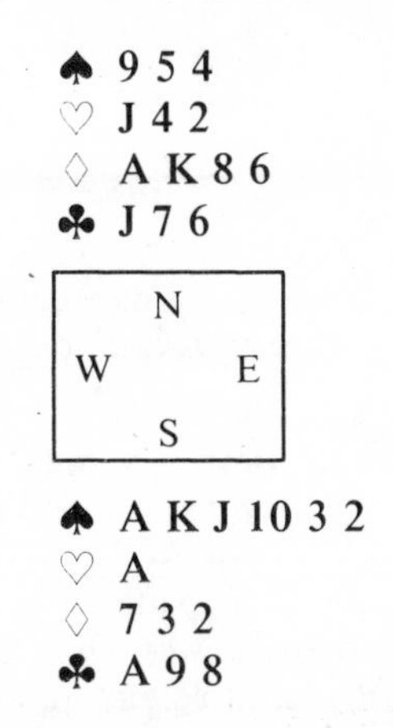

Both sides vulnerable. The bidding:

WEST	NORTH	EAST	SOUTH
	Garozzo		*Forquet*
3♡	Pass	Pass	4♠
Pass	Pass	Pass	

West led the 3 of clubs: six - ten - ace.

With two clubs and a diamond to lose, the contract seems to depend on picking up the queen of spades. In view of West's Three Heart opening, the odds favour cashing the ace of spades and if the queen has not appeared, crossing to dummy with a diamond to the ace to take the spade finesse.

When I cashed the ace of spades, lo and behold, East followed with a club. So, West had opened Three Hearts despite holding four spades to the queen.

How should South continue?

This was the complete deal:

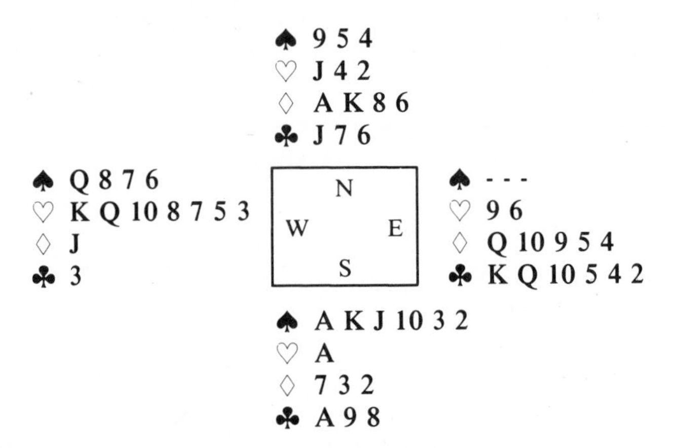

The only hope of success was to effect a diamond-club squeeze on East. For this to operate it was vital to prepare *a double rectification of the count.*

Having reached this conclusion, I cashed the ace of hearts and continued with the 2 of spades. West did best by winning the queen and returning the jack of diamonds. Winning dummy's ace, I led the jack of hearts (not the low one lest East hold the trick), discarding a club from hand. West won and put me back in dummy with the 9 of spades. I continued with a low heart on which I pitched a diamond. West won and returned a heart. After ruffing and drawing West's last trump, this ending was reached:

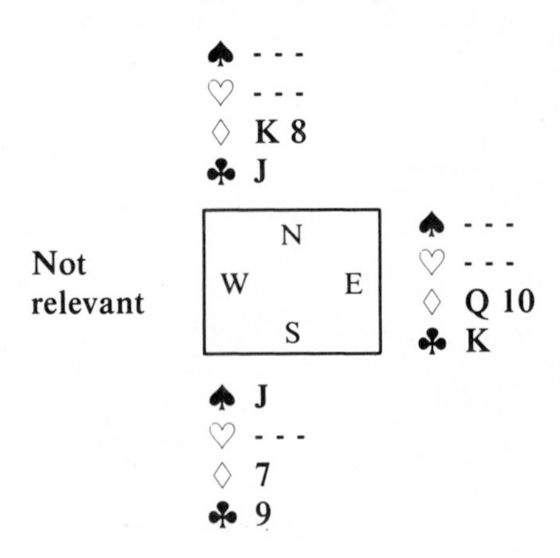

On the last trump I discarded the jack of clubs from dummy and East was duly squeezed in diamonds and clubs.

Are you satisfied with my line of play?

If you have answered in the affirmative, perhaps you would care to reconsider.

After the club lead taken by the ace, ace of spades, ace of hearts, queen of spades, ace of diamonds, jack of hearts won by the queen, spade to dummy's 9, this was the position:

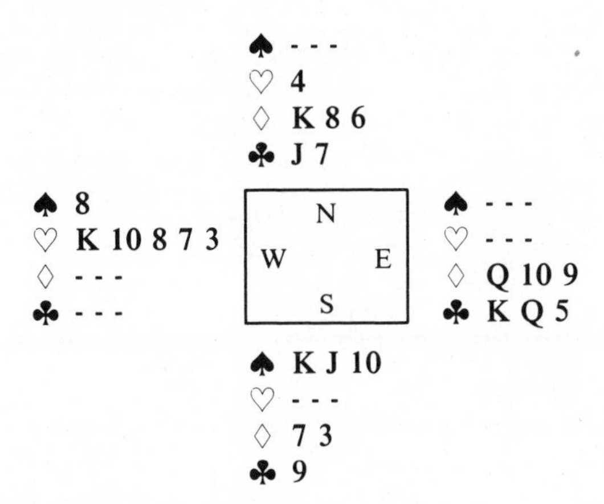

Did you spot the trap?

When South leads the 4 of hearts from dummy, pitching a diamond, West can let dummy hold the trick *by following with the 3!*

The contract must now fail as declarer is locked in dummy and cannot avoid losing two more tricks.

To avoid this the sure line is to play the 4 of hearts under the ace. Then West cannot underplay dummy's third heart, the 2.

An Avoidable Dilemma

During a pairs tournament played in Palma di Majorca, I landed in this Five Heart contract which at first glance seemed quite comfortable.

♠ K Q 7 6 5
♡ Q J 8 5
♢ 5
♣ A Q 5

	N	
W		E
	S	

♠ J
♡ K 10 7 6 4
♢ A K Q 8 7 4
♣ K

Both sides vulnerable. The bidding:

SOUTH	WEST	NORTH	EAST
Forquet		*Avarelli*	
1♡	Pass	1♠	Pass
3♢	Pass	4♡	Pass
4NT	Pass	5♢	Pass
5♡	Pass	Pass	Pass

West led the 3 of spades to East who took the ace and continued with the 10 of spades.

What would you have done in my position?

The early play had all the earmarks of a singleton lead and I therefore elected to trump with the king, a wise precaution when West played a club to this trick.

What would you have done next?

This was the complete deal:

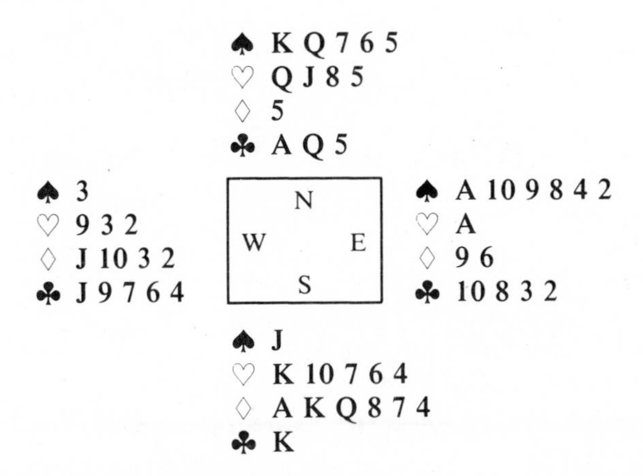

My problem was to guard against East holding the ace of hearts. (If West had the ace, my problems were over.) Had I automatically led a low heart to the queen, East upon winning the ace would have returned a spade, forcing me to choose between trumping with the 10 or with the 7. Following the odds, I would have ruffed with the 10 and then finessed dummy's 8, succeeding as the cards lie but failing if East had started with A-9 or even with A-9-x. A safer line of play was available. At trick 3 I led the king of clubs and overtook with dummy's ace in order to continue with a low heart from dummy. East rose with the ace but I was able to ruff his spade return safely with my 10.

An Unexpected Swing

When both tables play the same contract with the same opening lead and there is little choice in the play, it is rare for a swing to eventuate. This is not the case, however, when Benito Garozzo is involved.

Suppose you are my partner, East, with this layout:

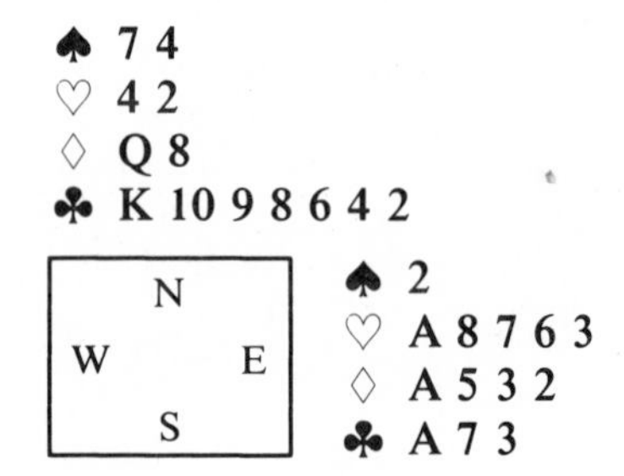

Both sides vulnerable. The bidding:

WEST	NORTH	EAST	SOUTH
Forquet		*Garozzo*	
Pass	Pass	1♡	Double
2♡	Pass	Pass	3♠
Pass	4♣	Pass	4◊
Pass	4♠	Pass	Pass
Double	Pass	Pass	Pass

West leads the 5 of hearts, taken by your ace, South following with the jack. The spade return is obvious and declarer on winning with the ace continues with the 4 of diamonds to the 7 and queen.

How do you plan the defence to achieve the best possible result?

This was the complete deal:

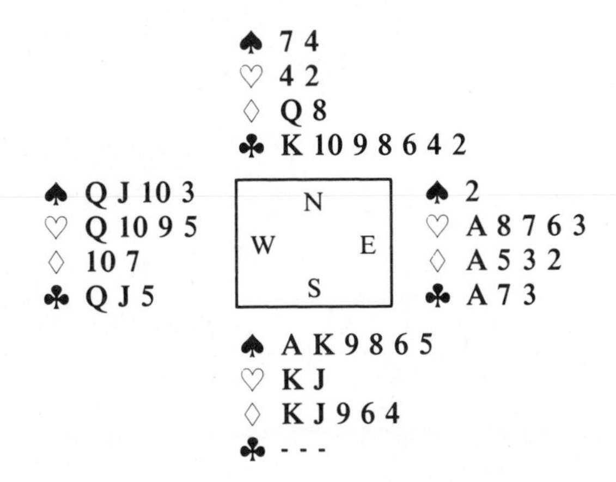

The hand arose in the 1963 World Championship during the match against the United States.

On the queen of diamonds, Benito played low and when declarer continued with the 8 of diamonds from dummy, my partner again followed low. Despite appearances, this second duck did not entail any risk. As South was marked with a spade-diamond two-suiter, the ace of diamonds could not disappear, since dummy had only one trump left.

Declarer, misled by this defence, placed the ace of diamonds with West. To restrict his losses, his problem was not to lose two diamond tricks. If West had started with A-10-x-x, nothing could be done; if he had started with A-x-x, it was vital to play an honour; finally, if West had ace-doubleton originally, it would be necessary to insert the 9. As this last play would also work if East started with 10-x-x, South did decide to play the 9.

The contract thus failed by two tricks (two trumps, one heart and two diamonds) which was worth 7 Imps, as Belladonna at the other table in the same contract was beaten by only one trick.

As Long As There Are No Further Problems

At any time during the play declarer is entitled to expose his cards in order to claim the contract or a certain number of tricks. However, upon showing his cards declarer is required to explain clearly his intended line of play.

Playing against a Roman team in the 1963 Italian championships, I was able to make a claim in a small slam after the sixth trick. I avoided doing this since the explanation would have taken longer than the play of the hand:

♠ 9 7 5 3
♡ A 7 4 2
◇ A J 9
♣ 5 3

	N	
W		E
	S	

♠ A K J
♡ K J 3
◇ K Q 8 7 6
♣ A Q

Neither side vulnerable. The bidding:

SOUTH	WEST	NORTH	EAST
Forquet		*Garozzo*	
1♣	Pass	1NT	Pass
2◇	Pass	2♡	Pass
2NT	Pass	3◇	Pass
3♠	Pass	4◇	Pass
6◇	Pass	Pass	Pass

West led the 8 of spades, East produced the 2 and on winning with the jack, I continued with three rounds of diamonds ending in dummy, West discarding a heart on the third diamond. I led a low heart from dummy and my jack lost to West's queen. He returned the 10 of hearts, won by my king as East pitched a club.

This was the position:

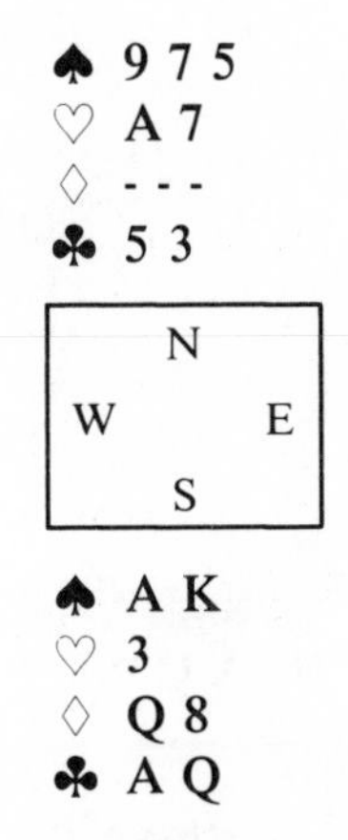

At this point I could have claimed the contract.

Can you see why?

This was the complete deal:

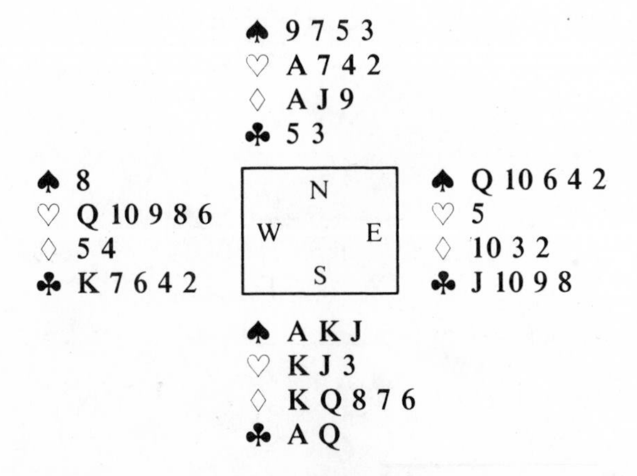

When I cashed the ace of spades I found that the suit was held by East. Then came the king of spades and the queen of diamonds to produce this ending:

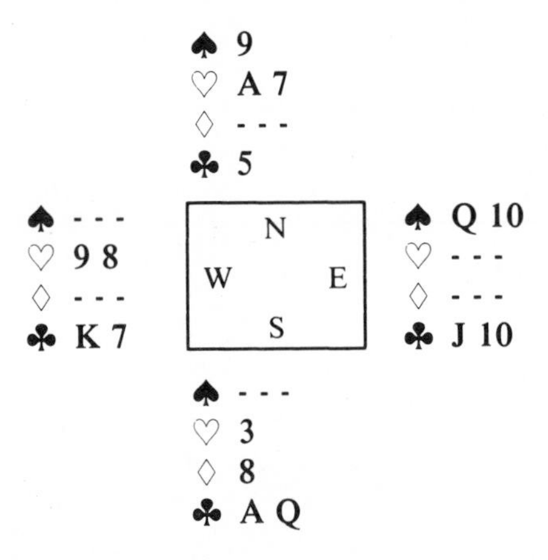

On the last diamond West had to discard a club to keep control of the hearts. I let go dummy's now useless 7 of hearts and East dropped the 10 of spades. When I led a heart to the ace, East now also had to discard a club to keep the guard in spades. Thus each opponent was left with just one club and it was child's play to drop the bare king in the West hand.

Suppose that the spades had actually been guarded by West. In that case, with seven cards to go, this would have been the layout:

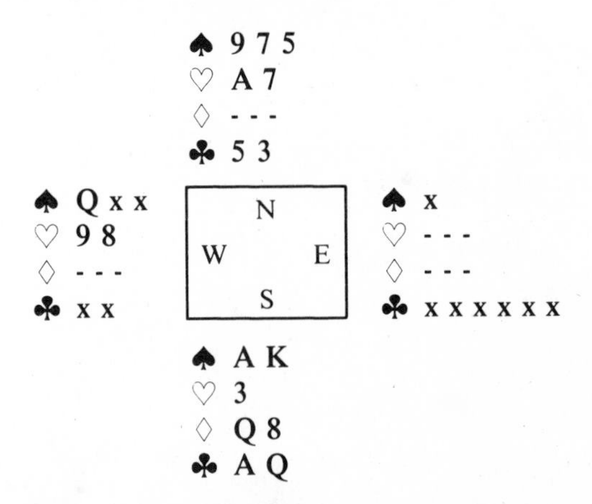

I would cash the ace and king of spades and upon learning that West had the spades controlled, I would have continued with two rounds of diamonds and the ace of clubs, squeezing West in spades and hearts. Once I have a count on West's hand, I would know that on my last two diamonds West is obliged to discard the two clubs he holds. If the king of clubs does not appear it would be just as good to retain a club in dummy and finesse against East's marked king.

An Obvious Double Squeeze But Yet . . .

In a pairs tournament in Beirut, Benito Garozzo, playing opposite Omar Sharif, was faced with this small slam in no-trumps:

♠ A K J 5
♡ 9 5
◊ A K Q 4
♣ K 3 2

	N	
W		E
	S	

♠ 6 4
♡ A 10 8 7
◊ 3
♣ A Q J 10 8 7

North-South vulnerable. The bidding:

WEST	NORTH *Sharif*	EAST	SOUTH *Garozzo*
	1♣	1♠	1NT
Pass	2NT	3♡	4♣
Pass	4◊	Pass	4♡
Pass	5♣	Pass	6♣
Pass	6NT	All pass	

There are twelve tricks on top. The problem is to make *thirteen* after the lead of the 2 of spades from West.

East's bidding ought to provide all the necessary clues. In order to notch up all the tricks, you need to execute a double squeeze: hearts-diamonds on West, hearts-spades on East.

How do you time the play to set up the squeeze?

After you have made up your mind, test your line on the complete deal:

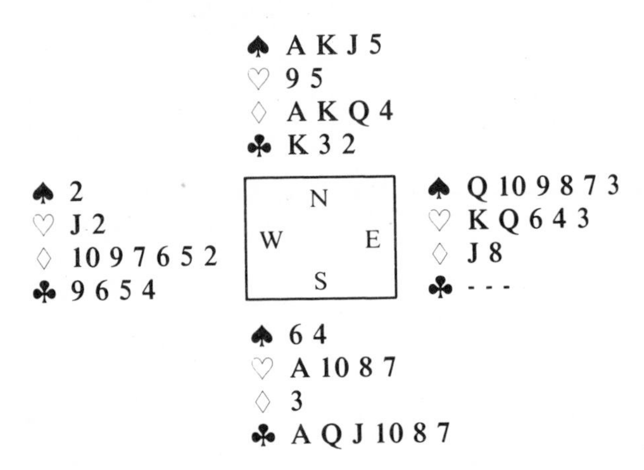

A number of declarers, at grips with the same problem, sought to set up the double squeeze in this order: ace of spades; ace, king and queen of diamonds; five rounds of clubs to reach this ending:

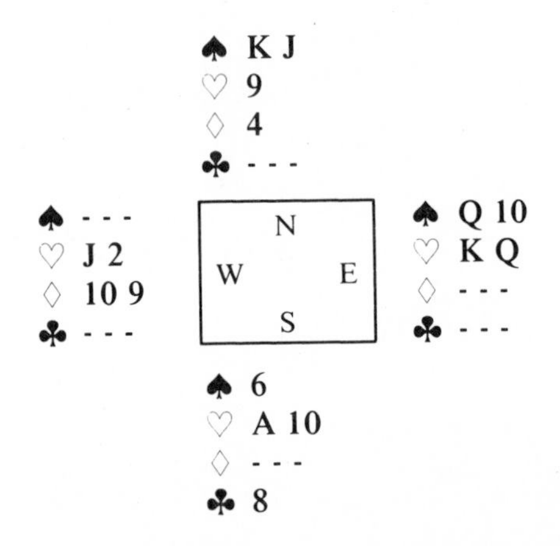

On the 8 of clubs West discarded a diamond and the dummy was squeezed ahead of East: if North let go the 9 of hearts, he would lose the communications necessary to squeeze West in the red suits; if he discarded the jack of spades, East could relinquish the spade guard, keeping just the hearts; if the 4 of diamonds were discarded, East could let the hearts go, as West with jack-doubleton can now control that suit. Thus declarers following this line managed no more than twelve tricks.

Garozzo, however, found the line to make *all* the tricks.

Winning the opening lead with the ace of spades, Garozzo cashed *the king of spades* and followed with five rounds of clubs to reach this position:

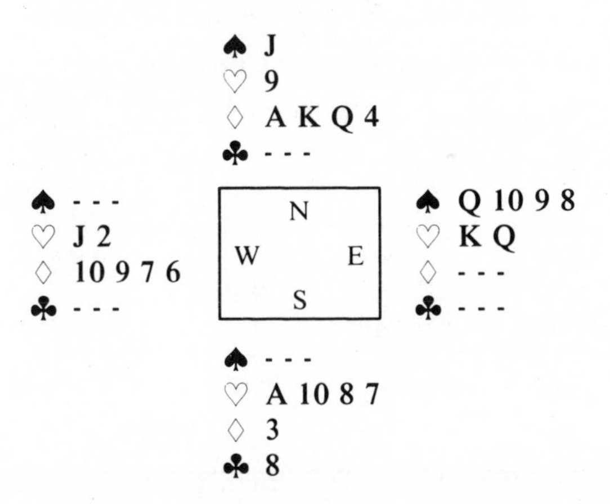

On the 8 of clubs West was forced to discard a heart in order to retain the diamond guard. Garozzo discarded the 4 of diamonds from dummy and played off two top diamonds, to produce this ending:

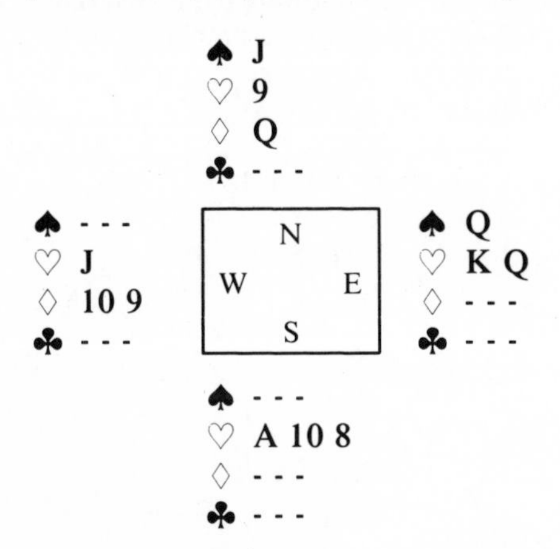

The queen of diamonds now squeezed East in spades and hearts.

Changing Tack

Suppose you are in my seat, South, with these cards:

♠ AKQJ108 ♡ KQ4 ◊ 9732 ♣ - - -

North-South vulnerable. The bidding:

WEST	NORTH	EAST	SOUTH
	Garozzo		*Forquet*
1◊	Pass	Pass	Double
3♣	Double	Pass	3♠
Pass	4◊	Pass	4♡
Pass	5♡	Pass	?

North's Four Diamonds and Five Hearts were cue-bids, implying support for spades. The cue-bid in hearts will be the ace, since South holds the king; the cue in diamonds shows first- *or* second-round control.

What would you bid now, Five Spades or Six Spades?

The decision to bid the slam is a borderline one, but that is what I did when confronted by this problem in a pairs tournament. West led the ace of clubs and when Garozzo tabled the dummy the slam looked laydown, as the ace of diamonds was bound to be with West:

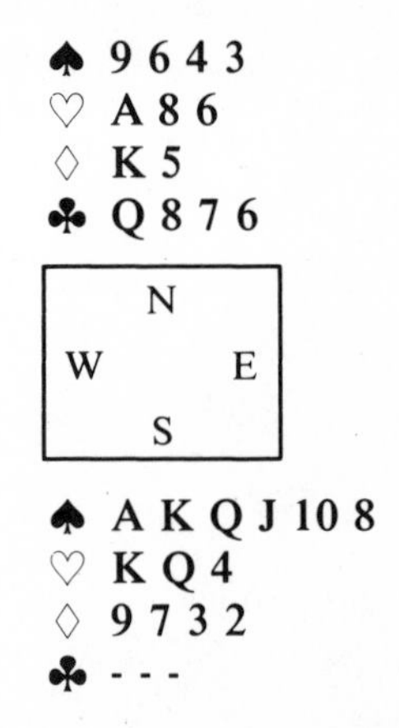

I ruffed the opening lead with the *ten* of spades (not yet foreseeing the subsequent developments but preserving maximum entries on general principles). On the ace of spades, West discarded a club. The 3-0 trump break presented problems. West had to have at least 5 diamonds, so that East's 7 would prevent my ruffing two diamonds in dummy. A different chance for success occurred to me.

How would you have continued in my position?

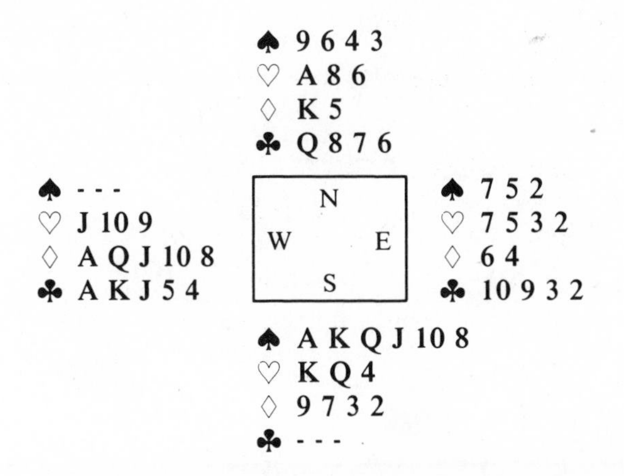

I continued with a diamond towards the king. West took the ace and returned the suit, won by the king. After ruffing a club in hand with the king of spades, I cashed three hearts and the queen of spades, leaving this ending:

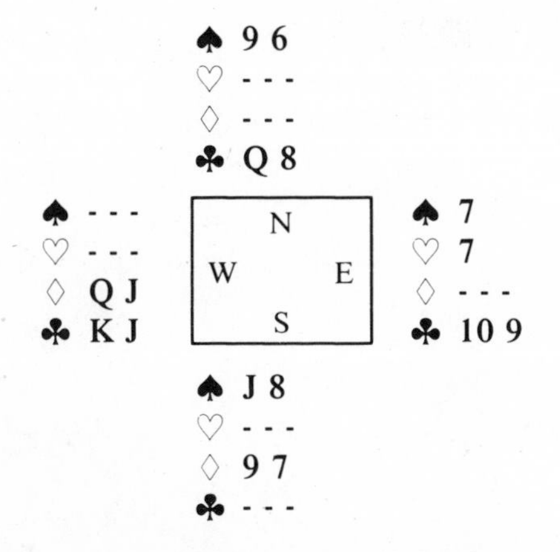

On the 8 of spades, West found himself squeezed: if he discarded a club I would overtake the 8 with dummy's 9 and set up a club winner by ruffing a club in hand; if instead West discarded a diamond, I would have kept the lead in my own hand by playing dummy's 6 and a diamond ruff in dummy would have made my hand high.

Variations

If at trick 3 West had not risen with the ace of diamonds the situation would have been slightly altered. The ending then would have been:

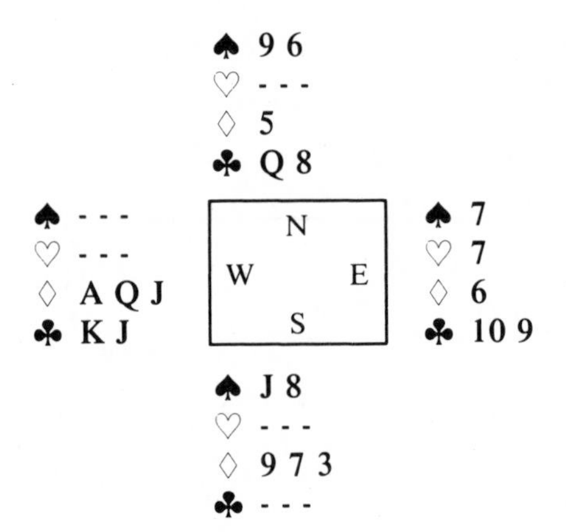

On the 8 of spades West is obliged to discard a diamond, for on a club discard, declarer overtakes the 8 with the 9 and ruffs a club. Now South plays a diamond and upon winning West has his choice of poisons: a diamond return sets up declarer's hand while either club provides dummy with the necessary winners.

A Nasty Surprise

In the match against Spain in the 1964 Olympiad, Garozzo found himself in the spotlight with a spectacular defence. Suppose you held his cards as West:

♠ K J
♡ 10 6 5
♢ J 7 3 2
♣ K 5 4 3

North-South vulnerable. The bidding:

WEST	NORTH	EAST	SOUTH
Garozzo		*Forquet*	
		Pass	1♠
Pass	2♡	Pass	2♠
Pass	4♣	Pass	4♠
Pass	4NT	Pass	5♡
Pass	6♠	All pass	

Four Clubs was an asking bid in clubs and Four Spades showed the ace of clubs; Four No-Trumps was Blackwood.

What would you have led as West?

The bidding suggested North held solid hearts and it seemed logical to set up a minor suit trick, hoping to use the king of spades as an entry. Which should be preferred, diamonds or clubs? In view of North's asking bid, Garozzo presumed that this must be North's weakness and so, notwithstanding South having shown the ace of that suit, he led the 3 of clubs. Dummy came down and West was looking at:

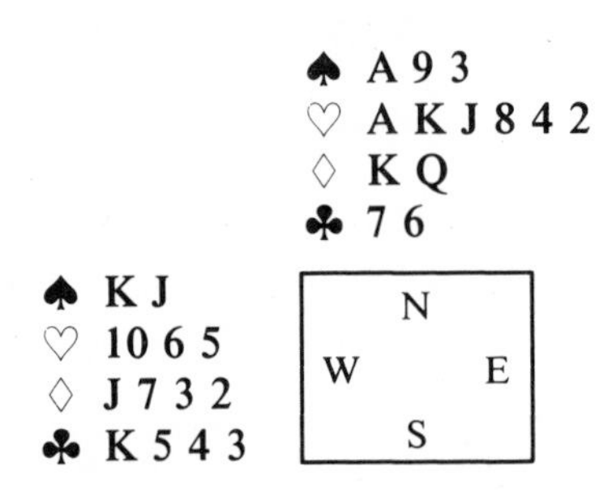

On the 3 of clubs I furnished the queen and South after winning the ace continued with the king and queen of diamonds, the ace of hearts and a heart ruff, the ace of diamonds on which dummy's second club was discarded, a club ruff and the king of hearts, discarding a club from hand. This position had been reached:

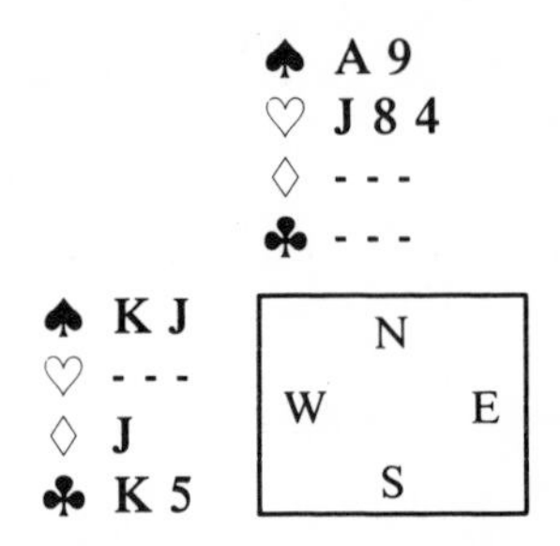

Declarer led a heart from dummy (on which I pitched the 10 of clubs) and ruffed with the 10 of spades.

How would you have defended in my partner's position?

This was the complete deal:

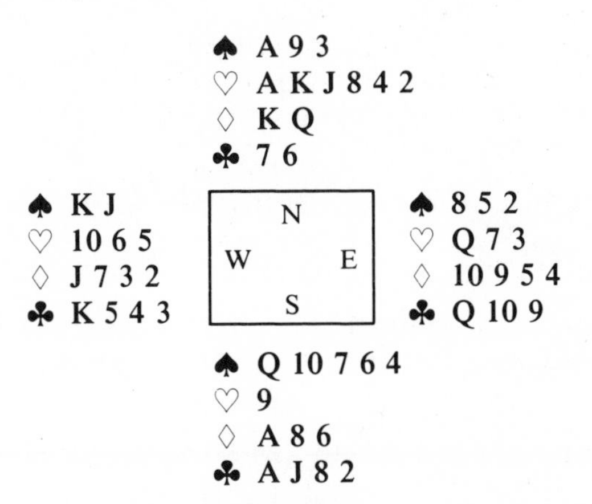

And this was the layout with five cards remaining:

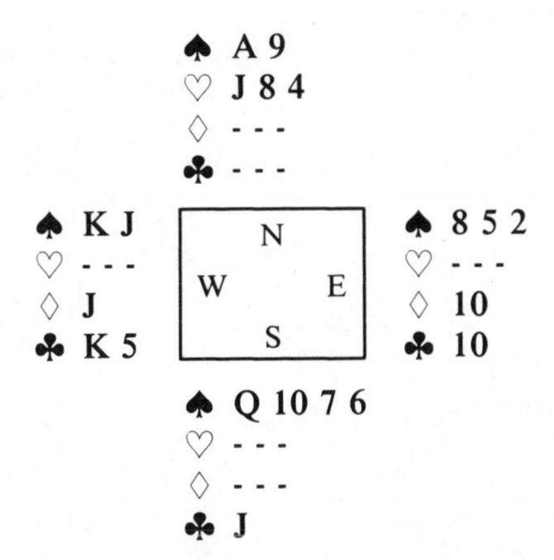

Garozzo overruffed the 10 with the *king* and returned the king of clubs. South, confident that the jack of spades was in my hand, ruffed with dummy's *ace* of spades to prevent my overruffing dummy's 9 with the jack. He then led the 9 of spades, finessing against *my* jack. I will never forget the look of surprise when Garozzo captured with 9 with the jack.

If Garozzo had overruffed declarer's 10 of spades with the *jack*, South would have been forced to ruff the club return with dummy's 9. The ace of spades would then have felled the king and the heart lead would have couped my 8-5 of spades under declarer's Q-7.

An Almost Unbeatable Contract

During an international pairs tournament in Naples in 1963, I found myself defending against Five Hearts on this deal:

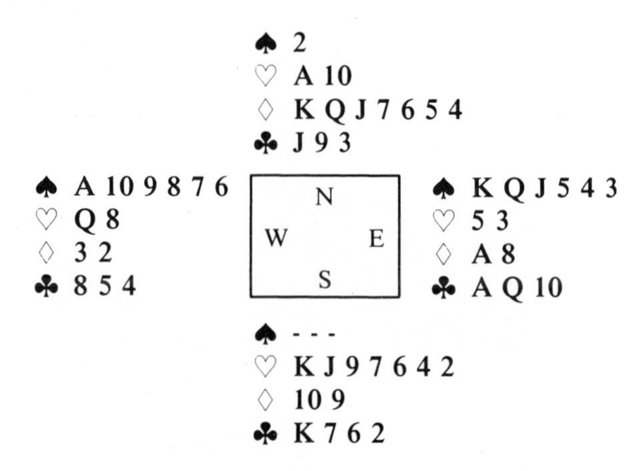

East-West vulnerable. The bidding:

WEST *Forquet*	NORTH	EAST *Garozzo*	SOUTH
		1♠	4♡
4♠	5♡	Double	All pass

Had I led a club, Garozzo could have forced out declarer's king and upon gaining the lead with the ace of diamonds, he would have been able to cash two clubs. Unfortunately, however, I started proceedings with the 3 of diamonds and after this lead, the contract was absolutely unbeatable.

Nevertheless we contrived to put declarer to a guess and his decision was not too lucky.

How could we give declarer a problem?

Garozzo won the lead with the ace of diamonds and cashed the ace of clubs. When I discouraged with the 4, my partner was on the horns of a dilemma: should he return a spade or a diamond? Garozzo knew I must hold the ace of spades but he was uncertain whether I held five or six spades. If I had five, would I have led a doubleton diamond rather than lay down the ace of spades to take a look at dummy? Hardly. Thus my partner concluded that if I had five spades to the ace, which would leave South with a spade also, the diamond lead would have been justified only if it had been a singleton.

Garozzo's return, therefore, was a diamond and declarer, winning with the ten, laid down the king of hearts, hoping for a 2-2 split. Had I followed low, South would have continued with a low heart to the ace and made the rest of the tricks. On the king of hearts, however, I followed with the queen without a tremor in an attempt to deceive declarer.

This play worked like a charm. Placing East with three trumps and me with the bare queen, South overtook the king with dummy's ace and led a high diamond. His plan was clearly to overruff East and re-enter dummy with the 10 of hearts.

Unluckily for him things did not go quite that way and when he discarded a club on the diamond, my ruff defeated the contract by one trick.

An Instinctive Move

In the 1964 Olympiad Teams semifinal the Blue Team and England produced one of their most exciting encounters, the Blue Team prevailing by the slight margin of 6 Imps. The English tried hand after hand to turn the tables but perhaps the most dramatic was this Four Spade contract:

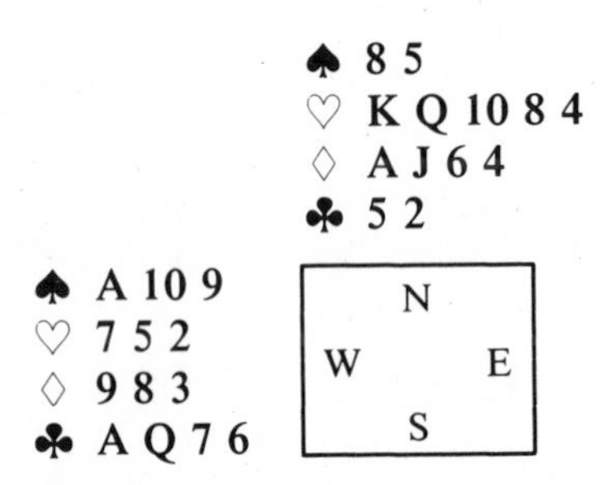

Neither side vulnerable. The bidding:

SOUTH	WEST *Garozzo*	NORTH	EAST *Forquet*
1◊	Pass	2♡	Pass
3♣	Pass	3◊	Pass
3♠	Pass	4♠	All pass

The bidding requires some explanation. The English pair was playing the 'Little Major'. The One Diamond opening was artificial and promised a spade suit. Two Hearts was not the usual forcing jump-shift but merely a positive response since One Heart would have been negative. The rest of the bidding was natural.

Garozzo led the 9 of diamonds. Declarer took dummy's ace and discarded a club from hand. Next came the 5 of spades: two - jack . . .

How would you have defended as West?

This was the complete deal:

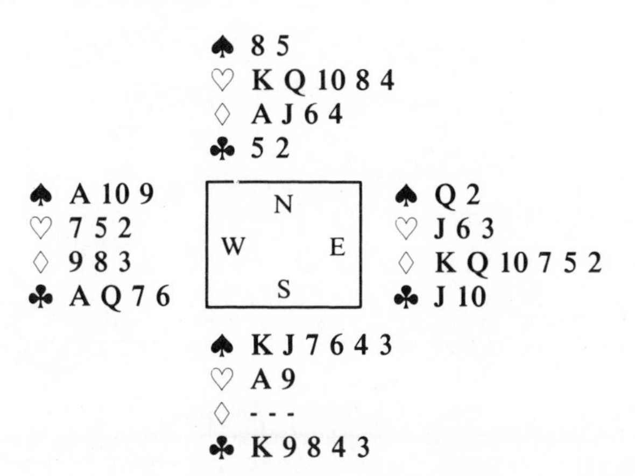

Had Garozzo taken the jack with the ace, the contract would have been unbeatable. On a club return, South would have made the king, cashed the king of spades and set about the hearts; on any other return, South would have won and continued with king and another spade, leaving West safely on lead.

Recognising the situation instinctively, Garozzo followed with the 9 of spades without a moment's hesitation. This led declarer completely astray and proved to be the killing move on the hand.

Had South continued with the king of spades he would still have made his contract but once the jack held, he placed me with the queen and ace. South therefore continued with the three top hearts, discarding another club, and then a spade. This would have succeeded if I had started with *three* spades to the A-Q and if the ace of clubs had been *doubleton*. The actual layout was, however, quite different and declarer lost two spades and three clubs, going two down.

Timely Assistance

This problem confronted me during a critical match in an Italian championship:

♠ K J 10 7 5 ♡ J 10 9 8 ♢ 7 ♣ K 8 5

I was dealer, with both sides vulnerable. I passed and my left-hand opponent opened One Diamond. My partner, Garozzo, doubled and next player passed.

What would you have called in my position?

To bid Two Diamonds to give partner the choice between spades and hearts was tempting but this would make partner declarer and could place my king of clubs in jeopardy on the opening lead. I therefore decided to bid Two Spades. Undeterred by my jump, my left-hand opponent also jumped, to Four Clubs. Garozzo bid Four Spades and this ended the auction.

This had been the bidding:

SOUTH	WEST	NORTH	EAST
Forquet		*Garozzo*	
Pass	1♢	Double	Pass
2♠	4♣	4♠	All pass

West led the queen of diamonds and Garozzo tabled the dummy:

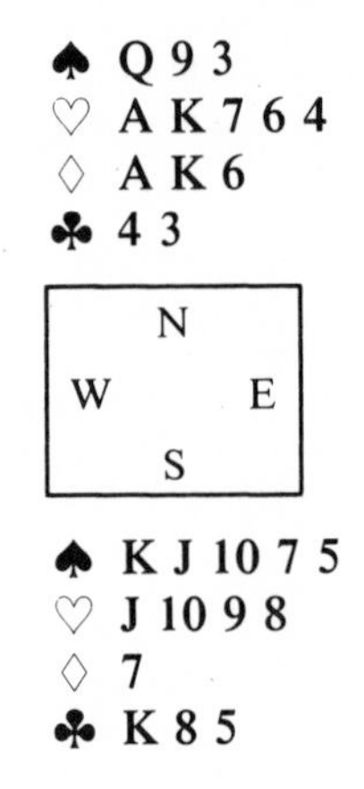

How would you plan the play?

This was the complete deal:

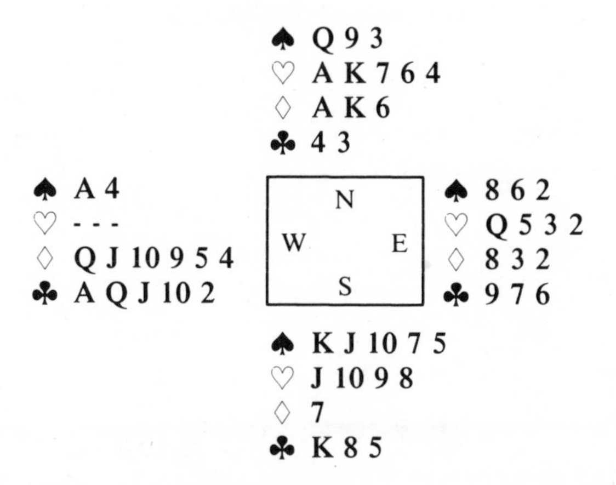

West's bidding provided the key to the play. His One Diamond opening coupled with his jump to Four Clubs when vulnerable opposite an obviously weak hand left me in little doubt that he had at least eleven cards in the minors and just as obviously, both missing aces. Hence I could tell twelve of his thirteen cards: eleven in diamonds and clubs plus the ace of spades. *If the thirteenth were another spade, I could guarantee my contract.*

The problem was to avoid letting East gain the lead with the queen of hearts for then the club lead would sink the contract.

On West's queen of diamonds I played *low in dummy*. He continued with a diamond to the king on which I discarded a heart. I led a spade to the king and West took the ace and played a third diamond. I discarded a second heart on dummy's ace of diamonds, cashed the 9 of spades and continued with the ace, king and 7 of hearts, ruffing when East covered with the queen. Dummy was re-entered with a spade to the queen and on the two established hearts in dummy I was able to discard two club losers.

The contract was made with the defence taking only the ace of spades, the ace of clubs and the queen of diamonds, a fair exchange giving them one red queen in place of the other.

An Unusual Ending

In an international pairs tournament in Dyvonne several years ago, I was East with the following problem:

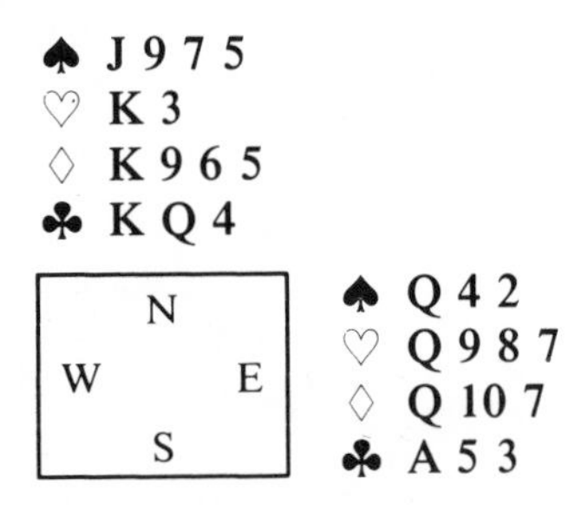

Neither side vulnerable. The bidding:

WEST	NORTH	EAST	SOUTH
Garozzo		*Forquet*	
		Pass	1♣
Pass	1♢	Pass	1♡
Pass	1♠	Pass	1NT
Pass	2NT	All pass	

My partner led the jack of hearts, holding the trick, and followed with the 10 of hearts. Winning with dummy's king, South continued with ace, king and another spade, all following. My heart return was won by declarer's ace, West furnishing the 4 and North discarding a diamond.

South then played the 2 of clubs: eight - king - *three*. When declarer played dummy's winning spade, this was the position:

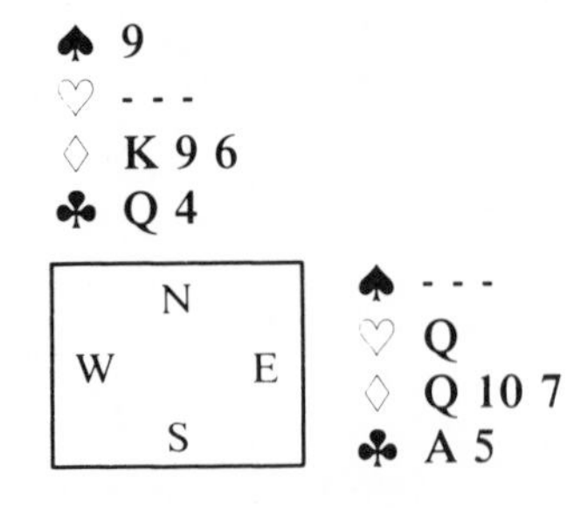

What would you have discarded in my position?

This was the complete deal:

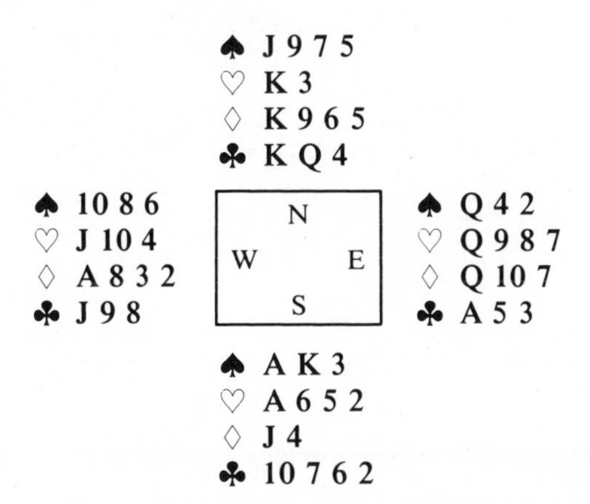

South had already shown up with the A-K of spades and the ace of hearts. If he had the ace of diamonds as well, he would certainly have bid 3NT and thus I concluded that my partner held the ace of diamonds. The *easy* discard was unquestionably a diamond and if Garozzo had the jack of clubs the contract would inevitably be beaten by *one* trick. Locked in dummy South would have to play diamonds or clubs and the defence would be able to take one spade, two hearts, two diamonds and a club (or one diamond and two clubs).

Visualising therefore the possibility of defeating declarer by *two* tricks, I elected to discard a club, baring the ace. Having to play from dummy and placing West with the ace of clubs, South chose to play diamonds, exactly as I expected. I won the queen, leaving this ending:

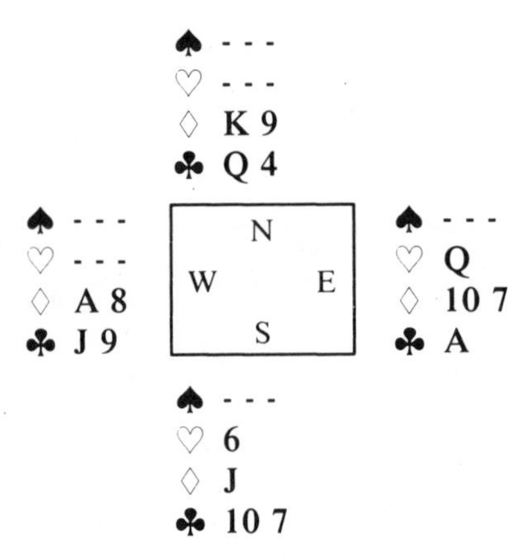

Declarer had taken six tricks but was unable to garner another. On the queen of hearts Garozzo discarded the 8 of diamonds and North was inexorably squeezed. The ending is a rare criss-cross squeeze in defence. If North discarded a diamond, I would lead a diamond to partner's ace, regain the lead with the ace of clubs and cash the established 10 of diamonds; if, instead, North let go a club, I would cash the ace of clubs and then put Garozzo on lead with the ace of diamonds to cash the jack of clubs.

Declarer thus went *two* down and we scored a deserved top. It was especially deserved because of the calculated risk I took in discarding a club rather than a safe diamond on the thirteenth spade. Had South divined the position, he could have made his contract by playing a low club at trick 9. He would then have scored both the queen of clubs and the king of diamonds.

Obviously in a teams event I would have been satisfied to defeat the contract by the straightforward discard of a diamond.

The Squeeze Or The Break?

Many years ago I played in the Mediterranean Cup in Algiers where the contestants were Algeria, Egypt, France, Libya, Morocco, Tunisia and Italy. After the qualifying rounds, France and Italy met in the final. The match was hard fought all the way and was ultimately decided by this deal:

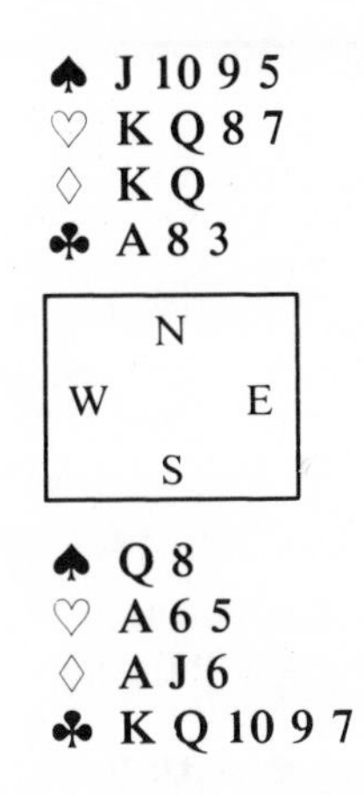

Suppose you are South faced with the problem of bringing in a small slam in no-trumps. Luckily West does not find the killing spade and leads instead the 10 of diamonds. Now if both clubs and hearts divide favorably, twelve tricks are there.

Winning the lead with the king of diamonds you play the ace of clubs (in case East has five clubs) and a club to the king. On the second round West discards a diamond, so you cross to the queen of diamonds, finesse the ten of clubs and cash two more clubs, West discarding another diamond and two spades and East a spade.

This is the ending:

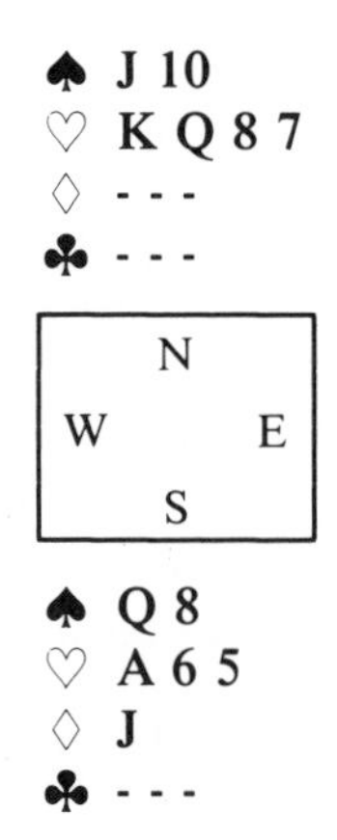

You still need five tricks to make your slam.

How do you proceed?

If hearts are 3-3 the slam is always there and if East has four hearts, he can be squeezed if he has both top spade honours. Therefore before testing the hearts, you play off the jack of diamonds, discarding a spade from dummy and East follows with *the king of spades*. Now is it not a simple matter to play the 8 of spades to East's ace? Out of diamonds, East is forced to return a heart and you are now home despite the bad break in hearts.

Do you agree with this line of play?

This was how the French South played the hand but I confess that I do not agree with his decision. This was the complete deal:

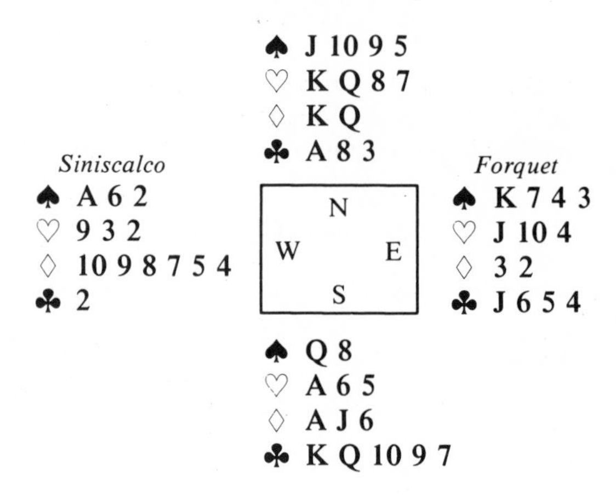

And this was the six-card ending:

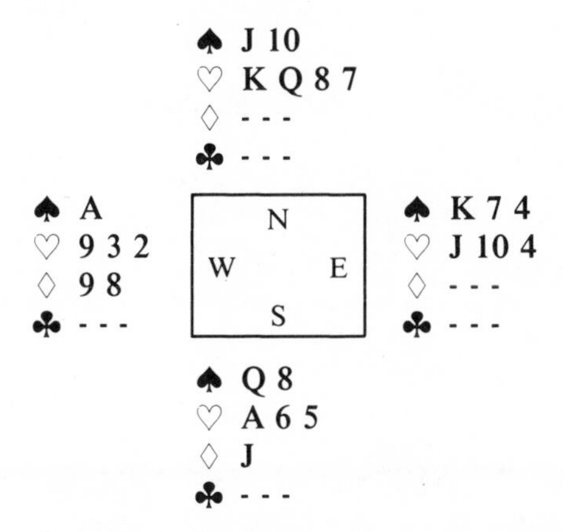

When South led the jack of diamonds, the position was quite obvious to me. Declarer did not want to restrict his chances to the 3-3 heart split and was giving himself the extra chance of a heart-spade squeeze. This would have been the ending if I would have held the A-K of spades and four hearts and was the position for which declarer was playing:

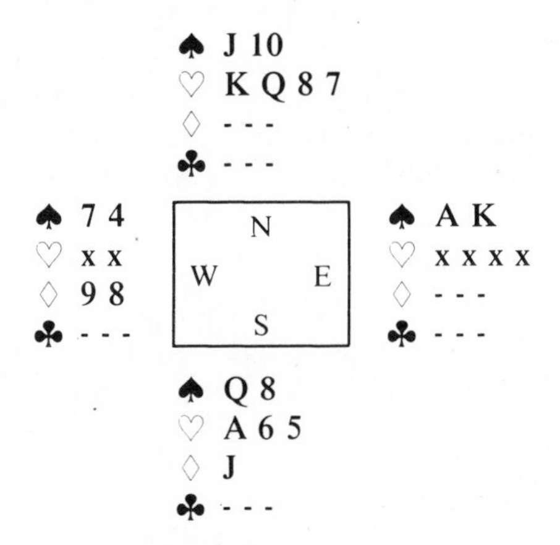

On the jack of diamonds I would have been forced to discard a spade honour to retain the guard in hearts and South would have made the queen of spades. Therefore when South discarded the 10 of spades on the jack of diamonds, I discarded my king of spades, giving declarer the impression that the squeeze was working. Declarer took the bait and rather than play for the break in hearts he chose to lead the 8 of spades. Imagine his chagrin when Siniscalco won the ace and then cashed the diamond to set the slam, with hearts 3-3 all the time.

A 'Chinese Coup' By Avarelli

The first time we played against the Chinese team (Taiwan) was at the 1964 Olympiad in New York. Belladonna who had studied our opponents' system stated that it held no special problems. "Watch out for Chinese coups, then," said Benito Garozzo jokingly just before the match.

The match ended well for us and sure enough, our victory included a 'Chinese coup' which Avarelli perpetrated on the following deal:

♠ A 10 4 3
♡ K J 4 3
◊ J 2
♣ A Q 2

N
W E
S

♠ K Q J 9 6
♡ 10 6
◊ K 9 8 7
♣ 9 6

Both sides vulnerable. The bidding:

WEST	NORTH	EAST	SOUTH
Belladonna		*Avarelli*	
Pass	1♡	Double	1♠
Pass	2♠	Pass	3♠
Pass	4♠	All pass	

Belladonna led the 2 of spades: 3 - 8 - king. The 10 of hearts was run and Avarelli won the queen, cashed the ace of diamonds and continued with the 10 of diamonds. South won the king and led a second heart. Belladonna who had previously played the 8 of hearts now followed with the 5. Dummy's king lost to the ace and Avarelli promptly returned a heart.

Put yourself in declarer's place in this critical position:

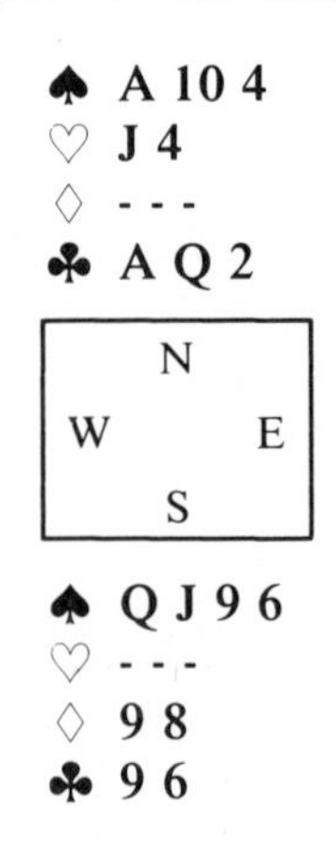

To succeed you cannot afford to lose another trick.

How would you have played on the heart return?

This was the complete deal:

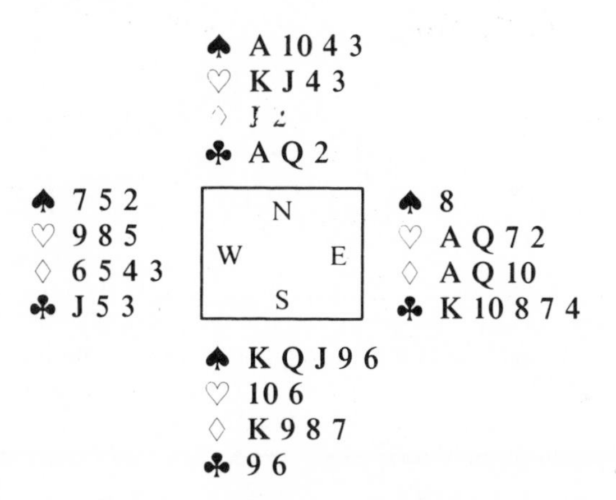

If on Avarelli's heart lead you decided to discard a club, you would have made your contract. The actual declarer, however, was not willling to risk this heart being ruffed if West had started with just a doubleton heart. He therefore ruffed with the queen of spades. The Chinese declarer reasoned that if spades were 2-2, the contract was laydown, while if they were 3-1, the marked ruffing finesse for the queen of diamonds would make the rest of the tricks just as surely.

The diamond finesse was *marked* from declarer's point of view since the queen of diamonds was clearly located with West in view of Avarelli's cash of the ace *followed by the ten with the bare jack in dummy.*

Thus declarer fell into the trap laid by Avarelli. After ruffing the heart return with the queen of spades, he cashed two trumps and tabled the 9 of diamonds, letting it run . . .

In the other room, the bidding went:

WEST	NORTH	EAST	SOUTH
	Garozzo		*Forquet*
Pass	1♠	Pass	4♠
Pass	Pass	Pass	

The same contract was reached but played by North. East led a trump and Garozzo winning in dummy, continued with the 10 of hearts, run to the queen. East paused to consider the situation. It was obvious that Garozzo was aiming to establish a heart winner to discard one of dummy's two clubs and thus East thought it best to set about the clubs at once. Hoping to find the queen of clubs with his partner, East switched to the 4 of clubs, thus solving all of my partner's problems.

From A Bottom To A Top

Several years ago Avarelli, Belladonna, Garozzo and I took part in an international pairs tournament at Dyvonne, organised by our friend, Tony Trad. After the first two sessions, our two pairs were in the lead. The third and final round would be decisive. This eventful deal towards the end proved to be the determining factor.

♠ 9 8
♡ 4 3 2
♢ A K Q J 9 8 7
♣ Q

	N	
W		E
	S	

♠ A K 4 3 2
♡ A 10 6
♢ 10 6
♣ A 8 7

Both sides vulnerable. The bidding:

SOUTH *Garozzo*	NORTH *Forquet*
1♠	3♢
3♠	4♢
4♡	4♠
5♣	6♢
6NT	Pass

Had this deal occurred at the beginning of the tournament we would probably have contented ourselves with the small slam in diamonds. Six Diamonds, as you have noted, would fail only if spades split 5-1 or 6-0. Otherwise by ruffing one or two rounds of spades, at least one extra spade trick can be set up to provide the twelfth trick.

As the hand arose late in the day and believing we were still trailing Avarelli-Belladonna, Garozzo decided to stake everything on bidding the slam in no-trumps.

West led the 7 of hearts and when I revealed the dummy, Benito's expression could not conceal the fact that things were desperate. No doubt my partner had hoped for a little more in my hand.

On the 7 of hearts, East played the queen.

How would you have planned the play in Garozzo's position to have a chance to bring in the slam?

This was the complete deal:

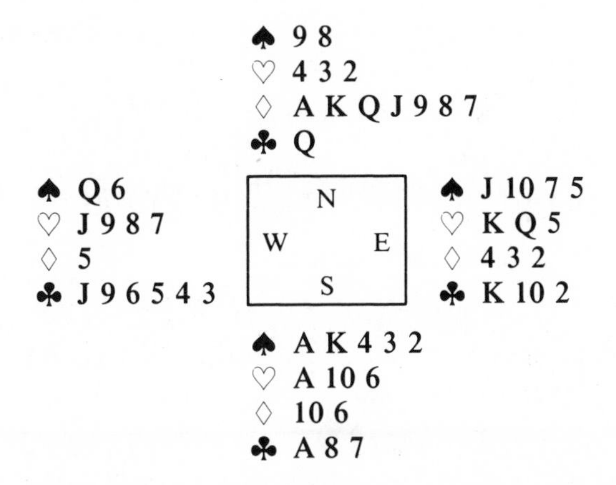

On the queen of hearts, Garozzo *played low* and East continued with the king of hearts. Winning with the ace, my partner continued with the ace and king of spades and then ran six rounds of diamonds. East erred beyond recovery by discarding . . . *the 5 of hearts.*

This discard enabled Garozzo to execute a double squeeze in this ending:

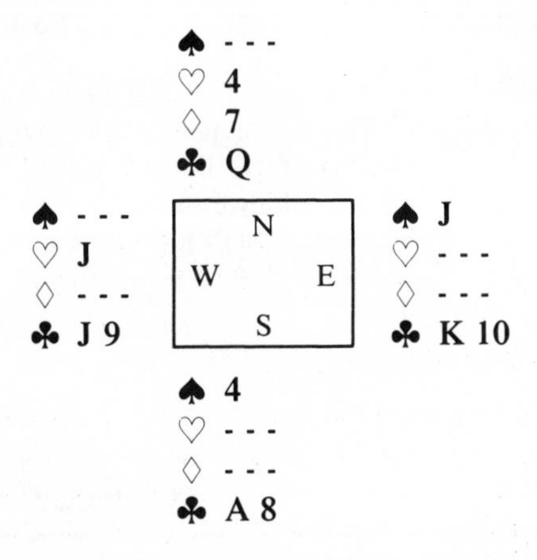

On the last diamond East was forced to discard a club to retain the guard in spades. South let go the now useless 4 of spades and West was squeezed in hearts and clubs.

Had East preserved the 5 of hearts together with the jack of spades, relinquishing his clubs, the squeeze would now have been inoperative. This triumph was sufficient to enable us to win the tournament.

Counting Is Not Too Tough

Most novices are handicapped by their failure to reconstruct the opponents' hands. Take for example the following deal which I played in an international pairs event in Cannes:

♠ Q 9 3
♡ K 9 7 5
♢ A Q 4
♣ K 8 7

	N	
W		E
	S	

♠ A K J 4 2
♡ A J 6
♢ 3 2
♣ A 6 5

North-South vulnerable. The bidding:

SOUTH *Forquet*	NORTH *Garozzo*
1♣	1NT
2♠	3♠
4♣	4♢
4♡	4NT
6♠	Pass

West led the 10 of spades and on winning the ace, I drew two more rounds of trumps, West discarding a diamond on the third round. Since it was pointless to put off the diamond finesse (if the fourth heart sets up, you can discard a club loser on that), I continued with a low diamond to the queen.

When this held, I cashed the ace of diamonds and ruffed the third diamond, East following to this trick with a club.

The success of the diamond finesse improved prospects considerably. At this stage the slam would succeed with the queen of hearts onside or if the 9 of hearts could be set up as a winner. Re-entering dummy with a club to the king, I led a low heart to my jack, which held the trick, East contributing the 4 and West the 2. With twelve tricks secure I could now pursue the thirteenth, depending on the heart position. I cashed the ace of hearts and East followed with the *queen*.

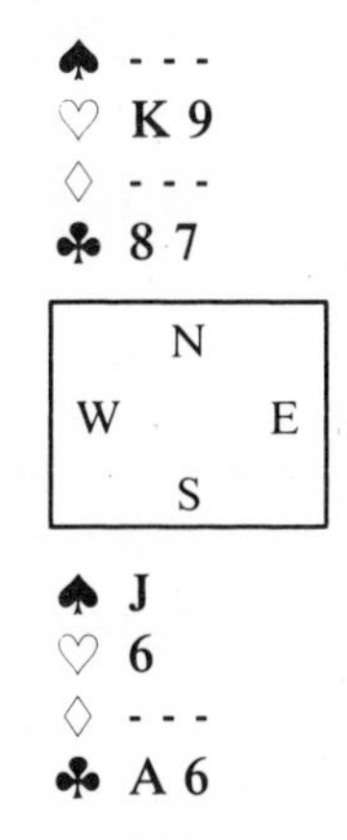

Now the problem was whether to finesse the 9 of hearts or whether to cash the king. The risk in finessing lay in East's having dropped the queen of hearts from an initial holding of Q-10-4, trying to lure me into finessing the 9 and losing to the 10. If the finesse of the 9 of hearts lost, the slam would fail since there would be no way back to dummy to score the king of hearts.

What would you have done in my position, taking into account that you are playing pairs where the overtrick can be of paramount importance?

After you have made up your mind, examine the complete deal:

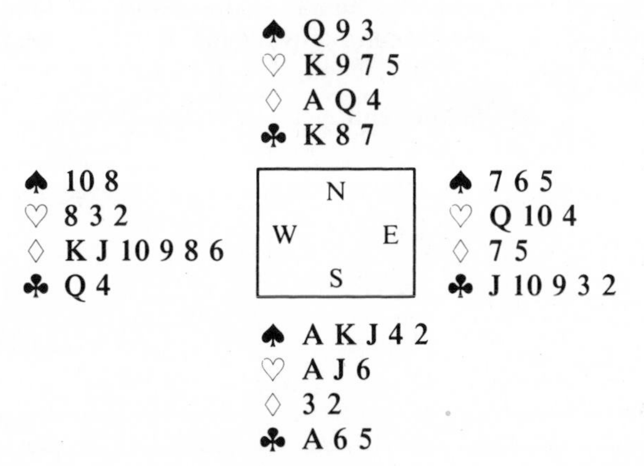

If you guessed the position correctly, take no credit. The solution to this problem is in fact a simple matter of arithmetic. South *must* first cash the ace of clubs to find the answer: if West follows to this trick, it means that he cannot hold more than three hearts (having already turned up with two spades, six diamonds and two clubs); if on the other hand, West fails to follow to the ace of clubs, it means he began with four hearts.

I cashed the ace of clubs and when West followed, a heart to the king dropped East's 10 and gave me all thirteen tricks.

A Double Dummy Problem

It is well known that situations which lend themselves to double dummy compositions rarely occur in actual play. The following deal, played by Benito Garozzo in the 1964 Olympiad against France, is therefore a rarity:

♠ Q J 8 5 3
♡ K 10 7
◊ K 6 2
♣ J 8

N
W E
S

♠ 10 9
♡ 9 8 5
◊ A J 10 8 5
♣ A Q 4

Neither side vulnerable. The bidding:

WEST	NORTH *Forquet*	EAST	SOUTH *Garozzo*
1♣	1♠	Pass	2◊
2♡	Pass	Pass	2♠
3♣	3◊	All pass	

West began with the 10 of clubs: jack - king - ace. Garozzo planned to establish the spades before the opponents broached the hearts and therefore led the 9 of spades. West rose with the king, East playing the 4, and switched to the ace and queen of hearts. Winning dummy's king, Garozzo pulled a low spade from dummy to the 10 but West won the ace, East playing the 2, and cashed the jack of hearts.

When West next led the thirteenth heart, this was the position:

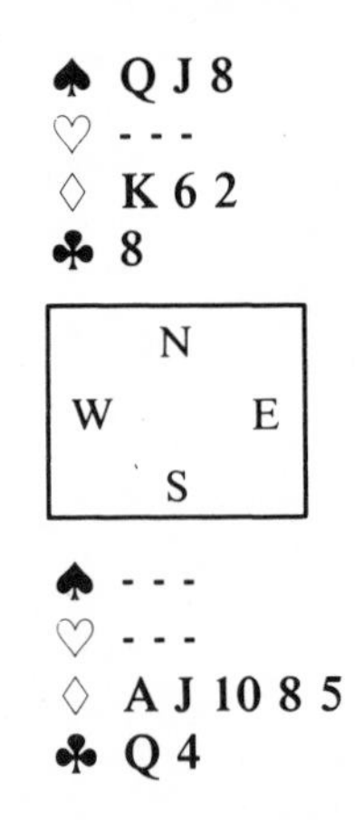

How would you have continued as declarer?

After you have decided, take a look at the complete deal:

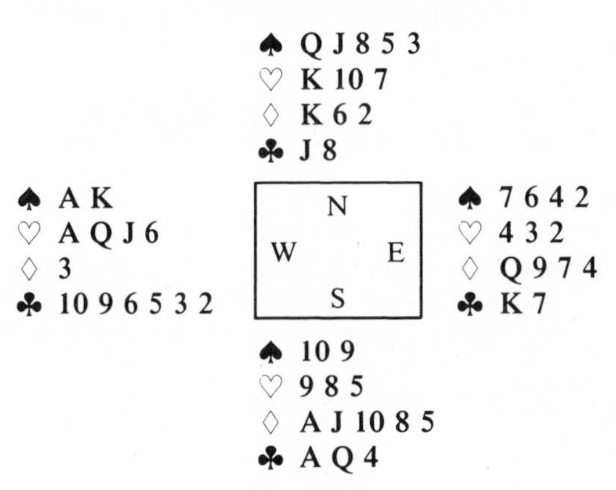

This was the layout at the end of trick 6:

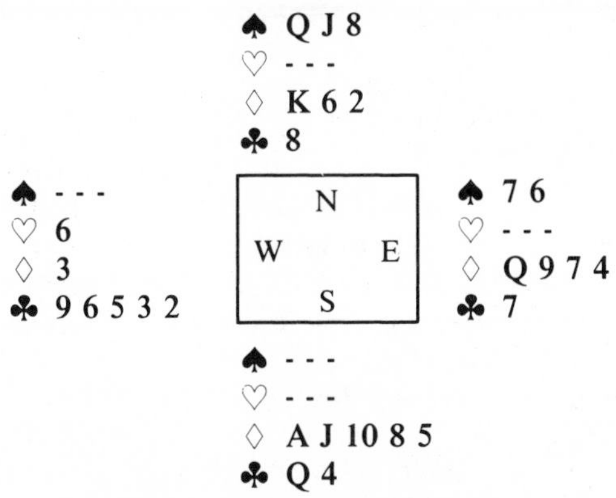

West has shown four hearts and on the bidding can be placed with six clubs (partly because of the rebid of such a weak suit, partly because of East's pass of Two Hearts with only three-card support, indicating that his support for West's first suit was even weaker). In addition, East's high-low in spades suggests that West began with just a doubleton. Add to this the fact that West has freely given declarer a ruff-and-discard with the thirteenth heart and you will appreciate Benito's conviction that trumps were breaking badly.

Garozzo realised that on the fourth round of hearts, East would discard his last club. Consequently he had to ruff this in dummy for if he ruffed in hand to discard a club from dummy, he would be unable to avoid losing a diamond trick to East.

Notwithstanding all of this, my partner managed to make his contract.

What was his line of play in this end-position?

Garozzo trumped the thirteenth heart with dummy's 6 of diamonds. East did best by discarding the 7 of clubs, but Benito *underruffed dummy with his 5 of diamonds!* He then led the 2 of diamonds to his jack, returned to dummy via the king of diamonds and discarded both his clubs on the queen and jack of spades. Down to just two cards with the lead in dummy, Garozzo had no difficulty in picking up East's queen of diamonds.

The Slam That Won An Olympiad

The final of the 1964 Olympiad teams between the United States and Italy was one of the most dramatic ever encountered by the Blue Team. The Americans cleared out to a 30 Imp lead early in proceedings but at the halfway mark, with the scores almost level, the following deal arose:

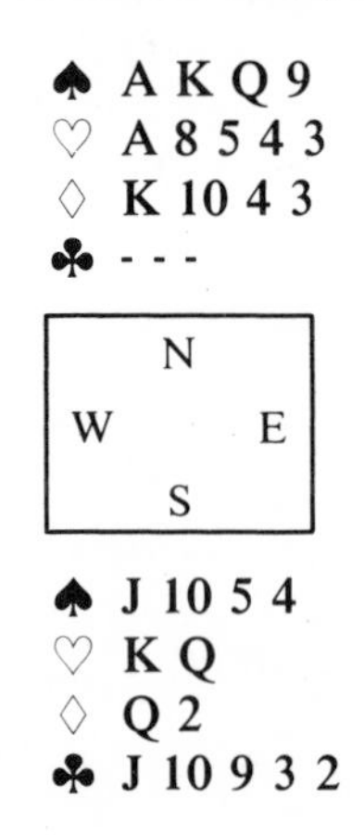

Both sides vulnerable. The closed room bidding:

WEST	NORTH *Forquet*	EAST	SOUTH *Garozzo*
	1♣	Pass	1♢
Pass	1♡	Pass	1♠
Pass	3♢	Pass	3♡
Pass	4♣	Pass	4♢
Pass	4NT	Pass	5NT
Pass	6♠	All pass	

South's One Diamond response was mandatory for in those days the systemic requirements for responding to the One Club opening were: One Diamond = 0-1 control, One Heart = 2 controls. After my game-forcing rebid of Three Diamonds, Garozzo upgraded his hand despite the One Diamond response and kept making forward-going moves.

Against Six Spades West led the ace of clubs. Garozzo ruffed and led a diamond to the queen which held the trick.

How would you have continued?

This was the complete deal:

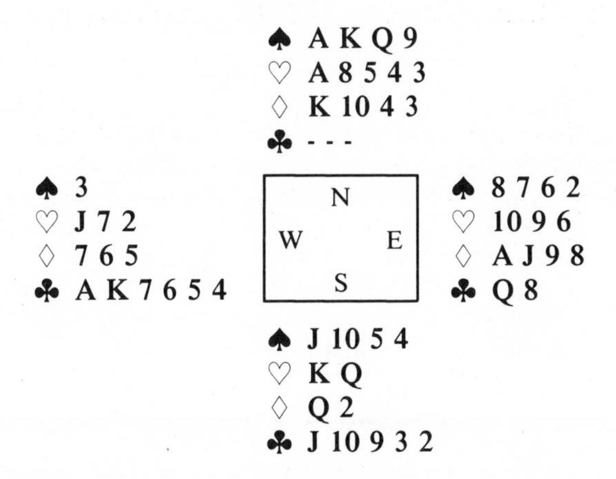

Benito cashed the king and queen of hearts, ruffed another club in dummy and led the ace of hearts, discarding his last diamond. When this stood up, he continued with a diamond ruff, club ruff, diamond ruff, club ruff and conceded just the last trick.

In the open room the Americans reached the same contract and Avarelli made the same lead, the ace of clubs. Declarer ruffed and led a diamond to the queen, just as my partner had done. Here, however, the US player committed a small error that cost the slam and 17 Imps. Instead of cashing the king and queen of hearts at once, he mistimed the play with a club ruff first and then the two heart honours. This error in timing made itself patent when South re-entered dummy by ruffing the third round of clubs, for on this trick Belladonna, East, was able to discard his third heart. When declarer then tried to cash the ace of hearts, Belladonna was able to ruff it and the contract could no longer be made.

Decision At Trick One

One of the hands that will always remain among the most vivid for Camillo Pabis-Ticci is the following, played in an international pairs tournament in Palma di Majorca in 1965. He was South holding this collection:

♠ Q 10 6 4 3 ♡ A Q 5 ◇ 8 7 5 3 ♣ 9

With both sides vulnerable, West opened Three Hearts. D'Alelio (North) doubled and East came in with Four Clubs.

What would you have bid in his place?

The value bid is probably Four Spades but Pabis is never inclined to hold back when there is the slightest excuse to push forward and accordingly he jumped to Five Spades. West passed and D'Alelio raised to Six Spades.

This had been the auction:

WEST	NORTH *D'Alelio*	EAST	SOUTH *Pabis-Ticci*
3♡	Double	4♣	5♠
Pass	6♠	All pass	

West led the 10 of clubs and when D'Alelio displayed dummy, Pabis wished he had settled for a more prudent Four Spades.

The lead of the 10 of clubs required a crucial decision: to cover or not to cover.

What would you have done in declarer's position?

This was the complete deal:

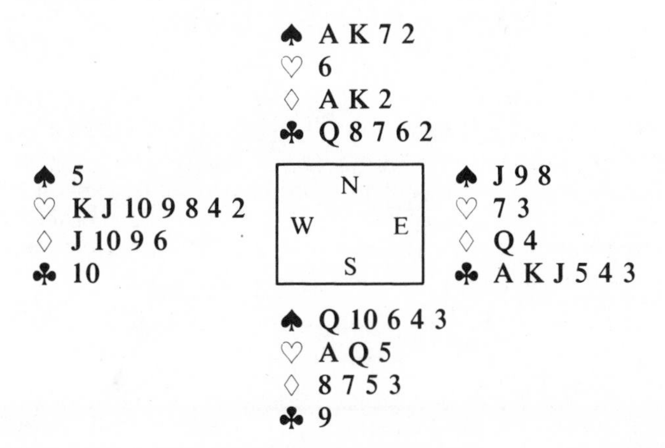

If declarer covered West's 10 of clubs with the queen, the club return might see declarer overruffed. Pabis therefore considered playing low from dummy but that could hardly improve the situation, since East would have the option of overtaking and returning the suit anyway or letting West hold the trick with the 10 of clubs. In the latter case a diamond switch by West would be unwelcome as it would reduce some of the possibilities of success.

Pabis who had spotted a remote chance of making the slam covered the 10 with the queen. East won the king and returned the 3 of clubs. Holding his breath, South ruffed with the 10 of spades and when this held he continued with the queen of spades and a spade to the ace. Next came the 8 of clubs - ace - ruff, diamond to the ace, 7 of clubs - jack - ruff, setting up the 6 of clubs as a winner. Returning to dummy with the king of diamonds, Pabis cashed the last two trumps to produce this ending:

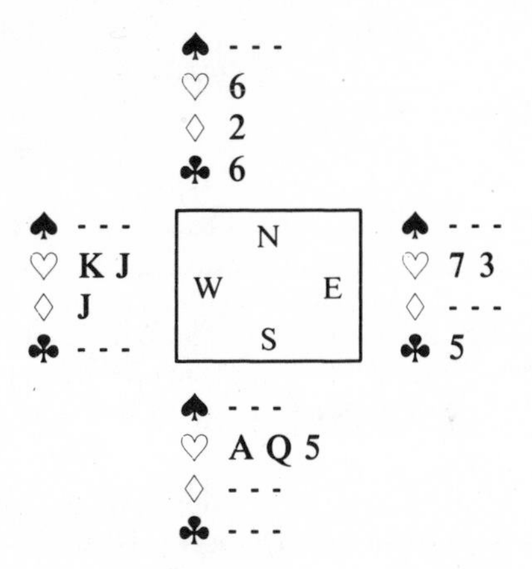

The 6 of clubs now squeezed West in hearts and diamonds. Six Spades made.

"Think First, Act Later"

Many years ago, playing with Eugenio Chiaradia, I found myself in a most difficult contract. I played quickly to the first trick, then sat and thought and thought and sat, contemplating the position which had become desperate. While I was thus engrossed, Eugenio who understood my problem even though he was dummy finally intervened and said, "It's useless to think now, you had to do it at the beginning."

This lesson was invaluable and I can assure you that those errors that I have committed subsequently were certainly not committed in haste.

Now, put yourself in my place as West on the following deal. South is playing Five Clubs doubled. Since it is a pairs event with game almost certainly on for us, then it is necessary at equal vulnerability to defeat declarer by three or more tricks to obtain a good score.

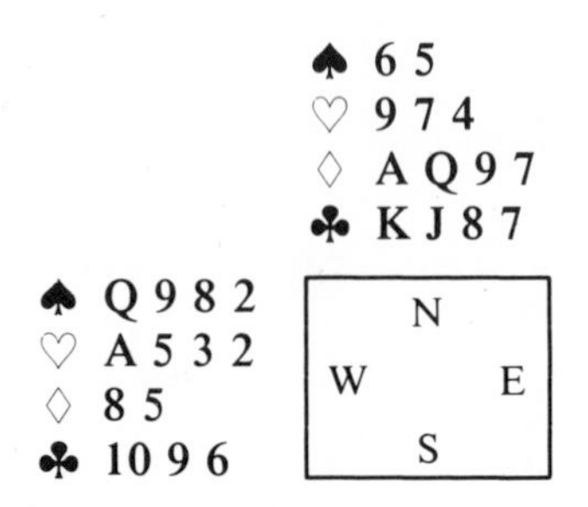

Neither side vulnerable. The bidding:

WEST	NORTH	EAST	SOUTH
Forquet		*Garozzo*	
		1◊	2♣
Pass	3♣	3♠*	4♣
4♠	Pass	Pass	5♣
Double	Pass	Pass	Pass

*Canape style, spades the longer suit

I led the 8 of diamonds: nine - ten - two. Garozzo switched to the ace and king of spades. Declarer ruffed the second spade and cashed three rounds of trumps, ending in dummy, East discarding three spades. Next came a low heart: eight - jack.

At this stage the defence has won two tricks and the ace of hearts makes three. The problem is to come to two more tricks.

How would you have planned the defence as West?

This was the complete deal:

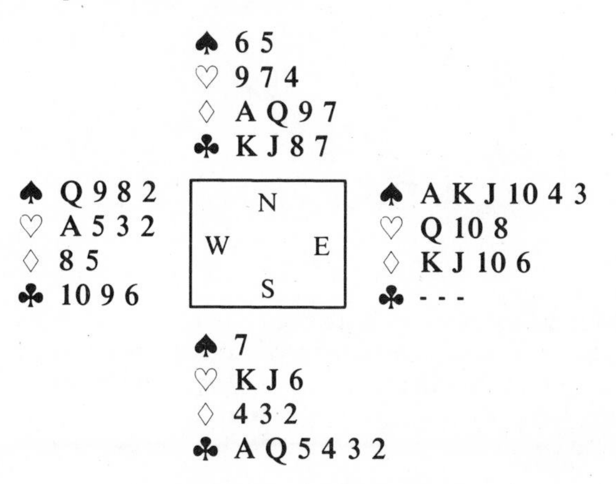

And this will be the position with six cards to go:

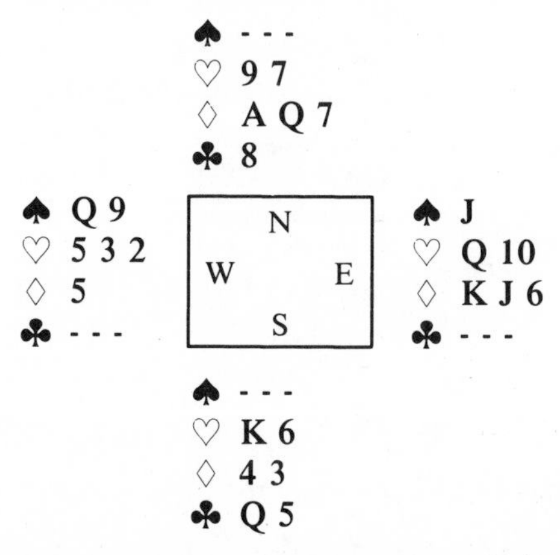

If, after winning the jack of hearts with the ace, you return a heart, South wins the king and plays a third heart, endplaying East and forcing a diamond return into the A-Q or a spade, giving declarer a ruff-and-discard; if you return a spade South can win the remaining tricks by ruffing in dummy while discarding a diamond from hand, and after a heart to the king, the last two trumps squeeze East in hearts and diamonds.

What then?

You should have thought of all of this first. Then this insoluble dilemma would not have arisen.

On the jack of hearts, *do not take the ace, but instead play low.* Then South cannot avoid losing three more tricks.

A Doomed Monarch

Many contracts succeed not just because of the favourable position of a key card but also by virtue of the number of cards accompanying it. In an Italian Teams Championship match between Rome and Florence, Avarelli and Belladonna landed in this optimistic Four Spade contract:

North-South vulnerable. The bidding:

SOUTH	WEST	NORTH	EAST
Belladonna		*Avarelli*	
1♡	2♣	Double	Pass
2♠*	Pass	2NT	Pass
3♠	Pass	4♠	All pass

*Canape style, shorter suit first

West led the king of clubs and switched to the 2 of diamonds.

How should declarer plan the play?

This was the complete deal:

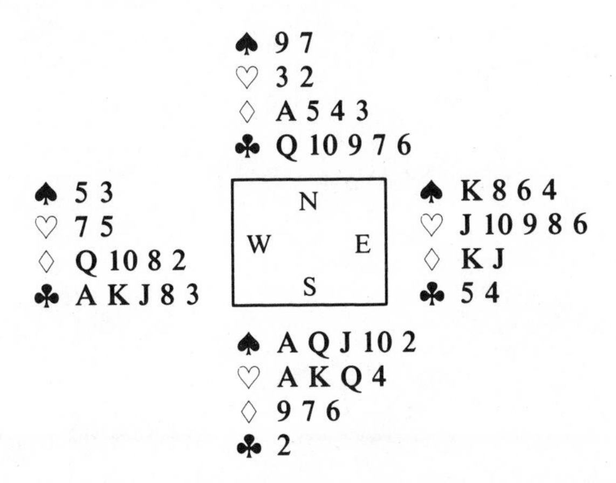

Two diamonds and a club were inescapable losers, so that the success of the contract appeared to hinge on the position of the king of spades. Since the heart loser had to be ruffed with one of dummy's only two trumps, it follows, does it not, that with only one finesse in trumps available, the success of the contract depends on finding East with precisely king *doubleton.*

Giorgio managed to find a line of play that would succeed even if East had *three or more* cards with the king of spades.

Upon winning the ace of diamonds, Belladonna ruffed a club and followed with the ace of hearts, king of hearts, heart ruff, club ruff, *queen of hearts ruffed* and a club ruff. At this stage declarer was left with the A-Q of spades and two losing diamonds. He simply exited with a diamond and had to make his two trump tricks in the end.

The Middle Is The Top

A brilliant defence by Eugenio Chiaradia in the 1959 European Teams Championship produced a decisive swing in favour of the Italian squad:

♠ A 2
♡ Q 4 3
♢ 7 6 4
♣ K 7 6 5 4

N
W E
S

♠ Q 3
♡ A 6 2
♢ A K Q J 10
♣ A 9 8

Both sides vulnerable. The bidding:

SOUTH	WEST *Chiaradia*	NORTH	EAST *Forquet*
1♢	1♠	2♣	Pass
2♠	Pass	2NT	Pass
3♢	Pass	3♠	Pass
4♣	Pass	4♢	Pass
4♡	Pass	5♢	All pass

West led the 3 of clubs: four - ten - ace. Three rounds of trumps saw East discarding a low heart on the third round.

How should declarer continue?

This was the complete deal:

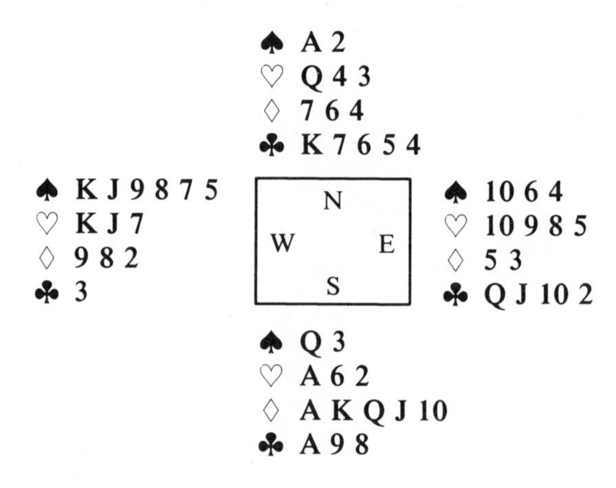

At the other table Walter Avarelli, South, faced the same problem. As the lead had all the earmarks of a singleton, ducking one round of clubs would not work for East's marked spade return would set the contract. By removing dummy's outside entry, the defence would be able to realise their three tricks, one club, one spade and one heart, before declarer could utilise dummy's fifth club.

After three rounds of trumps, Avarelli led the 2 of hearts (West must surely hold both the king of spades and the king of hearts to justify his intervention). West won the king of hearts and returned the same suit. Avarelli won in hand and now ducked a club, since he had a second entry to dummy. East's spade return was won by the ace and the king of clubs followed by a club ruff set up the fifth club. The queen of hearts provided the entry to dummy and the losing spade was discarded.

In the closed room declarer followed exactly the same play as Avarelli but Chiaradia outshone his counterpart. When at trick 5 South led the 2 of hearts, Chiaradia played low. When the queen won, this used up dummy's second entry prematurely so that declarer could not finish up as Avarelli did. Had he then ducked a club, my spade return would have put paid to the club suit and we would always have our three tricks.

Do you agree with all of this?

To answer this question you need to know what Chiaradia played when South led the 2 of hearts. Suppose he had followed with the 7. In that case, after winning the queen, declarer could have continued with the ace of hearts and a low heart, putting West on lead and forcing him to break the spades.

Foreseeing this ending, Chiaradia followed to the 2 of hearts with the *jack (!)* and when declarer came to hand with a heart to the ace, Chiaradia had no hesitation in pitching the *king* in order to unblock the suit.

At this stage the contract had become unmakeable. South tested the clubs but when they proved to be 4-1, declarer was forced to surrender after my spade return.

Killing Defence

During the 1965 Italian Championships Garozzo and I managed to defeat a 3NT contract that seemed laydown:

	North	
	♠ A 7 ♡ 3 ♢ Q 10 9 8 6 3 ♣ 7 6 3 2	
West ♠ 6 5 3 ♡ A J 6 5 4 2 ♢ K 5 ♣ Q 9	N W E S	

Both sides vulnerable. The bidding:

SOUTH	WEST	NORTH	EAST
	Forquet		*Garozzo*
2NT	Pass	3♢	Pass
3NT	Pass	Pass	Pass

I led the 5 of hearts: three - eight - king. Declarer continued with ace and another diamond.

How would you plan the defence in my position?

This was the complete hand:

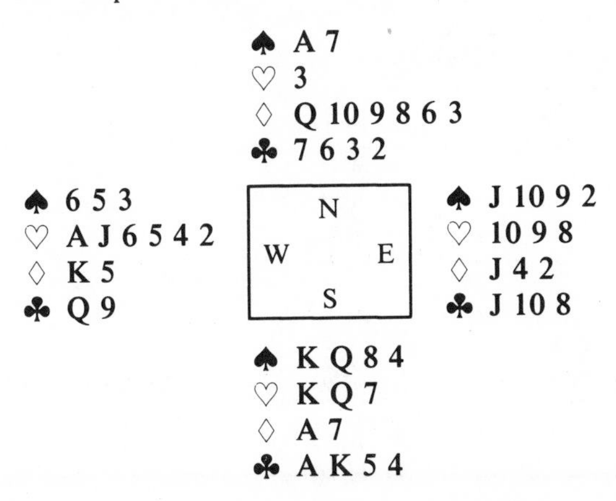

Partner's 8 of hearts at trick 1 marked declarer with the queen and 7, as well as the king. Hence in order to have a chance to defeat the contract, it was vital for East to gain the lead before declarer had the diamonds set up. Garozzo could not have a quick entry since the 2NT opening showed 21-22 points.

The only hope was to find East with the jack of diamonds three times.

Consequently under the ace of diamonds I dropped the KING to unblock the suit.

If you matched this play you have overcome the first hurdle in the defence. Nevertheless to defeat the contract the defence must still be razor-sharp.

Declarer won the second round of diamonds with the queen and when the jack did not drop, he had to abandon the diamonds and go for the clubs. If he could make three club tricks without giving East the lead, declarer would still succeed, with three spades, one heart, two diamonds and three clubs. The problem, therefore, was to avoid losing a trick to East.

Declarer led a low club from dummy: had Garozzo followed with the 8, South would have played low, forcing me to win the trick, but Garozzo played the 10. Declarer took the ace and I lost no time in ridding myself of the queen, else I could have been forced to win the second round of clubs. South re-entered dummy with the ace of spades and again led a club. Garozzo duly followed with the jack, again preventing me from being thrown on lead, this time with the 9, and South won the king. At this stage declarer's best chance would be to play king, queen and another spade, hoping to find me with the fourth spade but, disappointed at how little assistance had been received so far from the defence, South staked his contract on finding the 8 of clubs in my hand. When Garozzo won the club exit, he cashed the jack of diamonds and returned a heart: *three down*!

At the other table our teammates D'Alelio and Pabis-Ticci enhanced our success with a surprise result: *Six Diamonds bid and made!*

Here is the complete hand again:

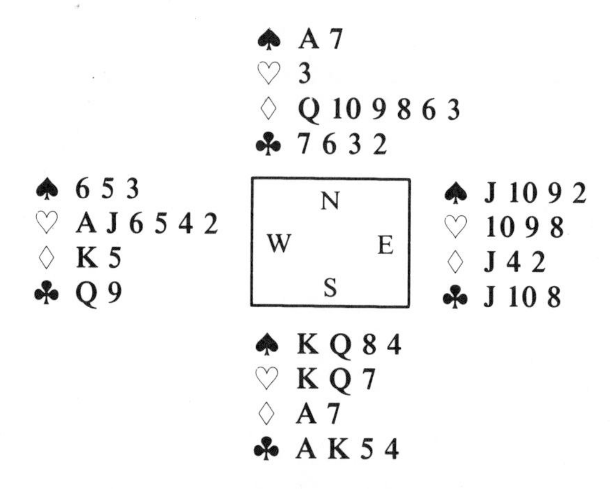

East had led the jack of spades and Pabis-Ticci, North, made the most of this lucky lead: three rounds of spades to discard the 3 of hearts; king of hearts - ace - ruff; ace and another diamond. Upon winning the king of diamonds, West returned a heart to dummy's queen, while North discarded a club loser. Coming to hand by ruffing the third heart, Pabis cashed the queen of diamonds to arrive at this end-position:

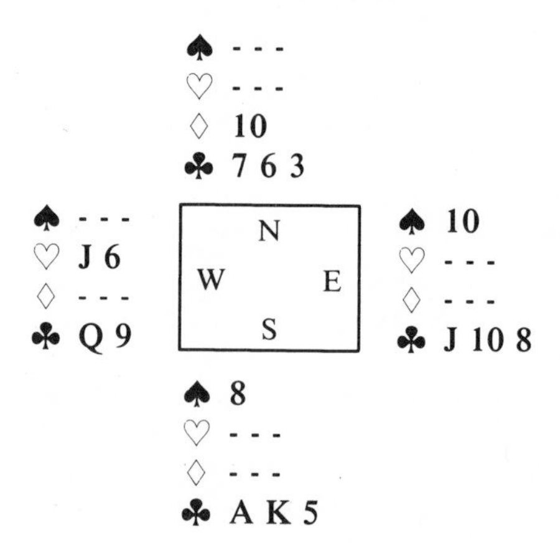

On the 10 of diamonds East was squeezed in spades and clubs.

The Password Is The Key

"Pass" is a legitimate call and can provide useful information. On this deal from a friendly match against a Rome team I had to bring in this contract of Four Spades:

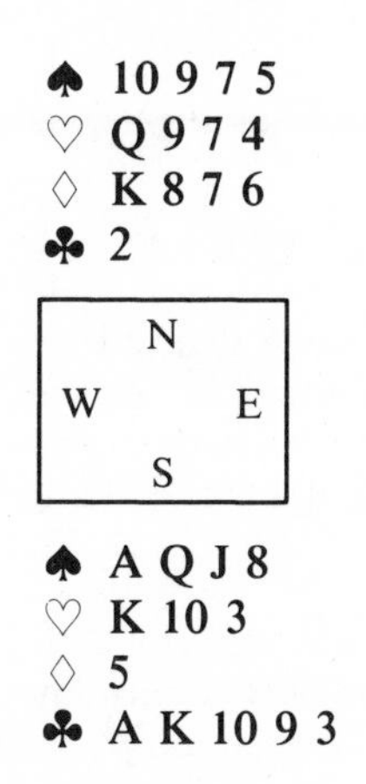

North-South vulnerable. The bidding:

WEST *Belladonna*	NORTH *Garozzo*	EAST *Avarelli*	SOUTH *Forquet*
		Pass	1♣
Pass	1◊	Pass	2♣
Pass	2◊	Pass	2♠
Pass	4♠	All pass	

Belladonna led the 2 of diamonds. I played low from dummy and Avarelli won with the 10. He switched to the ace of hearts, followed by the 2 of hearts.

What would you have done in my position to maximise your chances of making the contract?

This was the complete deal:

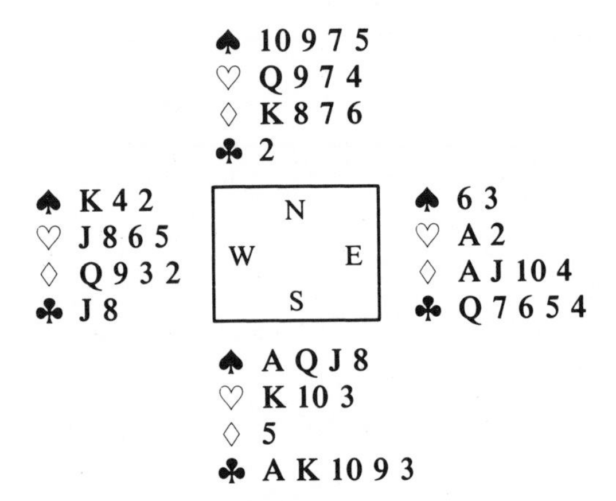

East had already shown up with the ace of hearts and no doubt the ace and jack of diamonds. In view of his original pass at favourable vulnerability, it was scarcely conceivable that he also had the king of spades. If I went for the spade finesse, West after winning the king would return a heart for East to ruff. To have any chance of making the contract, I would have to play ace and queen of spades, hoping against hope that East had started with no more than two trumps.

There was obviously more to the play than just this but a *sine qua non* of success was for East to have only two trumps. On Avarelli's ace of hearts, I unblocked my 10 and in with the king of hearts, I laid down the ace and queen of spades. Giorgio won the king and did best by returning his third trump. I won in hand with the jack and finessed dummy's 9 of hearts, coming down to the following ending:

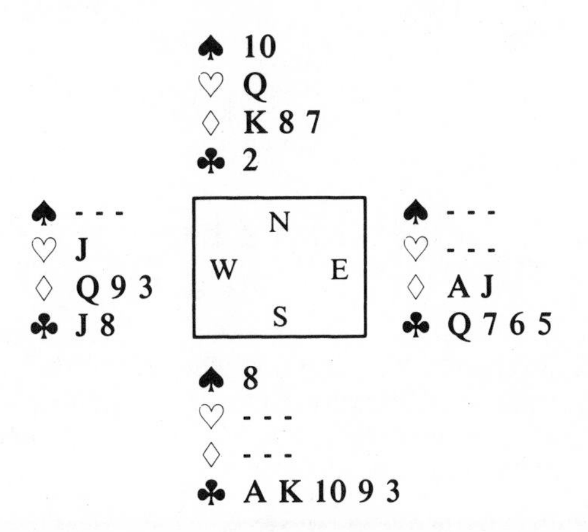

When I played the queen of hearts, Avarelli was squeezed: if he discarded a diamond, I would lead a low diamond, ruffing his ace and establishing the king; if instead he shed a club, I would have continued with ace, king and a third club, ruffing in dummy and setting up my own hand.

Variations

Had I failed to unblock the 10 of hearts, the communication problems would have precluded the squeeze.

If Belladonna had returned a diamond when on lead with the king of spades, I would have ruffed, taken the two heart tricks, finessing en route, cashed the ace and king of clubs and crossruffed the remainder.

Belladonna's Finesse

Giorgio Belladonna is wont to claim that when he needs to guess a finesse, he never has a problem. All joking aside, Giorgio really is endowed with tremendous flair and frequently gives the impression of playing as though he could see through the backs of the cards.

On the following deal the problem was to locate the queen of trumps. On this occasion Belladonna did not call upon his "intuition" but rather his expert technique.

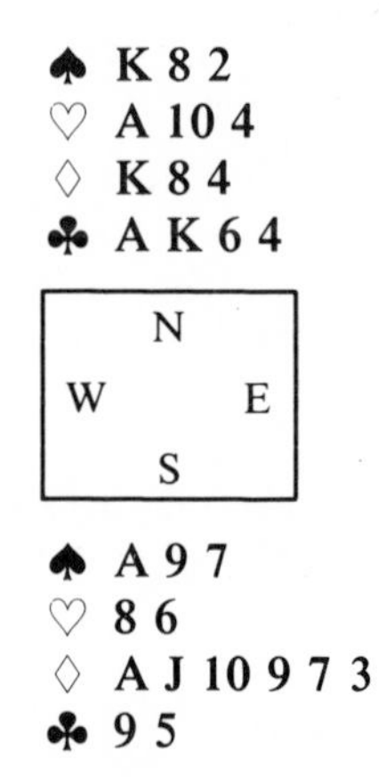

Neither side vulnerable. The bidding:

WEST	NORTH *Avarelli*	EAST	SOUTH *Belladonna*
	1NT	Pass	3◊
Pass	4◊	Pass	5◊
Pass	Pass	Pass	

No doubt 3NT would have been an easier contract, but after his partner's Three Diamonds, Avarelli naturally had visions of slam.

West led the jack of spades.

How would you have planned the play in Belladonna's position?

This was the complete deal:

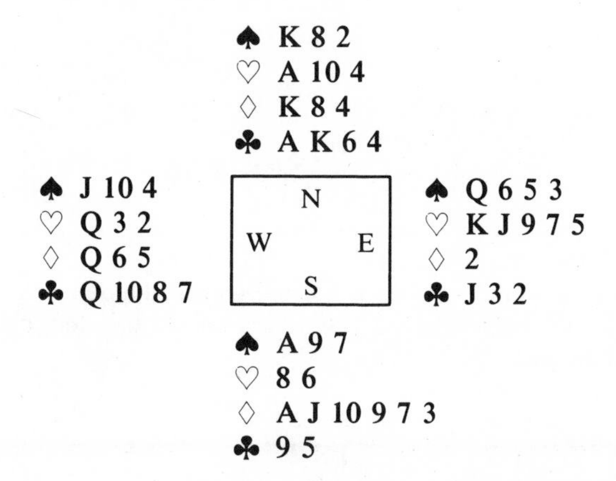

Winning the spade lead with the ace, Giorgio cashed the ace and king of clubs and ruffed a club in hand. He crossed to dummy with the ace of hearts and led dummy's last club. Had East followed, South would have discarded his heart loser but when East discarded on the club, Belladonna ruffed and gave up a heart. He won the spade return with the king and ruffed a heart to reach this end-position:

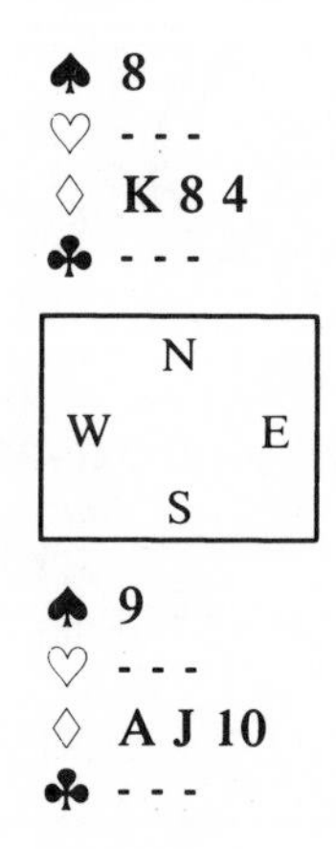

Bound to lose a spade and a heart, the contract had seemed to depend on finding the queen of diamonds. Giorgio's line did not locate the position of the queen of trumps, but his manoeuvres led to succeess irrespective of the position of the trump queen.

In the end-position Belladonna simply exited with a spade. It mattered not who won this trick or who held the queen of diamonds: the last three tricks had to be declarer's.

Invisible Solution

During a friendly match against a French team, I landed in an interesting contract of Two Spades, which resembles an old problem composed by Israel's Paul Lukacs:

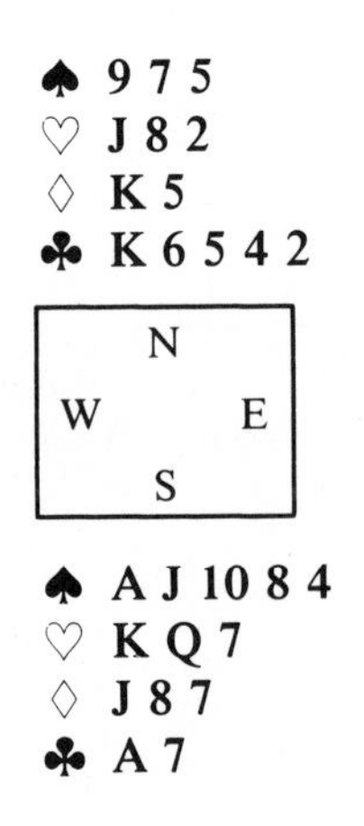

Both sides vulnerable. The bidding:

SOUTH	WEST	NORTH	EAST
Forquet		*Garozzo*	
1♠	Pass	1NT	Pass
2♠	Pass	Pass	Pass

After partner's 1NT response, I had two options: to underbid by repeating my spades or to overbid by raising to 2NT. After some thought I chose the first alternative.

West led the three of hearts, taken by East's ace, while I unblocked the king. On the six of spades return, I played low and West, after winning with the king, exited with the ten of hearts.

How should South proceed to have the best chance to make the contract?

This was the complete deal:

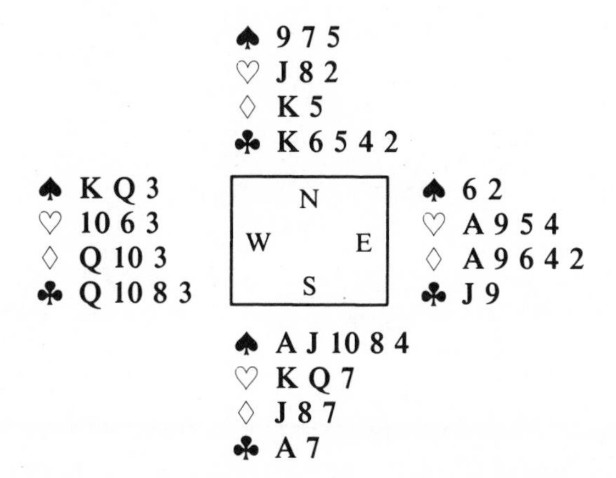

The problem lies in avoiding four more losers (three diamonds and a spade), which could occur if the opponents' cards all lay badly. Since in fact the cards did lie unfavourably, my safety play at trick four paid dividends.

Winning the heart return with dummy's jack, I continued with the five of diamonds from dummy. East played low and West won my jack with the queen. West was unable to play another round of trumps without losing a trick and I was therefore able to ruff the third diamond later in dummy.

Variations

Had the queen of diamonds been with East, the contract would have been equally safe since I would have been able to set up a diamond trick, whether East inserted the queen or whether East played low.

If at trick three I had captured the ten of hearts with my queen and had led a diamond to the king, the contract would have been beaten by a second trump lead by East. I then could not have avoided losing another spade and two more diamond tricks.

Ace Or King?

Very often one feels the need to ask, "From a suit headed by the ace-king, which do you lead, the ace or the king?" In a match against Switzerland during the 1964 Olympiad, Garozzo expressed his personal view on this subject. He held:

♠ A J 6 ♡ 8 5 3 ◊ A K 7 4 ♣ A Q 6

East-West vulnerable. The bidding:

WEST	NORTH	EAST	SOUTH
Garozzo		*Forquet*	
	Pass	Pass	1♠
1NT	2◊	Double	2♠
Double	Pass	Pass	3♣
Double	Pass	Pass	Pass

What would you have led in my partner's position?

The spade lead was out of the question and to start with a heart - with just three rags - was less than attractive. The ace (or the king) of diamonds seemed a lead that could do no damage but, as we will see, this lead would also have facilitated declarer's task.

With all this in mind, Garozzo selected the 6 of clubs, having also in mind the possibility of neutralising dummy's ruffing power. This decision worked out extremely well as I had the king and was able to win and return a club. Dummy was:

♠ 10 ♡ K 9 4 2 ◊ Q 10 8 6 2 ♣ 10 8 2

After winning the second round of clubs and cashing the third trump, how would you have proceeded as West?

This was the complete deal:

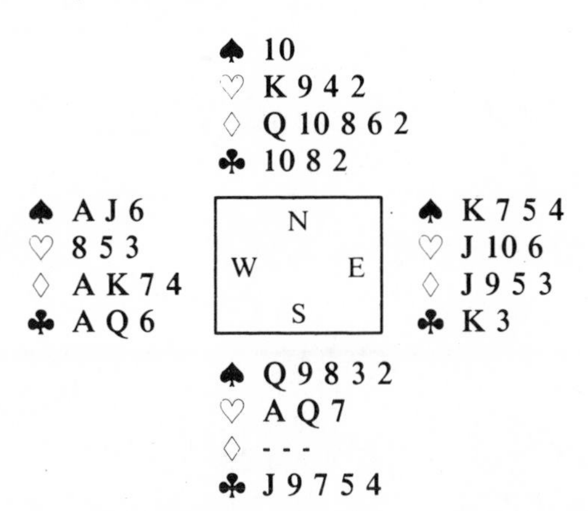

Divining the diamond position precisely by virtue of my penalty double of Two Diamonds, Garozzo switched to the 4 of diamonds, confident that declarer would not place him with both the ace and the king. South did insert dummy's 10, ruffed my jack, cashed four rounds of hearts and led a spade. Winning with the jack, Garozzo pursued his scheme by returning the 7 of diamonds! Declarer again took a deep finesse playing dummy's 8, but when I covered with the 9, declarer could not make more than his last trump.

The contract was thus scuttled by three tricks. At the other table, East-West played in 3NT, going one down.

An Additional Threat

During the qualifying rounds of the 1964 Olympiad, I was faced with the following slam:

♠ 5 4
♡ Q J 6
◊ A K J 5
♣ A 4 3 2

N
W E
S

♠ A K Q J 9 7
♡ 8
◊ 4 3
♣ K Q 10 7

East-West vulnerable. The bidding:

WEST	NORTH	EAST	SOUTH
	Garozzo		*Forquet*
	1◊	1♡	2♠
Pass	2NT	Pass	3♣
Pass	4♣	Pass	4♡
Pass	5◊	Pass	6♠
Pass	Pass	Pass	

West led the 10 of hearts and East, after capturing the queen with the king, switched to the 8 of spades. Winning the ace I drew two more rounds of trumps, dummy letting go a club and East a heart on the third round.

How would you have continued in my position?

This was the complete deal:

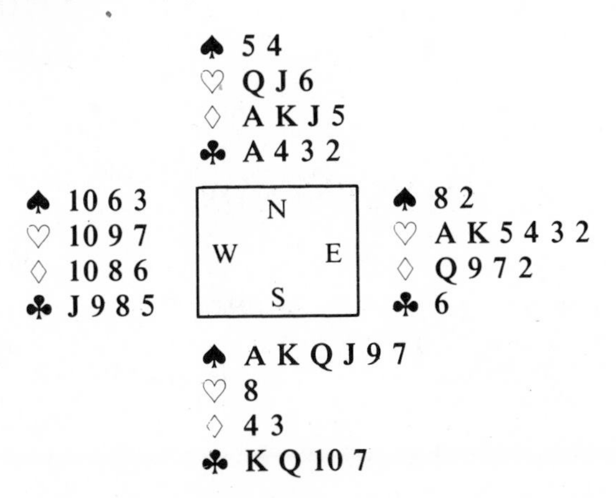

Prospects were extremely good. If clubs were 3-2 or if East held J-x-x-x, there would be no problems. If it was West, however, who held J-x-x-x, I would succeed if the queen of diamonds dropped (after ace and king of diamonds and a diamond ruffed) or if West were to succumb to a club-diamond squeeze. There was one further possibility, even though only a slender thread but still worth trying: if West had started with 10-9-7 in hearts, I would be able to transfer the control of the heart suit to him and use the 6 of hearts as an additional threat.

I therefore continued with ace of diamonds, jack of hearts-ace-ruff, king of diamonds, diamond ruff to reach this position:

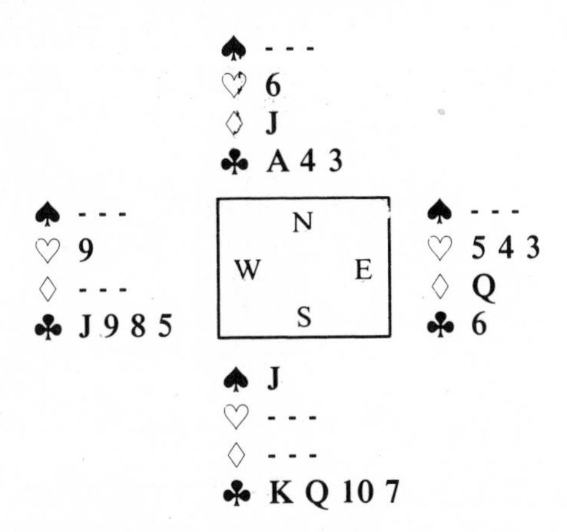

On my last trump, West in order to keep control of hearts had to let go a club. Note that if West had the queen of diamonds instead of the guard in hearts, the squeeze would have been just as effective.

D'Alelio's Sacrifice

Playing against a Spanish team at the 1966 Marbella Festival, Mimmo D'Alelio found a way to defeat a Five Diamond contract that at a certain point seemed unbeatable. This is what he held:

♠ A Q 10 9 ♡ 10 9 2 ◇ Q J 5 ♣ 10 4 3

The bidding:

SOUTH	WEST *D'Alelio*	NORTH	EAST *Pabis-Ticci*
1◇	Pass	2◇	Pass
2♠	Pass	3♣	Pass
3♡	Pass	4◇	Pass
5◇	Pass	Pass	Pass

The bidding was natural, with Three Hearts being a cue-bid.

What would you have led in D'Alelio's position?

To try to limit the forthcoming cross-ruff, Mimmo led a trump, although this could easily cost a trick. To retain some prospects of still making a trick in trumps, he tried to conceal his queen by leading the jack of diamonds. This was the layout:

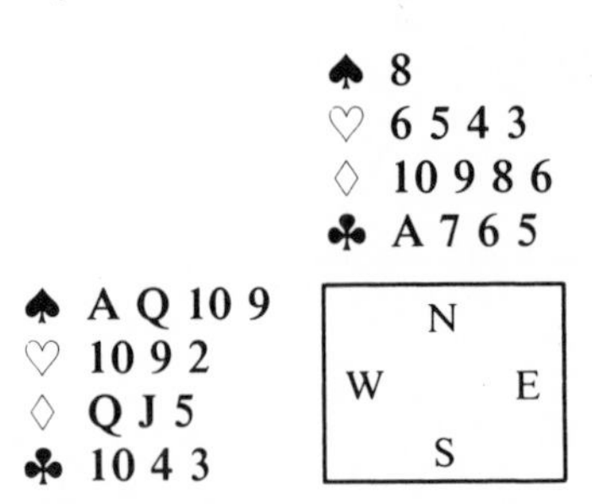

South won the diamond lead with the ace, East playing the 7. Declarer crossed to dummy with a club to the ace and led the 8 of spades: seven - jack - queen.

How would you continue?

This was the complete deal:

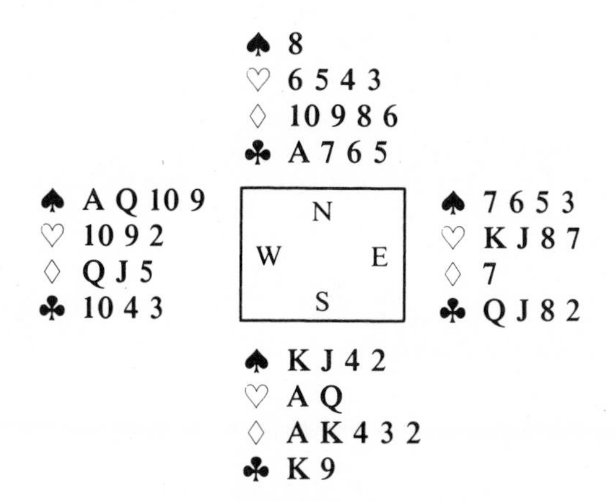

It seemed highly probable to D'Alelio that declarer had no losers in the outside suits and that the problem was to prevent declarer ruffing his remaining three spades in dummy. To return a diamond at this stage would remove one trump from dummy, to be sure, but it would also cost West his trump winner. Mimmo solved his problem by returning the *queen* of diamonds.

The contract now became unmakable thanks to the precious *five* of diamonds. If South elected to ruff two spades in dummy, not only would he have to give up a spade but the 5 of diamonds would have become the master trump; if instead declarer drew the 5 of trumps and then ruffed a spade, he would still have to give up two more tricks in spades later.

Note that any other defence by D'Alelio allows declarer home: on a heart or a club return, declarer ruffs the three spade losers in dummy, finesses in hearts and concedes a trump trick to West; had the return been the 5 of diamonds rather than the queen, South takes two spade ruffs in dummy, finesses in hearts, draws the last trump with the king of diamonds and concedes a spade at the end.

D'Alelio Never Forgives

During an Italian Championship Mimmo D'Alelio neatly exploited an opponent's error on this deal:

	North	
	♠ A K 3 2 ♡ A Q 10 9 ♢ K 7 5 ♣ 10 5	
West ♠ 10 8 ♡ J 6 4 2 ♢ A Q 2 ♣ Q J 9 7	N W E S	

Neither side vulnerable. The bidding:

WEST *D'Alelio*	NORTH	EAST *Pabis-Ticci*	SOUTH
	1NT	Pass	2♣
Pass	2♡	Pass	2♠
Pass	4♠	All pass	

South's Two Clubs was Stayman.

Mimmo led the queen of clubs to Pabis' ace. The 3 of clubs return was won by declarer's king. Declarer drew trumps in two rounds and then played king, ace and queen of hearts, Pabis discarding the 2 of clubs on the third round. Declarer came to hand with a trump and led the 3 of diamonds towards dummy's king.

How would you have played in D'Alelio's position?

This was the complete deal:

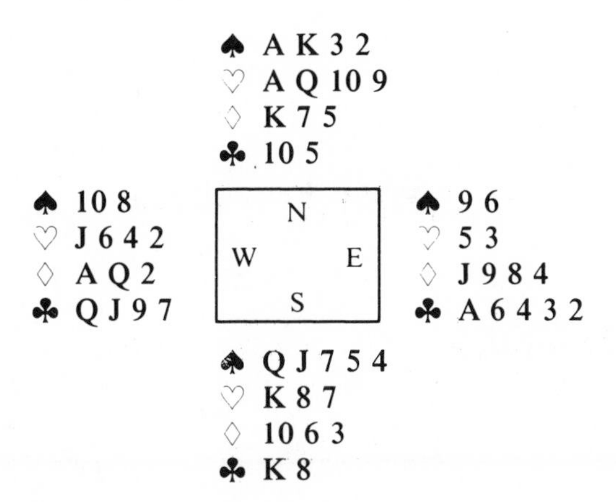

To defeat the contract required three more tricks. If Mimmo had risen with the ace, dummy's king would have been declarer's tenth trick while if he followed with the 2, South would play low in dummy, endplaying Pabis for a diamond to the king or a ruff-and-discard with a club. The only hope for three diamond tricks was to insert the *queen* and Mimmo duly played this card. Declarer tranced for a moment and finally decided to play for West to hold queen and jack in diamonds, playing low from dummy. Retaining the lead, Mimmo continued with the 2 of diamonds and following his plan, South ducked again in dummy, allowing Pabis to win with the jack.

The contract which was absolutely unbeatable thus failed by one trick.

Let's see how Benito Garozzo played the same contract at the other table: The first four tricks were identical but Benito managed the heart suit differently. He played the ace and king of hearts but on the third round, when he led low towards dummy and West played the 6, Benito without hesitation inserted dummy's 10. This play guaranteed the contract.

As the jack was with West, South was able to discard a diamond on the queen of hearts. Even if the 10 of hearts had lost to the jack in the East hand, East would thereupon have been endplayed and forced into leading a diamond up to dummy's king or giving a ruff-and-discard with a club return, the queen of hearts providing the resting place for the other diamond loser.

A Wise Precaution

Very often when one takes precautions to provide extra chances for success, the precautions prove unnecessary as the lie of the cards allows the contract to succeed in any event. Nevertheless, on some occasions the precautions taken will determine the result. Such was the case in the following deal which I played in Four Spades in the 1965 Italian Championships:

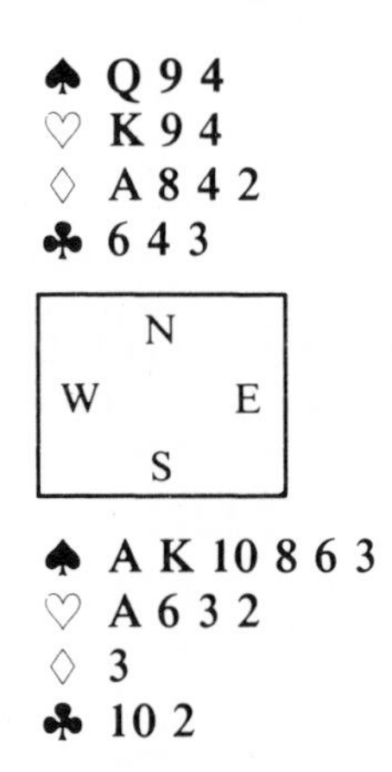

North-South vulnerable. The bidding:

SOUTH	WEST	NORTH	EAST
1♠	2♣	2♠	3♣
3♡	Pass	4♠	All pass

West led the 7 of hearts.

How would you plan the play in my position?

This was the complete deal:

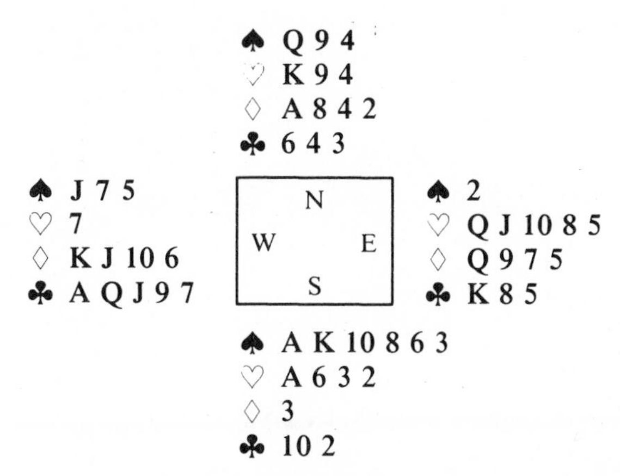

With two sure club losers, the problem was to avoid losing two hearts as well, assuming the suit did not divide 3-3. If they broke 4-2 I could start on the hearts before broaching trumps, planning to ruff the last heart in dummy. If West had started with only one heart, however, this would cost me two tricks in hearts. To protect myself against this risk I could draw just two rounds of trumps. If they were 2-2, my problems would be over while if they were 3-1, I could still survive if hearts were 3-3.

Nevertheless I scrapped both these lines since they seemed almost certain to fail: the heart lead, in the light of the bidding, was highly likely to be a singleton and if so, West was most likely to hold three spades.

Have you seen the solution?

Success required that I be able to ruff the fourth round of hearts in dummy without sustaining two heart ruffs on the way. I won the lead with the ace of hearts, crossed to dummy with a diamond to the ace and led the 3 of clubs.

As the cards lay, the contract was now unbeatable.

East followed with the 8 of clubs and West, winning my 10 with the jack, returned a trump. I won this in hand and led another club taken by East's king. East returned the queen of hearts. West let this go (he would have nothing to gain by ruffing) and upon winning the king of hearts, I led another heart. The defence thus could not prevent my ruffing the fourth heart in dummy and West was unable to receive two ruffs in hearts.

Variations

If at trick 3 East had risen with the king of clubs, the play would have developed along equivalent lines.

If at trick 2 I had led the 10 of clubs from hand, the defence would have prevailed as long as West did not play the ace or the 7 of clubs: any intermediate card would allow his partner two entries to provide two heart ruffs.

A Desperate Defence

Suppose you were West on the following deal:

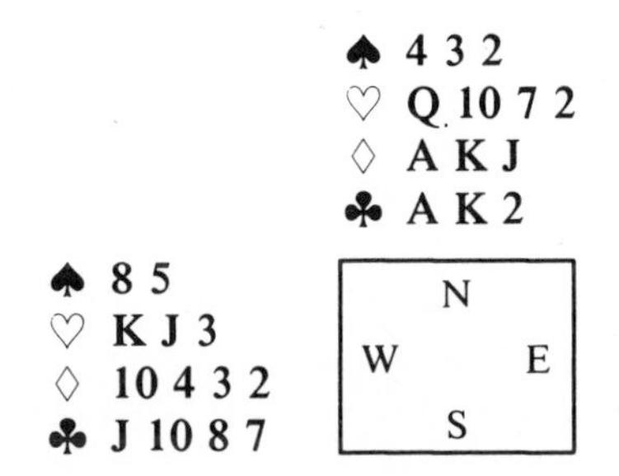

North-South vulnerable. The bidding:

WEST	NORTH	EAST	SOUTH
Forquet		*Siniscalco*	
		3♠	Pass
Pass	Double	Pass	3NT
Pass	Pass	Pass	

You lead the 8 of spades, East plays the jack and holds the trick as South plays the 10. The spade continuation is won by South's ace and declarer now plays ace of hearts and another heart.

How do you plan the defence?

This was the complete deal:

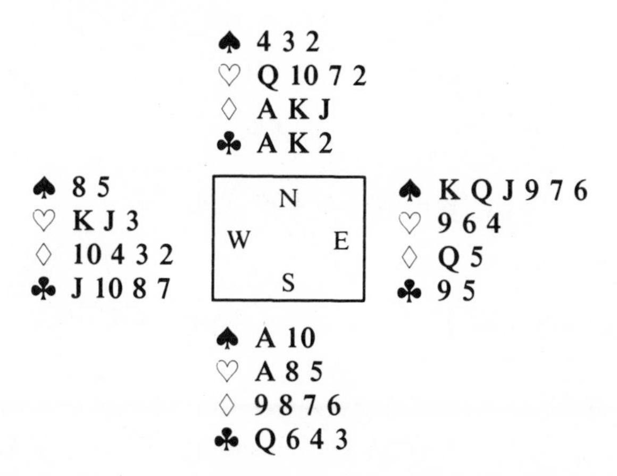

I was confronted with this problem in a European Championship many years ago. If declarer could garner three heart tricks, then if he held either the queen of diamonds or the queen of clubs, the contract would succeed. Since it was highly unlikely that my partner held both minor suit queens I sought to divert declarer from three heart winners.

When declarer laid down the ace of hearts, I dropped the king, creating the impression that I was unblocking the king to provide an entry to my partner's hand with the jack. My illusion succeeded for South cashed the ace of diamonds after winning the queen of hearts and ran off three rounds of clubs. Had clubs been 3-3 declarer would have had nine tricks, but when Siniscalco discarded a spade on the third round of clubs, declarer banked on the diamond finesse for the game-going trick. Siniscalco won the queen of diamonds, cashed three top spades and returned a heart.

You can visualise declarer's expression when the jack turned out to be in my hand.

The Revenge Of The Novice

Rarely does an expert fail in a contract that would be made easily by a lesser player. The following deal arose in an international teams tournament in Palma di Majorca:

♠ Q 4 2
♡ K Q 7 5
◊ 7 5 3
♣ 8 6 4

N
W E
S

♠ A K J 10 5 3
♡ A 8
◊ A K J
♣ A Q

Both sides vulnerable. The bidding:

Closed Room

SOUTH	WEST	NORTH	EAST
	Belladonna		*Avarelli*
2♠	Pass	3♠	Pass
4NT	Pass	5♣	Pass
5NT	Pass	6◊	Pass
7♠	Pass	Pass	Pass

Open Room

SOUTH	WEST	NORTH	EAST
Garozzo		*Forquet*	
1♣	Pass	1♡	Pass
2♠	Pass	3♠	Pass
4♣	Pass	4♡	Pass
5◊	Pass	5♡	Pass
7♠	Pass	Pass	Pass

By the time this deal was to be played in the open room, Belladonna who had completed his set wandered into the bridgerama room just in time to hear the expert commentator's prediction that the grand slam made in the closed room would produce a flat board since both the queen of diamonds and the king of clubs were onside for declarer. Belladonna interrupted and asserted that if West got off to a spade or a heart lead, Benito would go down in Seven Spades!

West did lead a spade and the outcome justified Giorgio's prediction.

How would you have planned the play in my partner's position?

This was the complete deal:

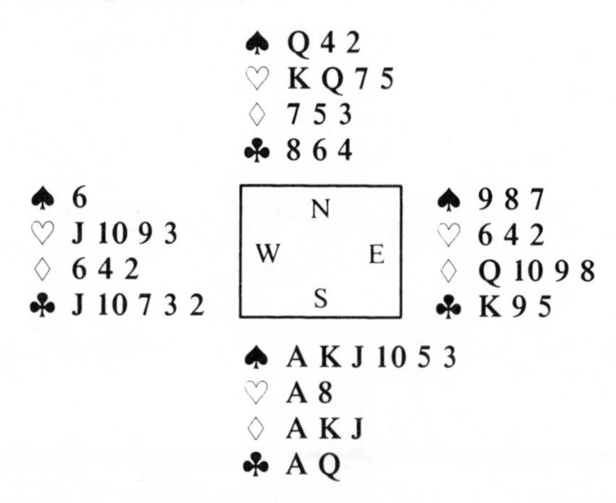

In the closed room the Spanish South received the same lead and after drawing trumps he laid down the ace and king of diamonds in the hope of dropping the queen. When this unlikely result did not eventuate, declarer played off three rounds of hearts, pitching the jack of diamonds, and fell back on the club finesse which worked.

How then did Garozzo go down?

Winning the trump lead, Garozzo ran all his trumps, the ace and king of diamonds and the ace of clubs, coming down to this ending:

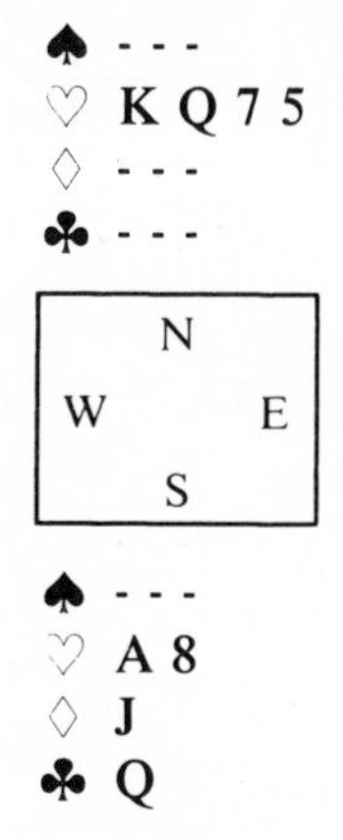

This would have been a winning position if the player with four or more hearts also held *either* the queen of diamonds *or* the king of clubs. To retain his guard in diamonds or clubs he would be obliged to reduce to only three hearts. The line chosen by the Spanish player worked in only one case, that of the king of clubs with East (the chance of the doubleton queen of diamonds would also have worked in Garozzo's line).

A Choice Of Finesses

This deal occurred at the Marbella international pairs tournament in 1966:

	North	
	♠ J 7 ♡ K Q 7 ♢ J 8 5 4 ♣ J 9 7 4	
♠ A Q ♡ 6 5 3 ♢ K Q 10 9 ♣ 10 8 3 2	N W E S	

Both sides vulnerable. The bidding:

SOUTH	WEST *Forquet*	NORTH	EAST *Garozzo*
1♠	Pass	1NT	Pass
3♡	Pass	4♠	All pass

On my lead of the king of diamonds Garozzo encouraged with the 7 and I continued with the 10. South ruffed with the 3 of spades, crossed to dummy with a heart to the king, on which my partner played the 2. He then led the jack of spades, letting it run.

How would you defend in my position to give yourself the best chance of defeating the contract?

Superficially the logical plan is to win the queen of spades and return a heart, intending to play a third heart when in with the ace of spades to give partner a heart ruff.

This defence, however, has a fundamental flaw: on the king of hearts, Garozzo had played the 2, showing that he had three cards in the suit, not a doubleton.

Consequently it was necessary to revise my defensive approach. South had shown up with four hearts and a diamond and would have 5 or 6 spades on the bidding. Accordingly he would hold two or three clubs. On the bidding he was a certainty to have two top honours in clubs. If he had the ace and the king, he could not be prevented from making his contract but if he had only the ace and queen . . .

This was the complete deal:

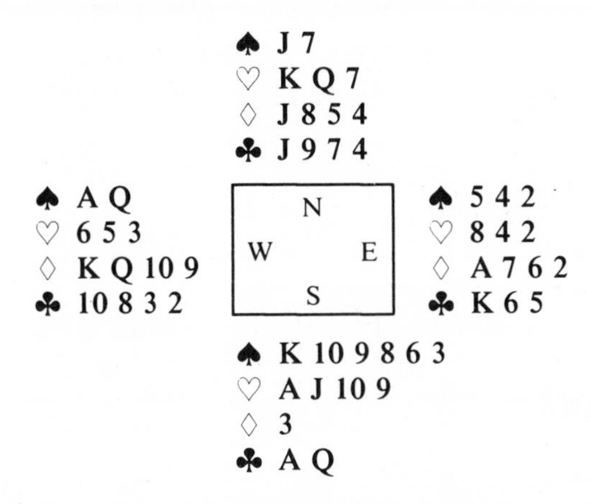

I won the jack of spades with the *ace*. Ruffing the diamond return, declarer returned to dummy with the queen of hearts. With no further entry he now had to choose between finessing for the queen of spades or for the king of clubs. Naturally he opted for the finesse *that had already proved successful*.

Winning the 10 of spades with the queen I played my last diamond and South could not avoid a club loser. The contract was thus defeated, the defence taking two spades, a diamond and a club.

Had I won the jack of spades at trick 4 with the queen, declarer would have made his game since he then would have utilised his last entry to dummy to take the club finesse.

The Swing That Did Not Materialise

On many occasions a contract can succeed on several different lines. On other occasions the superior line of play may not receive its just reward. On the following deal played during the 1966 Italian Championships, both North-South pairs arrived in the grand slam in hearts. Both pairs made the grand slam even though one declarer chose a line of play that was not best.

♠ Q 7 5
♡ 10 5 4
♢ A K 7 4
♣ A 8 7

N
W E
S

♠ A K 8 6
♡ A K Q J 9 6
♢ - - -
♣ Q J 4

North-South vulnerable. The bidding:

Closed Room

SOUTH	WEST	NORTH	EAST
1♡	Pass	2♣	2♢
2♠	Pass	3♢	Pass
6♡	Pass	7♡	All pass

Open Room

SOUTH	WEST	NORTH	EAST
Forquet		*Garozzo*	
1♣	Pass	2♣	2♢
3♡	Pass	4♣	Pass
4♠	Pass	5♢	Pass
5♠	Pass	7♡	All pass

The open room bidding requires some explanation. The jump to Three Hearts promised a solid suit and Five Spades was a grand slam try. North in addition to the five controls already promised held the queen of spades, a jewel after South had cuebid twice in spades, and consequently had no hesitation in bidding the grand slam. The closed room bidding was less scientific but equally effective.

At both tables the lead was the 6 of diamonds. If hearts had been 2-2, the hand would not be appearing in this book. Two clubs would be discarded on the ace and king of diamonds and the fourth spade, if not a winner, would be ruffed in dummy. Unluckily for South, East discarded a diamond on the second round of hearts.

How would you have planned the play as declarer?

After you have formed your plan, take a look at the complete deal:

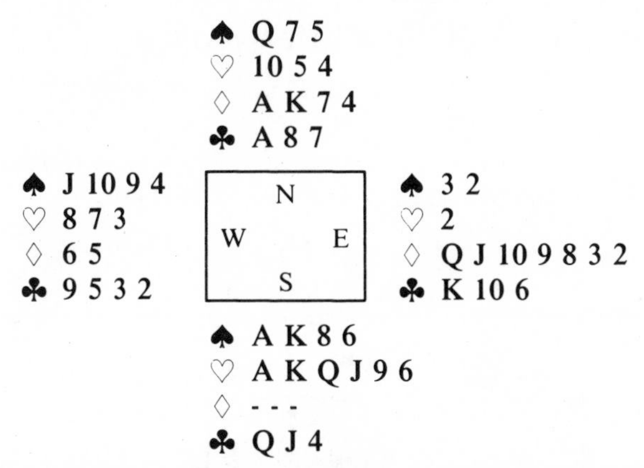

In the closed room declarer ruffed the opening lead, drew two rounds of trumps and rattled off four rounds of spades, ruffing the fourth in dummy. The grand slam thus made since West who held the trump length also had four spades. Clearly if West had started with only two spades, the contract would have failed.

In the open room replay I believed that East's Two Diamond intervention would certainly include at least six diamonds and the king of clubs. If so, I would be able to succeed without running the risk of West ruffing an early round of spades. The risk was not at all remote for East could easily have started with four spades, one heart, six diamonds and two clubs.

Winning the lead with the ace of diamonds, discarding a club from hand, I ran off five rounds of trumps, discarding two clubs from dummy. The ace and king of spades then produced this ending:

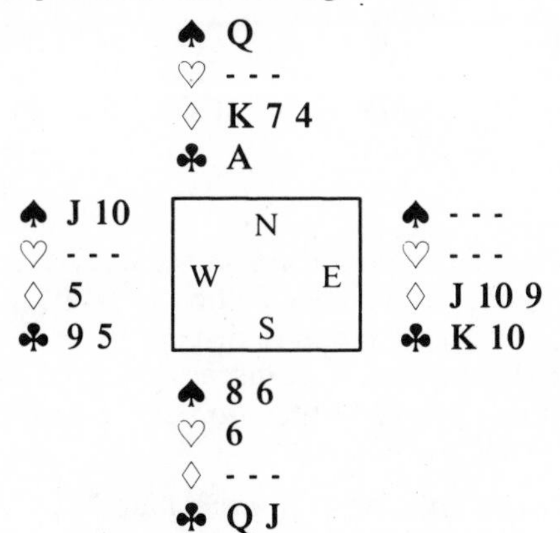

When I led a spade East was squeezed. If he discarded a diamond, I would ruff a diamond, making dummy high; if instead he let a club go, then the winning play would be to cash the ace of clubs and the king of diamonds to discard a spade.

Note that if East had started with four spades, the squeeze would have worked just as effectively. In this case East would have been squeezed in three suits while the line followed by the other declarer would have failed.

A Possible Recovery

During a teams tournament in Istanbul in 1966, Garozzo playing opposite Omar Sharif landed in a small slam on these cards:

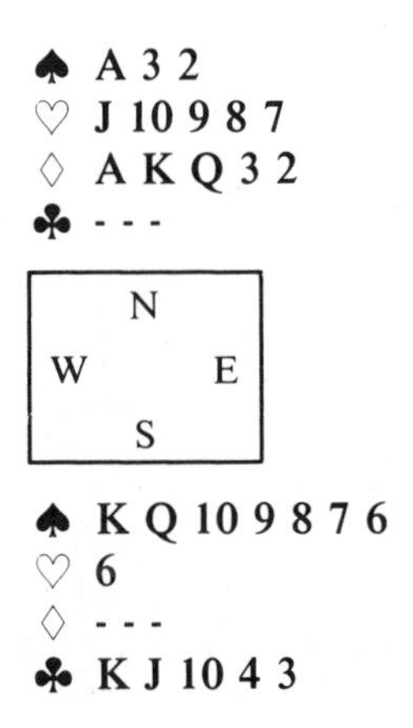

Both sides vulnerable. The bidding:

WEST	NORTH *Sharif*	EAST	SOUTH *Garozzo*
	1♡	Pass	2♠
Pass	3♠	Pass	4♣
Pass	4◊	Pass	4♡
Pass	5♣	Pass	5◊
Pass	6◊	Pass	6♠
Pass	Pass	Pass	

Both rooms reached this slam and at both tables West led the ace of hearts, East playing the 5, and continued with the 2 of hearts to East's king, ruffed by South. Declarer's problem was to dispose of his five club losers. Two could be ruffed in dummy and three discarded on the top diamonds. It was therefore vital only to pay close attention to the timing of these moves to guard against possible bad breaks.

How would you have played in South's place?

In the closed room declarer elected to start with a round of trumps and cashed the king of spades, *on which West played a club*. Declarer could not afford to ruff two clubs in dummy, lest the jack of spades with East score a trick. Nevertheless all was not lost.

How would you have continued?

This was the complete deal:

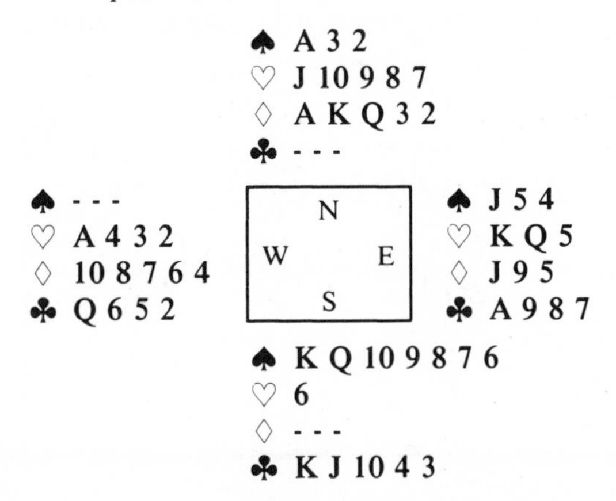

Declarer planned to set up a winning heart in dummy by taking a ruffing finesse against East's queen. He therefore continued with a club ruff; ace, king and queen of diamonds, to discard three clubs; jack of hearts - queen - ruff; spade to the ace; 10 of hearts, planning to pitch his last club. When East ruffed the 10 of hearts the contract was one down.

In the open room Garozzo preferred not to draw a round of trumps and after ruffing the king of hearts, he continued with a club ruff, three top diamonds to pitch the clubs, heart ruff, club ruff. This line naturally led to a happy ending and was certainly superior to the line chosen by the other declarer. The benefits flowing from cashing the king of spades were heavily outweighed by the attendant risks.

Still and all, South could yet have made the small slam after laying down the king of spades.

Have you spotted the winning play?

In view of the 3-0 trump split, rather than retain the lead, South should have *overtaken his king with dummy's ace.* This would succeed even if East began with only three hearts. The play would proceed: king of spades overtaken by dummy's ace; three top diamonds; heart ruff; club ruff; winning heart . . . If the heart lives, South rids himself of his last club and finesses against the jack of spades; if instead East ruffs the heart winner, South overruffs and ruffs his last club in dummy.

This plan also succeeds where East began with at least four hearts headed by the king and queen but with only two diamonds. When the third diamond is played, East may ruff or discard a heart. If he ruffs, South overruffs, crosses to dummy by ruffing a club, takes a ruffing finesse against the queen of hearts, ruffs the fourth club in dummy and ditches his last club on the established heart winner; if instead East discards a heart on the third diamond, the play follows the line previously examined.

Those Insignificant Low Cards

One of the rarest positions is the single suit squeeze. I was faced with this Four Heart contract during an Italian Championship:

♠ 7 5 4
♡ 5 4
◊ A Q 9 7
♣ 9 7 5 4

N
W E
S

♠ K 3 2
♡ A K Q J 10 7
◊ K 5 4
♣ J

Both sides vulnerable. The bidding:

SOUTH	WEST	NORTH	EAST
Forquet		*Garozzo*	
1♣	2♠	Double	Pass
3♡	3♠	4♡	All pass

West's Two Spades indicated at least six spades and a sound opening bid.

West led the ace of clubs and continued with the king, East following with the eight and the six.

How would you have continued after ruffing the second club?

The problem clearly consists of eliminating one of your three spade losers, the ace being obviously on your left. Suppose you start by drawing two rounds of trumps, all following. You now know that West started with at least six spades (from the bidding), two hearts and two clubs. If his last three cards are diamonds, your worries are over since one of the spade losers can be discarded on the thirteenth diamond. This is now the position:

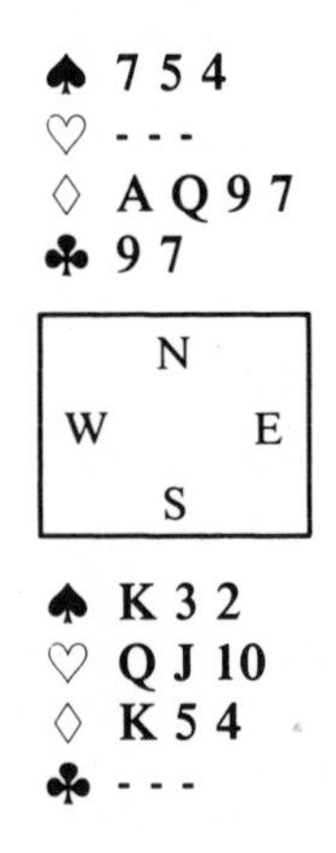

How do you continue?

If you have decided to draw the last trump, you have committed a serious mistake as you will have to discard a card from dummy before clarifying West's shape. Perhaps you wish to query the value of North's low spades. Why not discard one of them? Let's take a look at the complete deal and the rest of the play:

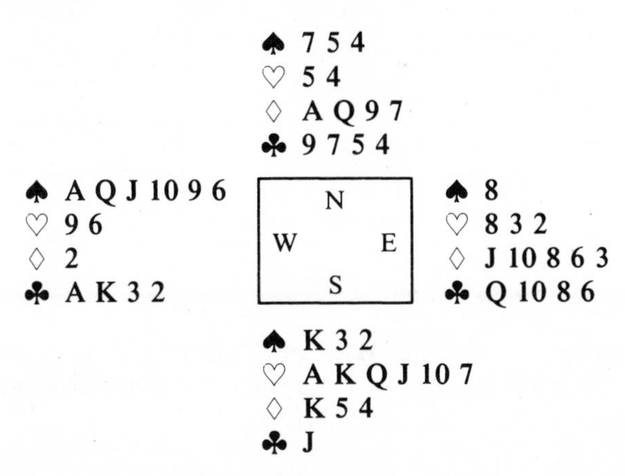

After ruffing the second round of clubs and drawing two rounds of trumps only, I crossed to dummy's ace of diamonds and ruffed another club. Once West followed with a club, the 3-3 break in diamonds could be discounted as West could hold no more than two diamonds (with two hearts and three clubs already seen and six spades on the bidding). Thus there was no hope of discarding a spade on the fourth round of diamonds and when I next drew the last trump, the low diamond discard from dummy was easy. I kept all three spades and a club.

On the third round of trumps West tried to guard against an endplay by discarding the queen of spades and when I cashed the king of diamonds he discarded the jack of spades.

This was the position immediately before I led my last diamond to dummy's queen:

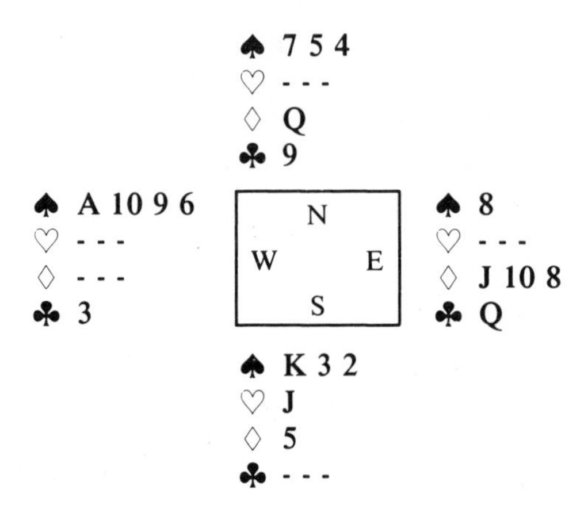

On the third round of diamonds, West let go the three of clubs and I came back to hand by trumping dummy's last club. It was at this moment that *West became squeezed in the spade suit itself.*

If he had discarded the six I would have continued with a low spade, putting West on lead and forcing him to lead up to my king of spades. If West had come down to A-10-8 in spades I would have had to lead a low spade in order to succeed. West did the best he could by discarding the 9 of spades and this left me with one final problem. Were West's last three cards the A-10-8 or the A-10-6 in spades? His hesitation before parting with the 9 of spades set me on the right track and I laid down the king of spades. West won the ace, cashed the 10 of spades but was then forced to concede the last trick to dummy's 7 of spades!

Chiaradia's Grand Slam

The following slam was played by Eugenio Chiaradia in the European Teams Championship many years ago:

♠ Q J 8
♡ A K 5
◇ K 6 5
♣ A Q 9 7

	N	
W		E
	S	

♠ - - -
♡ 6 4 2
◇ A J 10 9 8 7 2
♣ K 6 5

North-South vulnerable. The bidding:

WEST	NORTH *Siniscalco*	EAST	SOUTH *Chiaradia*
	1♣	1♠	1NT
Pass	2♣	Pass	3◇
Pass	4◇	Pass	4♠
Pass	5♡	Pass	5♠
Pass	5NT	Pass	6♣
Pass	7◇	All pass	

West led the 10 of spades: queen - king - ruff. Declarer's first problem was to decide how to handle the trumps to guard against Q-x-x in one hand. As East was known to have length in spades, Chiaradia elected to guard against West having the diamond length and accordingly laid down the ace of diamonds.

His decision was rewarded when East discarded a spade on this trick. Eugenio continued with two more rounds of trumps, picking up West's queen on the way, East discarding two more spades.

The next problem was to dispose of the loser in hearts. Chiaradia cashed the ace of clubs and came to hand with the king of clubs, East having followed with the 4 and the jack, West with the 2 and 3.

This was the position:

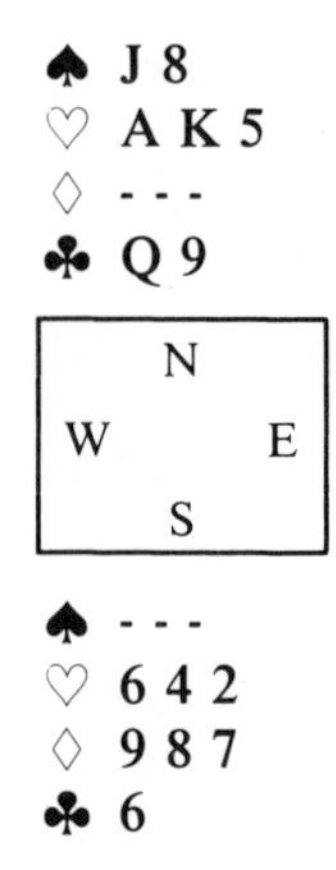

How would you have continued as declarer?

At the other table South wrestling with the same problem aimed to transfer control of the spade suit to West. He therefore played off the ace and king of hearts, jack of spades - ace - ruff, and another round of trumps. This was the three-card ending:

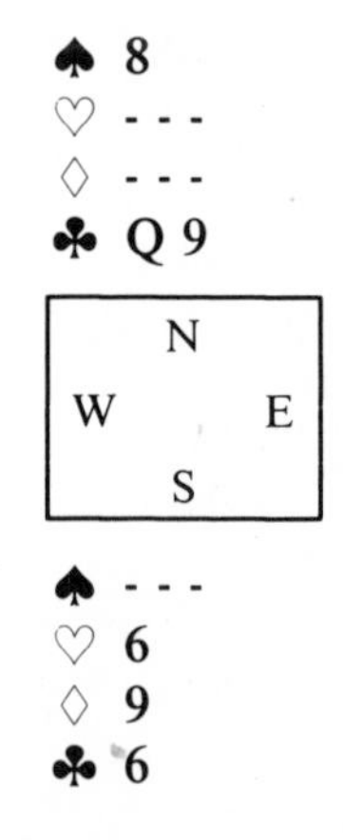

If in this ending West had started with the 9 of spades as well as four clubs, he would be squeezed; if on the other hand he had started with only three clubs (and East originally held J-10-x), West would be forced to retain the 9 of spades together with one club and then when South leads a club to the queen, the 10 would drop.

However, declarer failed to cater for the possibility that it was East who had started with four cards in clubs and hence his grand slam was consigned to perdition for the complete deal was:

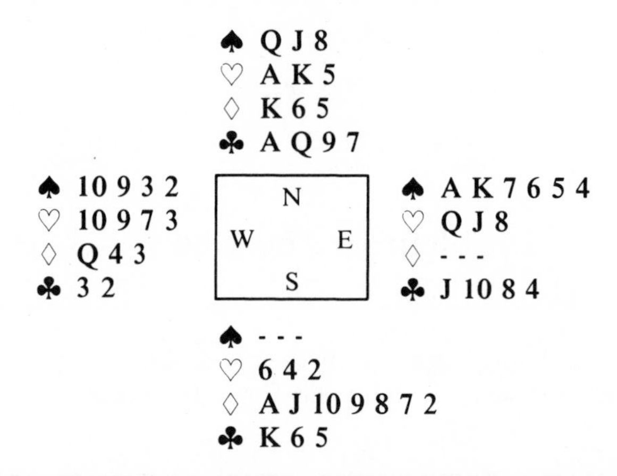

Chiaradia adopted a line of play which would ensure the grand slam, the only proviso being that West had the 9 of spades, almost a certaintly after the lead of the 10. Chiaradia drew trumps, cashed two top clubs and continued with a club to the queen and the last club from dummy, ruffed. This led to this position:

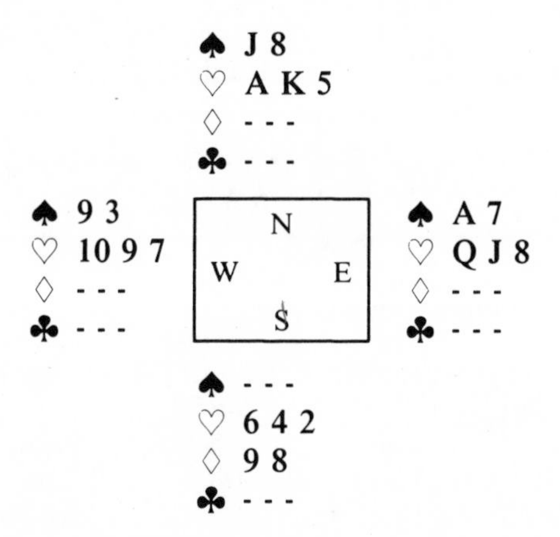

Eugenio now led the 9 of diamonds, discarding the 5 of hearts from dummy. West was forced to discard a heart, for if he let go another spade, South would have crossed to dummy with a heart and played the jack of spades, pinning the 9 and establishing the 8. Now it was East's turn to feel the pinch: if he discarded a spade, declarer would likewise have crossed to dummy with a heart, this time leading the 8 of spades and ruffing out East's ace; if he elected to pitch a heart, South would cash dummy's two heart tricks, thereby setting up his third heart as the thirteenth.

Problem In The Red Suits

During an exhibition match in the United States after the 1967 World Championships I was faced with this Four Heart contract:

♠ A 8 4
♡ K 7 5
♢ Q J 2
♣ A 8 7 5

	N	
W		E
	S	

♠ 9 7
♡ A Q 6 4 2
♢ A 6 5 4
♣ 6 3

North-South vulnerable. The bidding:

SOUTH *Forquet*	WEST	NORTH *Garozzo*	EAST
1♡	1♠	2♣	Pass
2♢	Pass	2♠	Pass
3♡	Pass	4♡	All pass

West led the 10 of diamonds and East covered dummy's queen with the king.

How do you play to give yourself the best chance of making the contract?

If diamonds are 3-3 the hand will present no problems (unless hearts break badly, in which case you will almost certainly fail). If, however, diamonds are 4-2 you will have to step gingerly in the red suits to ensure success.

This was the complete deal:

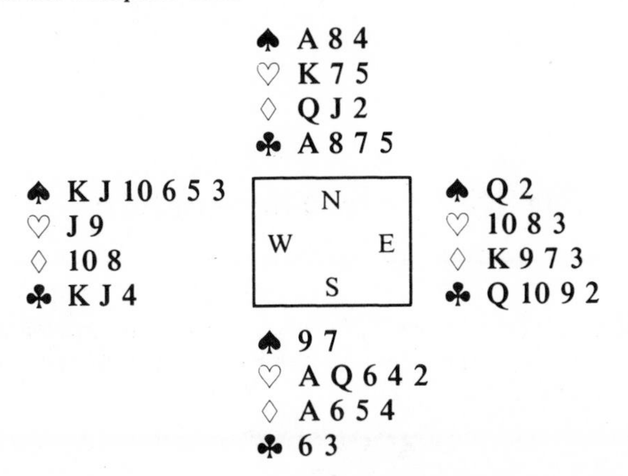

If after winning the ace of diamonds you play king and ace of hearts, jack of diamonds and give up a diamond, intending to ruff your last diamond in dummy, East upon winning the third diamond will simply return a trump and the contract will fail. If instead you continue at once with jack and another diamond, East upon winning will play back the fourth diamond: West's ruff with the 9 of hearts uppercuts dummy and promotes a trump trick for East.

How then should you play to make your contract?

The key is to duck the king of diamonds!

Whatever is returned, South will win, cash the king and ace of hearts and then play the jack of diamonds and ace of diamonds. If diamonds are not 3-3, declarer will still succeed if the player with only two diamonds began also with only two trumps. That was in fact the layout and I was thus able to ruff my fourth diamond in dummy and make the contract.

And now an additional question:

Can you see a way to defeat this contract?

This is how the bidding went at the other table:

SOUTH	WEST *Belladonna*	NORTH	EAST *Avarelli*
Pass	Pass	1♣	Pass
2♡	Pass	3♡	Pass
4♡	Pass	Pass	Pass

Here, too, the lead was the 10 of diamonds but when declarer played the queen from dummy, Avarelli produced the killing defence: *he played low.*

The contract can no longer be made. Declarer continued with ace and another diamond but Avarelli won the king of diamonds and continued the suit. Belladonna duly ruffed with the 9, promoting his partner's 10.

The Key Is In The Auction

Very often the result of a contract can depend solely on the opposition 's bidding Take for example this deal from the France-Italy match in the 1967 World Championship:

♠ A 8
♡ A K Q J
◊ Q 2
♣ K Q 5 4 3

	N	
W		E
	S	

♠ K 5 3
♡ 7 6 2
◊ K 5 4
♣ J 10 8 7

Neither side vulnerable. The bidding:

SOUTH	WEST	NORTH	EAST
Forquet		*Garozzo*	
Pass	Pass	1♣	Pass
1♡*	1♠	2♣	Pass
3♣	3◊	3♡	Pass
3NT	Pass	Pass	Pass

*6+ points, less than 3 controls

Put yourself in my position as South on the lead of the jack of diamonds.

How do you plan the play?

The problem is whether to rise with dummy's queen or whether to play low in both hands. Playing the queen will win if West has both missing aces, while it will lose if they are divided; playing low from both hands, vice versa, wins if the aces are divided provided that West holds six diamonds, while it loses if West has both aces.

The outcome of this deliberation appears to be that playing the queen offers the better chance. Once one takes the bidding into account, however, one can see that ducking in both hands is the superior move.

Second in hand, with neither side vulnerable, West passes originally and then, all on his own, he bids his two suits to the three-level. Without a doubt his suits must have good texture to afford such a risk. If in addition to these two strongish suits and good distribution, we place West with the two aces, how can we justify his pass on the first round?

Consequently this line of reasoning indicates that it is more likely that the aces are divided and accordingly I played low from dummy and my own hand at trick 1. This logic was wholly justified as can be seen from the complete deal:

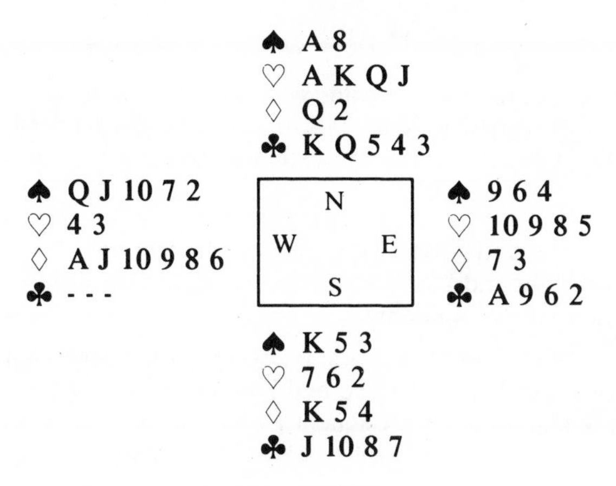

At the other table the bidding proceeded:

SOUTH	WEST	NORTH	EAST
	Belladonna		*Avarelli*
Pass	1♠	Double	Pass
1NT	2◊	3◊	Pass
3NT	Pass	Pass	Pass

The French South did not have the same data that I had and when Belladonna led the jack of diamonds, South had no hesitation in rising with the queen in dummy, naturally placing both missing aces in opener's hand.

Winning the trick, declarer led a low club from dummy. Avarelli elected to play low (had he taken the ace and returned a diamond, the contract would have been swiftly dispatched). Winning with the jack, declarer played three rounds of hearts, coming down to this position:

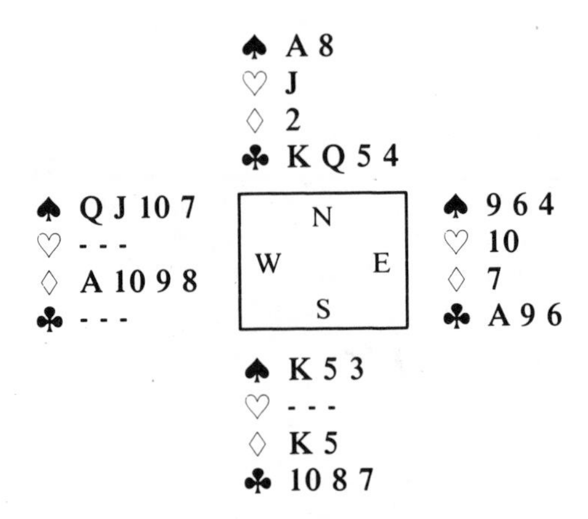

Suppose you are Belladonna, sitting West. When South plays dummy's last heart you are forced to let go a spade for if you let go a diamond, declarer can go after the clubs as you cannot take more than three diamond tricks.

What do you do then?

If the spade you discarded was the 7, declarer can continue with the ace of spades, king of spades and a third spade, putting you on lead and forcing you to lead up to the king of diamonds.

Foreseeing all these dangers Belladonna pitched the *queen* of spades and when South continued with the ace and king of spades, Belladonna duly dropped the *jack* and the *ten*! Consequently when declarer led his third spade, it was Avarelli who took the trick with the 9 and his diamond return ultimately defeated this keenly contested contract.

Help From The Bidding

Here is another example of how the opposition bidding can influence declarer's play. Take a look at this grand slam which I played in an Italian Championship:

♠ A K Q J 5
♡ K 7
♢ A 5 4
♣ A 7 5

	N	
W		E
	S	

♠ 7
♡ A Q J 10 3 2
♢ Q 7 6
♣ 6 4 3

North-South vulnerable. The bidding:

WEST	NORTH *Garozzo*	EAST	SOUTH *Forquet*
	1♣	2♣	Double
Pass	2♠	Pass	4♡
Pass	7♡	All pass	

The jump to Four Hearts showed a semi-solid suit, at least six cards long. Garozzo could therefore count thirteen tricks and had no hesitation in bidding the grand slam.

Winning the lead of the 10 of clubs with the ace, I could see that if spades were 4-3 the grand slam would be laydown. If the spade split was ugly, the thirteenth trick could only come from a squeeze.

I cashed the king of hearts to which all followed and hit the first snag.

How would you have continued?

Considering just dummy and my own hand, the best play would be to cash the ace of diamonds and then run all the trumps, thereby squeezing an opponent who held both five or more spades and the king of diamonds. Laying down the ace of diamonds first (Vienna Coup) allows the squeeze to operate against either East or West.

But how likely do you think it is that East began with five spades?

This reason (and another which we shall see shortly) made me decide not to cash the ace of diamonds. Instead, I ran four rounds of trumps, to which West followed with three diamonds and a spade while East played three hearts and a club.

What would you discard from dummy? And how would you play to maximise your chances of making the grand slam?

This was the complete deal:

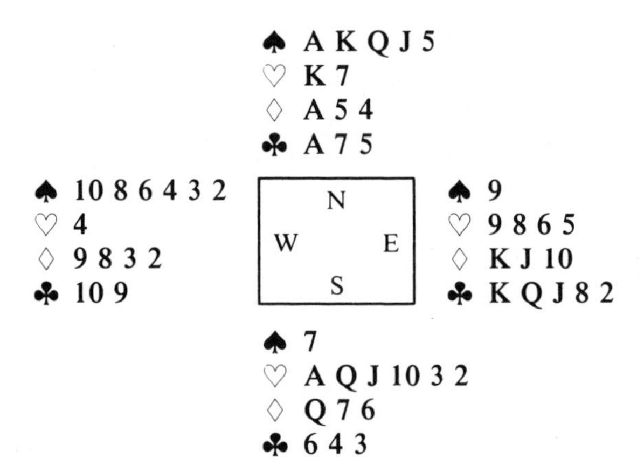

Once East had turned up with four hearts, to which could be added the five or six clubs and the king of diamonds from the bidding, it was pretty clear that the spades were not breaking and that despite the discard of one spade, West surely still had control of that suit. Consequently on the third, fourth and fifth rounds of hearts, I discarded two diamonds and a spade from dummy, coming down to this position:

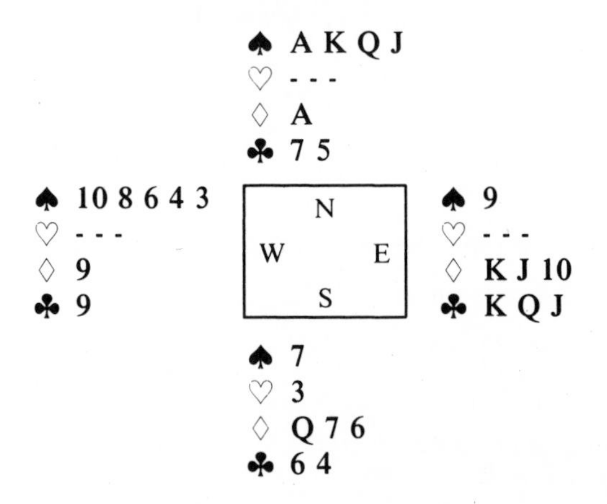

Three rounds of spades followed and this was the ending just before I led the jack of spades:

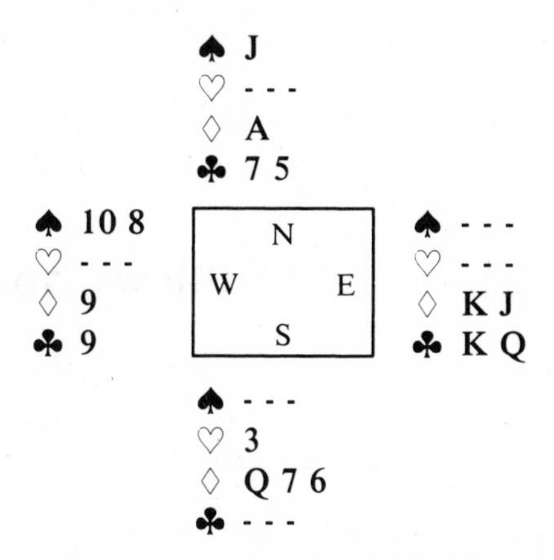

On the jack of spades East was well and truly squeezed. If he discarded the jack of diamonds, the ace of diamonds would have dropped the king and established the queen; if, instead, he decided to part with a club, I would have ruffed a club, setting up a club winner in dummy and the ace of diamonds would have served as the entry back to dummy.

After considerable agonising East chose the former poison and discarded the jack of diamonds.

It's An Ill Wind That Blows No Good

At the Marabella Festival in 1967, a bidding misunderstanding landed Garozzo in this miserable Five Diamond contract:

♠ A 10 9 2
♡ K Q J 5
♢ 8 6 5 4
♣ 10

	N	
W		E
	S	

♠ Q 7
♡ 10 8 3
♢ A Q 9 3
♣ A 4 3 2

Neither side vulnerable. The bidding:

SOUTH *Garozzo*	WEST	NORTH *Forquet*	EAST
1♢	1NT	Double	2♣
Pass	Pass	3♣	Pass
3NT	Double	4♣	Pass
4♡	Double	5♢	Pass
Pass	Double	All pass	

The bidding requires some explanation. My Three Clubs was a cue-bid searching for a major suit fit. When my partner produced 3NT, I felt my hand was not up to such a contract and repeated the cue-bid, now suggesting to partner that we play either Four or Five Diamonds. My message was not very clear and Garozzo took my Four Clubs as insisting on a major suit choice and accordingly bid Four Hearts. After West's double there was nothing left for me but to bid Five Diamonds.

West led the king of clubs and Garozzo won the ace, ruffed a club and led the king of hearts, which was allowed to hold. The queen of hearts was taken by West's ace and West returned the suit. With hearts 3-3, Garozzo was able to win in hand and ruff another club, come to hand with a diamond to the ace (East playing the 2 and West the 10) and ruff his last club (clubs were 4-4).

This was the ending:

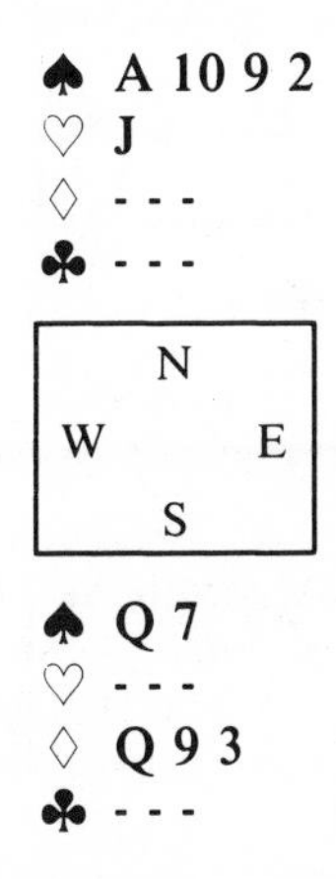

Garozzo continued with the jack of hearts on which East discarded a spade.

What would you have played from your hand?

This was the complete deal:

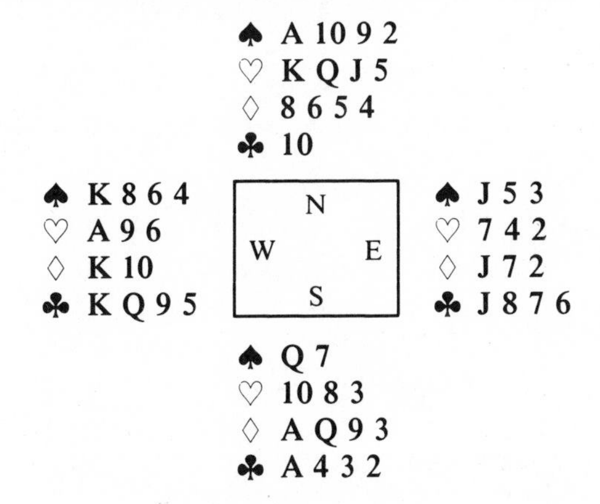

And this was the final layout in the five-card ending:

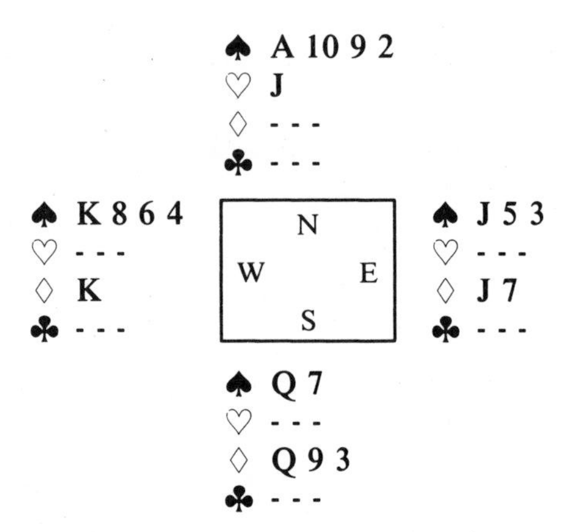

Garozzo ruffed the jack of hearts with the 3 of diamonds *to come down to the same number of trumps as East.* West overruffed with the king and returned the 4 of spades to the 10, jack, and queen. A spade went to the ace and when a spade was led from dummy, East who was down to J-7 of diamonds had to capitulate to South's Q-9.

The contract thus succeeded but only because of a serious error by the defence in the final position.

West after winning with the king of diamonds should have returned the *king* of spades! This would have prevented Garozzo from pulling off his trump coup.

An Unwanted Opponent

In the Italian Championships I frequently found myself pitted against Giorgio Belladonna: he with his Rome team and I with my Neapolitan team. I must confess, without wounding his pride too much, that Giorgio is far more acceptable as a teammate on the Blue Team than as an opponent.

This was one of our duels:

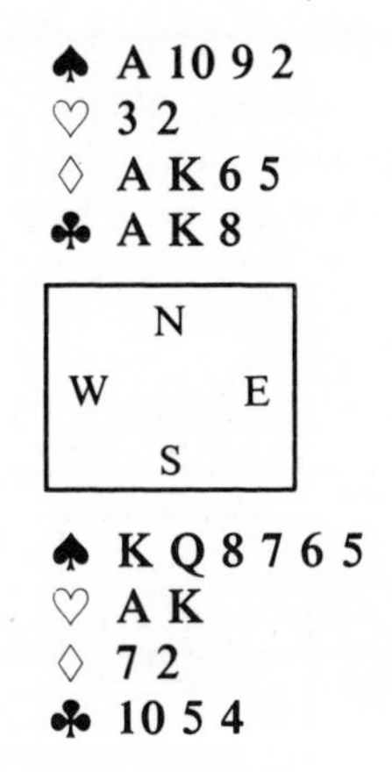

Neither side vulnerable. The bidding:

WEST	NORTH	EAST	SOUTH
R.Bianchi	*Garozzo*	*Belladonna*	*Forquet*
Pass	1♣	Pass	1NT*
Pass	2◊	Pass	2♠
Pass	3♠	Pass	4♡
Pass	4NT	Pass	5♡
Pass	5NT	Pass	7♠
Pass	Pass	Pass	

*Shows 4 controls, any shape

The contract was too high, no doubt, but if Garozzo's doubleton had been in clubs instead of in hearts, the grand slam would have been laydown.

Roberto Bianchi, West, led the 9 of clubs.

How would you have played to try to make this grand slam?

The lead of the 9 of clubs allowed me to place the queen and jack of clubs in Belladonna's hand. If he also started with four or more diamonds, the grand slam could be made via a trump squeeze. My plan was to cash four trumps and the two top hearts to produce this end position:

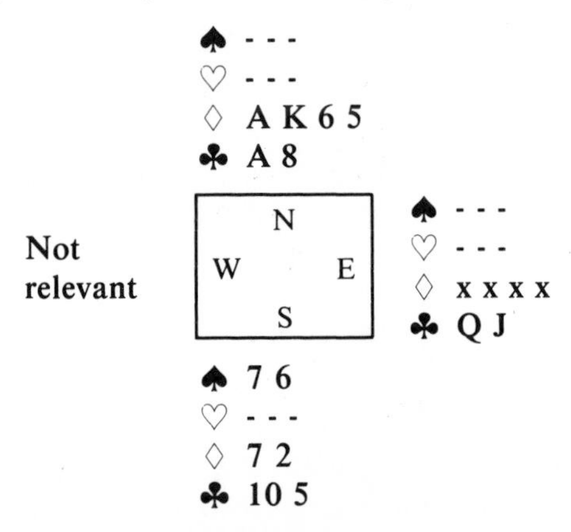

On the penultimate spade I would discard the 8 of clubs from dummy and East would be squeezed. If he discarded a diamond I would follow with ace, king and another diamond, ruffing; if instead he let go the jack of clubs, I would cash the ace of clubs, dropping the queen and setting up my 10.

I therefore won the club lead with the ace and cashed four rounds of trumps to which Giorgio followed with two hearts, a diamond and a club while Bianchi followed to three trumps and then pitched a heart. Both followed when I cashed the ace and king of hearts.

I had now reached the above ending and when I played the penultimate trump, discarding dummy's 8 of clubs, Belladonna, as ashen as the condemned climbing the gallows, dropped the jack of clubs. There was nothing left for me to do but cash the ace of clubs and . . .

This was the complete deal:

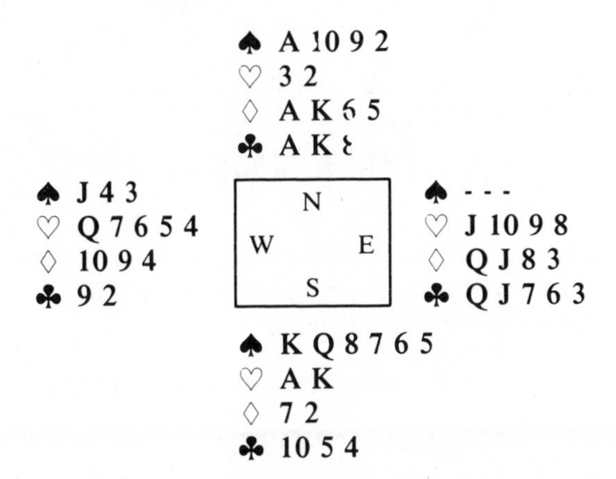

Obviously I failed by one trick since the *real* ending was:

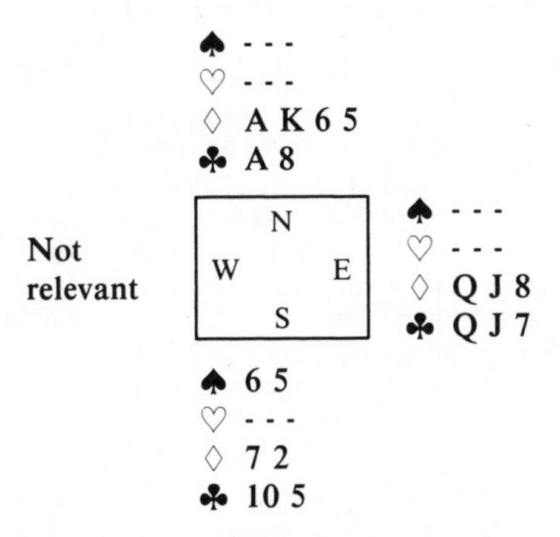

The squeeze had in fact operated but I could not tell that it had worked. What I did not know was whether Belladonna started with five diamonds and four clubs, or vice versa, and whether he had come down to a six-card holding of ◊ QJxx ♣ QJ or ◊ QJx ♣ QJx.

Giorgio's defence was unquestionably brilliant for he had seen from the outset that he would have to succumb to a trump squeeze. Consequently he planned to steer me on to the wrong track by making the diamond discard right at the start and then falsecarding with the jack of clubs in the critical ending.

A Brilliant Defence

In the United States v Italy match from the 1967 World Championships, the Americans reached this small slam:

♠ 4 3
♡ 10 6 2
◊ A 5 4 3
♣ A K 10 9

N
W E
S

♠ K J 9 8
♡ A K Q J
◊ K Q 7
♣ 8 5

Both sides vulnerable. The bidding:

WEST *Pabis- Ticci*	NORTH	EAST *D'Alelio*	SOUTH
	1♣	Pass	1◊
Pass	2◊	Pass	4NT
Pass	5♡	Pass	6NT
Pass	Pass	Pass	

Pabis-Ticci, West, led the 7 of hearts. South cashed his four hearts, discarding a club from dummy while West discarded a spade and a club. Crossing to dummy with a diamond to the ace, declarer led the 4 of spades: six - nine - five.

This was the position after South had won with the 9 of spades:

How should South continue?

This was the complete deal:

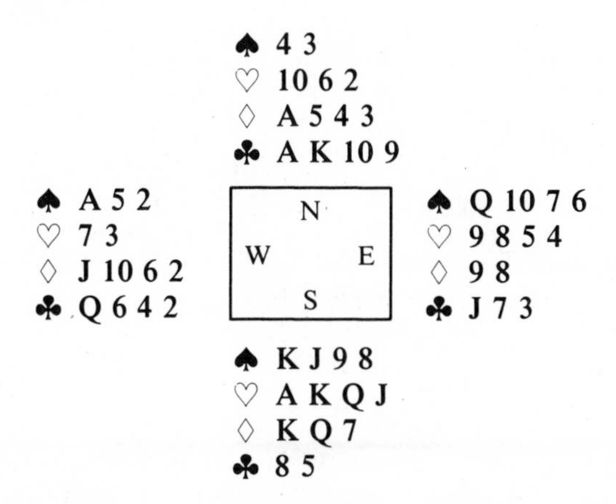

Pabis-Ticci's decision to play low on the 9 of spades led to the demise of the small slam. Note how it would in fact succeed if West had won the ace of spades at trick 6. West would do best by returning a club which is won by dummy's king, leaving this position:

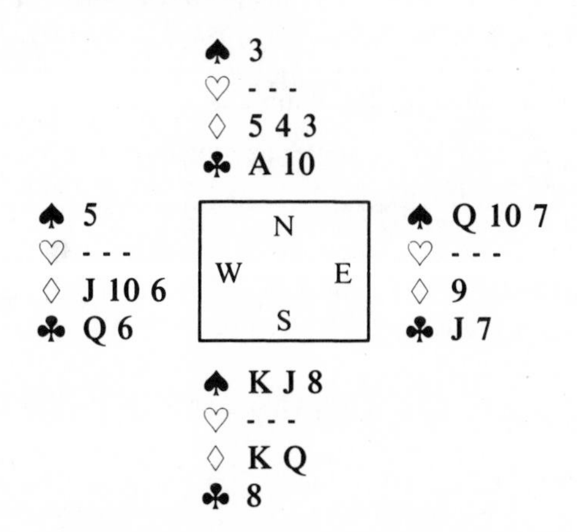

South repeats the spade finesse and cashes the king of spades, on which West must let go a club in order to keep the diamonds covered. Dummy now pitches a diamond and when South plays off the two top diamonds, East feels the pinch in spades and clubs.

Let's just go back to the position where declarer's 9 of spades has been allowed to hold the trick:

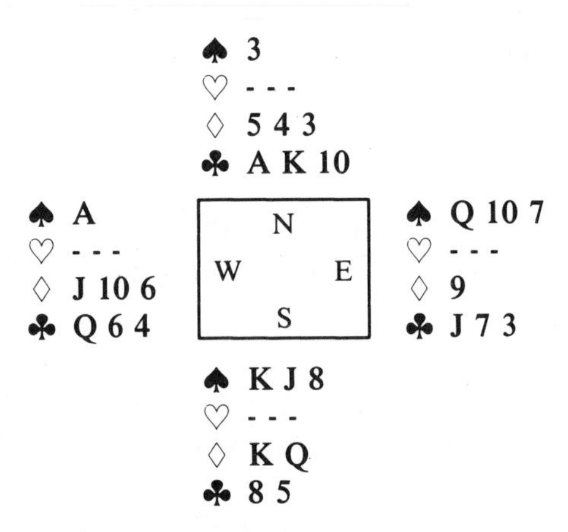

To make the slam one must place West with the ace of spades for if East started with all three spade honours, chances for success are almost nil. South's problem is the whereabouts of the 7 of spades: did East have Q-10 or Q-10-7 left in spades (leaving West with ace-doubleton or the bare ace respectively)?

South mispicked the position and played for the former position, namely that the remaining spades were 2-2. He crossed to dummy with a club to the ace and led the 3 of spades: seven - eight - ace. Pabis duly returned a club, destroying the vital entry for the double squeeze.

Had declarer played West to have the singleton ace left, he would have made his contract by playing the 8 of spades out of hand. In with the ace, Pabis could not have done better than return a club. Dummy's ace would win and declarer would come to hand with a diamond. The next diamond would force East to let a club go to preserve the queen-doubleton in spades, and then the king of spades would have done its work by squeezing West in diamonds and clubs.

In the open room Garozzo and I stopped in 3NT after this auction:

WEST	NORTH	EAST	SOUTH
	Garozzo		*Forquet*
	Pass	Pass	1♣
Pass	2♣*	Pass	2NT
Pass	3♣	Pass	3♡
Pass	3NT	All pass	

*Conventional, showing five controls

I had no problem passing Garozzo's 3NT because after he had shown five controls (two aces and one king) he could not have the queen of spades as well, for that would be 13 points with which he would not have passed originally.

He Who Hesitates Is Helpful

Each nuance in the bidding can provide precious clues for the subsequent play. In this example from an Italian Championship, Walter Avarelli used a slight hesitation by an opponent to pinpoint the way to success:

♠ A 5
♡ K 6
◊ A K J 5
♣ J 9 7 5 4

	N	
W		E
	S	

♠ K J 7 6 4 2
♡ J 9 8 5
◊ 10 9
♣ 10

East-West vulnerable. The bidding:

WEST	NORTH	EAST	SOUTH
	Belladonna		*Avarelli*
1♣	Pass	1♡	1♠
Pass	2NT	Pass	3♠
Pass	4♠	All pass	

Over West's 1♣ opening Belladonna could not come up with a good bid despite his 16 points and correctly elected to pass. After East's 1♡ response, Avarelli interposed 1♠, probably to suggest a lead, and was surprised to find, two rounds later, that he had been propelled into game. His surprise, however, did not prevent him from noticing the slight hesitation from West before he passed out the 4♠ bid.

The lead was the ace of clubs, followed by the 7 of diamonds, taken by the ace in dummy, East playing the 3 of clubs and the 6 of diamonds.

How would you have planned the play?

This was the complete deal:

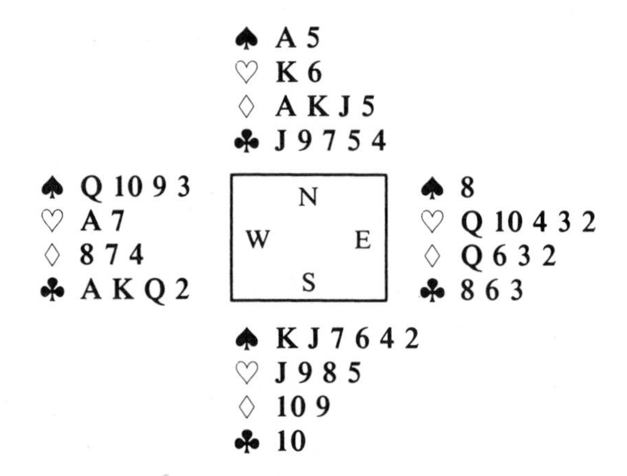

Avarelli deduced from the slight pause that trumps were not breaking and therefore set about a trump reduction play. After winning the ace of diamonds he ruffed a club and then led a heart towards the king. West took the ace and returned a diamond to dummy's king. Then came another club ruff, a heart to the king and a diamond ruff, leading to this ending:

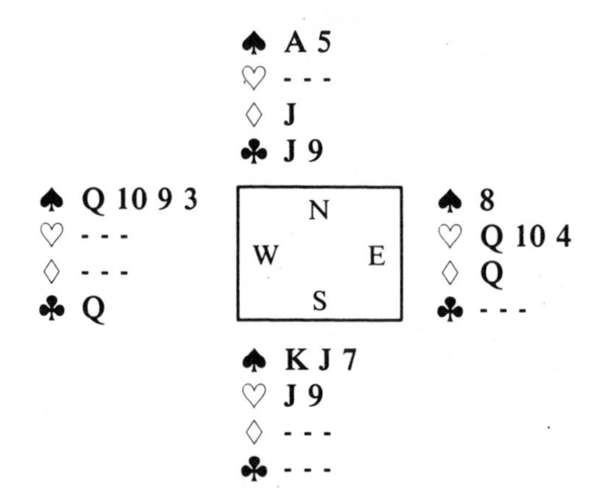

When Avarelli led the 9 of hearts, West was without resource. He decided to discard the queen of clubs, but declarer ruffed with the 5 of spades, cashed the ace of spades and continued with the jack of diamonds, discarding his last heart. West who was down to trumps only was forced to ruff and lead a trump into South's tenace.

Had West ruffed the 9 of hearts with the 9 of spades, Avarelli would have overruffed with the ace and led a club from dummy. East's best play would be to ruff with the 8 of spades and Walter, after overruffing, would have produced this ending:

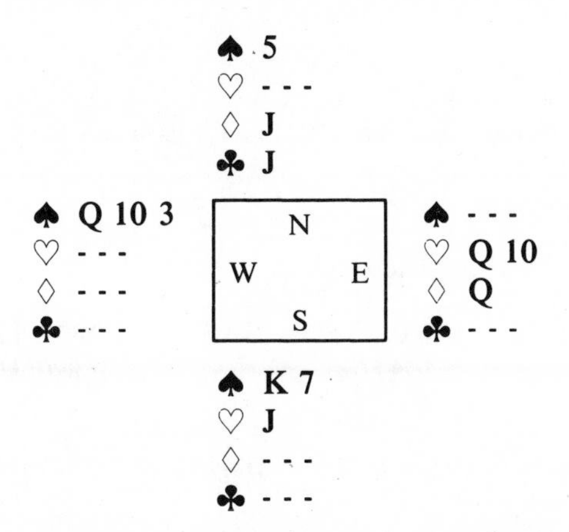

When South leads the jack of hearts West must trump with the 10, lest dummy's 5 score, whereupon West is once more forced to lead into South's tenace, this time the K-7.

Nine Never?

Suppose you are South, holding Camillo Pabis-Ticci's cards:

♠ A 10 9 7 6 ♡ K Q J 8 7 5 ◊ 3 ♣ 6

North-South vulnerable. The bidding:

WEST	NORTH *D'Alelio*	EAST	SOUTH *Pabis-Ticci*
	1◊	2♣	2♡
6♣	6♡	Pass	Pass
7♣	Pass	Pass	?

What call do you make?

Pabis thought for a long time. D'Alelio's pass, clearly forcing, looked to be based on a void in clubs and top cards in the other suits. Nevertheless the grand slam would almost certainly hinge on the spade suit.

After some deliberation Camillo decided, in view of the vulnerability, to try for the grand slam in hearts.

West led the 2 of diamonds and this was the layout:

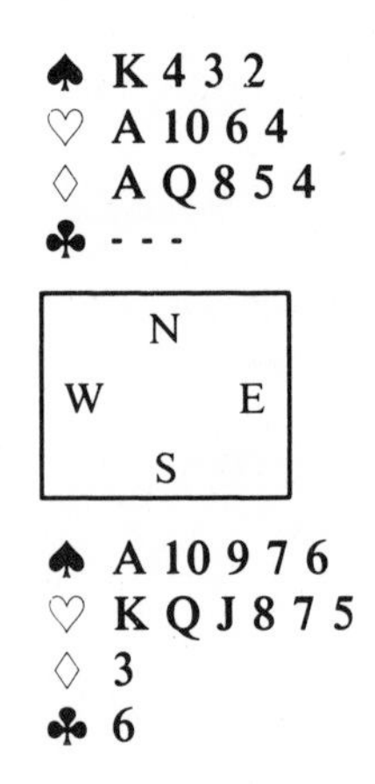

On the ace of diamonds, East played the 7.

How would you plan the play?

The success of the grand slam depends wholly upon the spade position. If spades were 2-2, declarer would make by playing for the drop; if, instead, spades were 3-1, South could still succeed provided that the singleton was an honour and South could determine which opponent held the singleton and which the honour third.

This was the complete deal:

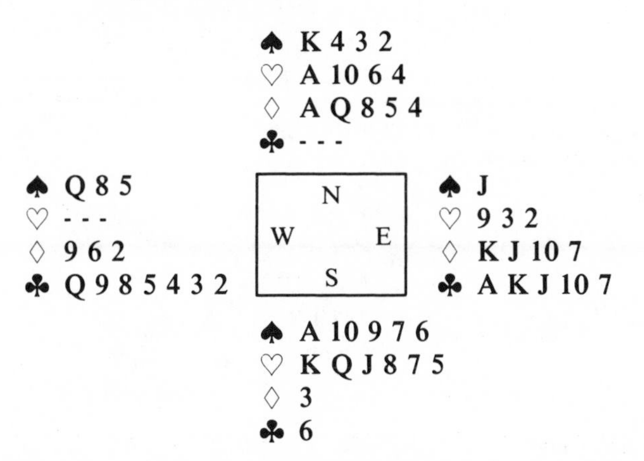

Pabis engineered the play so as to obtain a count of his opponents' hands. Winning the ace of diamonds, he ruffed a diamond with the king of hearts. Then came a heart to the ace, a diamond ruff, a heart to the 10, a diamond ruff and a third round of trumps.

East's hand was now almost an open book. He had turned up with three hearts, four diamonds and on the bidding was expected to hold five clubs. Hence he could have no more than one spade.

Accordingly Camillo laid down the ace of spades and when the jack dropped from East, he had no hesitation in finessing for the queen.

One Heart Or Two?

During a match against Egypt in a European Championship, I was faced with the following defensive problem:

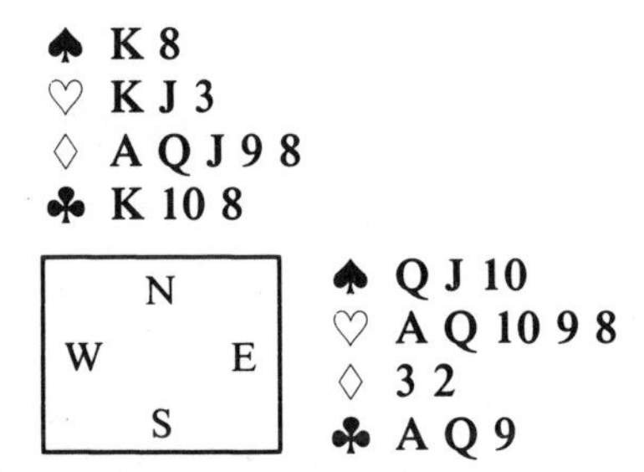

Both sides vulnerable. The bidding:

WEST	NORTH	EAST	SOUTH
Siniscalco		*Forquet*	
		1♡	1♠
Pass	2NT	Pass	4♠
Pass	Pass	Pass	

Siniscalco led the 4 of hearts and I took the jack with the queen, South following with the 2. Our system of leads is to play top from a doubleton and lowest from three or four cards in a suit bid by partner.

How would you have continued in my position?

This was the complete deal:

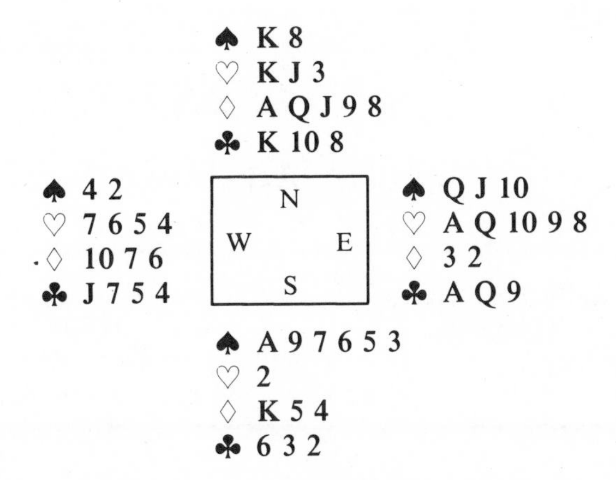

My problem was to ascertain the number of hearts my partner held. Once South followed with the two, my partner's four was the lead of the lowest card in hearts and that naturally excluded the possibility of a doubleton. While the lowest card can be a singleton, I could discount that since South would then have held four low hearts and would certainly not have jumped to Four Spades. Thus it boiled down to whether South had started with a doubleton or a singleton.

If South held a doubleton heart, we could defeat the contract by taking two hearts, the ace of clubs plus the trump trick, but if South had started with a singleton heart, it was vital to broach the clubs, for that was the only area that offered prospects of finding the setting trick.

To solve this cash-out problem, I continued at trick 2 with the ace of clubs which might extract some useful information from partner. He in fact signalled encouragement with the 7, indicating the likelihood of finding an honour card in his hand and simultaneously discouraging the heart continuation. I therefore kept on with the clubs and declarer could not avoid losing a spade, a heart and two clubs.

If at trick 2 I had made a passive return such as a trump, declarer would have made the contract by playing the king of spades, ace of spades and a third spade.

A Farsighted Move

The following 3NT was played by Giorgio Belladonna during an international tournament in Marabella in 1967. Commenting on the deal in *Figaro*, the noted French writer, Jose Le Dentu, said that the play found by Belladonna was beyond belief and that only a player given to fantasies would be able to conjure up such a trap.

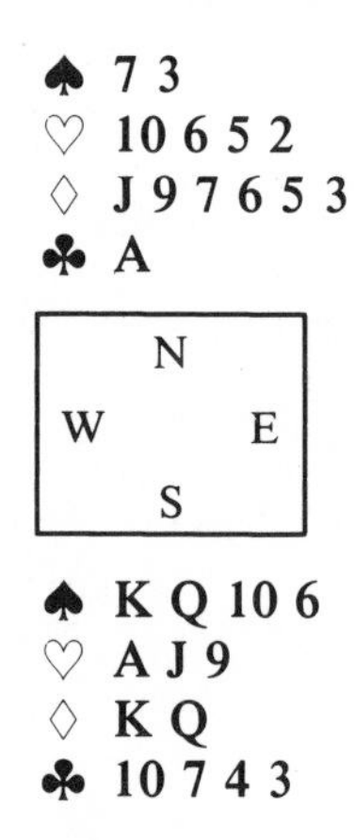

Neither side vulnerable. The bidding:

WEST	NORTH	EAST	SOUTH
	Avarelli		*Belladonna*
1♠	Pass	Pass	Double
2♠	3◊	Pass	3NT
Pass	Pass	Pass	

West led the 5 of spades and East played the 9.

How would you plan the play?

This was the complete deal:

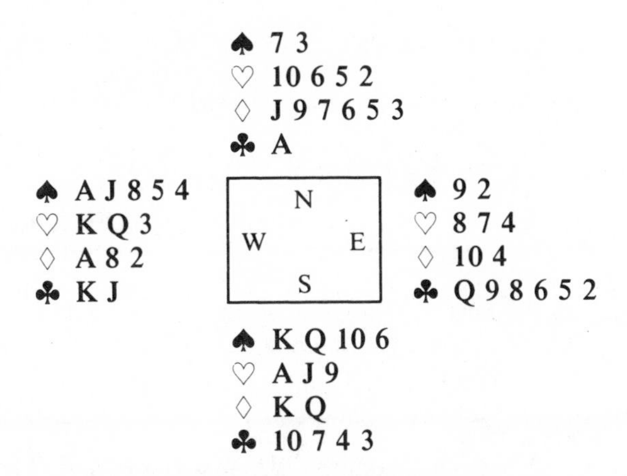

Belladonna won East's 9 with the king. This play appeared inconsequential but yet proved decisive in bringing in the contract, for West became completely unsettled as a result.

Belladonna continued with the king and queen of diamonds, West playing low. The contract now seemed hopeless. To establish the diamonds and return to dummy to cash them required *two* entries to dummy but where was there an entry other than the ace of clubs?

Belladonna continued with the 9 of hearts and West won the queen. It was at this point that the "strange" play of the king of spades at trick 1 paid dividends. West assumed that since South had not won the first trick cheaply, the 10 of spades was surely with East and so he mechanically returned the 4 of spades.

And so it came to pass that the SEVEN of spades was able to win a trick and the problem of finding a second entry had been solved.

The rest was routine for declarer. A diamond fetched West's ace and back came a club (best, for a spade or a heart gives South an overtrick). Belladonna thus made his game with two spades, a heart, five diamonds and a club.

Belladonna's play, brilliantly conceived as it was, should however not have succeeded in luring West into the trap. Once West had the lead with the queen of hearts, even if the 10 of spades could be placed with East with absolute certainty, it would have cost West nothing to continue with the ace and the jack of spades.

This would have returned to Belladonna the extra spade trick but he could have come to no more than eight tricks: three spades, two hearts, two diamonds and a club.

The Winnipeg Coup

At Winnipeg in one of the matches played by the 'Sharif Circus' against the 'Dallas Aces', Giorgio Belladonna produced a spectacular coup. Put yourself in his shoes as South with these cards:

♠ A Q 10 ♡ K 7 5 4 ◇ A K Q 10 7 6 ♣ ---

With neither side vulnerable, East on your right opens Four Clubs.

What call do you make?

Double seems the best bid, but Belladonna, never slow to step on the accelerator if the situation gives him half an excuse to do so, came in with Five Clubs. West passed and Garozzo bid Five Spades. East passed and Giorgio found himself faced with another difficult decision. The contract of Five Spades if North had only four trumps would be less than comfortable, but on the other hand Six Diamonds was just a stab in the dark.

After a very long trance Giorgio, bound to accept a risk whichever way he went, selected the contract that if successful would yield the best result, Six Diamonds.

This then had been the auction:

WEST	NORTH *Garozzo*	EAST	SOUTH *Belladonna*
		4♣	5♣
Pass	5♠	Pass	6◇
Pass	Pass	Pass	

West led the 8 of clubs and Garozzo put down the dummy:

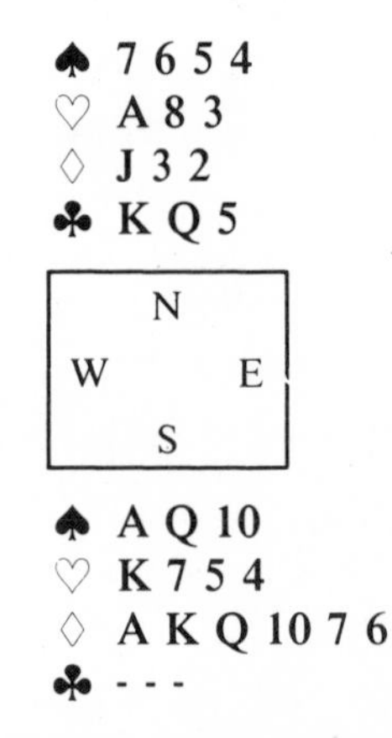

East covered dummy's king with the ace and Belladonna ruffed.

How would you have continued?

This was the complete deal:

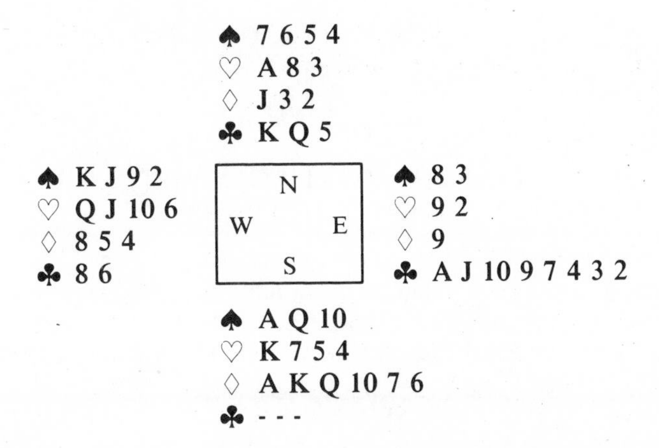

Given East's Four Club opening, Giorgio placed the king of spades on his left and set about the play in order to squeeze West in the likely eventuality that West had started with at least four spades and four hearts.

So, ruffing the ace of clubs, Belladonna continued with the ace of diamonds, a low diamond to the jack and the queen of clubs on which he discarded the 10 of spades. Then the trumps were run until this position was reached:

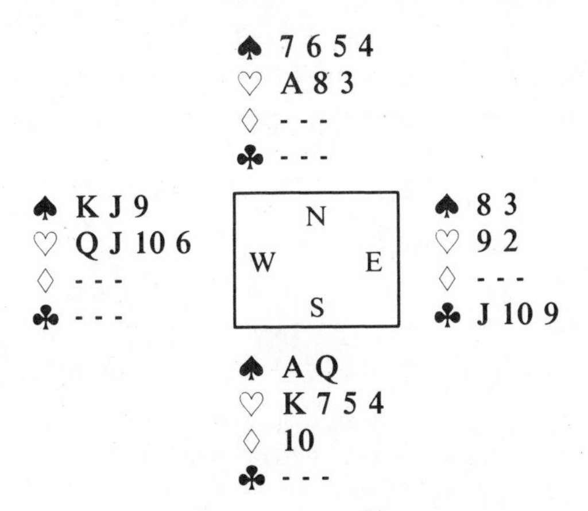

When Giorgio led his last trump West could not escape the squeeze. If he discarded a heart declarer would have continued with three rounds of hearts, setting up the fourth heart in hand and simultaneously endplaying West into leading into the spade tenace; if, instead, West discarded a spade, Giorgio would have thrown a heart from dummy and followed with the ace and queen of spades, setting up two spade winners in the North hand.

An Inverted Swing

When one side bids to a slam while the other stops in game, and one contract is defeated while the other succeeds, naturally the swing usually goes to the side that stopped in the lower contract. During the Italian Championships many years ago this deal gave rise to a singular swing in that the slam was successful while the game was defeated:

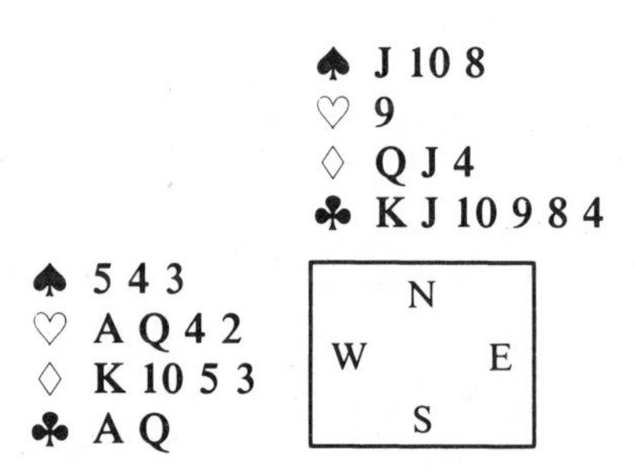

Neither side vulnerable. The bidding:

SOUTH	WEST *Forquet*	NORTH	EAST *Garozzo*
1♠	Double	2♣	2◊
4♡	Pass	4♠	Pass
Pass	5◊	Pass	Pass
5♠	Pass	Pass	Pass

My lead of the 3 of diamonds was won by Garozzo with the ace, South following with the 2. My partner returned the 6 of spades, run to dummy's 8. The 9 of hearts was now led: five - six - . . .

How would you defend to have the best chance of defeating the contract?

This was the complete deal:

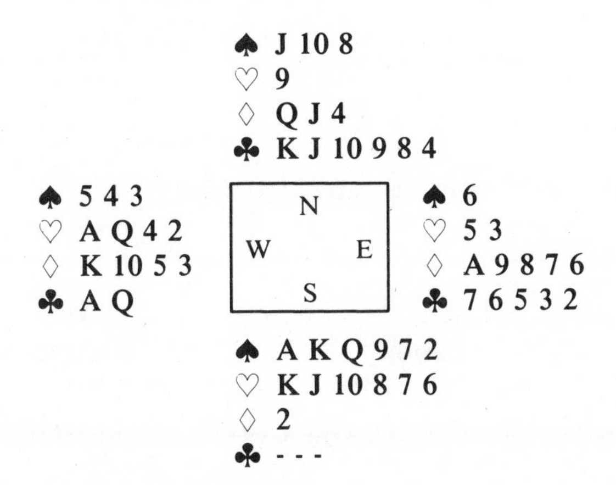

I won the 9 of hearts with the *ace* and returned a spade. Declarer, expecting the queen of hearts to be with East, continued with the king of hearts and a heart ruff, but when Garozzo showed out on this trick, declarer had to resign himself to one down.

Had I won the 9 of hearts with the queen South would have made his contract comfortably.

Let's see what transpired at the other table where our teammates did not apply the brakes until they had reached Six Spades (doubled, of course).

West began with the ace of clubs. South ruffed, crossed to dummy with a spade to the jack and the losing diamond disappeared on the king of clubs. Next came the 9 of hearts, ducked when East played low. West won with the *queen* and returned a trump. South won in hand and led the king of hearts, ruffing West's ace and thus making this highly optimistic contract.

An Inelegant Auction But Still . . .

The bidding does not always lead to the best contract. On the following deal from the Italian Championships several years ago, Garozzo and I reached a small slam in spades when in theory the heart slam was preferable:

♠ A K 8
♡ K 9 7 6 5 4
♢ A
♣ A Q 2

	N	
W		E
	S	

♠ Q 10 5 4
♡ A 2
♢ 9 5 4 3 2
♣ K 3

Neither side vulnerable. The bidding:

NORTH *Garozzo*	SOUTH *Forquet*
1♣	1♠*
2♡	2♠
3♠	4♣
4♢	4♡
4NT	5♠
6♠	Pass

*Three controls, any shape

There is no single blameworthy action in our reaching the wrong contract. Over my Two Spades Garozzo had a difficult choice. Normally in such situations, immediate support would show four cards in the suit but my partner was afraid that if he repeated his hearts, I would expect something better than just king six times. Hence he preferred the raise to Three Spades, feeling that although only three cards were held in the suit, there was adequate compensation in the two top honours.

The rest of the bidding was a series of cue-bids so that we could no longer find the best spot of Six Hearts.

West led the 3 of hearts, East played the 8 and I won the ace. This lead seemed an obvious singleton and I was elated at having avoided the small slam in hearts which could not be made if trumps were 4-1. I returned a low heart towards the king and when West discarded a diamond I continued the hearts ruffing with the 10 of spades, West discarding a club.

How would you have continued in my position?

This was the complete deal:

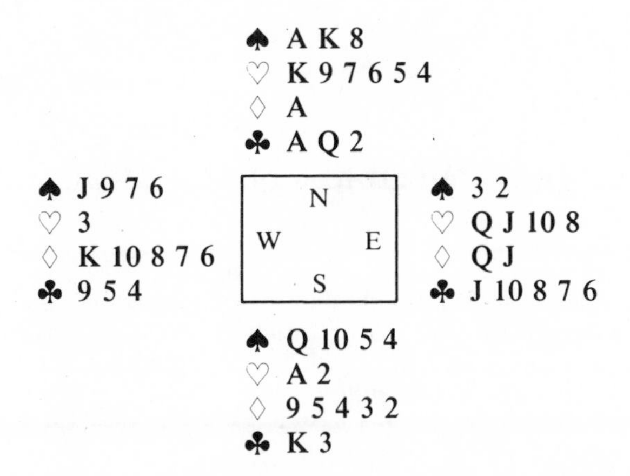

On winning with the 10 of spades, I continued with the queen of spades and a low spade to dummy. I then ruffed a fourth round of hearts with my last trump.

This was the end position with West still to play to this trick:

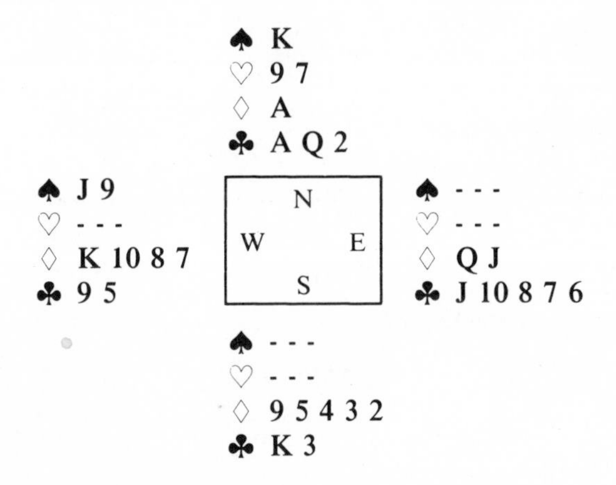

West is helpless. Whether he overruffs or discards, the slam is home.

Variations

If West had ruffed in at trick 2, my task would have been simple: three rounds of trumps, ending in dummy, ruff a heart and dummy is high.

If at trick 3 West had overruffed the 10 of spades with the jack, the slam would still succeed, for I would have ruffed the fourth round of hearts with the queen of trumps and then finessed against West's 9 of spades.

Indispensable Collaboration

On some hands you have to hope that the opponents will provide a little assistance. On the following deal which I played in an international tournament in Cannes in 1967, the contract could be made only if the opposition did not take a ruff in diamonds:

♠ K 7
♡ K 5 4
♢ A K Q 10 7
♣ Q 7 4

	N	
W		E
	S	

♠ Q 10 9 4 3 2
♡ 3
♢ 6 5 4
♣ K 10 2

North-South vulnerable. The bidding:

WEST	NORTH *Garozzo*	EAST	SOUTH *Forquet*
		Pass	Pass
2♡*	2NT	Pass	3♠
Pass	4♠	All pass	
*Weak			

West led the 2 of diamonds which I won with dummy's ace, East following with the 9.

How would you have planned the play?

The lead had all the characteristics of a singleton and consequently there was little hope of making the contract. If at trick 2 I played the king of spades, there would be no quick entry to dummy later to try for a finesse of the jack of spades. Furthermore, if East did have A-J-x in spades, then if I led the king of spades, East could not go wrong: it would be a simple matter to take the ace and give West the diamond ruff.

Accordingly I decided to lead the 7 of spades at trick 2. East played the 5 and my 10 lost to West's ace. The return was the queen of hearts. Naturally I played low from dummy to prevent East obtaining the lead easily and West, following his partner's encouraging 9, continued with the jack of hearts. Ruffing this, I crossed to dummy with a spade to the king, led the king of hearts, ruffing East's ace, and cashed the queen of spades, discarding a diamond from dummy.

This was the position:

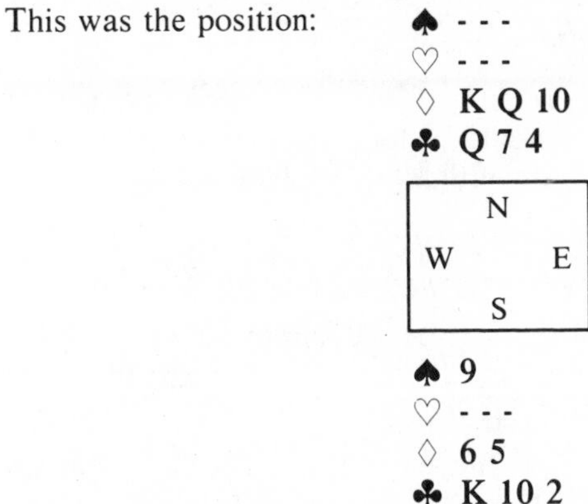

To make the contract I needed five of the last six tricks.

How would you proceed?

This was the complete deal:

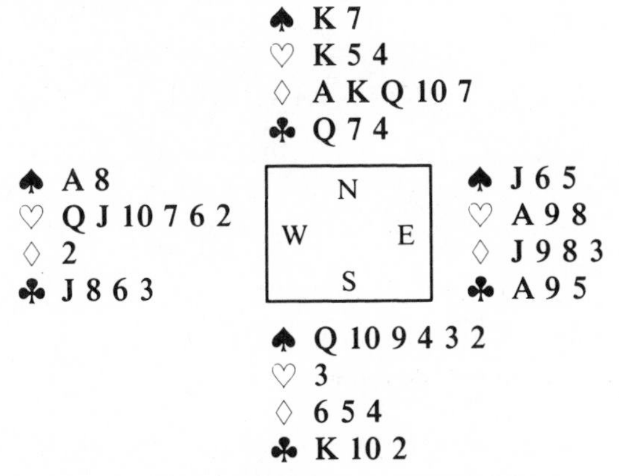

And this was the position with six cards remaining:

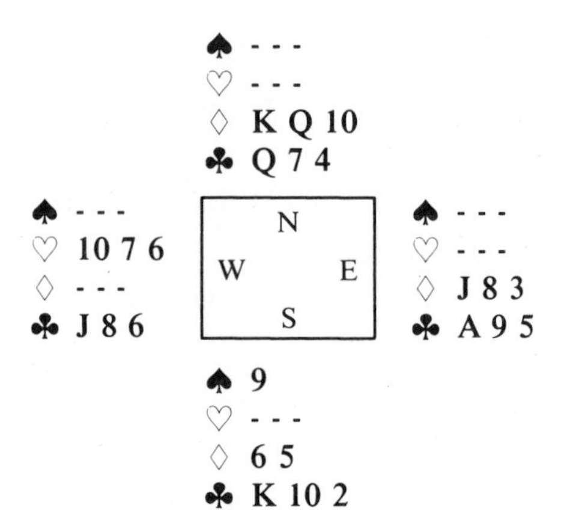

When I crossed to dummy with a diamond, West discarded the 6 of hearts, confirming that East had really started with four diamonds and that I would not be able to pitch a club on the fourth round of diamonds.

How would you manage the clubs to avoid two losers in the suit?

Do you let the fate of the contract hinge on finessing for the jack of clubs?

West has already shown up with the ace of spades and Q-J in hearts, thereby placing the ace of clubs with East in view of West's weak Two Heart opening. Once the ace is placed with East, the location of the jack is immaterial.

The 4 of clubs was led from dummy and on East's 5 I had no hesitation in rising with the king. Next came my last spade, discarding dummy's 7 of clubs.

This was the end position with East yet to find a discard on my 9 of spades:

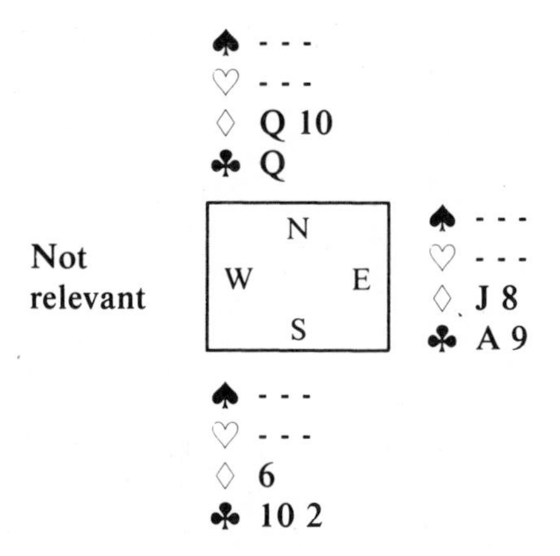

Forced to retain two diamonds East discarded the 9 of clubs. Naturally I simply played a club, putting East on lead with the ace and forcing him to lead into dummy's diamond tenace.

Pabis-Ticci Is A Grand Defender

During the 1967 Marbella Festival, the Blue Team faced a Spanish team in the Teams Semi-final. At the halfway mark the match seemed lost for us as our opponents had racked up a huge lead. In the second half things improved for our side but when the following deal arose towards the end of the match, I judged that we were still trailing:

♠ 5 3
♡ A 8 6 5 4
♢ 8 7 5
♣ A 10 4

N
W E
S

♠ A K Q 10 8 6
♡ 7
♢ A K Q
♣ K J 3

Neither side vulnerable. The bidding:

SOUTH	WEST	NORTH	EAST
Forquet		*Garozzo*	
1♣	Pass	1NT	Pass
2♠	Pass	3♡	Pass
3♠	Pass	4♠	Pass
4NT	Pass	5♣	Pass
7♠	Pass	Pass	Pass

Over my partner's Five Clubs I would normally have investigated his hand further but the state of the match drove me into bidding the grand slam. At worst, I thought, it should depend on the club finesse.

When West led the king of hearts and Garozzo put down dummy, I realised that the club finesse was not the sole requirement. I also had to hope for a favourable trump position.

How would you have planned the play?

This was the complete deal:

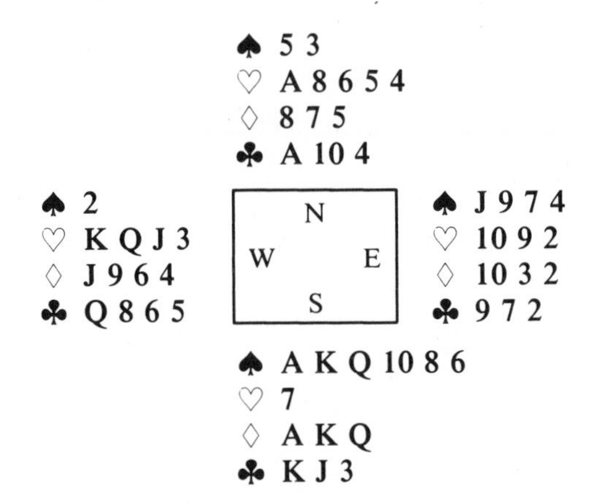

The problem of the club finesse could be postponed. The primary concern was to guard against a bad trump split. To prepare the groundwork in case East began with J-x-x-x in trumps, I won the ace of hearts and ruffed a heart at trick 2, initiating a trump reduction play, just in case. This proved to be a wise precaution when I cashed two top spades and found West discarding a club on the second round. I took three rounds of diamonds to reach this position:

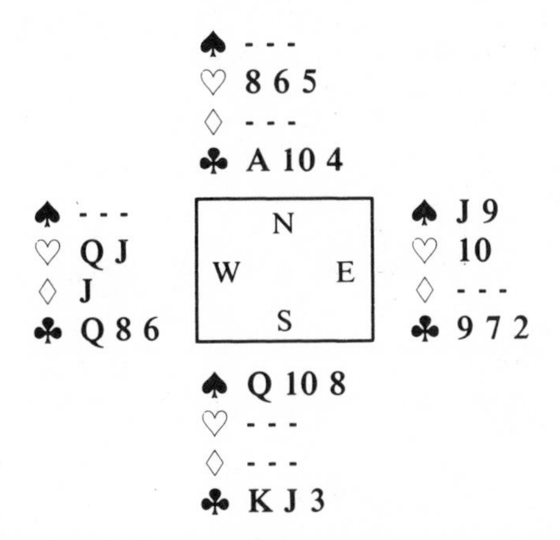

There was no longer any choice about the club finesse. It had to be through West to provide the necessary entries to dummy to shorten myself once more and then to lead from dummy to coup the jack of trumps. Accordingly I led a low club to the ten, ruffed a heart, cashed the king of clubs, led a club to the ace and came off dummy with a heart at trick 12. East's J-9 of spades was now trapped ahead of my Q-10 tenace.

The outcome of the match was a 7 Imp victory to us and the Spanish declarer had gone down in the grand slam on this deal. Proud of my trump reduction play, I made sure to point out to my teammates that the critical deal had been the grand slam which I made. However, Pabis-Ticci who had been West at the other table riposted, "Yes, indeed, that was the critical deal. Our South played the grand slam as you did, *card for card*. Just as well that when he led a low club towards dummy's A-10 I quickly inserted the queen . . ."

This fine play by Pabis-Ticci prevented declarer from securing two entries to dummy and thus the grand slam had to fail.

One Card Too Many

The following deal from the Italian Championships is one of the favourites of Guglielmo Siniscalco:

♠ 6 4 2
♡ J 10 8
◊ Q 8
♣ A K 5 4 2

	N	
W		E
	S	

♠ K J 7
♡ - - -
◊ A K J 10 9 6
♣ Q 9 8 6

North-South vulnerable. The bidding:

WEST	NORTH	EAST	SOUTH
	Chiaradia		*Siniscalco*
1♡	Pass	2♡	3◊
4♡	5◊	All pass	

West led the 7 of clubs.

How would you plan the play?

This was the complete deal:

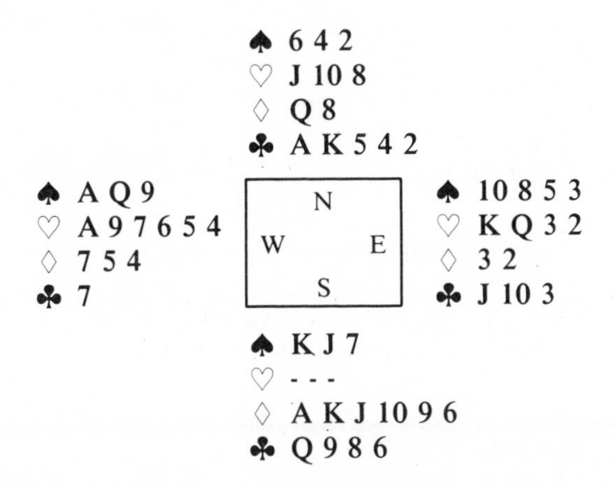

The problem would be trivial if declarer were able to cash five club tricks, but the likely 3-1 division, in view of West's probable singleton lead would mean that South would face a blockage on the fourth round of clubs which would be won in declarer's hand.

Siniscalco, however, found the answer. Winning dummy's ace he led the jack of hearts. East covered with the king and Guglielmo ruffed with the 9 of trumps. He crossed to dummy with the 6 of diamonds to the 8 and led the 10 of hearts. Again East covered and declarer ruffed East's queen, returned to dummy with a diamond to the queen and continued with the 8 of hearts. This time East was unable to cover and Siniscalco discarded his "inconvenient" *fourth* club. West won the 9 of hearts but could not prevent declarer from making his contract. Now South was able to cash *five* clubs and was simultaneously protected from a spade attack.

In commenting on the deal, an expert noted Siniscalco had run the risk of going down when the queen of spades might have been onside. (If trumps had been 4-1, declarer would have lost trump control and would not have been in a position to benefit from the spade finesse even if East had held the queen.)

This comment was valid but did not go far enough. The expert, in fact, forgot to add that Siniscalco's line of play was without question the superior one for two reasons: Firstly, in view of the bidding and the lead, diamonds were unlikely to be 4-1 and secondly, if East did not have two top hearts, South would not be severely shortened (since he could pitch a club one round sooner) and if East did have two top hearts, he could scarcely also hold the queen of spades (if so, what could West have had to justify the opening bid?).

Honour Cards Are Not The Only Important Ones

Frequently a seemingly insignificant card can prove to be of decisive importance. In a friendly match against a French team, I was West and had to face the problem of defending against this grand slam:

North:
♠ A K 7 5
♡ A K Q 8
♢ Q J
♣ Q 10 4

West:
♠ Q 10 8
♡ J 9 6 5
♢ 9 7 5 4
♣ 8 3

Both sides vulnerable. The bidding:

SOUTH	NORTH
1♢	1♡
2♢	2♠
2NT	4NT
5♡	5NT
6♢	7NT
Pass	

The bidding was natural with 4NT and 5NT being Blackwood.

I chose the 8 of clubs lead. East Garozzo, covered dummy's 10 with the jack and South won the ace. Three top hearts were then cashed, Garozzo discarding the 9 of clubs on the third round. The queen of diamonds came next, followed by the jack of diamonds, overtaken by declarer's king, as Garozzo discarded the 5 of clubs. On the next two rounds of diamonds, Garozzo continued discarding clubs, the 6 and the 7, leading to this end position:

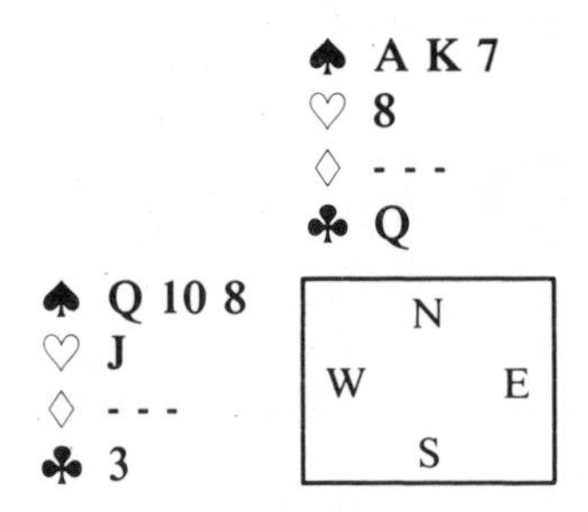

South now led his second last diamond, the 8.

What would you have discarded?

This was the complete deal:

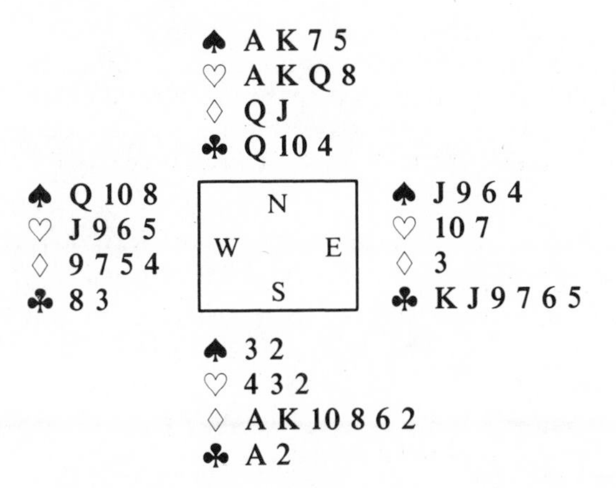

If on South's 8 of diamonds you decided to let go that insignificant 3 of clubs, you have just guaranteed the success of the grand slam. This would lead to this four-card ending:

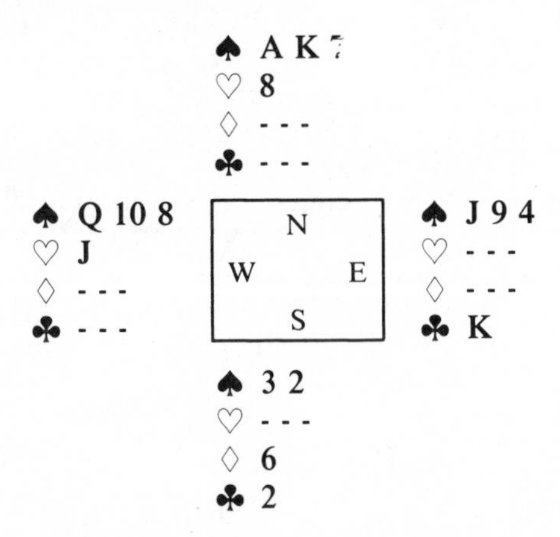

Now on South's final diamond, West has to discard a spade to hang on to the heart guard, whereupon North can let go the 8 of hearts, whose task has been completed, and East becomes squeezed in spades and clubs.

Foreseeing this double squeeze, I jealously guarded my 3 of clubs and instead discarded the 8 and the 10 of spades on the last two diamonds. Thus the grand slam was bound to fail.

Reading The End-Position

Sometimes declarer is able to produce a winning end-position but is unable to exploit the situation either because the opponents' carding has misled him or because it is impossible to determine the precise ending with certainty. On the following deal Benito Garozzo reached a most uncertain ending but his judgment allowed him to read the position precisely.

♠ 5
♡ J 9 5 4 3
◊ Q 9
♣ A J 10 8 5

N
W E
S

♠ A Q 8
♡ 10 8 6
◊ A K 10 7 5
♣ 7 6

Neither side vulnerable. The bidding:

SOUTH	WEST	NORTH	EAST
Garozzo		*Forquet*	
1◊	Pass	1♡	1♠
1NT	Pass	2♣	Pass
2NT	Pass	3NT	All pass

The final contract was certainly pushy but with Garozzo at the helm, it usually pays to bid one more!

West led the jack of spades, East encouraged with the 7 and after winning with the queen my partner continued by playing the 7 of clubs to the jack and East's king. Garozzo expected a spade return but after long thought East surprisingly returned the jack of diamonds.

Benito won with dummy's queen and led the 3 of hearts: two - ten - king. West returned the 10 of spades which declarer ducked and the next spade was taken perforce by the ace. South ran three diamond winners to which East followed with a diamond and two spades. This was the position:

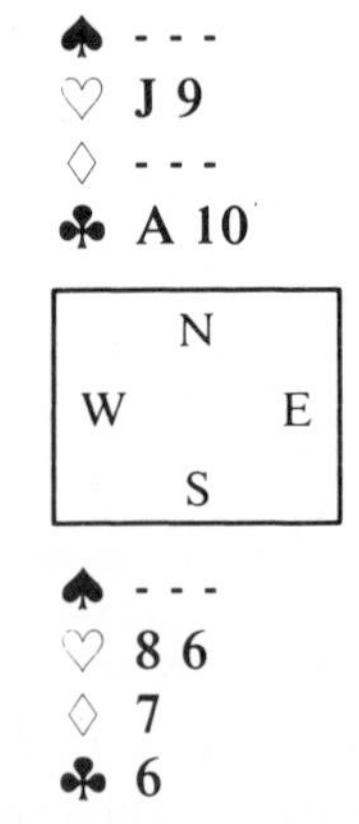

Needing three more tricks, Benito played off the last diamond. West hesitated and then threw a club. Dummy let go a heart and East played the ace of hearts.

How would you have continued? How confident are you about the remaining composition of the East-West hands?

When you have made up your mind, take a look at the complete deal:

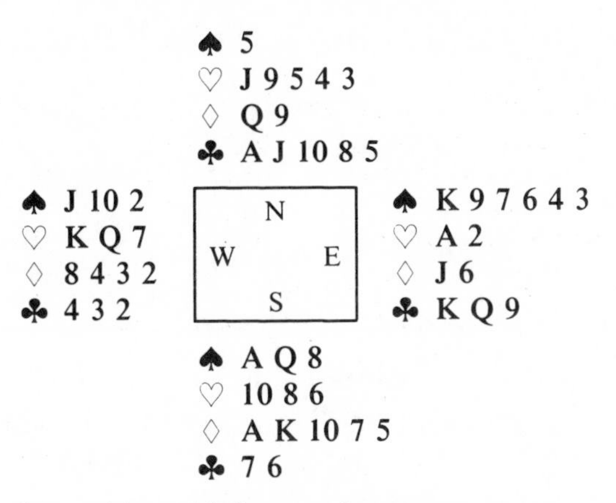

And this was the position with four cards to go:

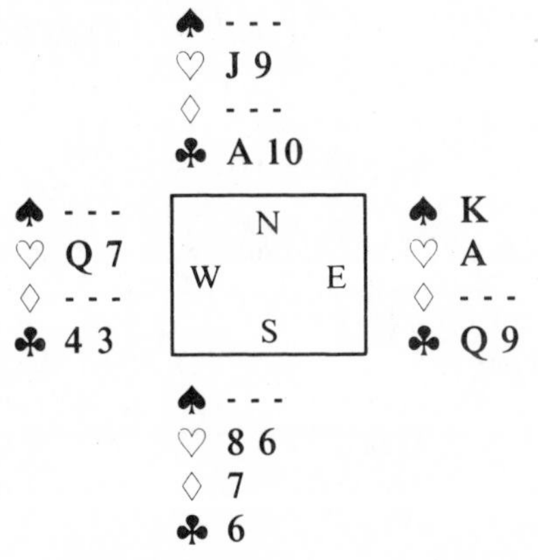

Garozzo read the ending perfectly even though both opponents had defended deceptively in winning in hearts and in clubs with the king instead of the queen. After the 7 of diamonds had fetched a club from West and the ace of hearts from East, Garozzo led a club to the ace and came off dummy with a heart. West won the queen but had to concede the last heart trick to South.

Reverting to the above four-card ending, *can South guarantee three winners?*

The answer is no. If on the last diamond West discards the 7 of hearts and keeps both clubs, South cannot avoid losing two more tricks. If dummy lets a club go, so does East, while if dummy pitches a heart, East discards the ace.

After the hand was over East explained the failure to return a spade at trick 3. He and his partner had adopted "Rusinow" leads (second honour from sequences) and when South turned up with the queen of spades, he also placed South with the 10, expecting West to lead the 10 first from a holding of J-10. (Most pairs using "Rusinow" play the top of touching honours in partner's bid suit and from two honours doubleton, such as K-Q, Q-J or J-10.)

Belladonna's Strip-Tease

During the 1968 Italian Championships Giorgio Belladonna produced a most unusual coup:

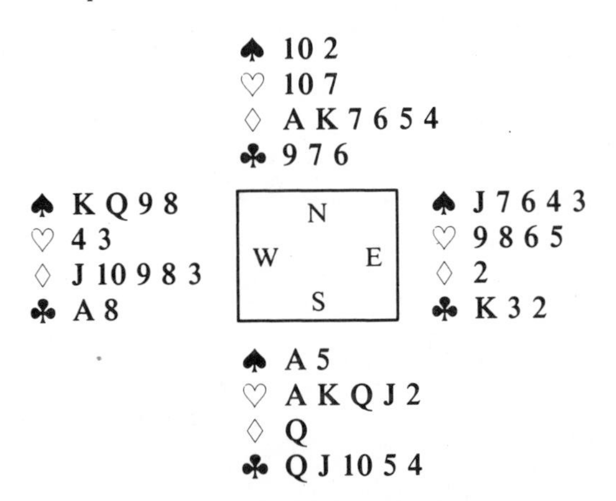

Neither side vulnerable. The bidding:

SOUTH	WEST	NORTH	EAST
Belladonna		*Avarelli*	
1♣	1◊	Double	1♠
2♡	2♠	Pass	Pass
3♣	Pass	4♣	Pass
4♡	Pass	5♣	All pass

West led the king of spades, won by the ace. Belladonna cashed the queen of diamonds and crossed to dummy with the 10 of hearts. When he played the ace of diamonds with the intention of discarding his losing spade, East ruffed with the 2 of clubs. Giorgio overruffed and played off the ace and king of hearts, now seeking to discard dummy's losing spade. This time West ruffed in with the 8 of clubs on the king of hearts and Belladonna overruffed with dummy's 9. The king of diamonds was led. To prevent the discard of declarer's spade loser, East was forced to ruff with the 3 of clubs and again declarer overruffed.

The *stripping* was thus complete. With both West's ace of clubs and East's king of clubs now bare and falling on the same trick, Belladonna had no problem making his game.

At the other table the contract was Four Hearts which was defeated after the lead of the king of spades. Declarer tried to establish the clubs but lost trump control.

Garozzo's Strip-Tease

On many occasions the opening lead guides declarer to the correct line. Take for example the following slam played by Benito Garozzo at the Deauville Festival in 1978:

♠ Q 7 4 2
♡ A K J 9
♢ 6 5 4
♣ K 3

N
W E
S

♠ A K 8 6 5 3
♡ 7 5 4
♢ A Q
♣ A 4

Neither side vulnerable. The bidding:

SOUTH	WEST	NORTH	EAST
Garozzo		*Belladonna*	
1♣	Pass	1NT	Pass
2♠	Pass	3♠	Pass
4♣	Pass	4♡	Pass
4NT	Pass	5♣	Pass
5♢	Pass	5♡	Pass
6♠	Pass	Pass	Pass

West led the 8 of hearts taken by the king, East playing the 6.

How would you plan the play?

This was the complete deal:

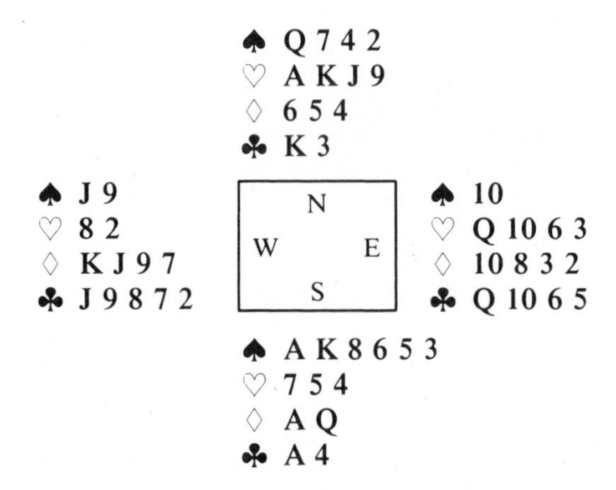

To begin with, taking into account only the holdings of declarer and dummy, the best line is to draw trumps and finesse the jack of hearts. If it holds, the contract is home, while if East wins with the queen and returns a diamond (best defence), South must elect whether to finesse the queen or play for the 10 of hearts to come down. The latter line is preferable since by winning with the ace of diamonds and running all the trumps and the clubs, you win not only if the 10 of hearts is coming down but also if you have been able to effect a diamond-heart squeeze.

I said *"to begin with"* since the lead of the 8 of hearts must affect your play. It indicates a singleton or a doubleton with West and consequently East has the hearts sewn up with the queen-ten four or five times. Thus the various favourable chances in the above line are reduced to nothing more than the king of diamonds being onside.

With all of this in mind, Garozzo embarked on a different line of play. He won the lead with the king of hearts, cashed the king of clubs and ran four rounds of spades to reach this position:

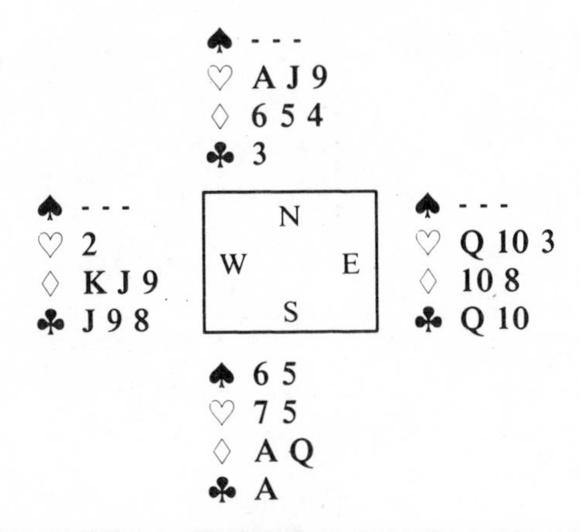

The ending lends itself to a double dummy problem:
With spades as trumps, South is on lead and has to make six tricks against any defence.

Even though East has the hearts twice held and the king of diamonds is offside, the slam is unbeatable provided that declarer is able to read the remainder of East's hand.

On the second last spade East discarded the 10 of clubs and on the last spade he let go the queen of clubs after some soul-searching. Garozzo then played the ace of clubs and to preserve his three hearts, East was forced to part with a diamond. Now the ace of diamonds did the last bit of stripping, reducing East to hearts only, so that when a heart was ducked to East's 10, East had to return a heart into dummy's K-J, providing declarer with the twelfth trick.

You have no doubt worked out that East has no defence. If with five cards to go, he comes down to a singleton in each minor, South cashes both minor aces, the order being irrelevant; if instead East comes down to two clubs, South must first cash the ace of diamonds, forcing a club out of East, and then of course the ace of clubs. As mentioned above, success will depend on determining precisely East's holdings outside hearts.

. . . And Finally My Own Strip-Tease

During the 1967 Italian Championships I was faced with this 3NT contract:

♠ 9 7 6 5
♡ 4 3 2
♢ K 9 7 5
♣ 10 9

N
W E
S

♠ A K 3 2
♡ A K Q
♢ A 4
♣ A 7 3 2

North-South vulnerable. The bidding:

SOUTH	WEST	NORTH	EAST
Forquet		*Garozzo*	
1♣	1♠	Pass	Pass
2NT	Pass	3NT	All pass

West led the queen of spades on which East played the 5 of hearts.

Despite having eight winners on top, prospects for a ninth trick were remote and success could come only from an endplay. Winning with the ace of spades, I continued with a low club. West won with the jack and returned the queen of clubs, which I allowed to hold. When West then produced the king of clubs, I took the ace, East having played 4, 5 and 6 on the club plays.

So far I knew that West had started with five spades and three clubs. If the remaining five cards were three hearts and two diamonds I would be able to draw them and then lead a low spade towards dummy, catching West in the endgame and forcing West to return the suit and give me my ninth trick.

I continued with the ace and king of hearts. On the king West pitched a spade, thus nullifying the above plan. This was the position:

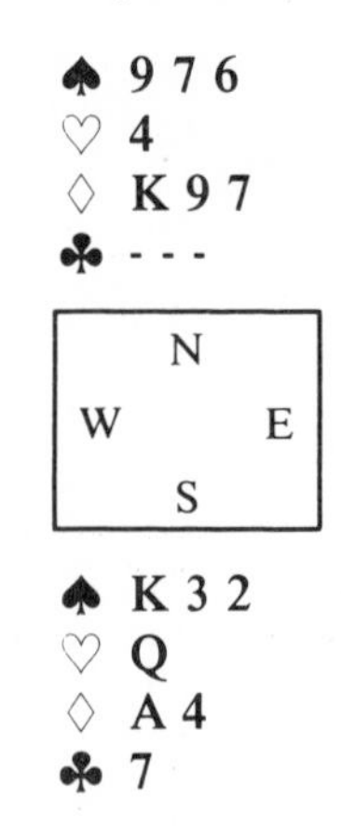

How would you have proceeded?

This was the complete deal:

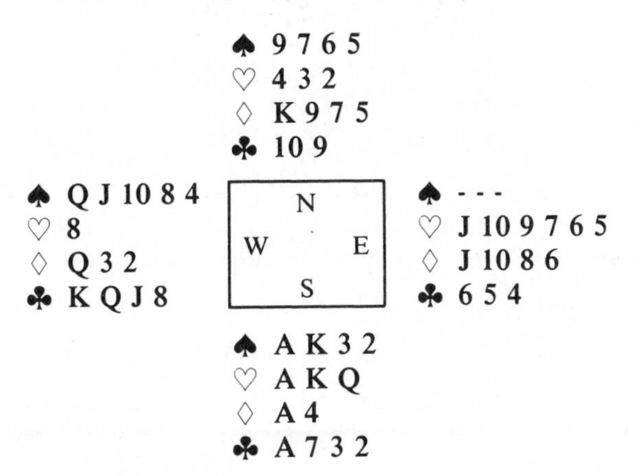

And this was the seven-card ending:

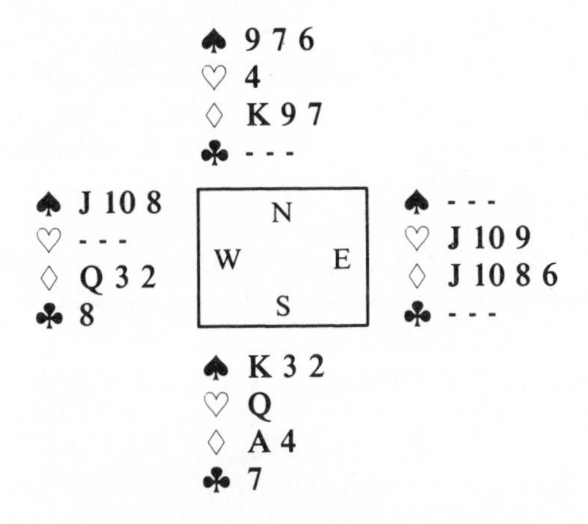

I knew that West had three spades left and the rest of his hand would be either four diamonds or three diamonds and the last club.

Which play would guarantee the contract?

I wonder whether your solution is the same as mine. I continued with the 7 of clubs, discarding a diamond from dummy. West won with the 8 and returned a diamond won by dummy's king. I crossed to hand with a heart to the queen, leaving this ending with West yet to find a discard on this heart trick:

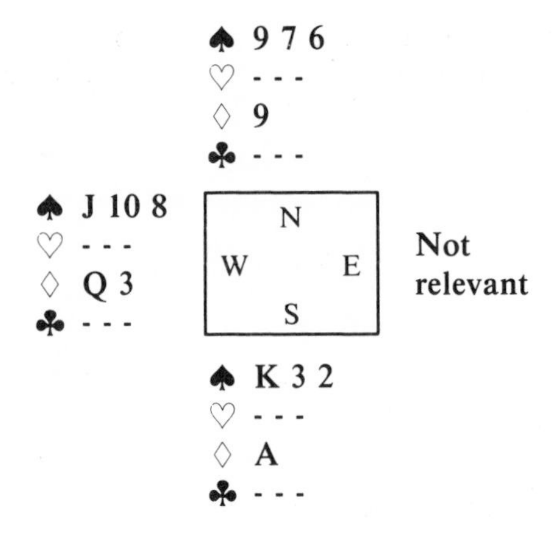

To keep three spades (lest I simply set up a spade winner), West had to part with a diamond. This however did not do him much good for I simply cashed the ace of diamonds, stripping West down to spades only, and led the 2 of spades. West could win the 10 of spades but now had to give me the extra trick via dummy's 9 of spades.

Let's re-examine that seven-card ending:

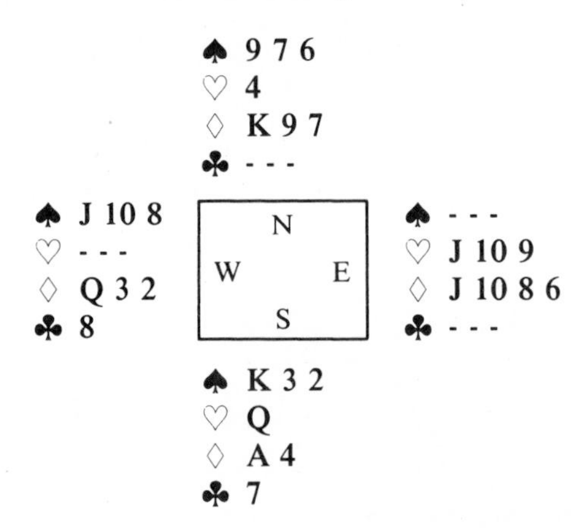

Suppose that instead of exiting with the club I had played the queen of hearts. As the cards lie this would have done equally well. Unable to pitch a spade or a club, West would have to let go a diamond. Then I could have continued with the king and ace of diamonds and a low spade.

However, what if West's last seven cards had consisted of three spades and four diamonds instead of three spades, three diamonds and the last club? This would have been the layout:

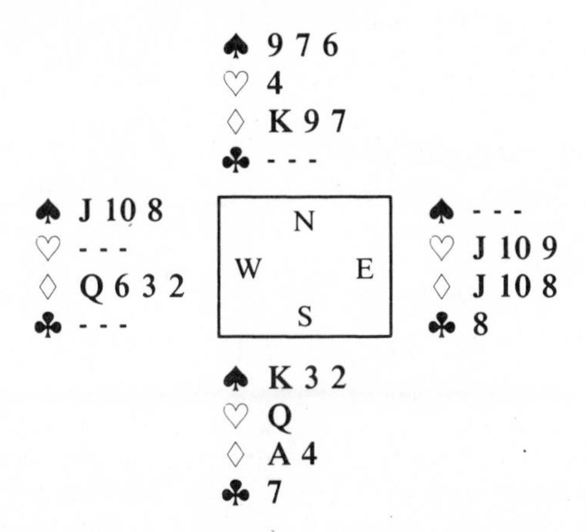

In this ending if I play off the queen of hearts, West would discard a diamond and the contract could be defeated (West naturally unblocking the queen of diamonds to avoid being thrown on lead).

If instead I exit with the 7 of clubs the contract cannot be defeated. East wins this but I win either red suit return to produce the line previously discussed: West would have to come down to just two diamonds and South cashes the top diamonds ending in hand and follows with a low spade towards dummy.

An Absolute Top

To score 3NT with two overtricks where even nine tricks are problematical represents a superb result without any doubt. Giorgio Belladonna achieved this in the Palma di Majorca pairs tournament in 1967.

♠ A 5
♡ A Q J
♢ Q 6 5 3
♣ K 10 9 4

N
W E
S

♠ K 8 3
♡ 10 9
♢ K 10 4 2
♣ A 8 7 5

Both sides vulnerable. The bidding:

WEST	NORTH *Avarelli*	EAST	SOUTH *Belladonna*
		1♠	Pass
Pass	Double	Pass	2NT
Pass	3NT	All pass	

How would you plan the play on West's lead of the 6 of spades? Do you win the first trick or do you duck? How do you handle the diamond suit?

This was the complete deal:

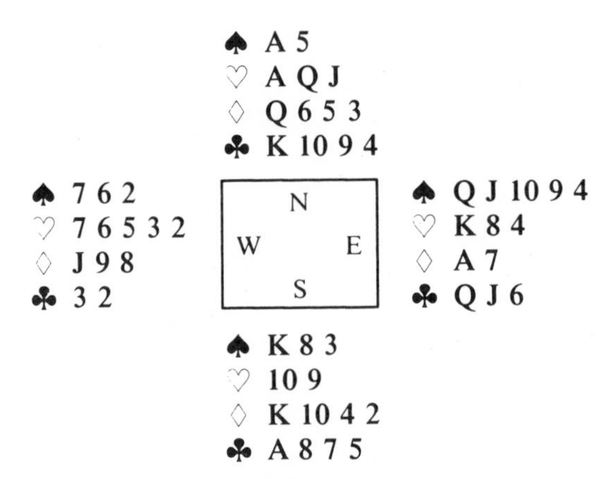

Belladonna did well to win the opening lead with the ace, since East with almost all the missing strength could not be kept off lead and the third round of spades could be useful for a throw-in later in the play.

In tackling the diamonds, since East is marked with the ace on the bidding, the best method is to lead low from dummy to the king. If East has played low and the king has won, lead low towards dummy: if the jack does not appear, play low from dummy. This line succeeds if East started with A-9, A-8, A-7, A-9-8, A-9-7, A-8-7, A-J; it loses only if East began with A-J-9, A-J-8, A-J-7.

Belladonna duly led a low diamond to the king and then low from both hands. Winning the ace, East returned the queen of spades, taken by the king. Giorgio cashed the two diamond winners, ending in hand. On the first of these East let go a heart without problem, but on the second he found himself in difficulty. Wishing to retain all three spades and unable to spare a club, he elected to bare the king of hearts.

Against some other players this might have worked but against Belladonna, the manoeuvre backfired. Giorgio deduced from the hesitation what had happened and led a low heart to the ace. When the king dropped, Giorgio cashed the queen and jack, on which East had to discard two spades to keep control of the clubs.

This was the four-card ending:

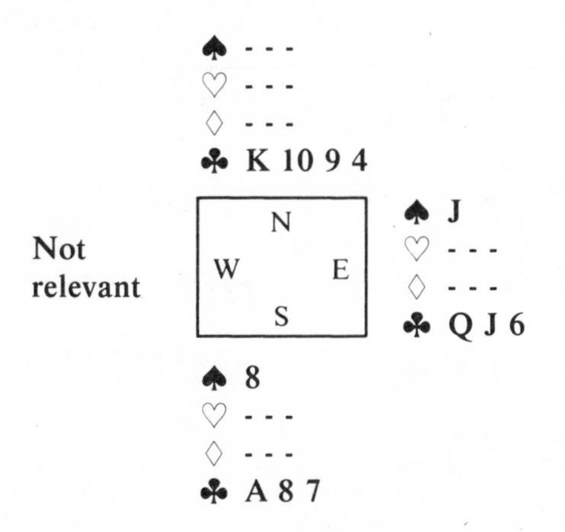

Belladonna continued with the 10 of clubs which East covered with the jack. Upon winning the ace, declarer led a spade to give East the lead with the jack and force him to lead a club into dummy's tenace.

3NT plus two. An absolute top.

Playing To The Gallery

Eric Jannersten, the famous Swedish journalist, commentating during the 1967 European Championships, had no hesitation in naming Giorgio Belladonna as the best player of the tournament. Jannersten was especially struck by the speed with which Belladonna relentlessly found the winning line.

On the following deal from the match against Sweden, Belladonna produced a scintillating defence:

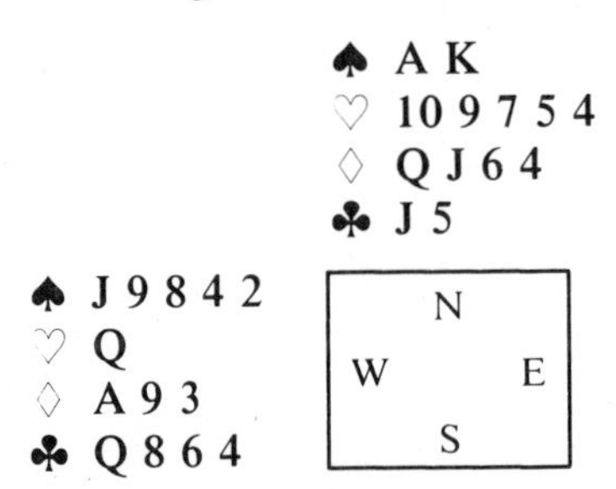

North-South vulnerable. The bidding:

WEST	NORTH	EAST	SOUTH
Belladonna		*Mondolfo*	
	Pass	1◇	2♣
Double	Pass	Pass	Pass

Giorgio led the queen of hearts: four - six - two.

How do you plan the defence?

This was the complete deal:

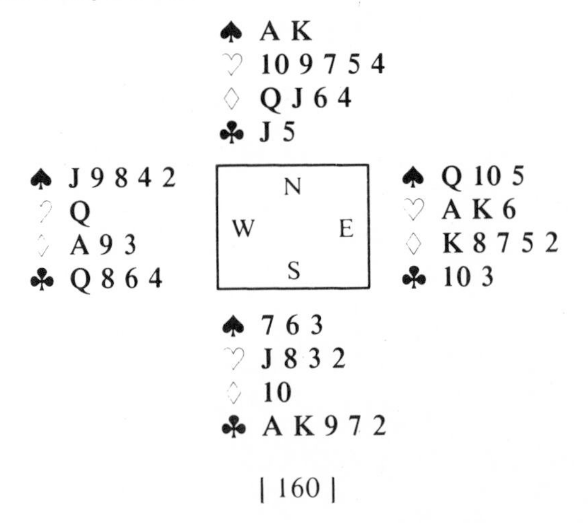

Giorgio continued with the *three* of diamonds. Mondolfo won the king and played his two top hearts on which Belladonna discarded the 9 and the ace of diamonds. East followed with a low diamond and South ruffed with the 9 of clubs (best). Had Belladonna overruffed with the queen, declarer would have had no difficulty in making the rest of the tricks, but Giorgio continued his brilliant defence by discarding a spade.

South could no longer avoid losing two more tricks. He led a low club towards dummy but Belladonna grabbed the queen and returned a spade. Locked in dummy declarer had to lose another trump trick.

Jannersten recounted that several spectators had thought that a less spectacular defence would have sufficed. The defence would in fact be able to shorten declarer's trump holding by leading diamonds twice and West would come to the queen of clubs and his fourth club as well.

Do you go along with this analysis?

Jannersten demonstrated that the Italian star had not been playing to the gallery when he discarded the 9 and the ace of diamonds. Had he instead discarded two spades on the ace and king of hearts, this would have been Belladonna's fate: East returns a diamond, South ruffs, cashes the ace and king of spades, ruffs a diamond to hand, ruffs a spade and comes to this ending:

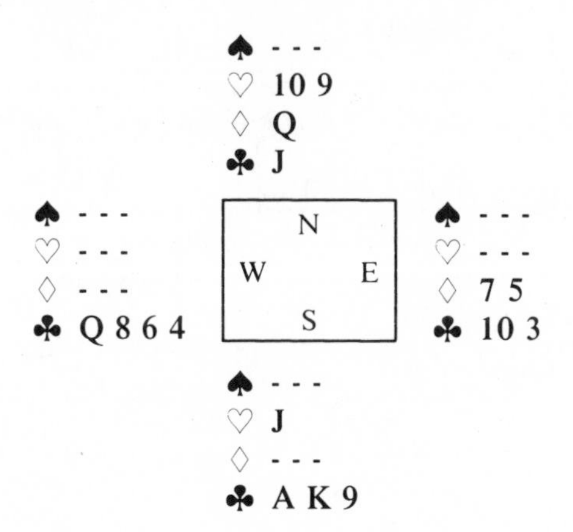

On the queen of diamonds South discards the jack of hearts. West ruffs but cannot prevent declarer making the last three tricks.

An Unforeseen Outcome

During a pairs tournament in Cannes I was faced with this 3NT contract:

♠ 5 4 2
♡ A K 9 4
♢ J 10 4
♣ A 10 5

N
W E
S

♠ Q 10 6 3
♡ Q J 10 5
♢ A 6
♣ K 8 7

North-South vulnerable. The bidding:

SOUTH	WEST	NORTH	EAST
Forquet		*Garozzo*	
1♡	Pass	2♣	2♢
Pass	Pass	3♡	Pass
3NT	Pass	Pass	Pass

Garozzo judged his hand too strong for a limit raise to Three Hearts and therefore chose Two Clubs first followed by a jump to Three Hearts. As this sequence was *forcing*, I could not drop Three Hearts and so suggested Three No-Trumps as an alternative to Four Hearts. Garozzo with his balanced hand and J-10-x in the opponents' suit accepted with alacrity and Three No-Trumps became the final contract.

West led the 9 of diamonds and East covered dummy's jack with the queen.

How would you plan the play?

The situation seemed hopeless with only seven tricks on top. If I won the ace of diamonds, then as soon as West obtained the lead, another diamond would spell defeat. The only hope was to play low on the queen of diamonds, giving East the impression that I had started with A-x-x.

East thought for some time and finally laid down the ace of spades. In compliance with his partner's 9, East continued with the jack. The queen lost to the king and West continued with the 8 of spades on which East discarded a diamond. The 10 of spades won, leaving this end position:

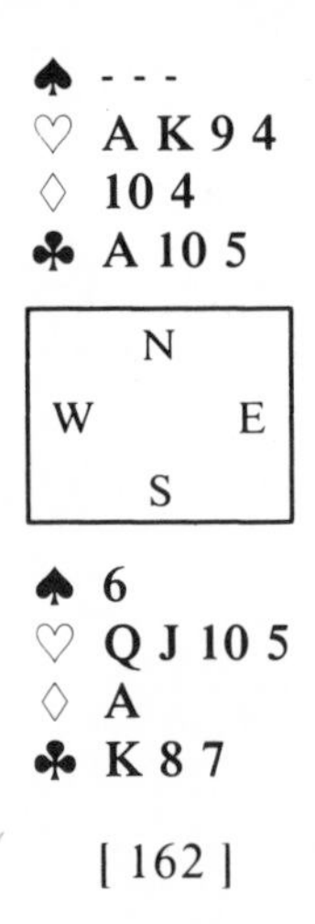

To make 3NT eight more tricks were required,with only seven in sight. The eighth trick would materialise only from some squeeze or an endplay. If I conceded the spade trick to West, I would be able to execute a squeeze on East but only if East began with the queen, jack and the NINE of clubs. If instead I cashed my four heart tricks first, I would succeed by throwing West on lead with the spade if West had started with the queen and jack of clubs with or without the nine. Accordingly I adopted this second line of play.

This was the complete deal:

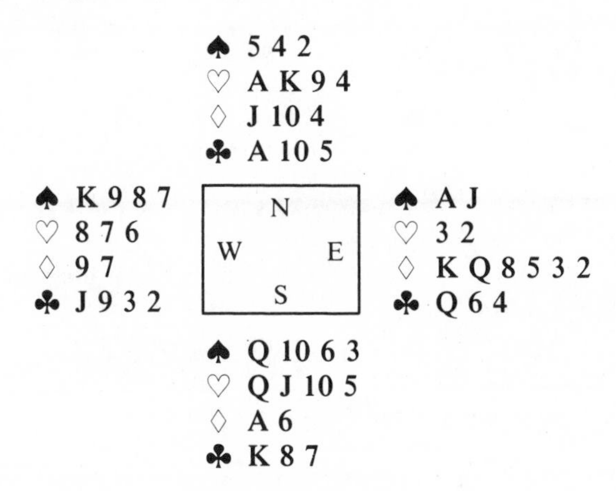

Cashing four rounds of hearts and the ace of diamonds, I threw West on lead with the spade. This was the three-card ending:

♣ A 10 5

♣ J 9 3 ♣ Q 6 4

♣ K 8 7

When West led the 3 of clubs, I played low from dummy and East was forced to play the queen. Winning the king I finessed dummy's 10 and thus produced my ninth trick.

Naturally you have noted that in this ending if West had returned the jack instead of the 3, he would have beaten the contract. Apart from this, there is a further point of technical interest: if West is a strong player, I would put up dummy's 10 on West's lead of the 3, for the 3 from a strong defender would be consistent with Q-J-3 but not with J-9-3 or Q-9-3.

A "Straightforward" Small Slam

During an exhibition match by the 'Omar Sharif Circus' in the United States, Benito Garozzo had to bring in this slam:

♠ K 6 3
♡ K Q 8 4 2
◇ 9
♣ 8 7 4 2

N
W E
S

♠ A 9
♡ A 5
◇ A K 8 5 3
♣ A Q J 10

North-South vulnerable. The bidding:

SOUTH	WEST	NORTH	EAST
Garozzo		*Belladonna*	
1♣	2♠*	Double	3♠
4◇	Pass	4♡	Pass
5♣	Pass	6♣	All pass

*Weak jump-overcall

West led the 5 of spades, East played the 10 and Garozzo won the ace. He continued with the ace and a low diamond, ruffing in dummy, and a club to the queen which held the trick.

How would you have continued?

This was the complete deal:

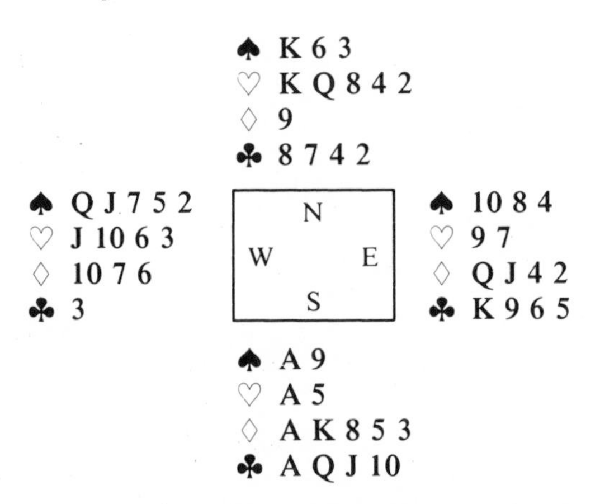

The apparently natural continuation seems to be to ruff another diamond in dummy and repeat the club finesse. But what if West has cunningly ducked the queen of clubs with king-doubleton? And what if the next club finesse loses and West plays a fourth diamond, allowing East to overruff dummy with the 9 of clubs?

Garozzo sought to guard against such possibilities by laying down the ace of clubs. Even if the king did not drop, the slam would be child's play if the clubs were 3-2.

When West showed out on the ace of clubs, the slam looked to be in grave jeopardy but Garozzo showed he had another string to his bow. He continued with the ace of hearts and a low heart to the king, reaching this position:

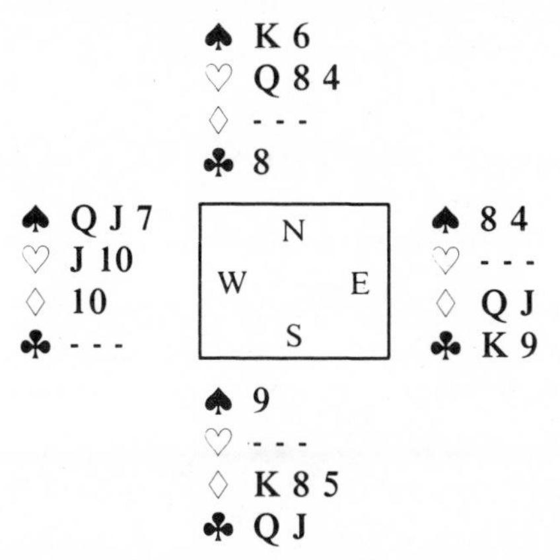

On the queen of hearts East considered the situation for a long time before discarding a diamond. Benito, likewise discarding a diamond, then took the king of spades, a spade ruff, a diamond ruff and when a heart was led from dummy at trick 12, he was bound to make his last trump *en passant*.

Variations

If East ruffed the queen of hearts with the 9, South would overruff and play king of diamonds, diamond ruff, king of spades, spade ruff.

If East ruffed the queen of hearts with the king of clubs and returned the 9 of clubs (best defence), Garozzo after winning this would cash the king of diamonds and arrive at this ending:

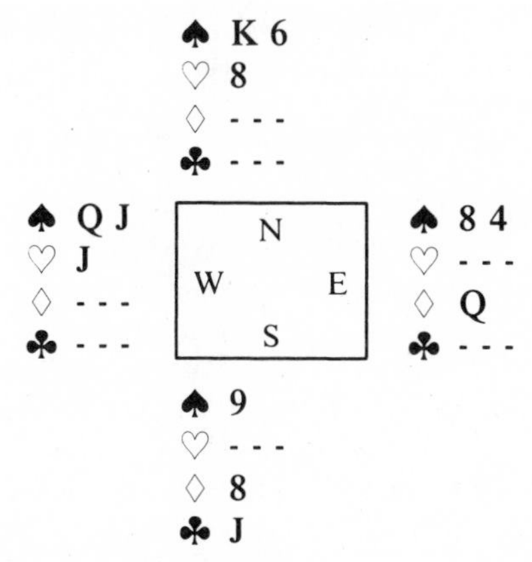

On the jack of clubs West must part with a spade to retain control of hearts. North's now useless 8 of hearts is discarded and East thereby becomes squeezed in spades and diamonds.

"Knowing The Theory Is Enough"

When you are one trick short, it is common to try to produce the extra trick by means of a squeeze. "Knowing the theory is enough and then each squeeze becomes easy," is a favourite dictum of Camillo Pabis-Ticci, for whom squeeze play holds no secrets.

This deal was played by Camillo during the 1967 Italian Championships:

♠ K Q
♡ A 3 2
◊ A Q J 3 2
♣ 8 5 4

N
W E
S

♠ A 10 7 6
♡ J 8 5
◊ K 10 8
♣ A K 10

Both sides vulnerable. The bidding:

WEST	NORTH	EAST	SOUTH
	D'Alelio		*Pabis-Ticci*
	1◊	Pass	1NT
Pass	2◊	Pass	3◊
Pass	3♡	Pass	3♠
Pass	4◊	Pass	4NT
Pass	5♡	Pass	6NT
Pass	Pass	Pass	

West led the 10 of hearts: two - queen - five. East returned the 2 of clubs.

How would you have proceeded?

This was the complete deal:

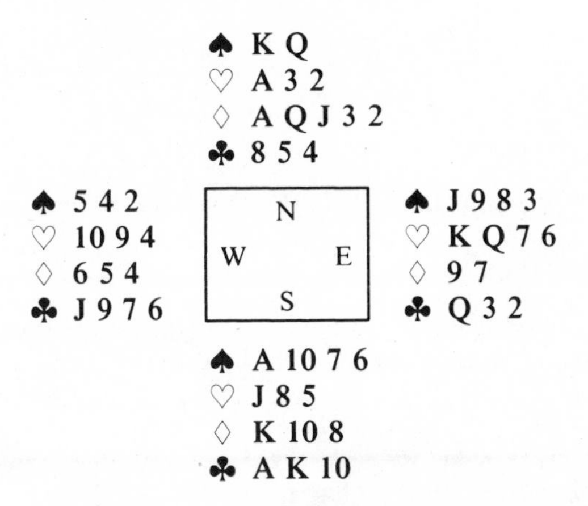

Winning the ace of clubs, Camillo cashed the king and queen of spades and five rounds of diamonds on which East had to let go two clubs as well as a heart in order to hang on to his guards in spades and hearts. South discarded first a club and then a heart. This was the position:

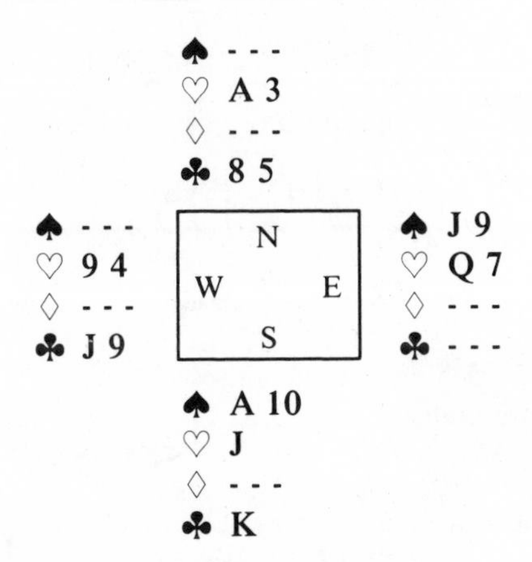

When Pabis led a club to the king, East had to part with a heart to keep the jack of spades guarded. Declarer continued with the ace of spades and West was squeezed in hearts and clubs.

Timing And Control

The following hand from an international teams tournament provides an excellent example of what is known in the game as "timing and control":

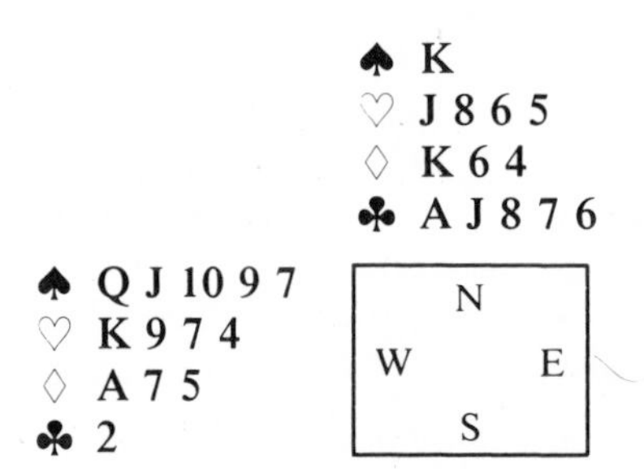

Neither side vulnerable. The bidding:

WEST *Siniscalco*	NORTH	EAST *Forquet*	SOUTH
	Pass	Pass	1NT (1)
Pass	2♣ (2)	Pass	2♠ (3)
Pass	3NT	All pass	

(1) 13-15 points, balanced
(2) Stayman
(3) Shows four spades and denies four hearts

Siniscalco led the queen of spades. Dummy's king winning, declarer continued with the 4 of diamonds: ten - queen . . .

How would you have defended in Guglielmo Siniscalco's position?

After you make up your mind, see how your plan would have fared on the actual deal:

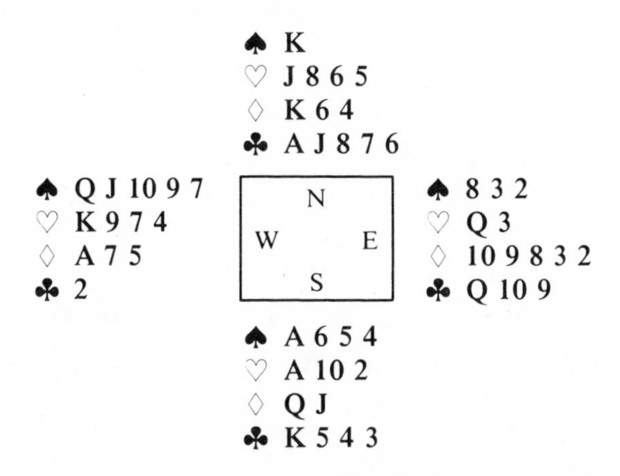

My *ten* of diamonds placed the jack with declarer and enabled my partner to come up with a brilliant defence. If Siniscalco won the ace, declarer would duck the spade return, thereby severing communications between the defenders. When I obtained the lead, I would be unable to put partner on lead. South would thus make 3NT via two spades, one heart, two diamonds and four clubs.

However, Siniscalco grasped the problem and allowed the queen of diamonds to win. This decision determined the fate of the contract. If South now broached clubs I would win the queen of clubs and force out the ace of spades before the ace of diamonds had been dislodged. As long as the ace of diamonds had not been removed, South could come to no more than eight tricks.

South therefore persevered with the jack of diamonds but Siniscalco did not falter. Had he won the ace of diamonds and returned a diamond, South could comfortably give up a club to my queen, since at most I could cash two more diamonds. Instead Siniscalco upon winning the ace of diamonds correctly returned the jack of spades, which South was obliged to duck (otherwise when I win the queen of clubs, I could play a spade to partner's hand).

After having acquired a trick in spades, Siniscalco went back to the diamonds and declarer had to hoist the white flag.

At the other table the bidding went:

WEST	NORTH *Chiaradia*	EAST	SOUTH *Luciani*
	Pass	Pass	1♠
Pass	2NT	Pass	3NT
Pass	Pass	Pass	

This time declarer was North, Eugenio Chiaradia. East led the 10 of diamonds, West winning and returning the suit. Chiaradia then played the king of clubs, a club to the ace, the king of spades and a third club. East returned a spade but declarer now had nine tricks in the bag.

Contrary To Nature

In a match in the 1968 Italian Championships Mimmo D'Alelio found himself in the following slam:

♠ A J 7 5 4
♡ A J 8 6
♢ - - -
♣ A K 7 3

	N	
W		E
	S	

♠ K Q 8 6
♡ Q 10 3
♢ 10 6 2
♣ J 6 5

North-South vulnerable. The bidding:

WEST	NORTH *Pabis-Ticci*	EAST	SOUTH *D'Alelio*
		1♢	Pass
2♢	3♢	4♢	4♠
5♢	6♠	All pass	

West led the queen of diamonds.

How would you plan the play?

In view of East's opening bid and his subsequent Four Diamonds, it is highly likely that the king of hearts will be in his hand. If declarer squanders an entry to hand to take this finesse, this might jeopardise the slam, as we shall see.

D'Alelio found a better line. Ruffing the lead in dummy, he next played a low heart from dummy! East won with the king and returned the 2 of spades, won by South's king, West playing the 10.

How would you have continued?

This was the complete deal:

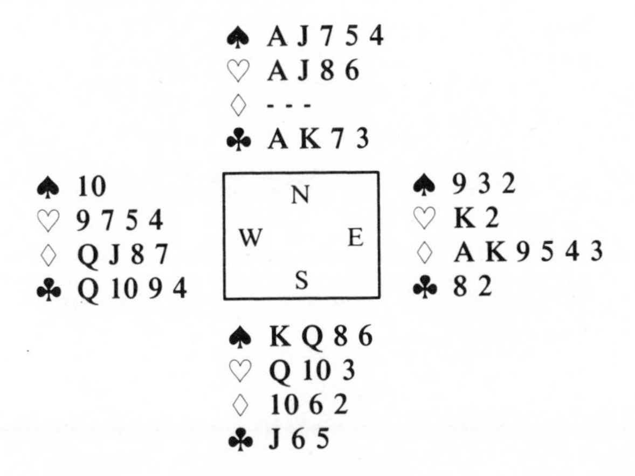

Mimmo read the situation precisely. He trumped a diamond with the ace of spades, returned to hand with a heart to the 10 and ruffed his last diamond with the jack of spades, reaching this position:

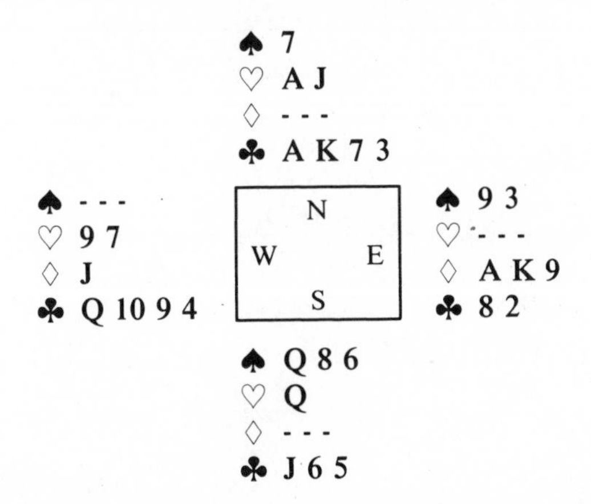

D'Alelio appreciated that West's 10 of spades had to be a singleton (else how could he have bid Five Diamonds?) and had no hesitation in finessing against East's 9. Drawing the last trump, he cashed the hearts and discarded his club loser on the fourth round.

Variations

If at trick 2 D'Alelio had come to hand with the king of spades to try the heart finesse, East upon winning the king would have returned a trump and the lack of communication between dummy and declarer would spell defeat for the slam.

The Two Queens Coup

This deal was played in the United States v Italy match in the 1968 World Teams Olympiad:

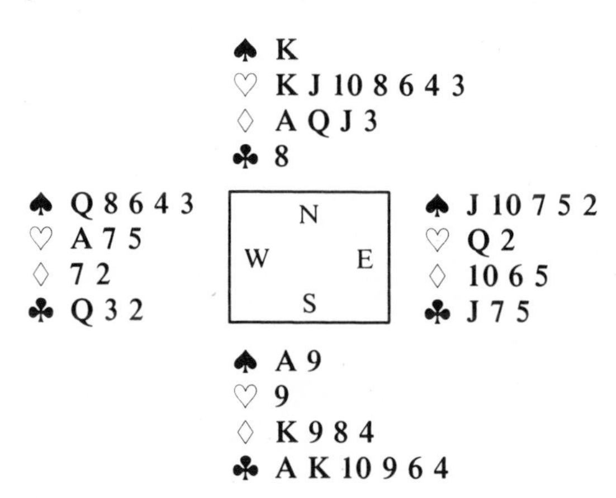

Neither side vulnerable. The bidding:

WEST	NORTH	EAST	SOUTH
Garozzo		*Forquet*	
	1♡	Pass	2♣
Pass	2♡	Pass	3◇
Pass	4◇	Pass	4♠
Pass	4NT	Pass	5♡
Pass	6◇	All pass	

Garozzo led the 3 of spades. Dummy's king won and declarer led the 3 of hearts from dummy. If South had the ace of hearts, the slam was unbeatable and so I rose with the *queen*, winning the trick. My club return was taken by the ace.

Undecided whether to set up the hearts or the clubs, South continued with the king of clubs. Garozzo, alive to the situation, dropped the *queen*, trying to create the impression that the clubs were 4-2.

This play achieved its aim as declarer decided to place me with the ace of hearts (strongly indicated by my play of the queen of hearts at trick 2). Drawing three rounds of trumps ending in dummy, declarer led the king of hearts, letting it run . . .

At the other table the bidding proceeded:

WEST	NORTH	EAST	SOUTH
	Avarelli		*Belladonna*
	1♢*	Pass	3♣
Pass	3♡*	Pass	4♢
Pass	5♢	Pass	6♢
Pass	Pass	Pass	

*Canape style, shorter suit first

The contract was the same but this time the declarer was *North*, Avarelli. East led a spade taken by the king. Declarer crossed to dummy with a club to the ace and led the singleton heart. When West rose with the ace, Avarelli had little trouble in bringing home the slam.

When There Are Too Many Trumps

During the match against Australia in the 1968 Olympiad, I was faced with this Four Heart contract:

♠ 9 8 7 6
♡ A 9
◊ A Q 8
♣ A 7 4 3

	N	
W		E
	S	

♠ 10 4 3
♡ K J 10 7 5 4 3
◊ 5 4
♣ 8

East-West vulnerable. The bidding:

WEST	NORTH *Garozzo*	EAST	SOUTH *Forquet*
		Pass	3♡
Double	4♡	Double	All pass

West led the king of spades and continued with the queen and the jack. On the third round, East won the ace of spades. Suppose that East switches to the 7 of diamonds: four - nine - queen.

How would you plan the play?

This was the complete hand:

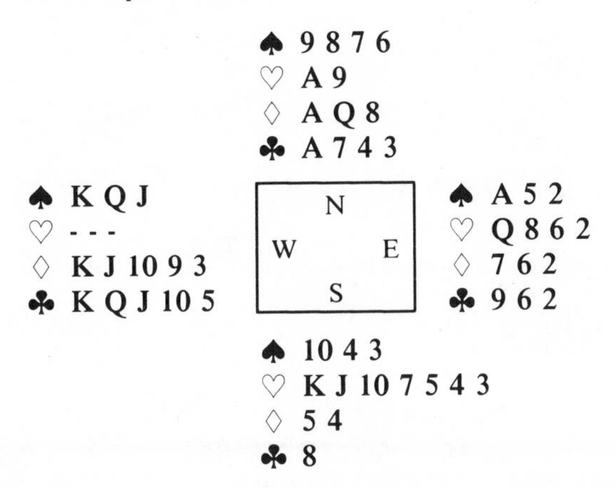

Given West's takeout double of Three Hearts and East's penalty double of Four Hearts, it is not hard to place East with Q-x-x-x in trumps.

In practice East returned a club after the third round of spades and I was able to make the contract this way: ace of clubs, club ruff, heart to the ace, 9 of hearts, club ruff, diamond to the queen, club ruff, diamond to the ace.

This was the ending:

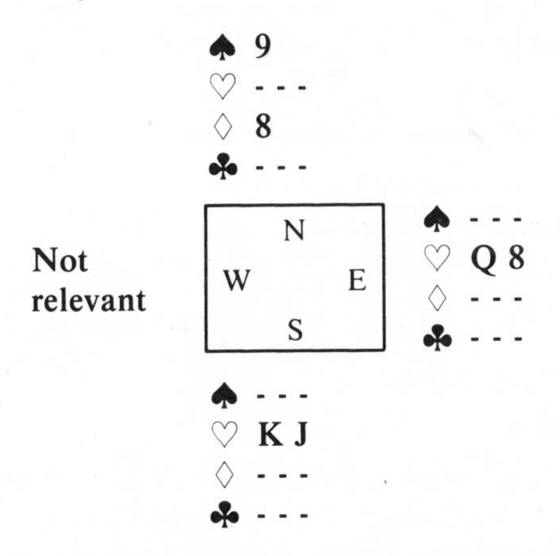

Playing either card from dummy it was easy to pick up East's queen.

Had East returned a diamond at trick 4, as was suggested at the start of the description of the play, it would have made life more difficult. The above line would not have been possible because of the shortage of entries to dummy.

The only play that would be successful would be to continue with the fourth round of spades at once, risking a possible overruff by West. Ruffing with the 7 of hearts would provide some protection against this possibility.

D'Alelio's Duck

During the qualifying rounds of the 1968 Olympiad I had to contend with the following 3NT:

♠ J 6 5
♡ 6 4
♢ A K 10 9 2
♣ K 5 4

	N	
W		E
	S	

♠ A K 2
♡ A Q J 2
♢ 6 5
♣ 10 7 3 2

Both sides vulnerable. The bidding:

WEST	NORTH	EAST	SOUTH
	Garozzo		*Forquet*
	1♢	2♠*	3NT
Pass	Pass	Pass	
*Weak			

West led the 4 of spades: five - seven - ace. I continued with a diamond to the 10 and East's queen. East switched to a low heart: queen - king - four, and West returned the 6 of clubs: four - queen - two. East led another low heart.

How would you have proceeded?

After you have settled on your plan, consult the complete deal to see how your approach would have fared:

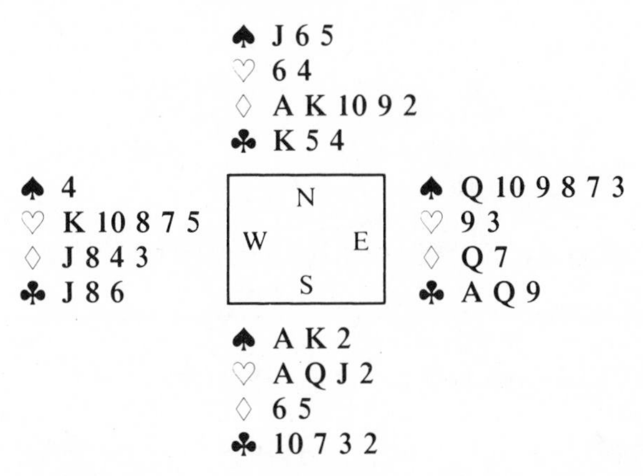

Winning the ace of hearts, I cashed the jack of hearts also, discarding a club from dummy. I then finessed the 9 of diamonds and ran two more rounds of diamonds to arrive at this ending:

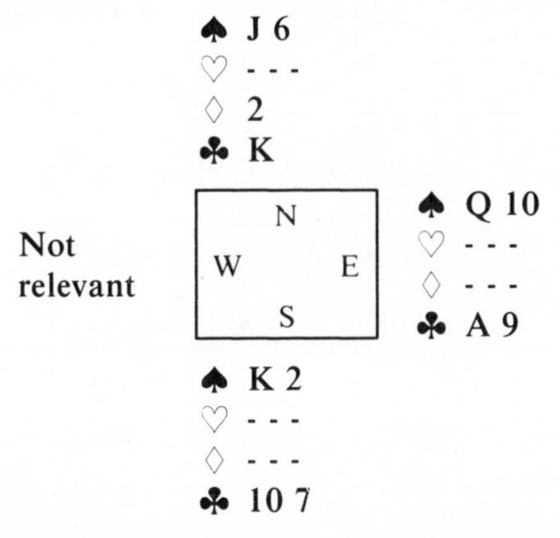

On the last diamond East was forced to discard a club to maintain the guard in spades. I too let go a club and continued with the king of clubs, endplaying East and forcing him to provide the trick I needed with the jack of spades.

At the other table the bidding proceeded:

WEST *Pabis-Ticci*	NORTH	EAST *D'Alelio*	SOUTH
	1◇	1♠	2NT
Pass	3NT	All pass	

West, Pabis-Ticci, also started with the 4 of spades and winning with the ace, declarer also tackled diamonds. Pabis signalled his four-card length by playing the 8, dummy's 10 was inserted and Mimmo D'Alelio *played low with the queen doubleton!*

This defence prevented declarer from making his contract.

An Indispensable Stepping-Stone

Suppose as South you hold the following cards:

♠ A K 3 ♡ A 7 ◊ A 9 8 7 6 ♣ 9 8 7

With neither side vulnerable, East on your right opens One Spade, you intervene with One No-Trump, West passes, your partner raises to Two No-Trumps and East passes.

What action do you take?

This problem confronted me during an international pairs tournament. Normally I would pass but as our score required a considerable boost, I decided to risk Three No-Trumps. West led the queen of spades and this was the layout:

♠ 9 5 2
♡ Q 10 8 6
◊ Q J 10 5
♣ K 10

N
W E
S

♠ A K 3
♡ A 7
◊ A 9 8 7 6
♣ 9 8 7

To recapitulate the bidding:

WEST	NORTH *Garozzo*	EAST	SOUTH *Forquet*
		1♠	1NT
Pass	2NT	Pass	3NT
Pass	Pass	Pass	

Prospects were anything but rosy. If the ace of clubs were onside, not only would the king of clubs provide a sorely needed trick but it would also be the required entry to dummy to enable the diamond finesse to be taken. The chance of the ace of clubs being on the left was, however, a futile hope since in view of East's opening bid and West's lead of the queen of spades, East could logically be placed with all the critical missing high cards.

How would you have planned the play?

This was the complete deal:

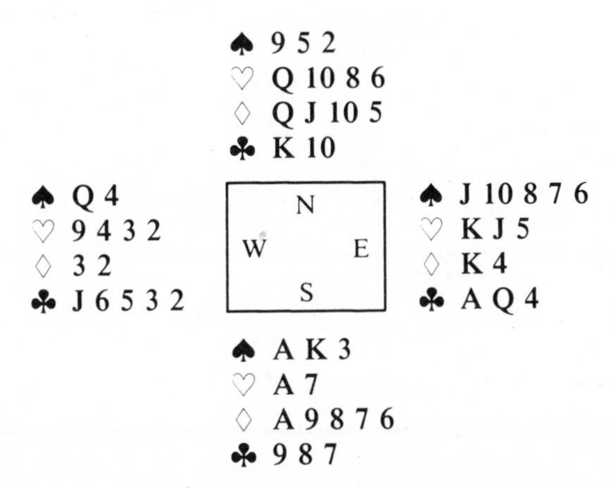

To make the contract it was necessary to bring in five diamond tricks. Then I still had to find an endplay to yield the ninth trick. But how was I to reach dummy to take the diamond finesse?

The only possibility was to use East as a stepping-stone in the hope that he had started with no more than five spades. Accordingly I won the ace of spades and continued with the king of spades and a third spade. East won this and cashed two more spades on which I discarded two clubs from hand and two hearts from dummy. If East had now switched to clubs or hearts not only would it give me the required entry to dummy but it would also give me my ninth trick. East did his best, therefore, by returning a diamond. Finessing against the king, I continued diamonds to reach this position:

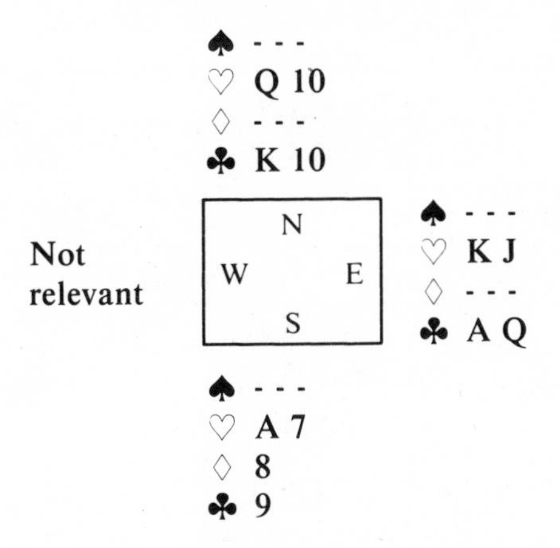

On the last diamond I discarded the 10 of clubs from dummy and East, to retain both hearts, had to bare the ace of clubs. I led a club forcing the heart return.

Enforced Co-operation

This deal arose during the qualifying rounds of the 1968 Olympiad:

♠ 8 7 2
♡ A 6 3
◊ 8 7 5 3 2
♣ 8 7

N
W E
S

♠ K J 9
♡ J 2
◊ A K Q 6
♣ A K Q 9

North-South vulnerable. The bidding:

SOUTH	WEST	NORTH	EAST
Forquet		*Garozzo*	
2NT	3♡	3NT	All pass

West started with the 6 of spades: two - four - nine. The contract seemed easy enough until I laid down the ace of diamonds only to find West discarding a heart. Had I continued diamonds to establish dummy's fifth card, East would have returned a spade and West would no doubt have cashed four more tricks in that suit (West would have to have a five-card suit to lead away from a holding like A-Q-10 into a Two No-Trump opener).

How would you have planned the play?

This was the complete deal:

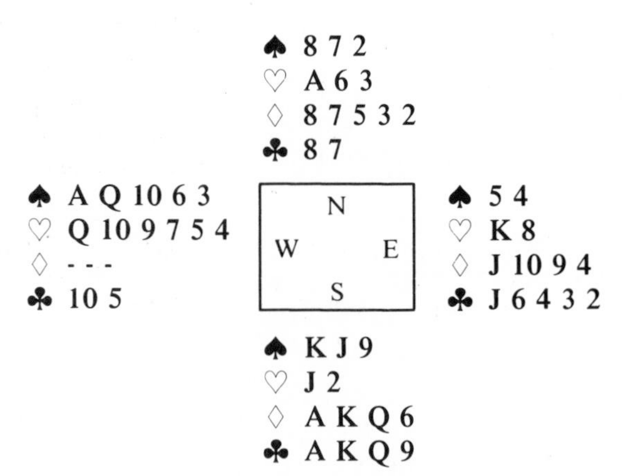

I cashed the ace and king of clubs and exited with the king of spades. West proceeded to cash the rest of the spades to produce this ending:

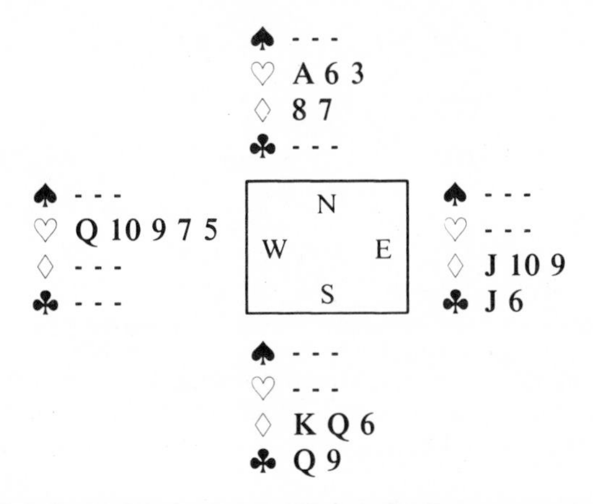

The enforced heart return was won by dummy's ace, simultaneously turning the screws on East in diamonds and clubs.

Variations

(a) Had I failed to cash two clubs before putting West on lead with the king of spades, I would have become squeezed. In order to retain the diamond menace, South is obliged to discard two hearts. This is all right if two clubs have been cashed since West with only hearts left returns to you the trick that has been abandoned. If the clubs are not extracted from West first, then West exits with the 10 of clubs and the ace of hearts is marooned.

(b) If West after winning the ace of spades and cashing just one more spade had switched to a low heart, I would have played low in dummy. After winning the heart continuation with dummy's ace, I would have played three rounds of diamonds. This would put East on lead and force a club return, allowing me to finesse the 9.

(c) If West after the ace of spades had cashed two more spades, East would have been forced to discard a heart to retain control in both minors. In this case I would win the heart switch with the ace and continue with three rounds of diamonds as above.

(d) If West after the ace of spades and just one more spade had led the queen of hearts, I could afford to rise with the ace, succeeding whether East plays low or whether East unblocks.

A Vital Overtrick

In a pairs tournament in Palma di Majorca several years ago, Avarelli and Belladonna scrambled to first place over Garozzo and Ferry Mayer thanks to the overtrick scored by Belladonna in this Five Club contract:

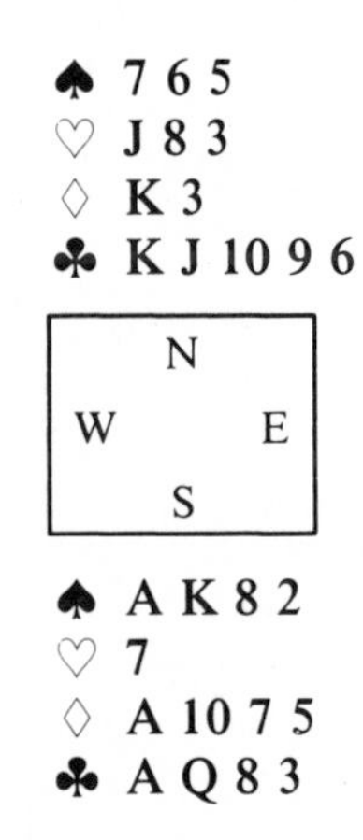

North-South vulnerable. The bidding:

SOUTH	WEST	NORTH	EAST
Belladonna		*Avarelli*	
2♣*	Pass	3♣	Pass
5♣	Pass	Pass	Pass

*Shows a 4-4-4-1 shape, singleton not yet disclosed.

West led the 10 of hearts and East upon winning the king switched to the jack of spades, taken by declarer's ace. Eleven tricks are there simply by ruffing two hearts in hand, but Belladonna engineered the play to produce twelve tricks.

How would you have continued at trick 3?

This was the complete deal:

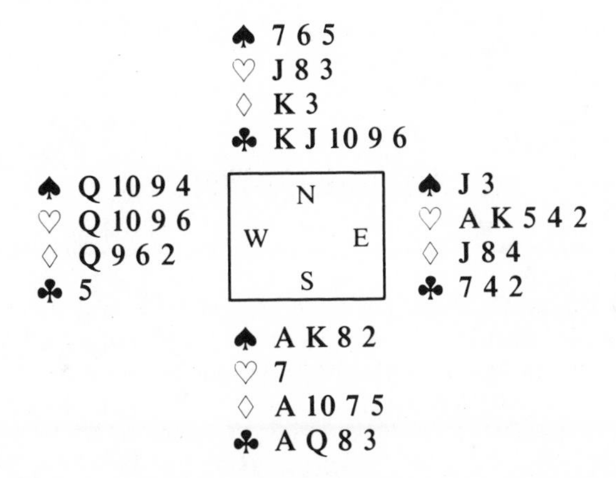

Belladonna continued with a low club to the jack, heart ruff, queen of clubs overtaken by the king and another heart ruff. He crossed back to dummy with a diamond to the king and cashed one more trump to reach this ending:

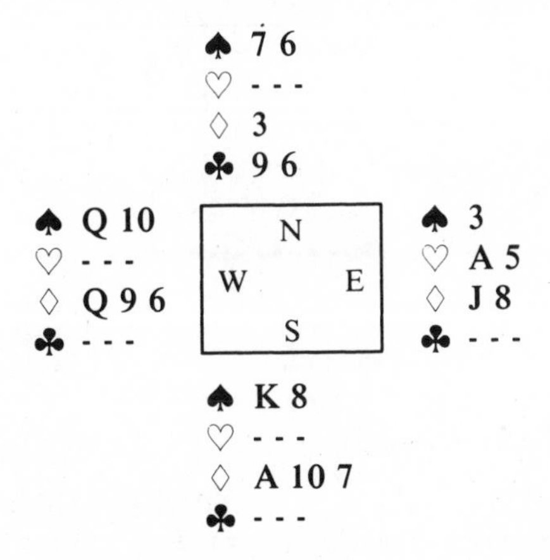

On the 9 of clubs Belladonna discarded the 8 of spades and West became squeezed. If he discarded a spade, declarer would have cashed the king of spades, establishing dummy's third spade; if instead he discarded diamonds, South's hand would have become high after ruffing a diamond in dummy, the king of spades acting as the entry back to hand.

A "Friendly" Defence

In the 1968 Italian Championships the match between Naples and Rome was particularly electrifying. After an even beginning, the match swung clearly to the Neapolitan Team in the latter stages, so much so that when the following deal arose Belladonna in desperation drove the bidding to a highly optimistic small slam:

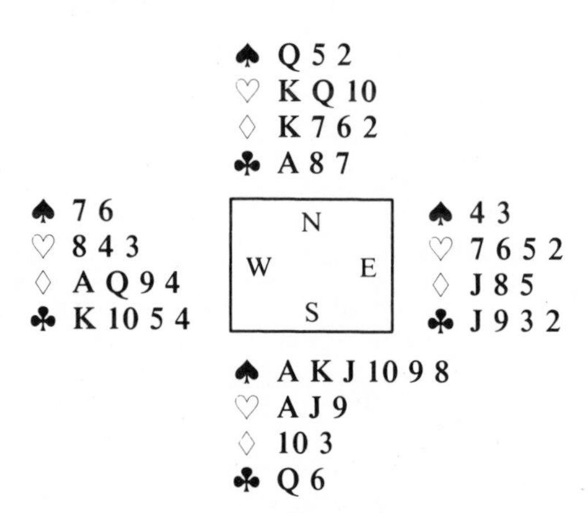

Both sides vulnerable. The bidding:

SOUTH	WEST	NORTH	EAST
Belladonna	*Forquet*	*Avarelli*	*Garozzo*
1♠	Pass	2NT	Pass
3♠	Pass	4♣	Pass
4♡	Pass	4♠	Pass
4NT	Pass	5♢	Pass
5♡	Pass	6♠	All pass

How would you have planned the play in this small slam after West had led the 7 of spades? And how would you have planned the East-West defence to defeat the slam?

After winning my trump lead in hand, Belladonna immediately led a low diamond. Had I taken this with the ace, the slam would have made easily. No matter what I return, Giorgio would win, draw a second round of trumps, play a diamond to the king and ruff a diamond, cash the hearts and run the spades to reach this position:

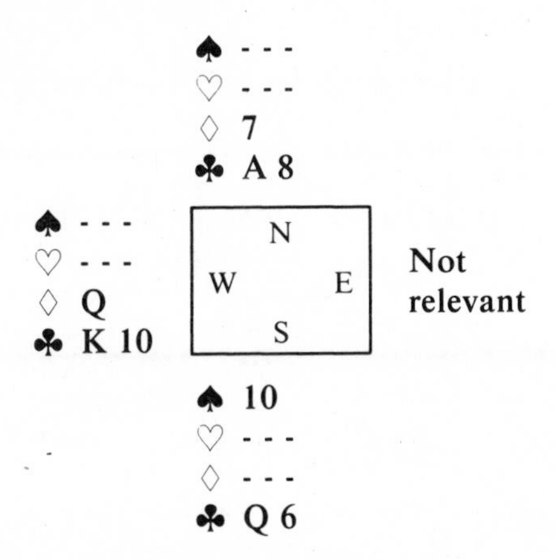

When the last spade is played, I would be squeezed in diamonds and clubs.

Accordingly I ducked the 3 of diamonds and Giorgio after winning with dummy's king continued with a low diamond from dummy. Had Benito carelessly played low, the 10 would have forced me to win the trick and then I could not have avoided the above squeeze. However, Benito was wide awake and reading the position perfectly, he promptly rose with the jack when the low diamond was led from dummy. Holding the trick, he returned a club destroying the entry to dummy which was vital for the squeeze to operate.

The Pabis-Ticci Variation

Suppose you are playing Four Hearts on this layout:

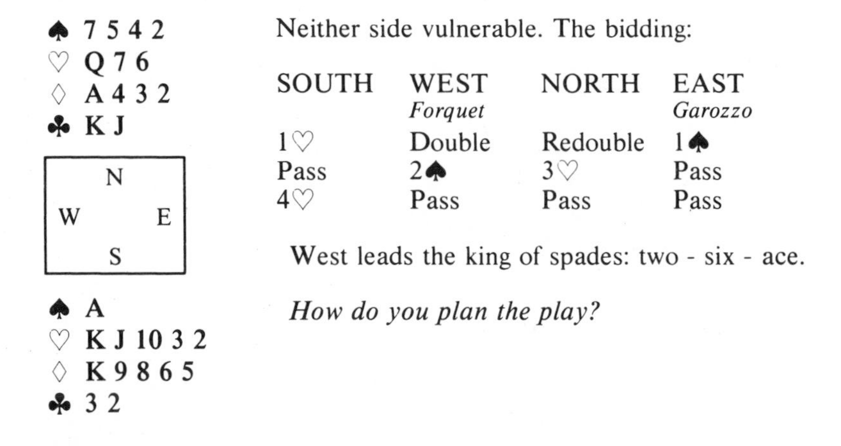

Neither side vulnerable. The bidding:

SOUTH	WEST *Forquet*	NORTH	EAST *Garozzo*
1♡	Double	Redouble	1♠
Pass	2♠	3♡	Pass
4♡	Pass	Pass	Pass

West leads the king of spades: two - six - ace.

How do you plan the play?

This was the complete deal:

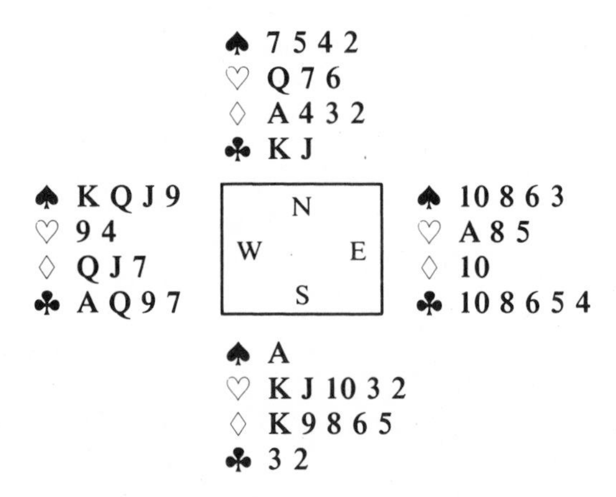

This deal arose in a teams match during the 1968 Italian Championships.

In theory South has ten tricks at his disposal: one spade, four hearts, four diamonds and a club. All the same, to realise all these tricks declarer must time the play extremely accurately.

At our table declarer failed to grasp the problem and ultimately lost trump control. Winning the lead he led a low heart to the queen and ace. Ruffing the spade return, South drew two more rounds of trumps and continued with the ace, king and a third diamond to my queen. I persevered with spades and declarer was forced to ruff with his last trump. The contract could no longer be made since South could not come to the club trick: when he led a club towards dummy, I rose with the ace and cashed my last spade.

Have you spotted declarer's error?

At the other table Camillo Pabis-Ticci was South in the same contract. He also won the spade lead and started on the trumps but with a slight difference. Instead of playing low to the queen he led the king and when East held off he continued with the jack. This time East won the ace and continued spades. Pabis ruffed and started on the diamonds, being very careful how to tackle the suit. As West had not led a diamond, a singleton diamond was more likely with East than West, if the suit did not split 2-2. Accordingly Camillo led a diamond to the ace and a diamond back towards the king. East could not gain by ruffing and Pabis won the king of diamonds, continuing with a low diamond taken by West who played yet another spade. This is the position after Camillo had ruffed this spade:

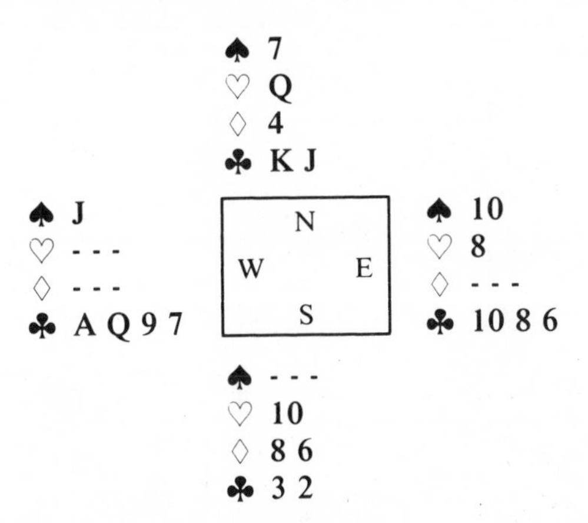

Camillo now led a club and West won the ace to play his last spade. Here, however, declarer had *control* and after ruffing, he crossed to dummy with a club to the king and the queen of trumps allowed the last trump to be drawn.

Try Not To Be Hurtful

When one is playing against opponents who are not too skilful one must exploit to the hilt their propensity for errors. In a pairs tournament at Dyvonne in 1968, I had to manage this small slam:

♠ A K 4 2
♡ A Q 6
◊ 7 5
♣ K 9 8 4

	N	
W		E
	S	

♠ 10 8 7 5 3
♡ K 7 5
◊ A Q 4
♣ A 5

East-West vulnerable. The bidding:

SOUTH	WEST	NORTH	EAST
Forquet		*Garozzo*	
1♠	Pass	2♣	Pass
2♠	Pass	4♡	Pass
4NT	Pass	5◊	Pass
5♡	Pass	6♠	All pass

The jump to Four Hearts showed strong spade support, control in hearts and denied first and second round control in diamonds (otherwise North's bid would have been Four Diamonds). Four No-Trumps was not Blackwood but showed slam interest and enquired as to further values, to which Benito's Five Diamonds promised third round diamond control (queen or doubleton).

The small slam needed no more to be a good bet: it would succeed either if spades were 2-2 or if the finesse for the king of diamonds worked.

Anyway, how would you play in my position to improve your chances slightly after West has led the jack of hearts?

This was the complete deal:

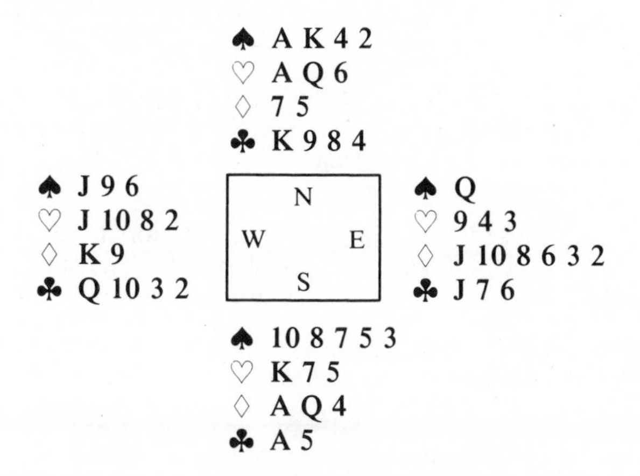

As you can see, the spades do not break and the king of diamonds is offside. Nevertheless, thanks to my little trap and West's great naivety, I managed to land the slam.

Winning the king of hearts, I laid down the *ten* of spades and West was kind enough to cover an honour with an honour. When East dropped the queen under the ace, the position was pretty clear. Judging that East was not good enough to drop the queen from Q-9, I came to hand with a club to the ace and led the 8 of spades, finessing when West played low.

After the tournament Garozzo was recounting to Belladonna how I had been presented with this gift for a top board. Giorgio protested that this should not be treated as an absolute top since exactly the same thing had happened at his table. "Eh," replied Benito, "I did not realise that *you* were sitting *West*!"

Garozzo's Personal Brand Of Simplicity

"Why make easy things difficult?" is a criticism that is frequently heard at the table, especially at rubber bridge.

Now, it is true that one should strive to avoid unnecessary complications but it is also true that experts generally consider hands more deeply than the average player and the expert's "complications" are almost invariably based on some logical and technical justification.

Those who preach simplicity will certainly not be enamoured with the style of Benito Garozzo who on almost every deal, no matter how seemingly simple, will succeed in producing something rather special.

Take for example this mundane Four Spade contract which my partner played against the United States in the final of the 1968 Olympiad:

♠ K 4
♡ A 5 4 3 2
♢ A 7 6 3
♣ J 7

N
W E
S

♠ A 10 9 7 5 2
♡ K J
♢ K J 5
♣ Q 3

Neither side vulnerable. The bidding:

SOUTH	WEST	NORTH	EAST
Garozzo		*Forquet*	
1♠	2♣	2♡	Pass
2♠	Pass	3♠	Pass
4♠	Pass	Pass	Pass

West leads the king of clubs, ace of clubs and switches to the 3 of spades: four - queen - ace.

How would you have continued?

The natural line seems to be to set up a heart winner in dummy to obviate the diamond finesse. To cope with a 4-2 break (if they are 3-3, there is no problem), it is necessary to start with the king of hearts, ace of hearts and a third heart ruffed. If the hearts are indeed 4-2, declarer enters dummy with the king of spades, ruffs another heart and the ace of diamonds will provide the needed entry to reach the established heart winner.

Garozzo however foresaw that this line of play incurred some risk. If on the third round of hearts from dummy East follows, should declarer ruff high or low? If you ruff low, you may find West overruffing with the 8 and this would cost the contract if West began with 8-doubleton in trumps. If instead you ruff with the 10 or 9 you would lose an extra trump trick if trumps are 4-1.

This was the complete deal:

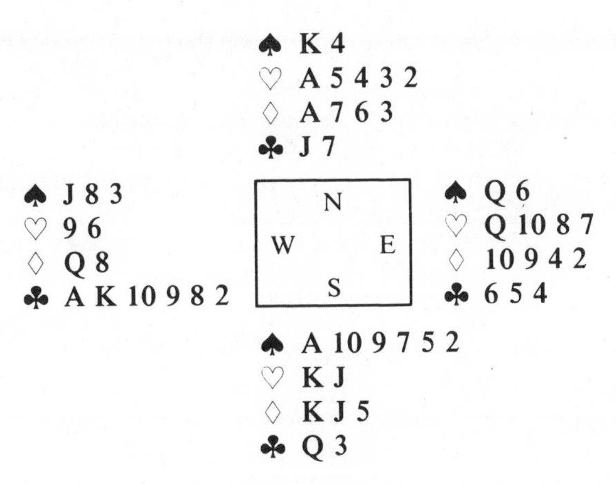

As you will have noticed, declarer would succeed whether he ruffs the third heart low or with the 10, since West started with *three* trumps to the jack.

My partner however decided to forsake the straight and narrow and "complicate matters" by adopting a different line of play. Winning the queen of spades with the ace, Benito continued with a second trump won by the king. Next came the king of hearts, a heart to the ace and a third heart, ruffed. West overruffed and returned a club.

At this point the contract seemed doomed since declarer lacked the entries to set up the fifth heart and return to dummy to cash it, while if declarer tried the diamond finesse, that too was destined to fail.

Garozzo, however, read the position perfectly. Ruffing the club return, he played another round of spades on which East discarded a diamond. This was the ending:

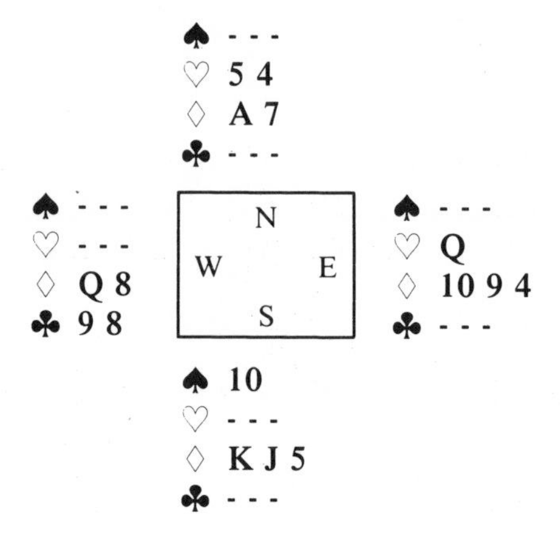

When Benito played his last spade, discarding a heart from dummy, East was forced to let go another diamond in order to hang on to the queen of hearts. My partner continued by playing a diamond to the ace and a diamond back towards the king, East following with the 9 and 10. Benito had no problem in rising with the king and dropping the queen of diamonds offside. East's remaining card was known to be the queen of hearts so that the queen of diamonds had to be in West's hand.

A Matter Of Control

The following deal arose in Palma di Majorca in 1969 during a match against a Danish team:

♠ 6 2
♡ 10 9
◊ A 8 7 4 2
♣ K 8 7 3

	N	
W		E
	S	

♠ K Q 10 9 5 4
♡ 8
◊ K 3
♣ A Q 5 4

Both sides vulnerable. The bidding:

SOUTH	WEST	NORTH	EAST
Forquet		*Garozzo*	
1♠	Pass	1NT	Pass
3♣	Pass	4♣	Pass
4♠	Double	All pass	

West led the 6 of hearts. East won the ace and returned the 3 of hearts.

How do you plan the play to maximize your chances of making the contract?

This was the complete deal:

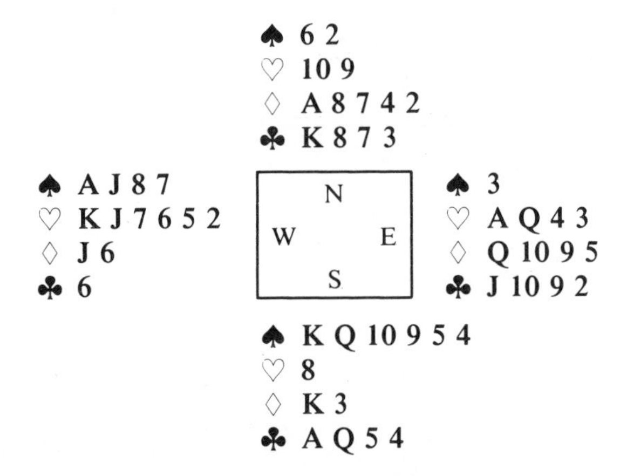

West's double heralded a foul trump break which required careful play to avoid losing trump control. If after ruffing the second heart I had led the king of spades, West would play low and the contract would now fail even if the clubs had been 3-2. If South then continues with the queen of spades, West would take the ace and force declarer with another heart. Declarer is down to *two* trumps, the same as West. If South now abandons trumps, West will trump with the low trump, while if South perseveres with spades, West wins with the jack and the next heart demolishes South.

Therefore in order not to lose trump control, I led the *ten* of spades after ruffing the second heart. If West won this with the jack, dummy's trump would prevent his shortening me again. West decided to duck this and I continued with the king of spades which West won, returning a heart. After ruffing, I cashed the queen of spades and reached this position:

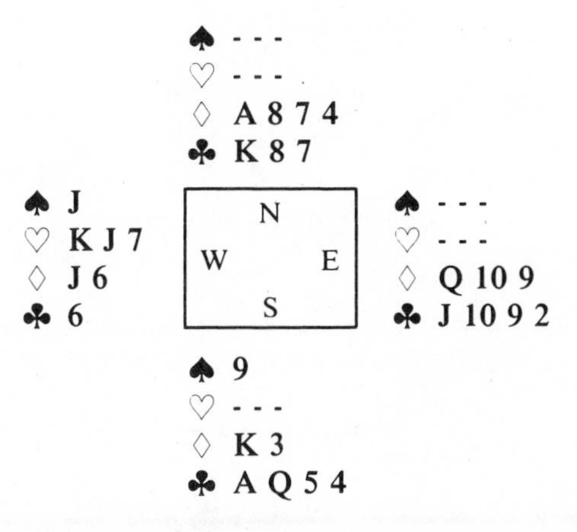

I proceeded to tackle the clubs, playing a club to the king and back to the ace. Had clubs been 3-2, the hand would be over while if West had started with a singleton club, this play might induce him to make a mistake.

West did indeed ruff the ace of clubs, a mistake, whereupon the contract became unbeatable. This was the ending:

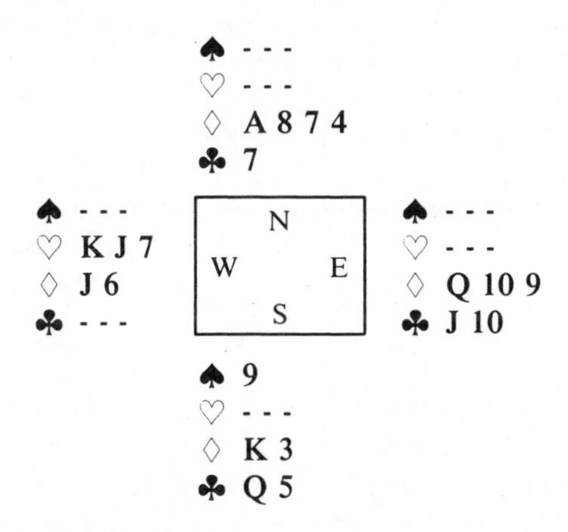

West returned a heart and East was automatically squeezed in diamonds and clubs. Had West returned a diamond, I would have won in hand and produced the same effect by leading the 9 of spades.

West's error in ruffing the ace of clubs is a common one. Had he patiently allowed me to cash my winners, I would have been forced to concede a club in the end as well as the jack of spades.

A Mundane Contract

During an international tournament I had to play this Four Spade contract:

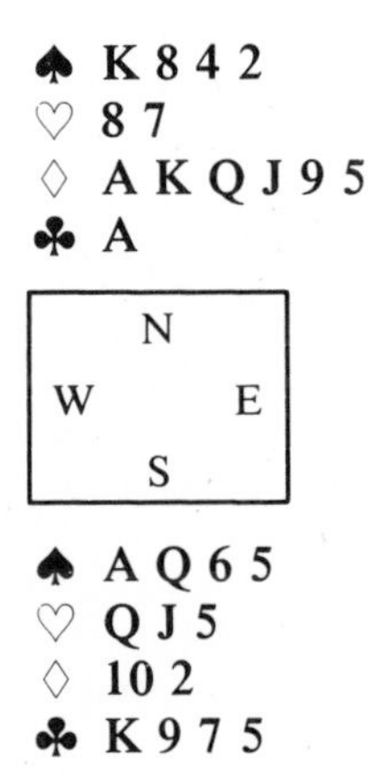

Both sides vulnerable. The bidding:

WEST	NORTH *Garozzo*	EAST	SOUTH *Forquet*
	1♣	Pass	1♠*
Pass	2♢	Pass	2♠
Pass	3♠	Pass	3NT
Pass	4♣	Pass	4♠
Pass	Pass	Pass	

*3 controls, any shape

If I had held the king of hearts instead of the king of clubs, I would have bid Four Hearts over Four Clubs. Consequently Garozzo was able to pass Four Spades in comfort, knowing in view of my denial of heart control that we had two losers in hearts.

West led the ace of hearts, the king of hearts and a third heart. The contract seemed routine until I cashed the ace of spades . . . East produced a club . . . West had started with J-10-9-7-3!

How do you plan the play to give up only one more trick?

This was the complete deal:

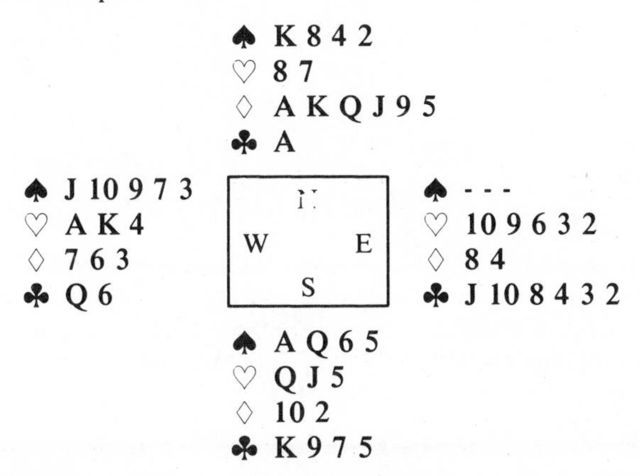

West had turned up with five spades and three hearts at least. If his remaining cards were three diamonds and two clubs or even four diamonds and a club, he could not prevent me from making my contract, notwithstanding the two apparent losers in trumps.

My continuation was ace of clubs, ace of diamonds, king of diamonds, queen of diamonds ruffed in hand, and the king of clubs, pitching a diamond from dummy. This was the ending:

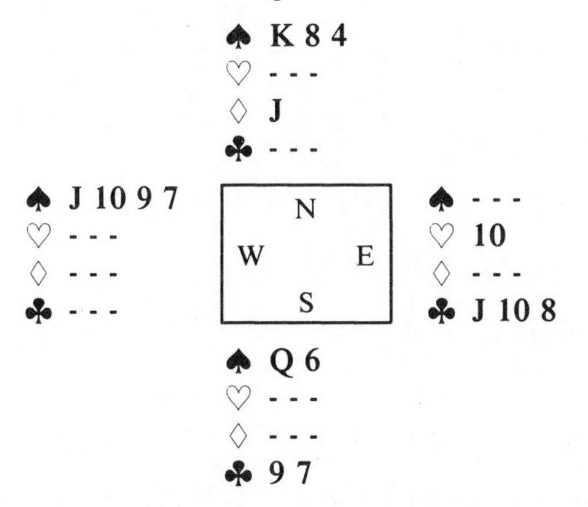

When I played the 9 of clubs West had to ruff high to prevent my winning cheaply with dummy's 8 of spades. I discarded the jack of diamonds on this trick and West was forced to return the 10 of spades. Winning with the queen, I was able to finesse the 8 on the next round, thus making the contract.

If West had started with four diamonds and a singleton club, the contract would have succeeded just the same. I would have cashed three diamonds instead of two (after taking the ace of clubs), ruffed the fourth round of diamonds and then led a club. The ending would have been the same.

An Extra Chance

Rather than stake everything on the outcome of a finesse, a competent player ought to check whether there might not be some superior line of play. Take, for example, the following 3NT contract from the 1968 World Teams Olympiad:

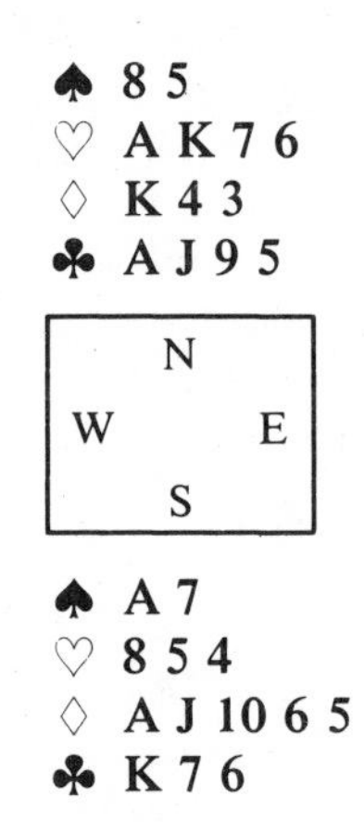

Both sides vulnerable. The bidding:

WEST	NORTH	EAST	SOUTH
Belladonna		*Avarelli*	
	1♡	Pass	2♢
Pass	3♣	Pass	3NT
Pass	Pass	Pass	

Belladonna started with the king of spades and continued with the queen, Avarelli playing the 4 and the 2.

How would you plan the play?

If you opt for the diamond finesse, the outcome of the contract will depend solely on the position of the queen of diamonds. Instead declarer should contemplate two other possible lines which offer additional chances. The first is to play off the ace and king of clubs hoping to find East with queen-doubleton (in this case declarer is able to procure nine tricks without the agony of the diamond finesse; one spade, two hearts, two diamonds and four clubs); the second is to cash the ace and king of diamonds hoping to drop the queen, reverting, if it has not appeared, to the club suit, playing the king and then finessing the jack, hoping for four tricks there.

After long deliberation declarer elected to tread the first path and cashed the ace and king of clubs. This play was successful insofar as Avarelli, East, produced the queen of clubs on the second round. Declarer then played off the king and ace of diamonds, but when this queen did not drop, he continued with a low club to the 9 in dummy, finessing against the 10 *marked* in Belladonna's hand.

This was the complete deal:

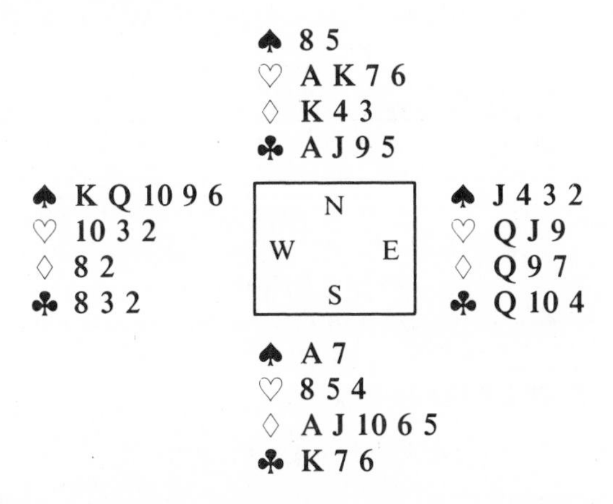

You can of course picture declarer's chagrin when the 9 of clubs lost to Avarelli's 10. The contract thus failed by two tricks, as the defence came to four spades and a diamond as well.

It must be stressed that declarer appreciated the risk which his line entailed against a defender of Walter Avarelli's calibre. This can be seen from declarer's trying to drop the queen of diamonds before taking the club finesse in an attempt to avoid a possible trap set by East.

At the other table Camillo Pabis-Ticci faced with the same contract and the same problem followed the same approach. Winning the ace of spades at trick 2, he also led a club to the ace and a club back to the king. When the queen of clubs did not appear, however, Camillo reverted to the diamonds, playing for the queen of diamonds to be with East. When this finesse succeeded, he had ten tricks.

Squeeze Or Throw-In

In the 1969 European Championships, Giorgio Belladonna had to contend with the following slam:

♠ 9 8 5
♡ A K J 5
◊ 10 9 4
♣ Q 10 3

	N	
W		E
	S	

♠ A K 6 4
♡ 8
◊ A K Q J 8
♣ A 9 8

Both sides vulnerable. The bidding:

WEST	NORTH *Mondolfo*	EAST	SOUTH *Belladonna*
		2♠	Double
Pass	3♡	Pass	4◊
Pass	4♡	Pass	6◊
Pass	Pass	Pass	

East's Two Spade opening showed a weak two-suiter in spades and hearts and accordingly Mondolfo's Three Heart and Four Heart bids were clearly strength-showing cue-bids.

How would you have planned the play after West leads the 4 of hearts?

Giorgio won the ace and cashed five rounds of diamonds, to which West followed with four trumps and the 4 of clubs while East played a trump, two spades and two hearts. This was the position:

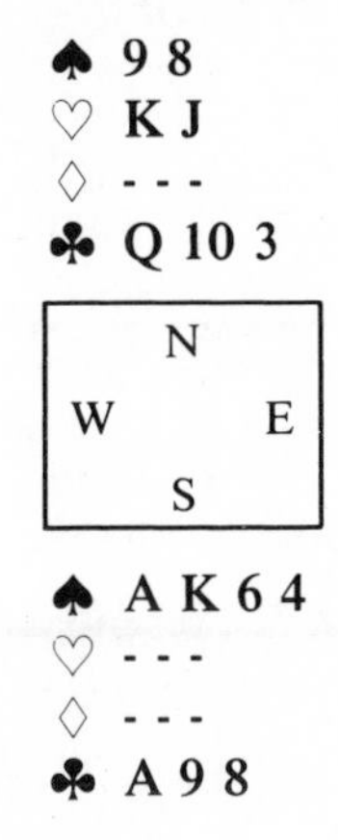

How would you have continued?

This was the complete deal:

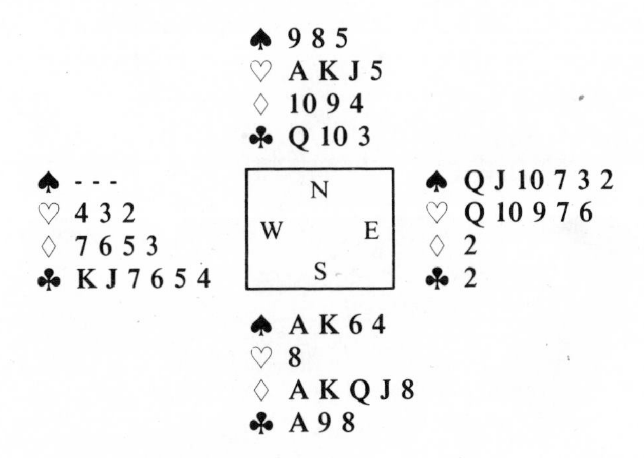

The complete seven-card ending looked like this:

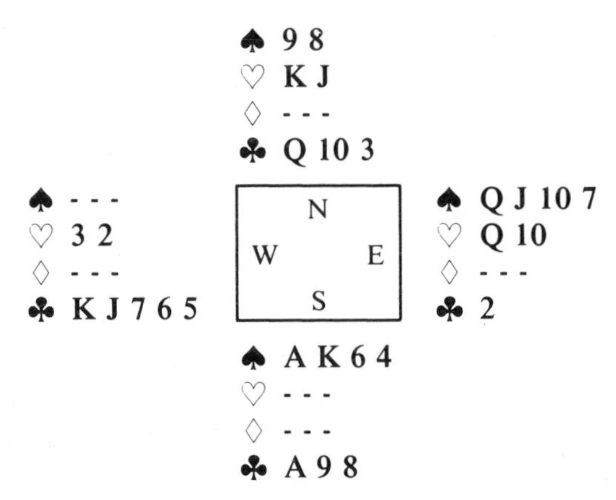

At this stage, the problem can be presented as a double dummy problem: At no-trumps, South is to lead and win six tricks against any defence.

Let's suppose that South leads a low club and West wins with the king. West returns a heart (a club comes to the same) which South wins with dummy's king. A club to the ace and a club to the queen leaves this position:

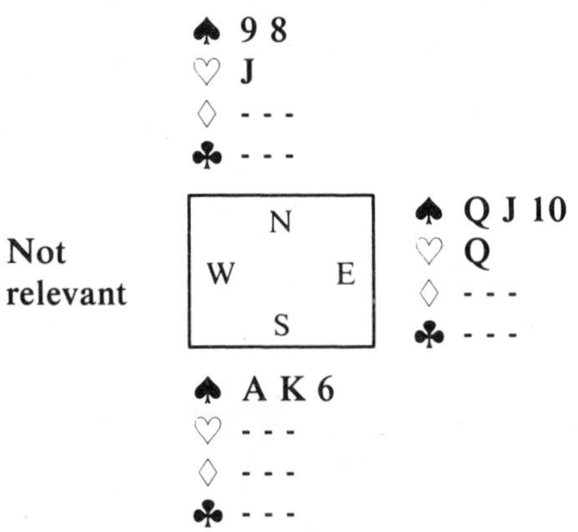

East still has to make a discard on the queen of clubs and is thereby squeezed in spades and hearts.

Did you spot the error?

The above line will come to grief if West ducks the low club lead from South. Dummy will win the trick but the squeeze will be inoperative as there is no further entry to dummy's hearts.

Belladonna naturally found the correct solution in the seven-card ending: *ace of clubs first* and then a low club: if West wins with the king, we have already seen how the squeeze in spades and hearts operates on East; if West plays low, South wins dummy's queen and East must discard a spade to retain the heart control. South then plays three rounds of spades and East wins the third round only to find himself forced to lead into dummy's heart tenace.

An Invisible Defence

In partnership with Garozzo, Mimmo D'Alelio won the Beirut Pairs tournament several years ago. This was one of the deals that contributed to their success:

♠ A Q 10 6 4
♡ K J 2
◊ A J 6 5 3
♣ - - -

N
W E
S

♠ - - -
♡ A Q 10 8 7
◊ K 7 2
♣ Q 10 6 5 4

North-south vulnerable. The bidding:

SOUTH *D'Alelio*	WEST	NORTH *Garozzo*	EAST
1♡	Pass	2◊	Pass
2♡	Pass	2♠	Pass
3◊	Pass	3♡	Pass
4♡	Pass	5♣	Pass
5♡	Pass	6♡	All pass

West led the 5 of spades and dummy's queen held the trick, D'Alelio discarding a club.

How would you have planned the play?

Mimmo cashed the ace of spades, discarding another club, and came to hand with a spade ruff. Then he followed with a club ruff, a diamond to the king and a diamond towards dummy. His plan was to take the two top diamonds and then crossruff to the end. However, when Mimmo led the second round of diamonds, *West discarded the king of spades.*

How would you have continued?

This was the complete deal:

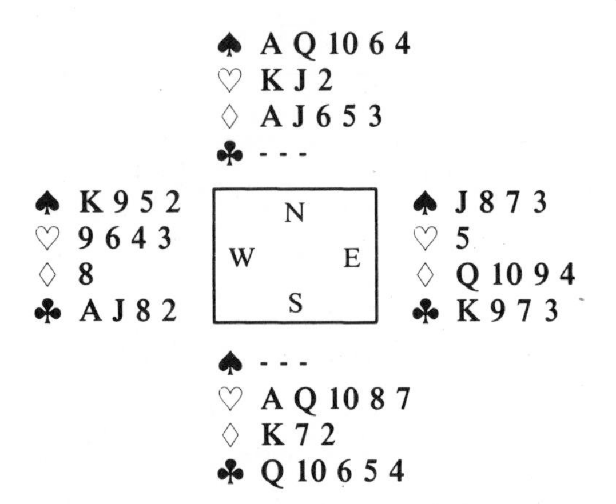

And this was the position after D'Alelio had taken the second round of diamonds with dummy's ace:

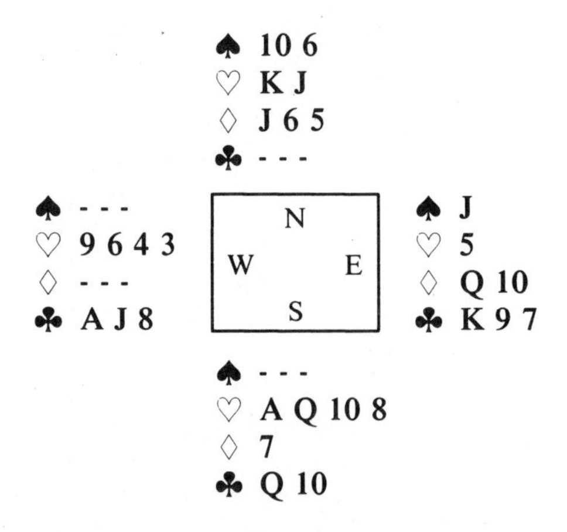

Mimmo ruffed a spade with the ace of hearts, ruffed a club in dummy, ruffed another spade with the queen of hearts and ruffed his last club in dummy.

This was the ending:

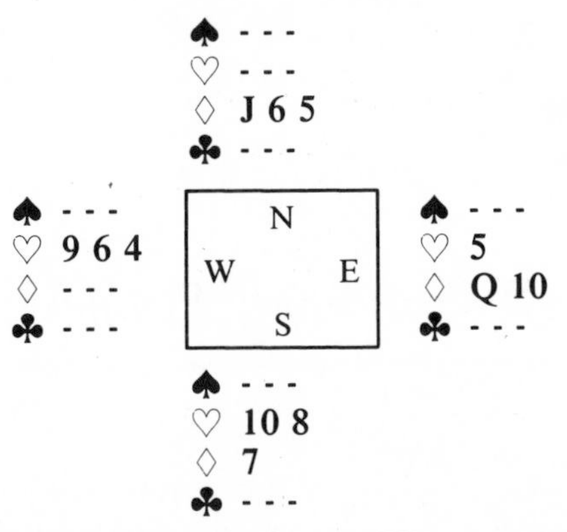

D'Alelio led a diamond from dummy and West could not help ruffing his partner's winner and then leading into South's tenace.

However, suppose that on the second round of diamonds, West had ruffed. This would be the position:

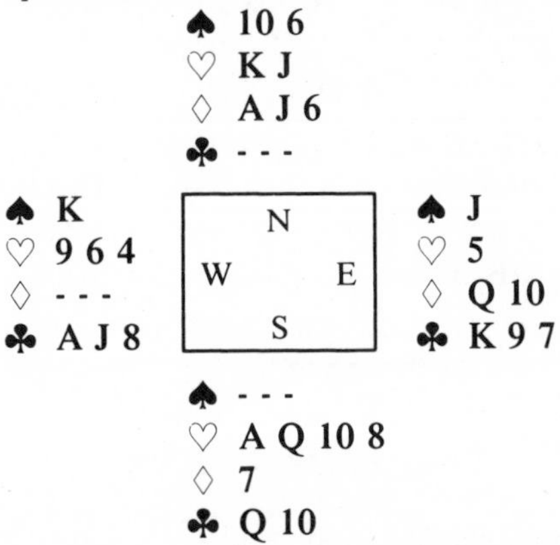

West's best return would be a trump. D'Alelio could counter this by winning with the queen, ruffing a club in dummy and ruffing a spade in hand. After drawing trumps, the last club would be discarded on dummy's winning spade, using the ace of diamonds as the entry.

Was the slam then unbeatable after the original spade lead?

No. West would have been able to defeat it if on the last two spades which declarer ruffed with the ace and queen, *he had underruffed each time*. Then the above three-card ending would not have been reached, for West's last three cards would have been two hearts and a club. Accordingly when South exits with a diamond, West would have been able to discard the club, leave East on lead with the diamond and thereby come to the setting trick with the 9 of hearts.

Variations

If at trick 3 South had played the king of diamonds and led a low diamond from hand, the line of play would be equivalent to the above and would lead to the same conclusion as described above.

An Extraordinary Promotion

The promotion of a trump card is a common enough occurrence but when the trump that is promoted is the *five*, it is worth recounting the story. This deal arose in the 1969 World Championships in the match against the United States:

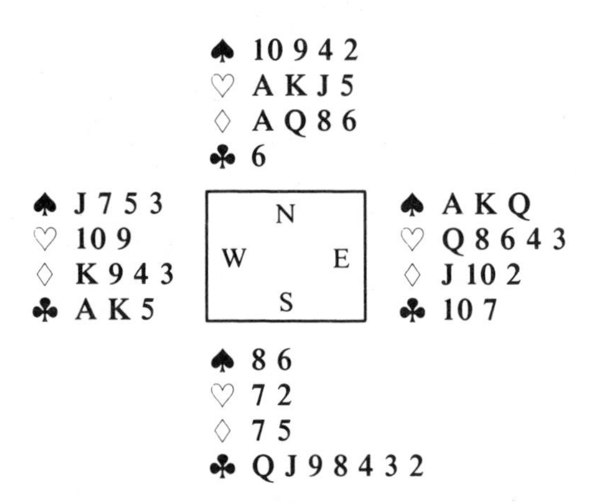

North-South vulnerable. The bidding:

SOUTH	WEST	NORTH	EAST
	Forquet		*Garozzo*
Pass	Pass	1♡	Pass
1NT	Pass	2♢	Pass
3♣	Pass	Pass	Pass

Winning my spade lead with the queen, Garozzo played off the king and ace, South ruffing the third round. South crossed to dummy with a heart to the king and led the 6 of clubs: seven - nine - king. Seeing an outside chance of having my five of clubs promoted, I returned the jack of spades and Garozzo duly cooperated by ruffing with the 10. South overruffed with the jack and continued with the queen of clubs.

This play sealed the fate of the contract. Winning with the ace of clubs, I returned a heart, locking declarer in dummy. This was the position:

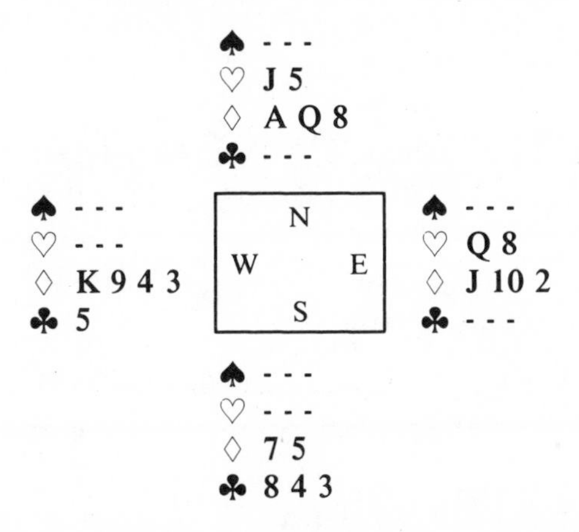

South had to play another heart to try to return to hand (both to draw the last trump and to take the diamond finesse), but his 3 of clubs was overruffed by my 5. Declarer should have succeeded either by taking the diamond finesse when he had the chance or by cashing both of dummy's top hearts earlier (so that I would be unable to lock him in dummy), but the American declarer evidently hoped to obviate the diamond finesse and preferred to try first for the queen of hearts to drop.

On The Verge Of A Grand Slam

Playing with Leon Yallouze in Faro, Portugal, in 1969 Benito Garozzo landed in this small slam in spades:

♠ A Q 7 6 5 4
♡ K 2
♢ A
♣ A K J 2

N
W E
S

♠ K 8 2
♡ A 7 5
♢ J 8 5 4 3
♣ 8 3

North-South vulnerable. The bidding:

NORTH	SOUTH
Yallouze	*Garozzo*
1♣	1♠
2♠	3♠
4♣	4♡
4NT	5♠
5NT	6♣
6♢	6♠
Pass	

The bidding, highly scientific, requires some clarification. Garozzo's One Spade response was artificial and promised three controls, any shape. Four Clubs and Four Hearts were cuebids and Five Spades over Four No-Trumps indicated no further slam interest. Six Clubs over Five No-Trumps showed third round control (queen or doubleton).

Enthused by this development, Yallouze invited the grand slam by bidding Six Diamonds. If he had held the queen of clubs, Benito would no doubt have accepted the invitation but with the doubleton club and only three trumps, he contented himself with the small slam.

West led the 6 of clubs, taken by the ace. Garozzo cashed the ace of spades, East playing the 3 and West the 9.

How would you have continued?

This was the complete deal:

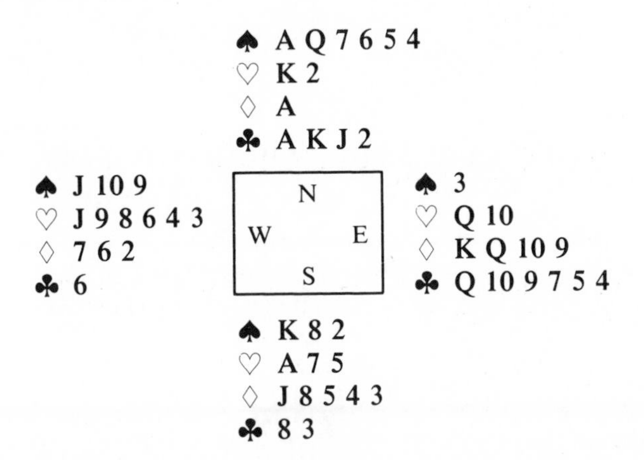

Garozzo came to hand with a heart to the ace and led his second club. It would have simplified declarer's task if West had ruffed but he did his best by discarding a heart. Upon winning dummy's king Benito continued with a club and trumped in hand with the king.

Had declarer ruffed low, West would have been able to overruff and return a trump. Crossing back to dummy with a diamond to the ace, Garozzo ruffed the last club in hand. West was able to overruff this time but it was the only trick for the defence.

A Slam From The Right Side

During the international teams tournament played in Faro, Portugal, in 1969 Avarelli managed to steer home this tricky slam:

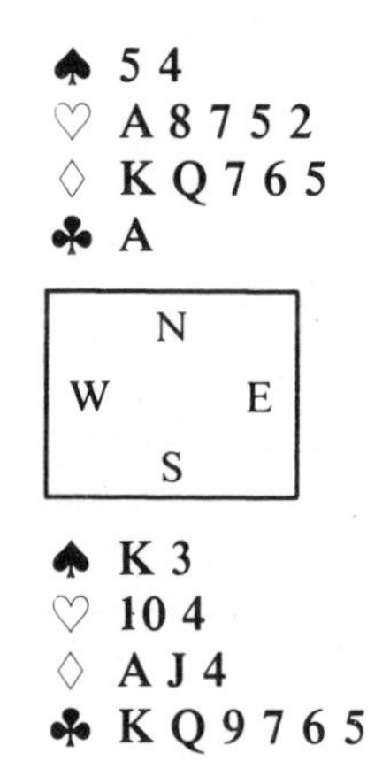

Both sides vulnerable. The bidding:

SOUTH	WEST	NORTH	EAST
Avarelli		*Belladonna*	
1♢	Pass	2♡	Pass
3♣	Pass	4♢	Pass
4♠	Pass	5♣	Pass
5♢	Pass	6♢	All pass

West led the 3 of hearts which Avarelli took with dummy's ace, East producing the 9.

How would you proceed?

This was the complete deal:

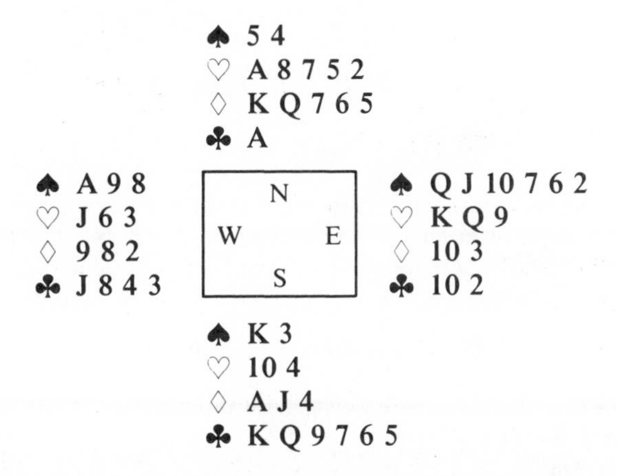

The contract seems to depend on diamonds and clubs dividing perfectly but Avarelli found a small additional chance that allowed him to make the contract notwithstanding the 4-2 break in clubs. Winning the ace of hearts and cashing the ace of clubs, Walter continued by playing the king of diamonds and a low diamond to the ace. Then, before drawing the last trump, he played off the king and queen of clubs, discarding dummy's two spades. This move could not cost the slam for if the opposition had ruffed a top club, this would mean that the clubs were not 3-3, in which case the slam could not have succeeded even if the last trump had been drawn.

The clubs turned out to be 4-2 but Avarelli was in a position to benefit from his fine early technique. He led a heart and East won the 10 with the queen. The spade return was ruffed in dummy and the heart ruff established the rest of the hearts. A spade ruff to dummy and the queen of trumps did the rest.

Without detracting in the slightest from the brilliant play that landed this slam, there was an opportunity for the defence to defeat the slam.

Have you spotted it?

At trick 1 East must unblock one of his top honours under the ace. Later in the play this would have enabled West to win the 10 of hearts with the jack and the trump return would have prevented declarer from setting up the heart suit. (Declarer would of course have placed pressure on East by ruffing a spade to dummy and leading the heart from dummy rather than from hand, but East should find the duck, reasoning that if South did hold the jack of hearts, there would be no defence to defeat the slam.)

At the other table the slam was reached with North as declarer. The queen of spades swiftly despatched this contract.

An Inspired Recovery

One of Italy's toughest matches in winning the European Championships in 1969 was against Sweden. At the end of the first half, Sweden led by 63 Imps to 17 and seemed certain to win the match. In the second half, however, the Italian players produced a grandstand recovery to snatch a 75-71 win.

This was the deal which contributed most to this successful comeback:

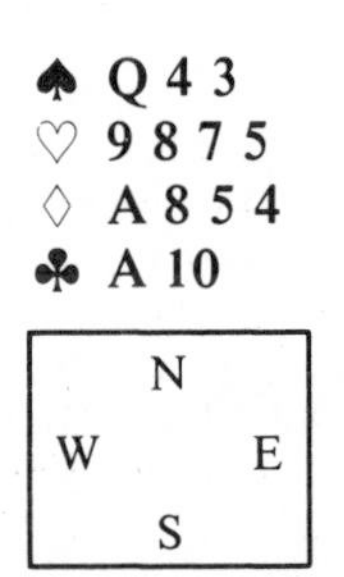

♠ K 10 7 6 2
♡ 4
◊ K J 10 9 2
♣ K 3

Both sides vulnerable. The closed room bidding:

SOUTH *Belladonna*	WEST	NORTH *Garozzo*	EAST
1♠	2♡	2♠	2NT
3♠	4♣	4♠	Double
Pass	Pass	Pass	

West's lead was the ace of hearts, East playing the jack. West followed with a heart to his partner's king, which Belladonna ruffed. A low spade to the queen saw West discard a club and East, after winning the ace, returned the 9 of spades. Capturing the 9 with the 10, Giorgio continued with the jack of diamonds and once more West discarded a club.

This was the position:

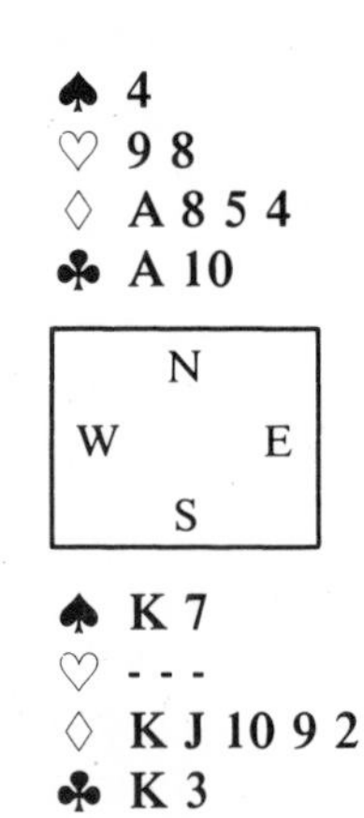

How would you have continued?

This was the complete deal:

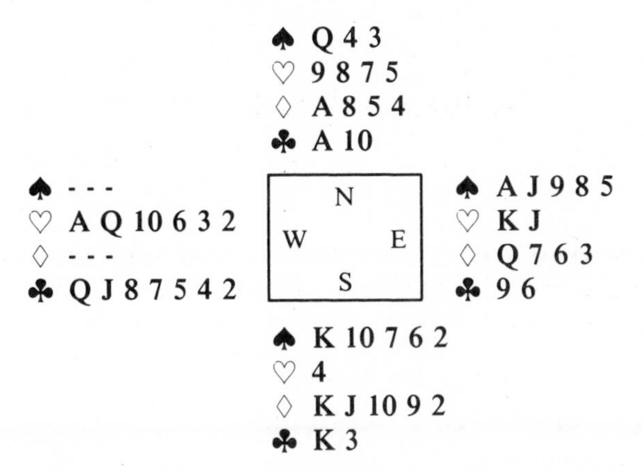

The layout of the cards was by now clearly marked and the contract could not fail. West had started with seven clubs and six hearts while East began with five spades, two hearts, four diamonds and two clubs.

Giorgio covered the jack of diamonds with the ace and continued with the 8 of diamonds, running it when East played low. Then came two more rounds of diamonds, finessing East's queen, the king of clubs and a club to the ace, leading to this ending:

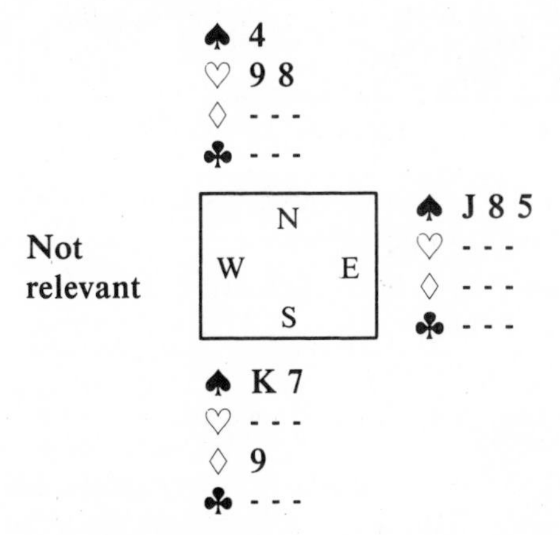

Belladonna led a heart from dummy and East was without recourse. If he ruffed with the 5, South would overruff with the 7; if instead he ruffed with the 8, which is what happened, South would leave East on lead by discarding the 9 of diamonds, forcing East to lead a spade and give South a marked finesse for the last two tricks.

In this way Giorgio made this Four Spade contract with a combined total of only 20 high card points and despite all five trumps being in one hand.

This brilliant result was, however, surpassed by Bianchi and Messina in the open room. Here is the complete deal again:

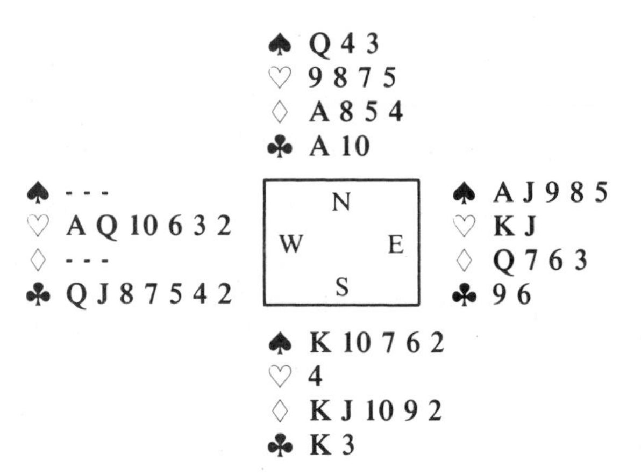

This was the bidding at their table:

SOUTH	WEST	NORTH	EAST
	Messina		*Bianchi*
1♠	4♡!	Double	Redouble!
Pass	Pass	Pass	

The bidding of the Italian pair had its basis no doubt in the state of the match and was an out and out gamble.

North led the ace of diamonds and Messina, after ruffing, continued with the jack of clubs. North took the ace and continued diamonds. Ducking in dummy, declarer ruffed in hand and played a second club, won by South's king. South now led the king of diamonds.

Had Messina ruffed this, he would have lost control of trumps but he prudently guarded against the probable 4-1 break in trumps by discarding a club on the king of diamonds.

The contract thus succeeded, the defence taking just three tricks (two clubs and a diamond). After the match Messina confessed to having suffered a thousand deaths before deciding to let the king of diamonds go. It is true that safety first demanded that the king of diamonds be conceded but the situation in the match was so desperate that it was no easy matter to relinquish the possibility of a redoubled overtrick.

Fortunately prudence prevailed.

At Odds With Sound Technique

It is not necessarily always correct to rely exclusively on the best mathematical line. Playing with Rafael Munoz of Spain in the International Pairs Tournament in Palma di Majorca in 1969, I had to contend with this rather unappetising slam:

♠ - - -
♡ A 9 5 3
♢ A Q 7 6 5
♣ Q 10 9 8

N
W E
S

♠ A 10 8 7 5 2
♡ - - -
♢ J 3
♣ A 7 4 3 2

Neither side vulnerable. The bidding:

WEST	NORTH	EAST	SOUTH
	Munoz		*Forquet*
Pass	1♢	Pass	1♠
2♡	Double	Pass	4♣
Pass	6♣	All pass	

At whose feet should we lay the blame for this highly optimistic slam? Probably my Four Clubs is at fault but this was my first game with Munoz and I was afraid that a mere Three Clubs would not have made a significant enough impression as to the playing strength of my hand.

How would you plan the play after West's lead of the king of hearts?

Before you finalise your plan you should know that over the Six Club bid by my partner, East, before passing, gave us the third degree as to the significance of the bidding so that one could not help feeling that East was on the verge of a penalty double.

This was the complete deal:

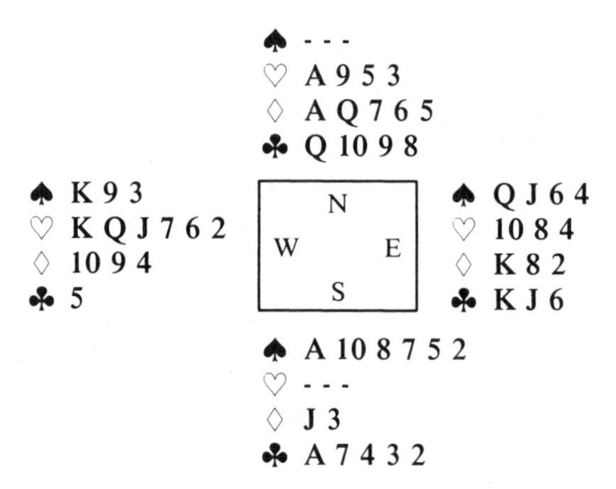

Technique would indicate ruffing the lead in hand and leading the jack of diamonds but in view of East's inquisition I thought the king of diamonds was far more likely to be on my right. Accordingly I adopted a different approach.

I won the lead with the ace of hearts and discarded a diamond from hand. Then came the ace of diamonds, a diamond ruff, ace of spades,a spade ruff, a diamond ruff and a spade ruff.

This was the position:

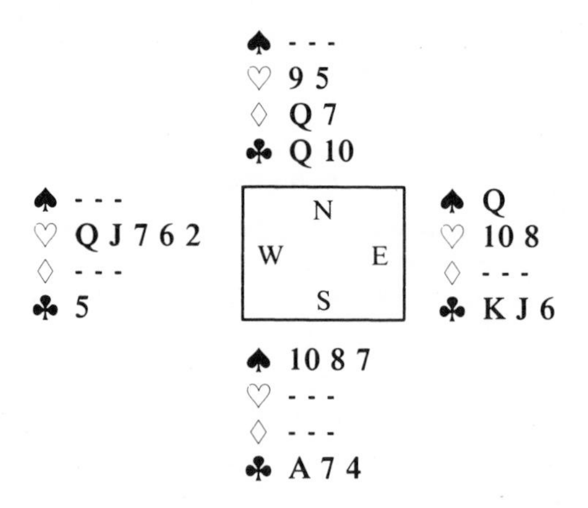

My continuation of the queen of clubs was covered by the king and taken by the ace. A spade ruff led to this ending:

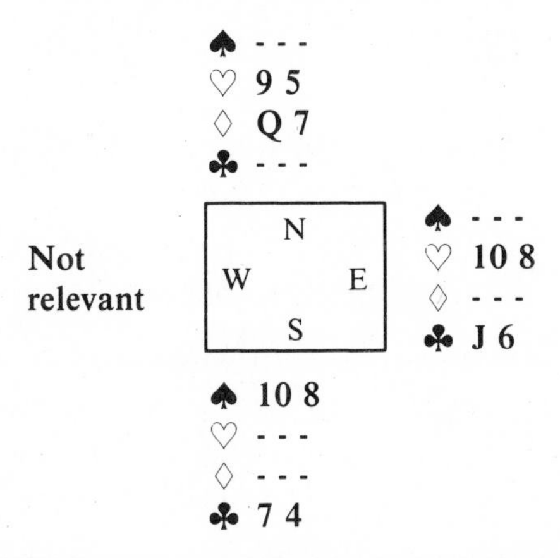

I played dummy's queen of diamonds and East had no defence. If he ruffed with the jack of clubs, that would be his last trick; if he ruffed with the 6, I would overruff with the 7 and continue spades; finally, if he discarded hearts on the two winning diamonds, I in turn would discard my two spades and the heart from dummy would lead to my twelfth trick.

An inattentive critic objecting to this line might claim that if East had not covered the queen of clubs with the king, the contract would have been unmakable because of entry problems. Let us go back to the six-card ending at the bottom of the previous page. Suppose the play proceeds queen of clubs from dummy, ducked all round; queen of diamonds, ruffed by East and overruffed by South, spade ruff in dummy leaving this ending:

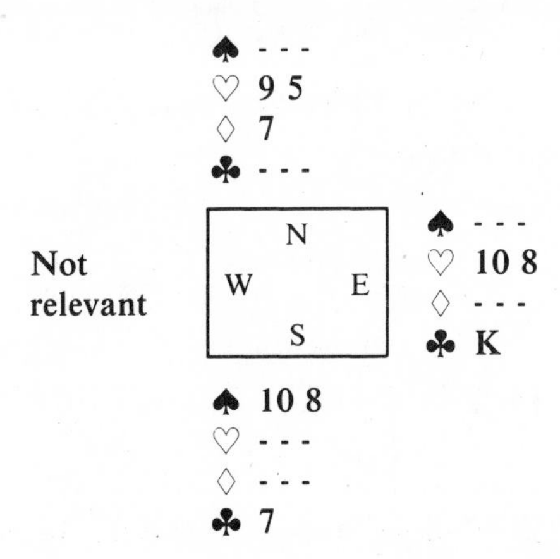

When the 7 of diamonds is led from dummy, East is again without defence: if he ruffs, South's last trump provides the entry to the winning spade, while if East discards, South simply ruffs a heart for the twelfth trick.

Acclamation For The Double Squeeze

This fascinating slam was played in the 1969 International Teams tournament in Palma di Majorca in a match against a Swedish team:

♠ A Q
♡ Q 9 2
♢ A 7 6 4
♣ A K 4 3

N
W E
S

♠ 7 6 5 4
♡ A K J 10 7
♢ K 2
♣ 6 5

Neither side vulnerable. The bidding:

Closed Room

WEST	NORTH	EAST	SOUTH
	Garozzo		*Forquet*
	1♣	Pass	1NT*
Pass	2♣	Pass	2♡
Pass	2NT	Pass	3♡
Pass	4♢	Pass	4NT
Pass	5♣	Pass	6♡
Pass	Pass	Pass	

*Four controls, any shape

Open Room

WEST	NORTH	EAST	SOUTH
Avarelli		*Frendo*	
	1♣	Pass	1♡
Pass	2NT	Pass	6♡
Pass	Pass	Pass	

How should South plan the play after a trump lead from West?

This was the complete deal:

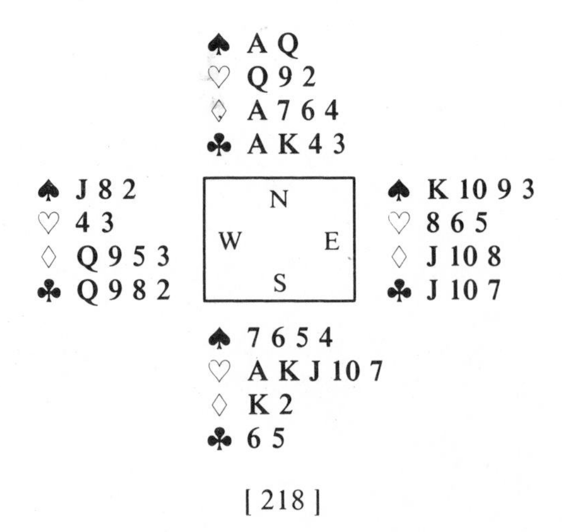

In the open room the Swedish South won the lead in hand and immediately took the spade finesse. Had this succeeded, declarer would have made all the tricks by ruffing two spades in dummy. The king was, however, offside and upon winning Frendo duly returned a trump leaving South in dire straits, with dummy having but one trump to cater for South's two spade losers.

How did the Swedish player prevail and make the slam after all?

Winning the trump return, South cashed the ace of spades, came to hand with a diamond to the king and ruffed a spade in dummy. He continued with the ace of diamonds, a diamond ruff and this was the position after one more trump had been cashed, discarding a club from dummy:

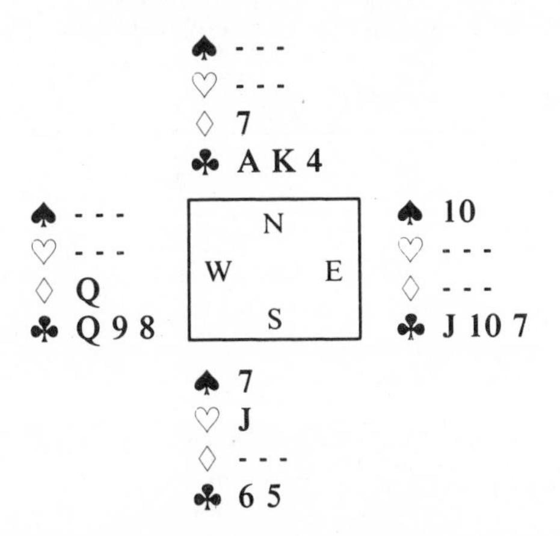

When South led his last trump Avarelli was forced to pitch a club to preserve the diamond guard, whereupon North's 7 of diamonds which had fulfilled its task was also discarded, producing a squeeze in spades and clubs on East.

The audience warmly applauded this double squeeze but I felt that the following line was superior. Winning the trump lead in hand and appreciating the risk that the spade finesse entailed, I chose to set about a dummy reversal.

I continued with the king of diamonds, a diamond to the ace, a diamond ruff, a club to the ace, a diamond ruff, a club to the king, a club ruff, a spade to the ace and a final club ruff. Thus four of the trumps in hand had been used to ruff all of dummy's minor losers. With three cards remaining, dummy held two top trumps and the queen of spades and the defence could win only one trick.

Hidden Pitfall

It is not always easy to detect the dangers that a contract presents. Take for example the following deal from a match in Palma di Majorca in 1969, played against a Danish team:

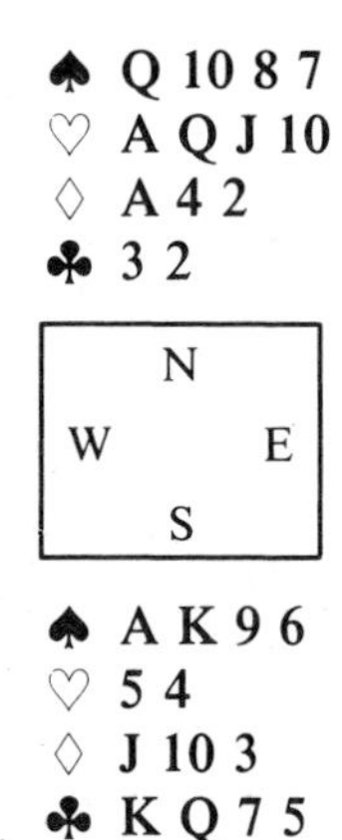

East-West vulnerable. The bidding:

SOUTH	WEST *Forquet*	NORTH	EAST *Garozzo*
1♠	Pass	2♡	Pass
2NT	Pass	4♠	All pass

When South played low from dummy on my lead of the 6 of diamonds, Garozzo won the king of diamonds and returned the 8: jack - queen - ace. Declarer cashed the ace of spades, to which I followed with the jack, and continued with the queen of spades on which I discarded the 5 of diamonds. East was therefore known to have started with four trumps and to avoid the risk of a diamond ruff (the sequence of play in the diamond suit suggested a 5-2 split), declarer drew the remaining trumps ending in hand.

This was the position:

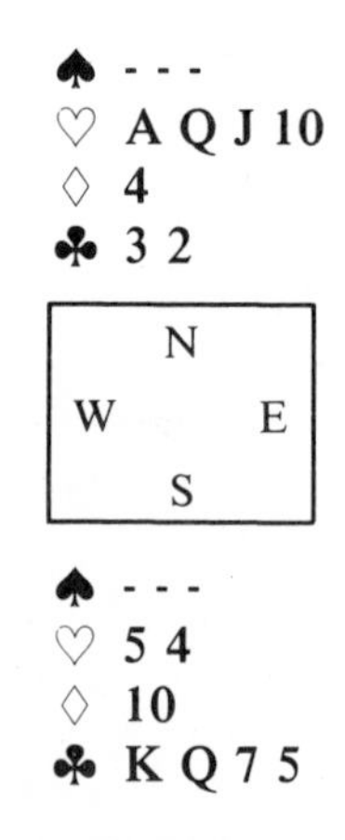

To make his contract South needed five more tricks. He led a low heart to the queen . . . that won . . . and a low club to the king . . . that also won.

How would you have proceeded?

This was the complete deal:

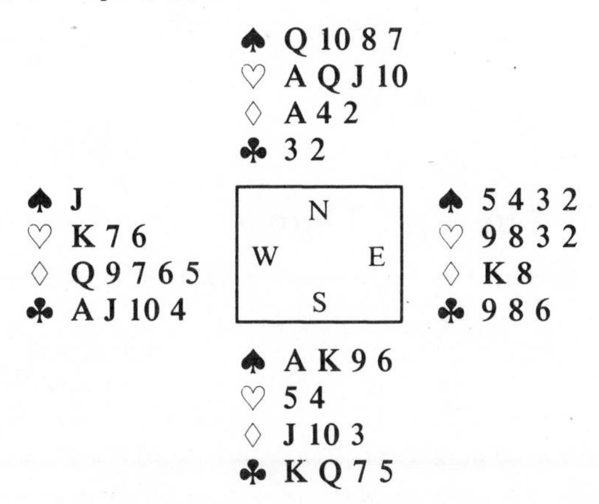

Double dummy it would be child's play to make eleven tricks by repeating the heart finesse but at the table declarer did not come to even ten tricks. After the king of clubs had won, declarer had nine sure tricks and the tenth could come by repeating the heart finesse or by repeating the club finesse.

The Danish declarer tranced for a considerable time and finally entrusted his fate to the clubs, believing that it would be tougher for me to duck his king of clubs than it would be for Garozzo to duck dummy's queen of hearts. Consequently he led a heart to the ace and a club to the queen, the upshot being one short.

My defence was obvious enough since I could place South with the queen of clubs for two reasons: firstly, if South had not held the queen of clubs, then after the heart finesse had won, he would have come to hand with a diamond, not a risky club to the king, and secondly, because without the queen of clubs, South would not have had an opening bid.

The final decision of the Danish player cannot be criticised but as you are about to see, the earlier sequence of plays can be.

At the other table Walter Avarelli found himself in the same contract and the first three tricks were identical. At this point, however, Avarelli came to a decision that allowed him to obviate the above dilemma in the ending. Figuring that if East had the king of hearts and West had the ace of clubs the contract would not succeed (if trumps are drawn, East would duck the first round of hearts — if trumps are not drawn, East would win the king of hearts and take a diamond ruff, using West's ace of clubs as the entry), Avarelli elected to try the heart finesse at once. Winning with dummy's queen, Walter procured the tenth trick by continuing with the ace of hearts and a heart ruff with the king of spades followed by drawing East's trumps. This line secured ten tricks via two diamonds, two hearts, a heart ruff, four spades and one club (in practice, eleven tricks were made as the king of hearts dropped on the third round of hearts).

Easier At The End Than At The Beginning

One does not have to be an expert or an international star to know the squeeze, the Vienna Coup, the strip-and-throw-in or the other techniques of the end-game. The real difficulty lies in recognizing these positions from the outset and following the correct sequence of plays to ensure that the proper ending is reached.

During the International Pairs at Dyvonne in 1969, Benito Garozzo found himself in charge of this Five Club contract:

♠ K J 10 6 5
♡ 7 6
♢ 5 4
♣ 8 7 6 5

N
W E
S

♠ 7
♡ A K 9 4 3
♢ A K 6
♣ K Q J 9

East-West vulnerable. The bidding:

SOUTH	NORTH
Garozzo	*Forquet*
1♣	1♢
1♡	1♠
2♣	3♣
3♢	3♠
5♣	Pass

West led the ace of spades and continued with the 2 of spades. Garozzo inserted the jack which won the trick, East having followed with the 3 and the 4.

How would you have planned the play?

This was the complete deal:

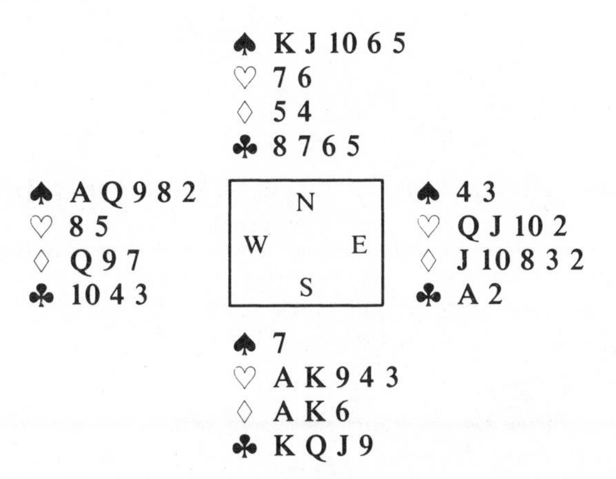

On the jack of spades Garozzo discarded a heart and continued by *ruffing a spade in hand*. Next came the king of clubs. East won the ace and switched to a diamond. Taking the ace, Garozzo cashed the queen and the jack of clubs, followed by the ace and king of hearts, to reach this ending:

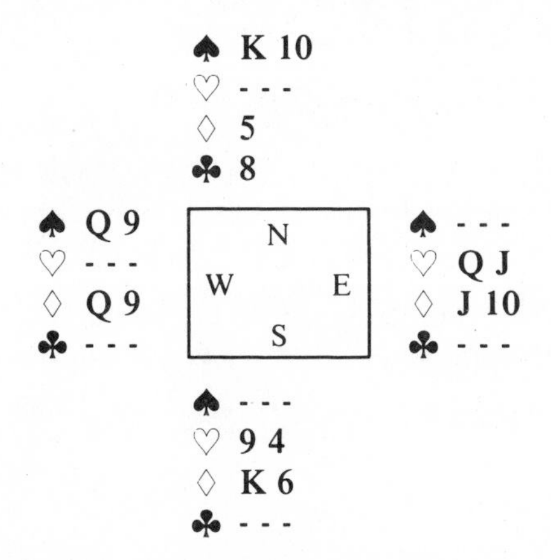

The 4 of hearts came next. If hearts had been 3-3, that would have been the end of the matter. When they happened to be 4-2, Garozzo was just as successful given that it was East who held the four hearts (which was highly likely in view of West's known length in spades and clubs).

On the 4 of hearts, West was forced to part with a diamond to hold on to the guarded queen of spades. Garozzo ruffed in dummy and when the king of spades was cashed, it was East's turn to feel the pinch, namely in hearts and diamonds.

Two Apparently Equivalent Defences

In an international pairs tournament in Cannes in 1969 I had to produce just the right defence to defeat a Four Heart contract:

	♠ J 7 6 5 ♡ J 5 ◇ Q 4 ♣ A 10 9 5 4	
♠ A 9 8 2 ♡ K 4 3 ◇ 3 ♣ K Q 8 7 2	N W E S	

Neither side vulnerable. The bidding:

SOUTH	WEST *Forquet*	NORTH	EAST
4♡	Pass	Pass	Pass

On my diamond lead, North played the 4, East the jack and South won the ace. He continued with the 2 of diamonds towards dummy's queen.

How should West defend to have the best chance of defeating the contract?

This was the complete deal:

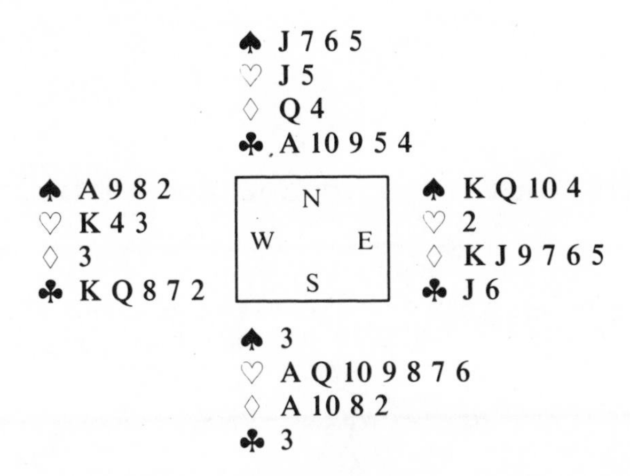

Declarer's line of play revealed his hand. Clearly South had started with A-10-x-x in diamonds and intended to concede a diamond to the king and to ruff a diamond in dummy.

Therefore I ruffed the diamond at trick 2 and underled my ace of spades to try to put partner on lead. This succeeded and when he won the queen, partner duly returned the 2 of hearts. Thus the contract had to fail as declarer could negotiate only one ruff in dummy and still had to lose the king of hearts and the king of diamonds.

This Four Heart contract was reached and defeated at a number of other tables, although by means of a different defence. West declined to ruff the diamond at trick 2 and when East won the king of diamonds, the switch was naturally to a trump. South won the ace, ruffed the 8 of diamonds with the jack of hearts, came to hand via the ace of clubs and a club ruff, and continued with the queen of hearts. Upon winning the king of hearts, West likewise underled the ace of spades and was able to ruff the diamond return from East.

The two defences which we have seen appear equivalent but in fact South can counter the second defence and make the contract.

Have you worked out how?

Winning the heart return with the ace, South can continue with the ace of clubs, a club ruff, a diamond, ruff and then a club, *discarding his lone spade*. The effect of this "scissors coup" is to sever the communications between the defenders and consequently West is unable to put East on lead to receive the diamond ruff.

When Does A Guard Become A Menace?

In the qualifying rounds of the 1969 World Championship Camillo Pabis-Ticci's brilliance brought in this Three Diamonds doubled:

♠ 7 3 2
♡ 9 8 7 2
♢ 6
♣ Q 10 9 4 3

	N	
W		E
	S	

♠ A 10 9
♡ K 3
♢ K Q J 5 4 2
♣ A K

Both sides vulnerable. The bidding:

WEST	NORTH *D'Alelio*	EAST	SOUTH *Pabis-Ticci*
	Pass	Pass	1♢
1♠	Pass	2♡	3♢
Pass	Pass	Double	All pass

West led the king of spades, East following with the 4.

How would you plan the play?

Prospects are far from rosy. The double suggests trumps are not breaking and in addition the absence of any entry to dummy not only bars access to the queen of clubs but also precludes your leading up to the king of hearts.

Camillo won the ace of spades and continued with the king of diamonds. East won the ace and continued with a club to declarer's ace. The queen and the jack of diamonds provided a welcome surprise: trumps were 3-3. Both opponents followed to the king of clubs and when Camillo played off his last three diamonds West discarded two spades and a heart and East let go two clubs (what would be the point of retaining a guard in dummy's long suit if South did not have an entry to dummy?) and a heart.

This was the position:

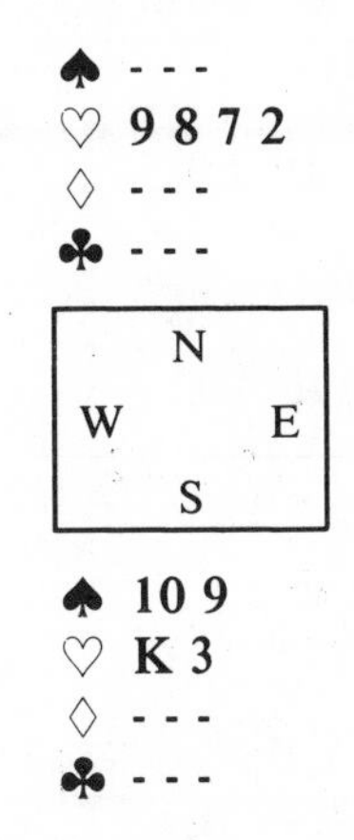

To make the contract declarer had to win one more trick.

What would you have done?

This was the complete deal:

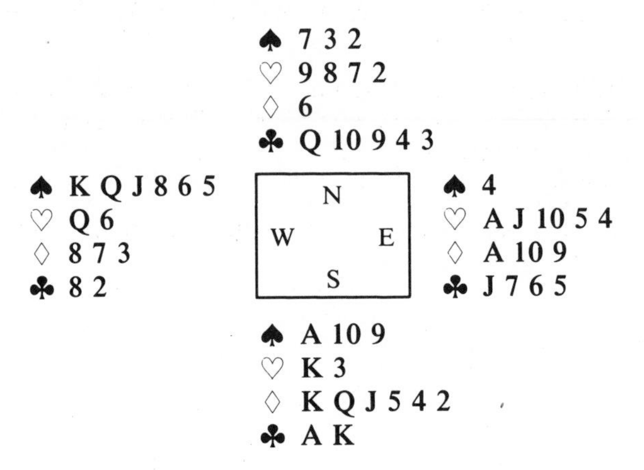

Camillo read the ending perfectly as:

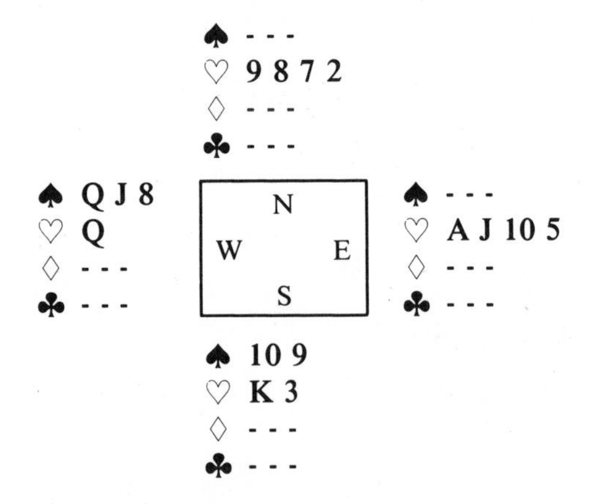

He continued with the king of hearts and East was forced to concede the final trick to dummy's last heart.

Have you worked out how the contract can be defeated?

West could have done no better. If in the four-card ending he had retained two spades and two hearts, South would have thrown West in with a spade and compelled a heart lead up to the king.

The error was East's for he should not have discarded all his clubs. It is true that there was no point in keeping a *guard* in clubs as South had no entry to dummy, but all the same East's fourth club operated as a *menace* against dummy which would have been squeezed by declarer!

Let us take a look at the five-card ending with East hanging on to a club:

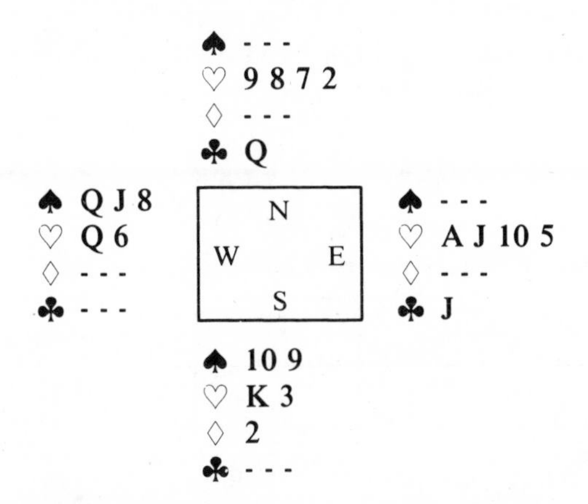

On the last diamond West discards a heart and North, forced to play ahead of East, finds himself in an insoluble dilemma. If he discards the queen of clubs, East lets the 5 of hearts go, while if North pitches a heart, East retains the fourth heart and pitches the jack of clubs.

After the hand was over Camillo pointed out to Mimmo D'Alelio that this was the first time that he had to wait until trick thirteen to reach dummy!

There Is Always One Better

This slam was played by Mimmo D'Alelio in the International Pairs tournament in Marbella in 1970:

♠ A 10 4
♡ K 10 6 5
◇ A 8
♣ K J 10 8

	N	
W		E
	S	

♠ K Q 8 6 3 2
♡ 8
◇ Q 9
♣ A Q 6 3

Neither side vulnerable. The bidding:

SOUTH	WEST	NORTH	EAST
D'Alelio		*Pabis-Ticci*	
2♠	Pass	2NT	3♡
3♠	Pass	4◇	Pass
4♡	Pass	4NT	Pass
5◇	Pass	6♠	All pass

West led the 3 of hearts, Mimmo played low from dummy and East, upon winning with the 9, switched to the 5 of spades.

What is your plan of play to bring this slam home?

This was the complete deal:

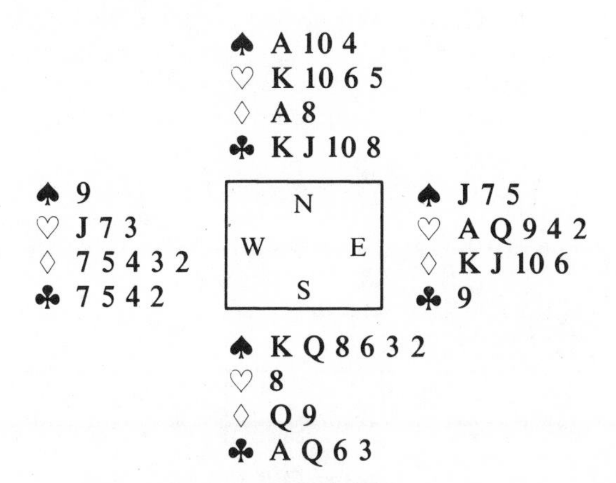

The only chance of success was to find East with the king of diamonds in addition to the ace of hearts, quite likely on the bidding. Therefore Mimmo won the spade switch and continued with four more rounds of trumps and three rounds of clubs, coming down to the following ending:

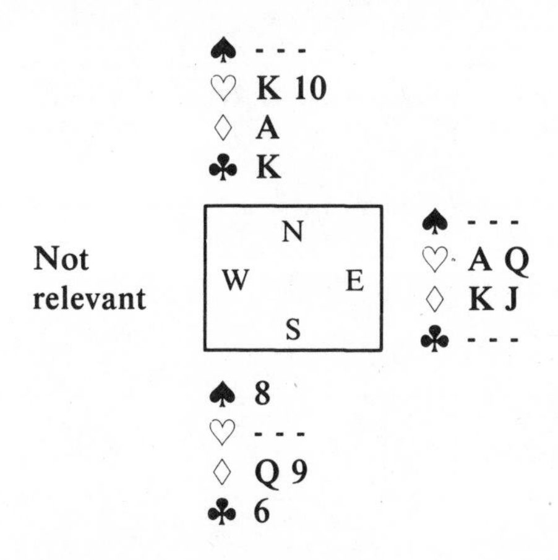

When D'Alelio played a club to dummy's king, East was squeezed in the red suits: if he discarded the queen of hearts, South would have led the 10 of hearts, ruffing out East's ace and setting up dummy's king, while if East discarded the jack of diamonds, the ace of diamonds would be cashed and declarer's hand would be high.

This result gave D'Alelio almost a top as many North-South pairs played in the easier Six Clubs and those who had played in Six Spades had failed, the majority having received a diamond lead. At one table, however, the small slam was played in no-trumps and with North as declarer, this contract proved unbeatable. Here is the complete deal again:

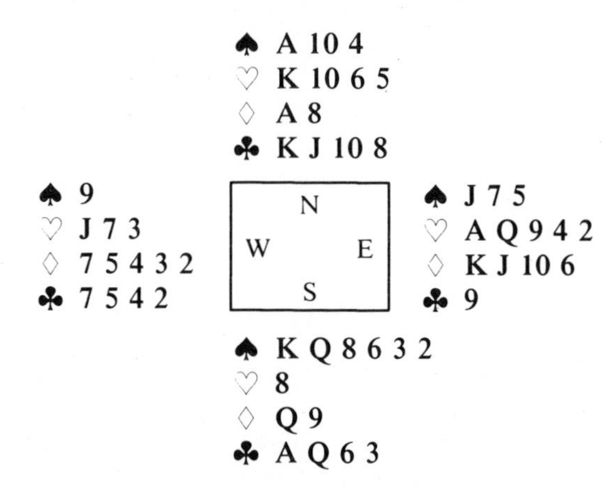

If East leads a red suit, that gives declarer the twelfth trick at once. East did lead a black suit but all the same declarer made the slam by cashing ten tricks in the black suits and arriving at this ending, with East yet to make his discard at trick 10:

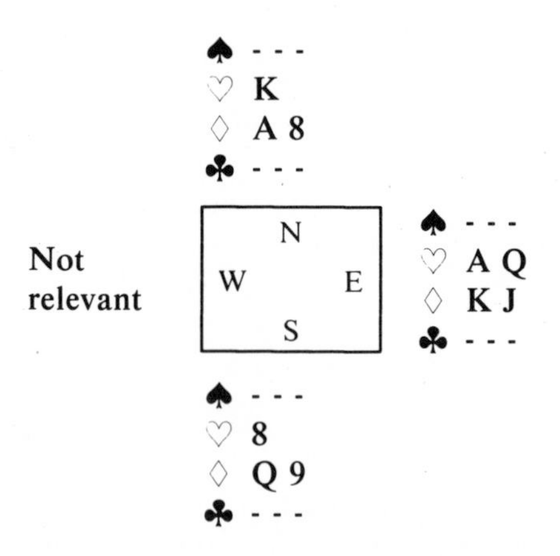

In order to retain the protected king of diamonds, East had to throw the queen of hearts. North then exited with the king of hearts and East on winning with the ace had to open up the diamonds.

Garozzo Under Pressure

Put yourself in my place as North with these cards:

♠ Q J 10 ♡ Q 7 3 ◊ A 9 3 ♣ Q 9 4 3

North-South vulnerable. The bidding:

WEST	NORTH *Forquet*	EAST	SOUTH *Garozzo*
	Pass	Pass	1♠
Double	Redouble	3♣	3♠
5♣	?		

What action would you take?

I faced this problem during a match from the qualifying rounds in the 1969 World Championships. In all probability I ought to have doubled West's Five Clubs, but in view of my strong spade support, hitherto undisclosed, the vulnerability and the possibility of finding Garozzo void in clubs, I elected to pass, a forcing pass of course, to leave the final decision up to my partner. As he was indeed void in clubs, Garozzo had not the slightest hesitation in bidding Five Spades which became the final contract.

West led the king of clubs and this is what Benito saw:

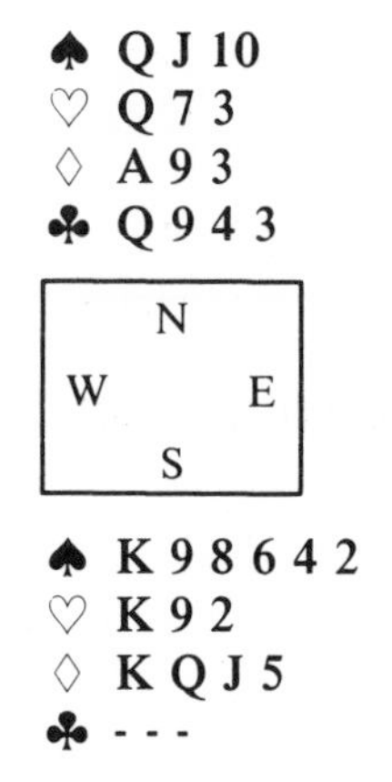

Benito ruffed the king of clubs lead and played a low spade to the queen. East took the ace and returned a trump, while West showed out, discarding a heart.

How should declarer have continued?

This was the complete deal:

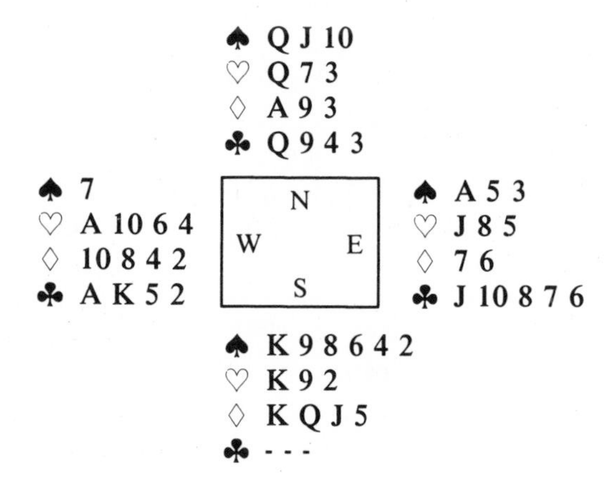

If East had started with four diamonds, South would have been able to discard a heart from dummy on the fourth round of diamonds and could subsequently ruff his third heart in dummy. This possibility was promptly discarded by my partner as it was highly unlikely on the bidding that West had started with just one spade and only two diamonds.

Benito took a different approach. Winning the spade return in dummy, he continued with a club ruff, *a diamond to dummy's nine, finessing West's ten,* a club ruff, a heart to the queen (West could not gain by rising with the ace), and a fourth club ruff.

This was the ending:

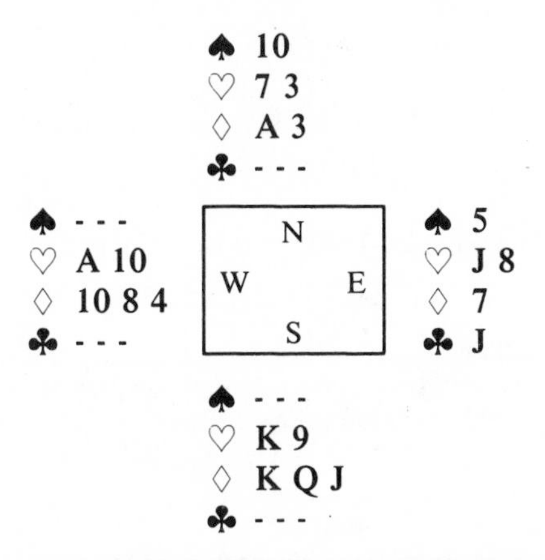

Garozzo crossed to dummy with a diamond to the ace, drew the last trump, discarding a heart from hand and then continued the diamonds. He thus succeeded brilliantly, conceding just the ace of spades and the ace of hearts. However, the defence missed two opportunities to defeat declarer.

Have you spotted them?

East had the first chance. At trick 2 he ought to have played low on the queen of spades. Were South to lead a second round of trumps, East would win and play a third round of spades, leaving declarer without recourse. On the other hand, after East ducks the queen of spades, South could have continued with a club ruff, a diamond to the 9 and a club ruff. At this point South would have had three options to enter dummy but none of these would be crowned with success. In fact, (a) if he had led a spade to the jack, East would take the ace and return the suit, thus removing declarer's last trump; (b) if he had played a heart, East upon gaining the lead with the ace of spades later would return a heart, taking two tricks in that suit; (c) if instead South played a diamond to the ace, East when in with the ace of spades would put partner in with the ace of hearts and receive the diamond return to ruff.

The second chance to defeat the contract was missed by West. If on the first round of diamonds West had inserted the 10, he would have deprived declarer of a vital entry to dummy.

A Reasonable Risk

At duplicate pairs the need to win the greatest possible number of tricks may sometimes require that the safety of the contract be jeopardised. In a national pairs tournament in Naples in 1970, I was faced with this Three No-Trumps:

♠ 4 3 2
♡ 10 9 5
♢ A 7 5
♣ A K Q 5

	N	
W		E
	S	

♠ A 10 9 5
♡ K Q 7
♢ K 8 4
♣ J 7 6

North-South vulnerable. The bidding:

WEST	NORTH	EAST	SOUTH
	Garozzo		*Forquet*
	1♢	1♠	2♣
Pass	3♣	Pass	3NT
Pass	Pass	Pass	

My Two Clubs was a temporising as well as a strategical move. Foreseeing the likelihood of reaching Three No-Trumps, I made the bid which might divert the opposition from leading clubs, as I feared that this suit might be the weak point in the hand (little did I know!). Over Two Clubs West took time out to query the significance of the One Diamond opening and was informed that my partner need have no more than three cards in that suit.

How would you plan the play after the queen of diamonds lead by West?

After determining your line of play, take a look at the complete deal:

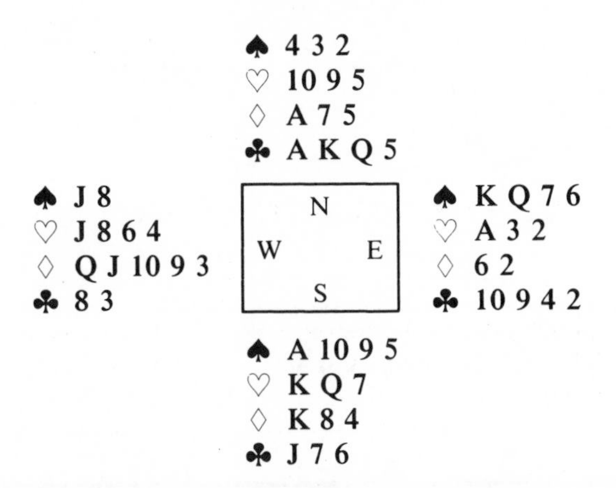

On the queen of diamonds lead I took time to take stock of the situation. The ace of hearts had to be with East to justify the One Spade intervention and consequently nine tricks were secure (one spade, two hearts, two diamonds and four clubs). Nevertheless what was going to happen at those tables where West did lead a spade? Very likely those declarers would wind up with an overtrick so that I was headed for a poorish result if I brought in only nine tricks.

First of all, to have a chance of making ten tricks, one cannot afford to duck a diamond, for then the defence would easily come to four tricks (two spades, one heart and one diamond). In addition it is necessary to set up a second spade trick, bearing in mind that the entries to dummy do not permit you to lead spades and hearts towards hand as often as required.

West's inquiry about the One Diamond opening tended to confirm that he held five diamonds (at least) and accordingly it was vital to eliminate his possible spade entry at once, in case he held a singleton or doubleton honour. In fact, if you play hearts before spades, East could rise with the ace, return a diamond and thus set up the diamonds while West still has an entry in spades.

Having taken all these factors into account, I won the opening lead with the *king* of diamonds and led the 10 of spades *from hand*. Had West ducked smoothly I would have had to pick the position but West took the jack of spades and persevered with the jack of diamonds. Winning with dummy's ace, I led a heart to the king, crossed to dummy with a club to the ace and again led a heart. East took the ace and returned the suit to my queen. After cashing three more clubs, I reached this ending:

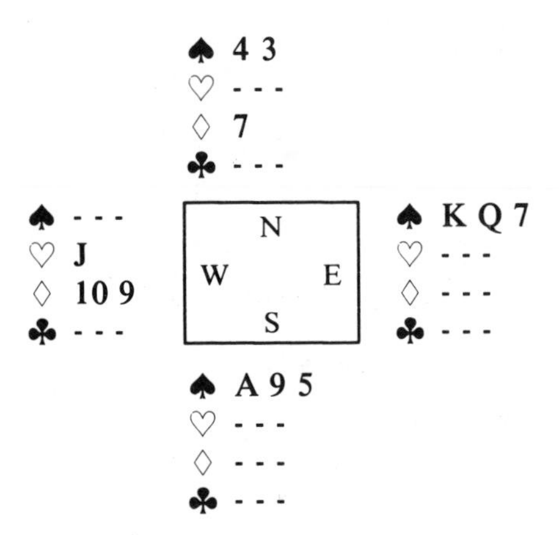

I led the 4 of spades from dummy and when East inserted the queen, I let him hold the trick, thus forcing him to provide a spade finesse on the next trick.

Entry Prohibited!

In a pairs tournament played in Paris with Omar Sharif I found myself defending against Three No-Trumps:

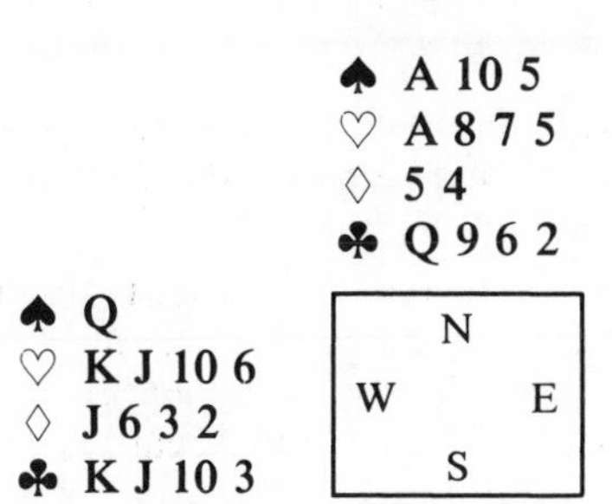

North-South vulnerable. The bidding:

WEST	NORTH	EAST	SOUTH
Forquet		*Sharif*	
		3♠	3NT
Pass	Pass	Pass	

I led the queen of spades: five - six - seven.

How would you continue?

This was the complete deal:

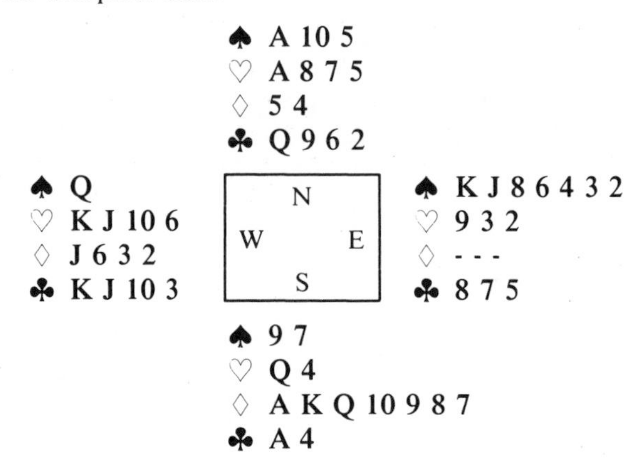

In view of North's high card strength as well as my own, it was obvious that South had punted 3NT on the basis of a long solid diamond suit, the ace of clubs and probably also the queen of hearts.

In order to remove declarer's entries to hand, I switched to the king of clubs. South won the ace and played the ace of diamonds (had this not been a pairs event, ducking a round of diamonds would have been a marked safety play but at pairs, South's play seems correct). When Omar discarded a spade on the first round of diamonds, declarer continued with the king, queen and 10 of diamonds, discarding a club and a spade from dummy. Winning the jack of diamonds, I persevered with the jack of clubs, taken by dummy's queen.

This was the ending with South needing four more tricks to make the game:

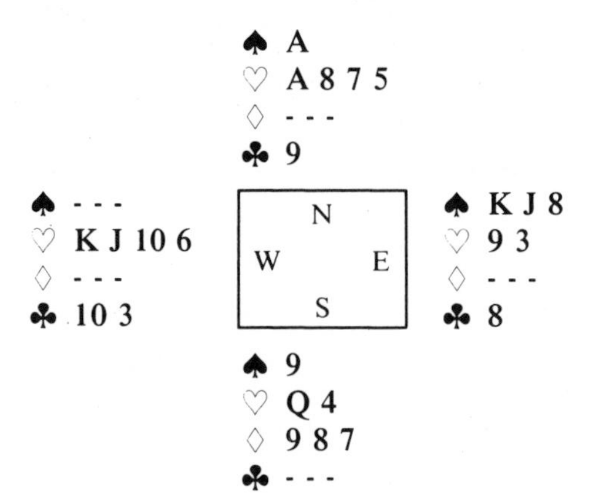

South led the 9 of clubs from dummy, discarding a diamond from hand and expecting me to win with the 10. I followed with the 3, for had I taken the 10, I would have been able to cash the 3 of clubs but then would have been forced to open up the hearts, giving declarer the sorely needed entry to hand. Locked in dummy, South could not avoid losing three more tricks.

The contract was in fact defeated in this manner but it is worth noting that declarer missed a number of chances to make his game.

Apart from ducking the first round of diamonds, explained above as being unattractive in a pairs tournament, South would have succeeded had he taken the ace of spades at trick 1. Likewise, after winning the ace of clubs, if he had crossed to dummy and led a diamond from there, he would have seen the necessity for ducking the first round (had East followed he would of course have played the ace of diamonds, succeeding on any diamond division). Finally, if on the king of clubs he had dropped the 6 from dummy instead of the 2, he would have been able to reach this position:

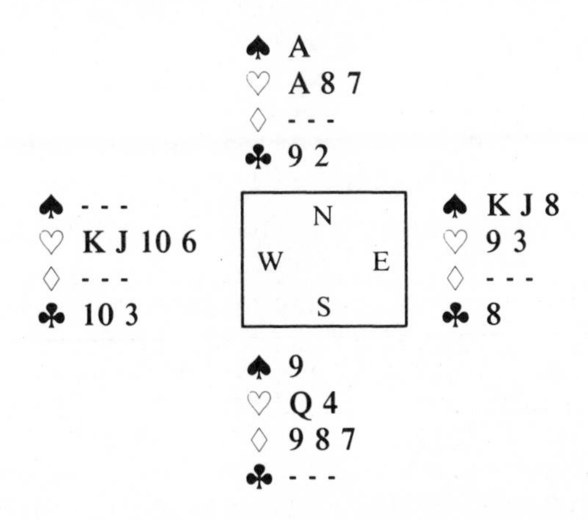

In this ending I could not have escaped the lead in clubs and the subsequent fatal lead in hearts. On the other hand if North had kept the 6 of clubs instead of the 2 and in the above position had 9-6 left, I would have been able to avoid the throw-in by taking the club exit with the 10 and returning the 3.

Similarly, declarer could have succeeded if dummy's last six cards had been ♠A ♡A875 ♣2 or even ♡A875 ♣92, the critical card being the ♣2.

Where There's Life, There's Hope

However desperate a situation seems, one must never give up until every possible chance, however slight, is exhausted. In an international pairs tournament in Naples in 1970 I was faced with a 3NT contract that because of the bad break in diamonds and because of the lack of vital entries seemed destined to fail.

♠ A Q 9 7 6 5
♡ A K
♢ A 5
♣ K 5 4

N / W E / S

♠ - - -
♡ J 7 5
♢ K 9 8 6 4 3
♣ A 9 6 3

Both sides vulnerable. The bidding:

WEST	NORTH *Garozzo*	EAST	SOUTH *Forquet*
	1♣	Pass	1♠*
Pass	2♠	Pass	3♢
Pass	3♠	Pass	3NT
Pass	Pass	Pass	

* 3 controls, any shape

West led the queen of clubs. Winning with dummy's king, I continued with the ace of diamonds, East playing the 10, and a low diamond towards hand. Had East followed I would have had at least ten tricks at my disposal. Unfortunately East pitched a spade. I inserted the 9 and after winning the jack, West continued with the jack of clubs. I let him hold this trick and he then switched to the 2 of hearts.

How would you have proceeded?

This was the complete deal:

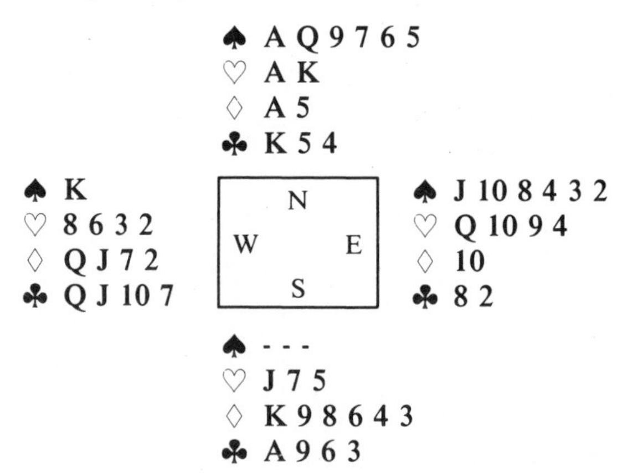

The situation was almost hopeless. The only chance was to find the king of spades singleton or doubleton. If this remote possibility did come about, not only would it provide an extra trick in spades, my eighth, but it would also enable me to set up some position in the endgame to produce the ninth trick.

I played a low spade from dummy and West won with the king! Winning the heart return in dummy, I cashed the ace of spades, reaching this ending:

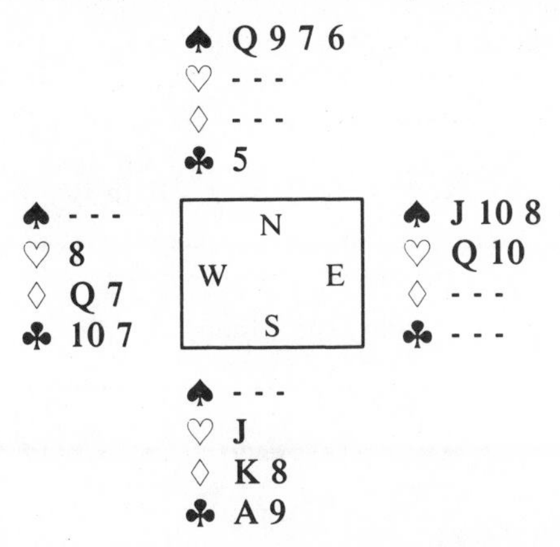

On the queen of spades I discarded the jack of hearts and West in order to keep both minor suits guarded had to pitch a heart also. Naturally I continued with a club to the ace and the 9 of clubs, forcing West to lead into my diamond tenace.

The contract thus succeeded but a different defence would have led inexorably to defeat.

Have you spotted the error committed by the defence?

West after winning trick 3 with the jack of diamonds, ought to have returned a heart without first leading the jack of clubs. Then the end position would have been:

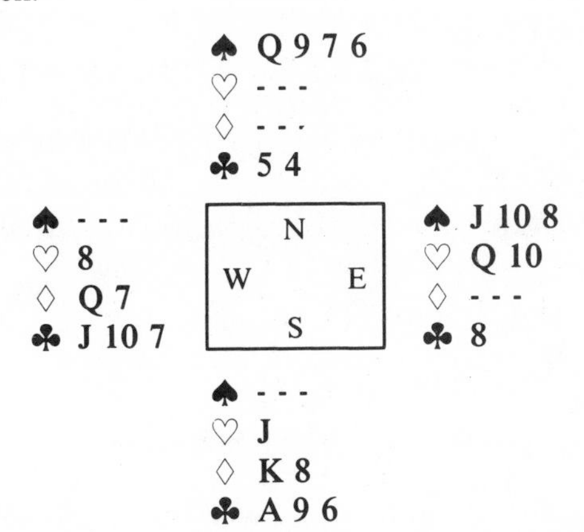

In this ending, when the queen of spades is cashed West would have a safe discard in the 7 of clubs, still retaining control in both minors and still having the 8 of hearts to reach partner.

A Poisoned Finesse

In a recent World Championship, I found myself defending against this 3NT contract:

♠ 4 3 2
♡ Q 10 9
♢ Q J 2
♣ 10 8 7 6

♠ 10
♡ K 8 6 5
♢ 9 8 7 6 3
♣ Q 4 2

	N	
W		E
	S	

Both sides vulnerable. The bidding:

SOUTH	WEST	NORTH	EAST
	Forquet		*Garozzo*
2NT	Pass	3NT	All pass

As West, I led the 9 of diamonds and dummy's queen was covered by East's king which held the trick. East returned the 10 of diamonds which was won by dummy's jack and declarer continued by leading the 10 of hearts from dummy: three – four – . . .

How would you have planned the defence to try to defeat this contract?

This was the complete deal:

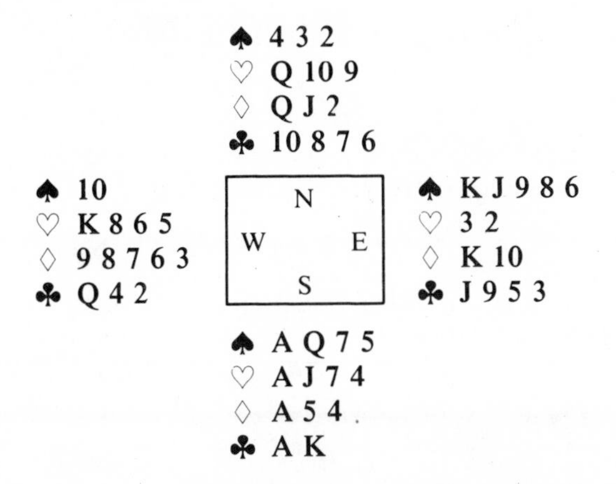

In view of the sparsity of entries in dummy I thought it best to give declarer the impression that the heart finesse was working so that dummy would be used solely to "pick up" the king of hearts. Accordingly I played the 5 of hearts, letting dummy's 10 hold the trick. Declarer continued with the 9 of hearts, ducking in hand and I too ducked again.

From South's point of view the contract looked safe and sound: one spade, four hearts, two diamonds and two clubs. Naturally he continued with the queen of hearts but when Garozzo showed out declarer had to resign himself to one down, being unable to reach dummy to take the spade finesse.

At the other table the bidding went:

SOUTH	WEST	NORTH	EAST
D'Alelio		*Pabis-Ticci*	
1NT	Pass	2♣	All pass
2NT	Pass	3NT	

The first two tricks were identical but when D'Alelio ran the 10 of hearts, West won it with the king. D'Alelio thus was able to enter dummy later with a heart to take the spade finesse for the ninth trick.

D'Alelio's Winning Move

In an international tournament played in Palma di Majorca in 1973, Mimmo D'Alelio pulled off this spectacular coup:

♠ 9 8 7
♡ 7 6 4 2
◇ K 2
♣ A K 5 4

N
W E
S

♠ A K 5 4
♡ 3
◇ A Q J 10 4 3
♣ 7 6

Neither side vulnerable. The bidding:

SOUTH *D'Alelio*	WEST	NORTH *Pabis-ticci*	EAST
1◇	2♣	Double	2♡
2♠	Pass	3◇	Pass
4◇	Pass	5◇	Pass

West led the ace of hearts and switched at trick 2 to the 2 of spades to East's 10.

How would you have planned the play?

This was the complete deal:

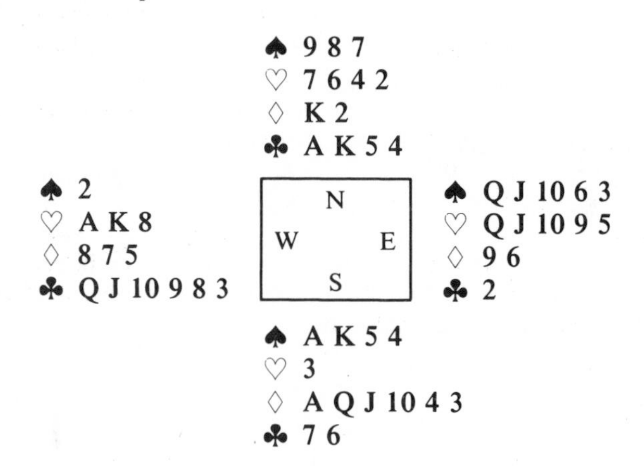

If West had continued at trick 2 with another heart, D'Alelio in all probability would, after ruffing, have played off the ace and king of spades, intending then to concede a spade and ruff the fourth spade with the king of diamonds. The surprising 2 of spades from West, however, was clearly a singleton and so D'Alelio chose a different line of play.

After winning with the ace of spades, he continued with the ace of diamonds and a diamond to the king. Ruffing a heart, he led a club to the ace, ruffed the third heart and played two more rounds of trumps.

This was the ending:

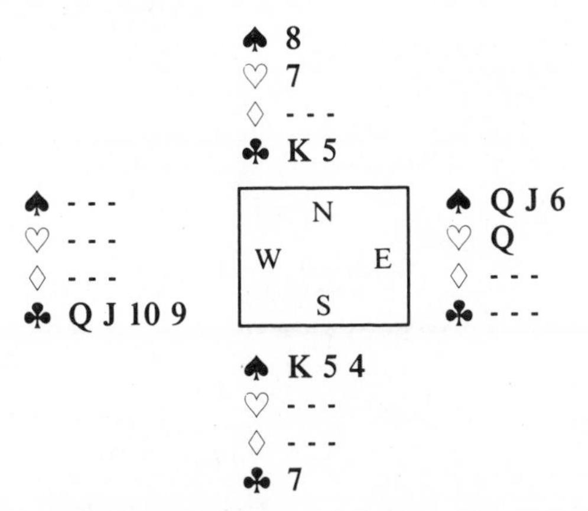

To bring in the contract D'Alelio had to make three of the last four tricks. Even looking at all four hands, the solution would escape a number of players. As he had only two tricks available via the two black kings, the third could come only from a spade-heart squeeze on East.

If declarer plays a club to the king, the squeeze will not operate for East has a safe discard with a spade. But D'Alelio came up with the brilliant solution (aided by a slight defensive error) which allowed him to rectify the count.

He played the 7 of clubs and played dummy's 5(!) under West's 9. East discarded a spade on this but the forced club continuation from West, taken by dummy's king, now effected the spade-heart squeeze.

Have you found the defence's error?

West ought to have preserved fiercely that 3 of clubs. Then in the four-card ending he would have held Q-J-10-3 and on declarer's 7 of clubs, West would have been able to play the 3! In that case declarer would be helpless and the contract would be bound to fail.

Danger From The East

Playing with C. C. Wei, the creator of the Precision Club system, in a tournament in New York, Benito Garozzo did not let his partner down in this Four Spade contract:

♠ A J 5
♡ A Q J 9
◇ Q 10 9
♣ 10 5 4

	N	
W		E
	S	

♠ K Q 10 9 8 7 6 4
♡ 10 2
◇ - - -
♣ K 7 6

East-West vulnerable. The bidding:

WEST	NORTH *C.C. Wei*	EAST	SOUTH *Garozzo*
		1◇	4♠
Pass	Pass	Pass	

West led the 3 of diamonds and dummy's 9 was covered by East's king.

How do you plan the play?

If West could be relied on to hold the king of hearts, there would be no problem, but if it is with East, the latter on gaining the lead would broach the clubs putting South in jeopardy. Some declarers, prepared to rely on the protection afforded by the 10 of clubs, played simply and mechanically: ruff the lead, two rounds of trumps, 10 of hearts, running it when West plays low. East takes the king of hearts and returns the queen of clubs.

What do you play on this, the king or a low card?

If you elected to play low and East then continued with a low club, what would you play now, the king or low again?

In these situations, with the defence needing three club tricks, a good defender is obliged to return the queen or the jack (for if he returns a low card, declarer simply ducks it and the defence cannot come to more than two club tricks). The queen or jack would be led from combinations headed by the Q-J, Q-only, J-only and even A-Q or A-J (with these last two combinations, the defender first leads the lower honour and follows with a low card next, hoping that declarer will duck twice).

Therefore, going up with the king wins whenever East has led the queen from Q-x-x or A-Q-x, while ducking twice will gain only when East has led from Q-J-x. Consequently many declarers covered the queen of clubs with the king (for if East had led from the ace, they would make the rest of the tricks) but the contract thus failed since the complete deal was:

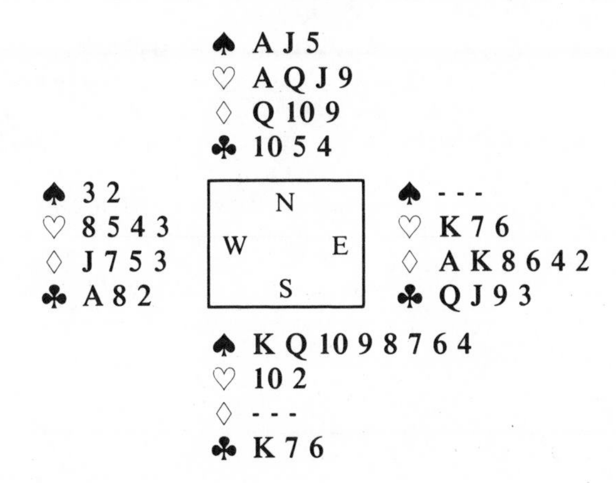

Garozzo managed to avoid this problem entirely by means of a superior line of play. After ruffing the first round of diamonds with the 6 of spades, he continued with the 7 of spades to dummy's jack and the queen of diamonds, covered by the ace and ruffed with the 8 of spades. Next came the 9 of spades to dummy's ace and the 10 of diamonds was led, South discarding a heart when East could not cover the 10.

This was the position:

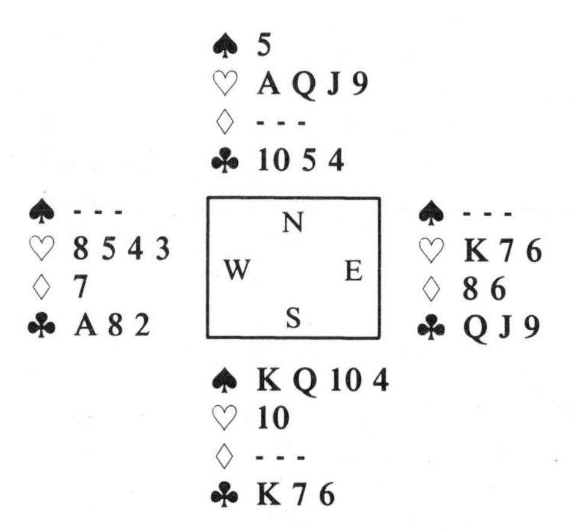

When West won the jack of diamonds, Garozzo had succeeded in preventing East obtaining the lead. West returned the 3 of hearts but Garozzo had no further problems. Winning dummy's ace, he continued with the queen of hearts, ruffing East's king with the 10 of spades. Finally the carefully preserved 4 of spades allowed him to cross to dummy's 5 of spades and two clubs were discarded on the two winning hearts. The contract was thus made with an overtrick.

A Gala Debut

In the 1973 World Teams Championships I played for the first time with Benito Bianchi. As part of our training schedule we competed in a teams event a couple of months before the championship began. I must say that Benito's debut was outstanding, worthy of the other Benito who had been my great partner for more than ten years. Just take a look at the masterly care he put into this Four Heart contract:

♠ K Q 5
♡ K 2
♢ 7 6 5
♣ 7 6 5 4 3

	N	
W		E
	S	

♠ A 7 4 3
♡ A 9 8 7 6 5 4
♢ K 4
♣ - - -

Both sides vulnerable. The bidding:

SOUTH *Bianchi*	WEST	NORTH *Forquet*	EAST
1♠	Pass	1NT	Pass
3♡	Pass	4♡	All pass

West led the 2 of clubs to East's ace. Without doubt declarer's prospects are very, very rosy: a 2-2 heart split, a 3-3 spade split or finally a successful diamond finesse, any one of these would allow the contract to succeed. Bianchi, however, did not content himself with just these chances and chose a line of play with additional chances.

How would you have planned the play?

Bianchi ruffed the opening lead, crossed to dummy with a spade to the king and led a low diamond to his king. Obviously if the ace had been onside, that would have been the end of this story but it was not to be and West took the king with the ace, returning the 8 of clubs.

How would you have continued?

This was the complete deal:

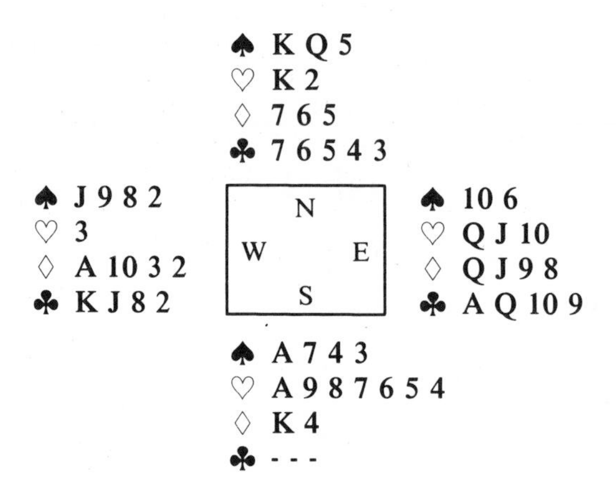

Bianchi ruffed the club return and continued with the 4 of diamonds! He won the heart switch with the king and cashed the queen of spades, reaching this position:

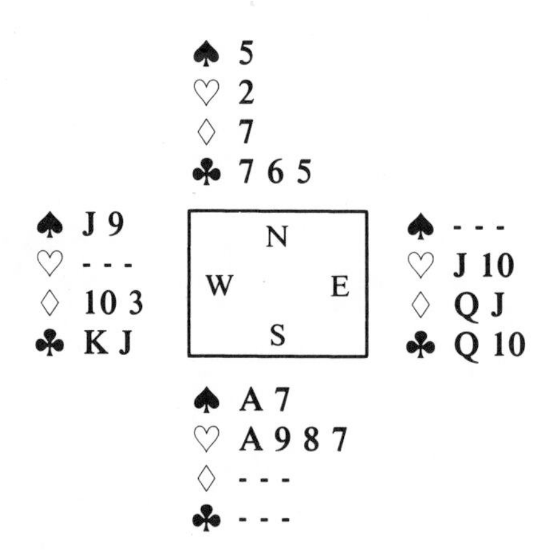

When the 5 of spades was led from dummy, East was without recourse: if he ruffed, he would be using his trump winner to ruff South's losing spade; accordingly he discarded a club but this was also to no avail. Bianchi won the ace of spades and ruffed the fourth spade with dummy's 2 of hearts. The defence thus could come to only three tricks: one heart and two diamonds.

Without doubt you have noted declarer's superlative technique. Bianchi's line would have succeeded if either of the major suits had divided favourably and also if one of the defenders had started with four spades and three hearts or, as in the actual case, East had started with two spades and three hearts. To cater for this last case, however, it was critical to lead the second round of diamonds to sever the communications between the defenders. In fact if Bianchi had not played it just so, East could have ruffed the third round of spades, led a low diamond to West's 10 and received another spade ruff.

Had the defenders led two rounds of hearts early, the contract would have failed but this does not detract from declarer's fine play.

Garozzo's Devilry

In an international pairs event in Rabat, Morocco, in 1973, Garozzo was the hero on the following small slam:

♠ A 10 8 3
♡ J 7
◊ A
♣ A K J 7 4 2

	N	
W		E
	S	

♠ Q J 9
♡ A Q 10 8 4 3
◊ J 2
♣ Q 5

Both sides vulnerable. The bidding:

SOUTH	WEST	NORTH	EAST
1♡	Pass	3♣	Pass
3♡	Pass	3♠	Pass
4♡	Pass	4NT	Pass
5◊	Pass	5NT	Pass
6♣	Pass	6♡	All pass

What line of play would you adopt after West leads the king of diamonds?

The problem revolves around not losing a trick in hearts and a trick in diamonds. To prevent this South must give up a trick to the king of hearts (if such a loss is necessary) while dummy still has a trump to cater for the losing diamond. As the lack of entries precludes your ruffing the second diamond at once, you, South, decide to play a low heart from dummy to your queen: if West wins this with the king, the jack of hearts will take care of a diamond return, while on a trump return you can later discard the diamond and the spades on the winning clubs; if instead the queen of hearts holds the trick, you ruff the diamond loser in dummy, come to hand with the queen of clubs and continue with the ace and the 10 of hearts (trusting trumps to divide normally).

This line of play seems clearly best but your plan is in urgent need of revision when at trick 2, on the low heart from dummy, East plays the king.

How do you continue after this development, bearing in mind that you are competing in a pairs tournament?

After you have formulated your plan, examine the complete deal:

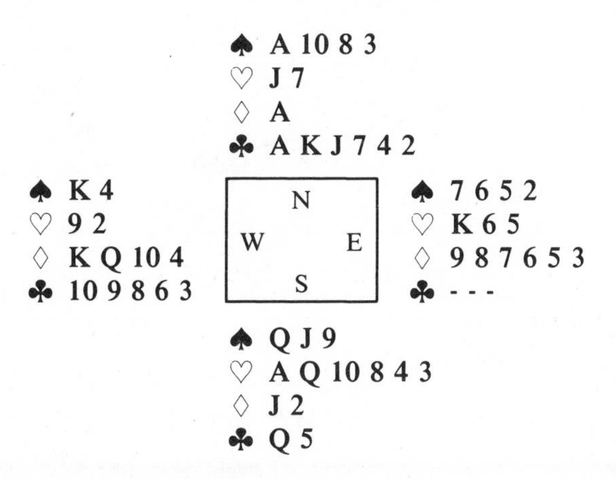

Garozzo was the East player, of course.

Declarer thought (and who can blame him?) that East's king was singleton and so he continued with a low heart to the jack, the aim being not to lose a trick to the 9-x-x-x apparently with West. No doubt he was a little surprised when West followed to the second round of trumps with the 9 and . . . Garozzo produced the 5. No doubt the surprise was even greater and considerably more painful when East turned up with a third trump with which he unkindly ruffed the low club led from dummy when declarer attempted to return to his own hand.

Garozzo thus reaped the reward of his brilliant defence and after ruffing the club he was able to cash a diamond trick for one down.

If East had been a mere mortal and had played a low heart at trick 2, South in following his original plan would have won the queen and after ruffing the diamond loser, he would have tried to return to hand with a club to the queen. East could ruff this but it would be the defence's sole trick.

Benito Garozzo's brilliant defence finds its source in his extraordinary ability to reconstruct the unseen hands. His defence, however, would probably not have succeeded had it arisen in a teams event. In this situation a good declarer, renouncing the chance of an overtrick by capturing the 9 of trumps, would have continued at trick 3 with a diamond ruff and a club. East would have ruffed this but no return would have endangered the contract.

As the deal arose in a pairs event, however, where an overtrick can be of paramount importance, declarer's line of play cannot be condemned or even criticized. I can aver, however, that if I found myself in this declarer's shoes and knowing the devilry of which Benito is capable, I would perhaps have renounced this *sure* overtrick . . .

An Extra Chance

This slam played and made by Mimmo D'Alelio in an international teams tournament is particularly spectacular.

♠ K 10 9 8
♡ 10 9 7
◊ A 4 3
♣ A 8 7

N
W E
S

♠ 2
♡ A K Q J 5 4 3 2
◊ K 10 9
♣ 9

Both sides vulnerable. The bidding:

SOUTH	WEST	NORTH	EAST
D'Alelio		*Pabis-Ticci*	
1♡	Pass	1♠	Pass
4♡	Pass	5♡	Pass
6♡	Pass	Pass	Pass

The One Heart opening followed by the jump to Four Hearts shows a more powerful hand than a Four Heart opening. Pabis-Ticci with 2½ tricks made a slam try by raising to Five Hearts and D'Alelio was more than happy to accept his partner's invitation.

West led the queen of clubs, won by dummy's ace. A heart to the ace was followed by the 2 of spades on which West played the jack.

How would you have continued?

This was the complete deal:

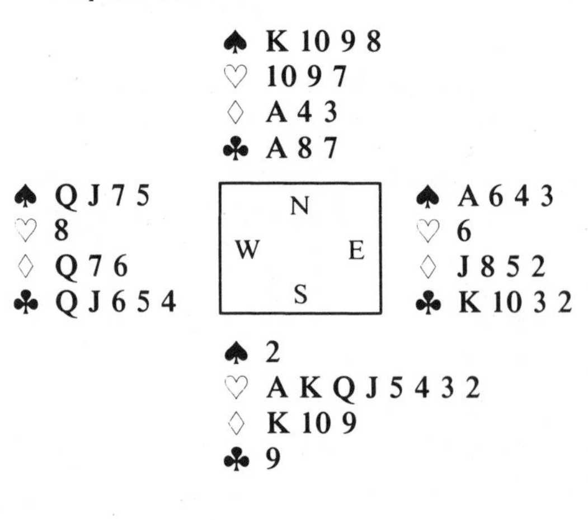

The problem was not to lose a diamond trick. If the ace of spades had been well-placed, either the king of spades would win a trick or it would provide a diamond discard later in the play. Once however West had played the jack of spades, it was reasonable to place the ace of spades with East and in order to eliminate the diamond loser declarer had to revise his initial plan.

Without seeing all the cards, there are two possibilities to set up a spade trick: firstly, if you place East with A-x-x (or shorter), duck the jack of spades and then ruff two low spades from dummy, planning to drop the ace; alternatively, if West began with Q-J-x, South would have to cover the jack with the king and again ruff two more rounds of spades. D'Alelio opted for the second line as it afforded him an extra chance.

East took the king of spades with the ace and returned the king of clubs. After ruffing, D'Alelio crossed to dummy with a heart to the 10, ruffed a spade, played a heart to dummy's 9 and ruffed another spade.

The queen had not dropped but declarer had another string to his bow. One more round of trumps produced this ending:

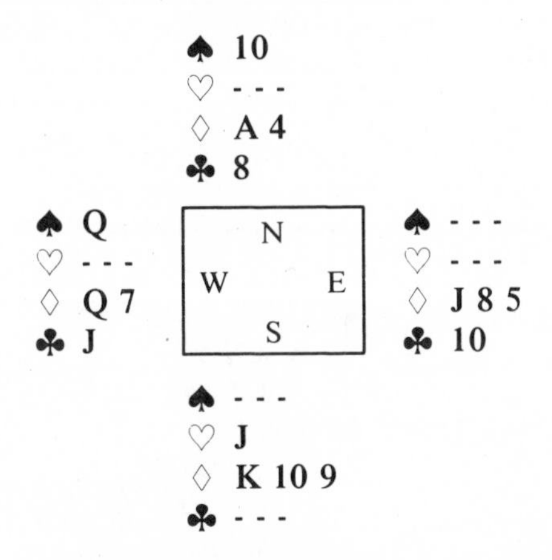

When D'Alelio cashed his last trump West discarded the 7 of diamonds, North pitched the 10 of spades which had fulfilled its duty and East let go the 10 of clubs. D'Alelio led a diamond to the ace, on which West dropped the queen, and continued with absolute confidence by finessing against East's jack of diamonds, as West's last two cards were marked.

Variations

If West had discarded the jack of clubs on South's last trump, South would have discarded dummy's 10 of spades and East would have been subjected to a squeeze in the minors.

No Risk Attached

The following Four Spade contract played by Camillo Pabis-Ticci in a match in the 1974 Italian Cup was not especially difficult. Nevertheless at the table declarer had to apply himself to come up with the best line of play:

♠ Q 8 4
♡ A K 7 6
♢ A 8 4 2
♣ 3 2

N
W E
S

♠ K J 10 9 7 5
♡ 5
♢ 7 5
♣ K 7 6 5

SOUTH	WEST	NORTH	EAST
Pabis-Ticci		*D'Alelio*	
2♠	Pass	4♠	All pass

West led the jack of clubs. East took the ace and returned the queen of clubs.

How would you have planned the play?

This was the complete deal:

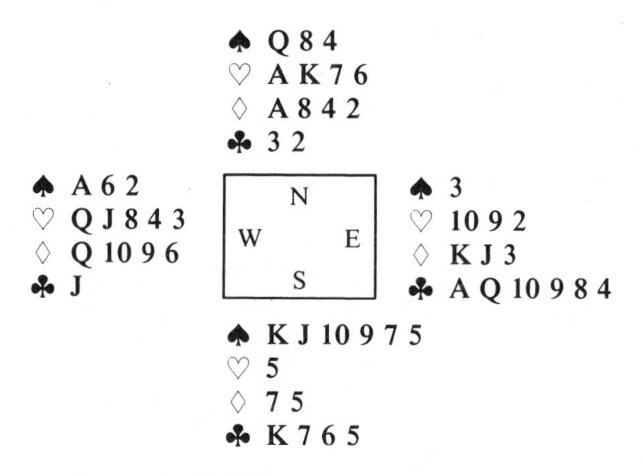

If South covers the queen of clubs with the king, West ruffs and continues with ace and another spade. The contract is now in jeopardy because declarer, with three tricks already lost, can ruff only one of his two club losers.

Pabis-Ticci guarded against this possibility by ducking the queen of clubs! The defence duly switched to the ace and another spade but declarer made his contract easily by ruffing his remaining club loser.

Variations

Without question Pabis-Ticci's line is by far the best but nevertheless it is interesting to note that with the actual distribution (East having only three hearts), the contract would be unbeatable even if South had covered the queen of clubs with the king.

Have you worked out how?

After ruffing the king of clubs West does best by continuing with ace and another spade. South wins this in hand, ruffs one club in dummy, cashes the ace and king of hearts, discarding a diamond, ruffs a heart and cashes two more spades to come to this ending:

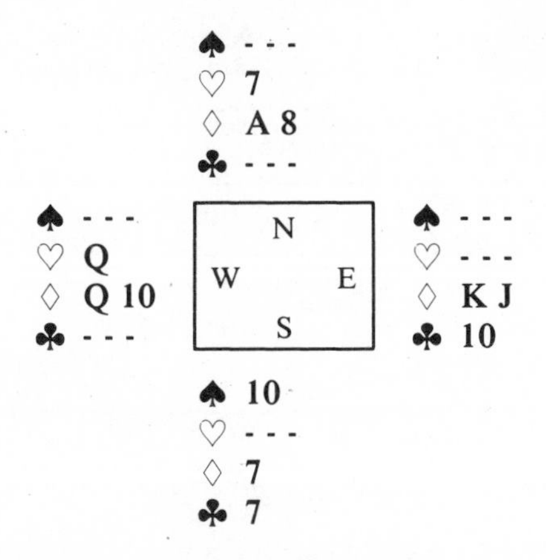

On the last spade West must throw a diamond to keep the cover in hearts. The 7 of hearts is now discarded from dummy whereupon the screw is turned on East in the minors.

Obviously if East had started with four or more hearts the above ending would not have been possible because West would have retained the diamond control and East would have held on to the control in the other two suits.

Garozzo Keeps Control

During the 1974 Italian Championships Garozzo landed this Four Spade contract thanks to a simple but ingenious manoeuvre:

♠ 10 2
♡ 2
♢ A K Q J 4
♣ A Q 5 4 3

	N	
W		E
	S	

♠ Q J 9 8 4 3
♡ A 9 8 7
♢ 3 2
♣ 6

Neither side vulnerable. The bidding:

WEST	NORTH	EAST	SOUTH
	Belladonna		*Garozzo*
	2♣	Pass	2♠
Pass	3♢	Pass	3♠
Pass	4♠	All pass	

West led the king of spades and switched to the king of hearts.

How should declarer plan the play?

This was the complete deal:

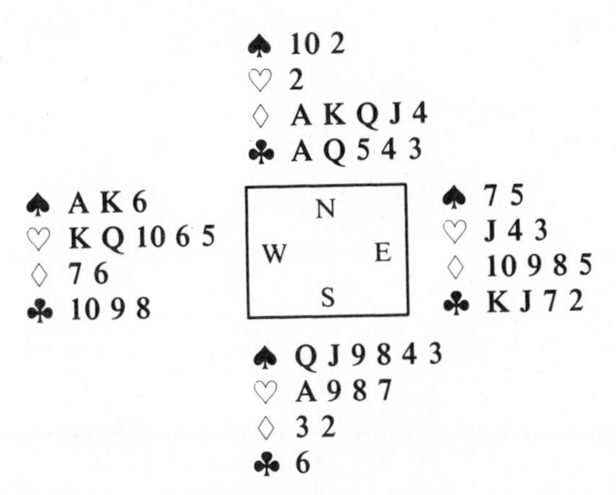

At the other table, South was in the same contract after the same start. Winning the king of hearts with the ace, South continued with a heart ruff and the top three diamonds, discarding a heart on the third round. This would have succeeded had diamonds been 3-3.

Unfortunately for declarer, West had started with only two diamonds and was able to defeat Four Spades by ruffing the queen of diamonds and cashing the ace of spades and a heart.

Benito Garozzo made the contract by means of a neat move: he allowed West's king of hearts at trick two to hold the lead! West was left without recourse. He continued the hearts, which was best, but Benito ruffed in dummy and continued with the ace of clubs, a club ruff to hand and a top spade. The ace of hearts, zealously retained, kept control of the danger suit.

Five-Card Conundrum

The following 3NT arose during the pairs tournament at the VII International Festival at Cannes:

♠ K 8 2
♡ A 7 3 2
♢ J 7 4 3
♣ 6 5

N
W E
S

♠ A 7 6
♡ Q 10
♢ A 10 6
♣ A K J 4 3

Both sides vulnerable. The bidding:

SOUTH *Forquet*	WEST	NORTH *Avarelli*	EAST
1NT (1)	Pass	2♣ (2)	Pass
2NT (3)	Pass	3NT	All pass

(1) 16-18 points
(2) Major suit enquiry
(3) Maximum hand, no four-card major

West led the jack of spades and, left on lead, continued the suit. Winning with dummy's king, I took a successful club finesse and followed with three more rounds of clubs. West followed twice and then discarded the 4 and the 6 of hearts.

Upon winning the queen of clubs, East returned the queen of spades, won by my ace. I cashed the fifth club, on which West discarded the 8 of hearts and East the 5 of diamonds. This was the position:

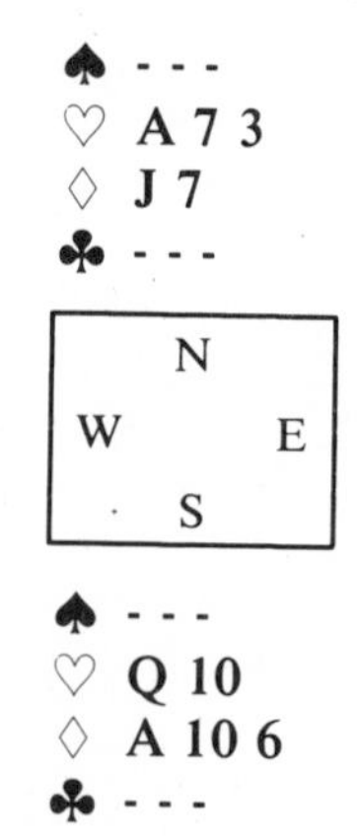

West certainly held the thirteenth spade and the discards placed the king of hearts with East.

How would you have continued to produce the three tricks still required?

Make a firm decision as to which card you intend to lead next before taking a look at the complete deal:

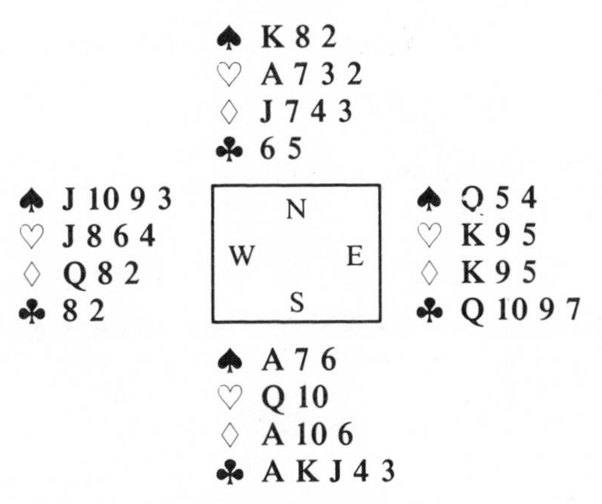

This was the five-card ending:

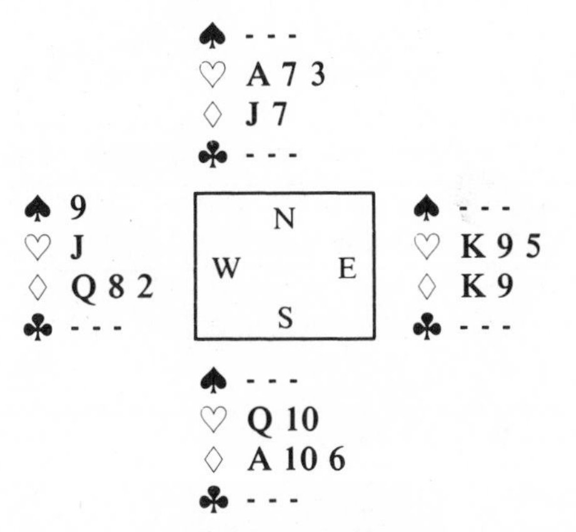

The actual position is a genuine double dummy problem:
At no-trumps, South is to lead and make three tricks against any defence.

The defensive discarding allowed me to diagnose the above ending and I laid down the ace of diamonds. If East had followed with the 9, I would have continued with a low diamond, endplaying East and forcing a heart return away from the king. East, after some thought, unblocked the king of diamonds. This fine move did not, however, prevent the success of the contract.

I now cashed the ace of hearts (to draw West's last heart) and continued with the jack of diamonds. West won the queen, cashed the 9 of spades but had to concede the last diamond to me.

You have no doubt realized that if instead of cashing the ace of diamonds, I had led a low diamond at trick 9, East after winning the king of diamonds would have returned the suit. My best play then would have been to rise with the ace and continue with the queen of hearts. East would win this and return the 5 of hearts, defeating the contract because of the blockage in the heart suit. The upshot would have been that I would become a stepping stone to West's last diamond instead of vice versa.

Precise Technique

During the international teams tournament held in Alicante, Spain, in 1974, I found myself in this Four Spade contract:

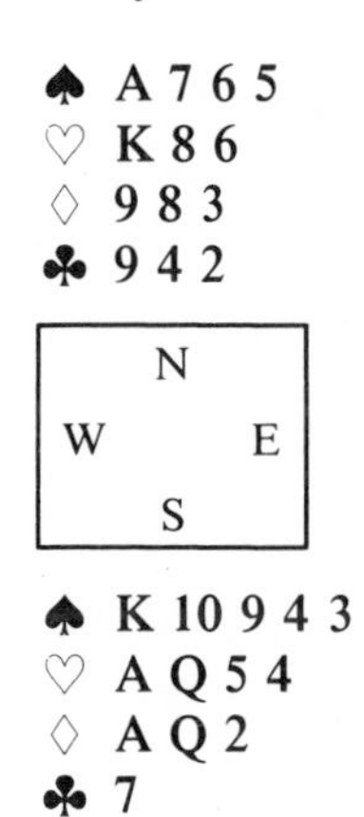

Both sides vulnerable. The bidding:

SOUTH	NORTH
Forquet	*B.Bianchi*
1♠	2♠
3♡	4♠
Pass	

West led the king of clubs and continued with the 5 to East's ace. Afer ruffing, I cashed the king of spades to which both opponents followed low and crossed to dummy with a spade to the ace, West discarding a diamond.

How should declarer continue?

If you have elected to ruff dummy's third club, you are on the right track, but your problems are far from over. Here is the position:

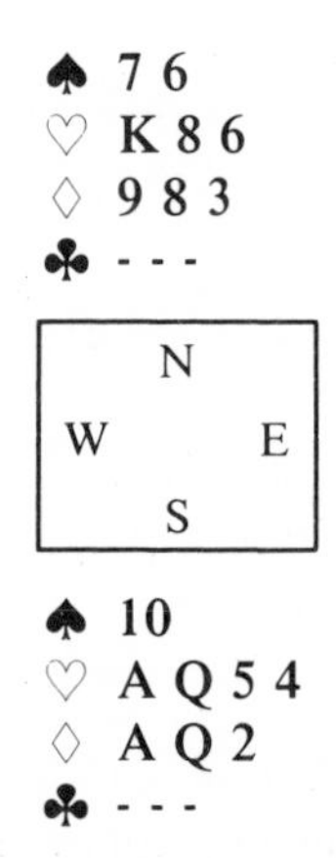

How would you have continued?

Decide on your next move before looking at the complete deal:

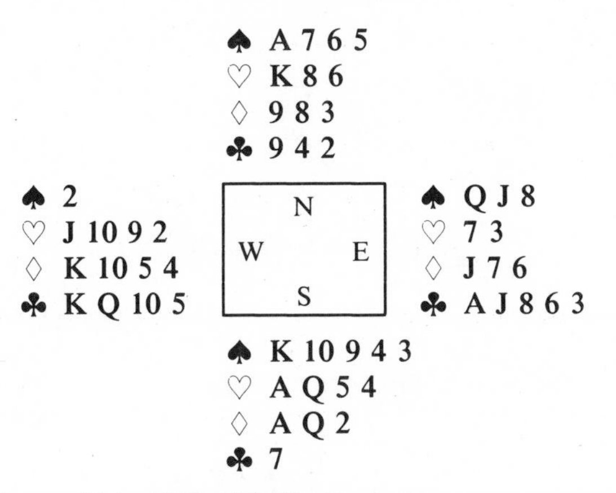

This was the position after trick 5:

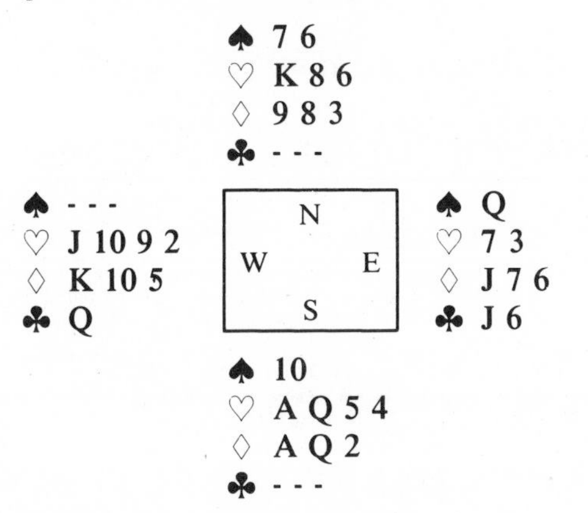

The problem, obviously, was to guard against the king of diamonds being offside if the hearts were not 3-3.

Have you spotted the solution?

My continuation was the ace of hearts and a low heart to the king. It was vital that the third lead of hearts come from dummy. East did best by discarding a club (had he ruffed, I would have been able to pitch a diamond from dummy later on the queen of hearts) but despite this I was well placed in bringing the contract home. Winning the queen of hearts, I continued with the fourth round of hearts, discarding a diamond from dummy. This time East had no way out: if he left West on lead, West would have to lead a diamond into my A-Q or concede a ruff-and-discard, while if East ruffed with his master trump, this would have given me my tenth trick immediately.

At the other table South in the same contract went down. Declarer was not to blame, however, as Avarelli unkindly prevented him from developing my line of play. At trick 1 Avarelli overtook Pabis-Ticci's king of clubs and returned the 6 of diamonds. That was curtains for declarer.

All Or Nothing

The following slam arose at the Venice Bridge Festival of 1974, won by the Lancia Bridge Team (Avarelli, Belladonna, Garozzo, Sharif and Forquet):

♠ A K J 9 4
♡ A 7 6 5
◊ 3
♣ 10 9 7

	N	
W		E
	S	

♠ 7 6 5 2
♡ K J
◊ A K
♣ A Q 8 3 2

North-South vulnerable. The bidding:

WEST	NORTH *Sharif*	EAST	SOUTH *Forquet*
3◊	Double	5◊	6♣
Pass	Pass	Pass	

West led the 3 of spades.

How should South plan the play?

The lead was obviously a singleton and so with a sure loser in spades, the slam seemed to hinge on the double finesse in clubs. I regretted not having reached the spade slam (should I have bid Six Diamonds instead of Six Clubs?). The spade slam requires the finesse for the king of clubs only, not for both the king and the jack of clubs.

Winning the ace of spades I led the 10 of clubs and let it run. West won the jack and exited with the queen of diamonds to my ace.

How would you continue?

This was the complete deal:

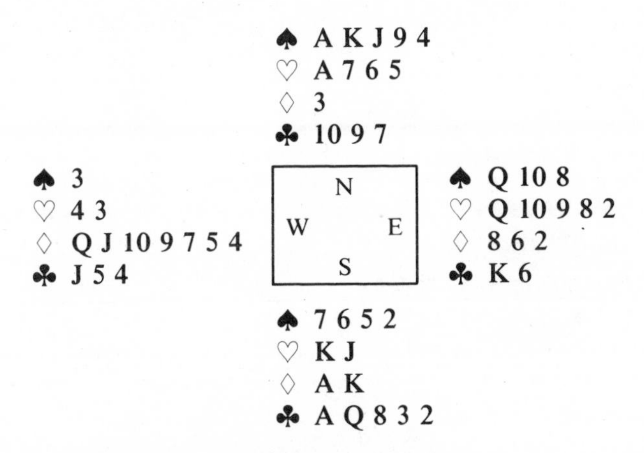

My first impulse was to ruff the king of diamonds in order to repeat the club finesse. While this move would have provided the best chance of picking up the king of trumps, it would have precluded any possibility of catching East in a spade-heart squeeze.

I therefore reviewed my plan and decided to go for all or nothing.

Ruffing the king of diamonds, I used this entry to take the heart finesse, not the trump finesse. When the jack of hearts won, I crossed my fingers and laid down the ace of clubs. When East obligingly dropped the king, I felt it was all over bar the shouting.

Two rounds of trumps produced this ending:

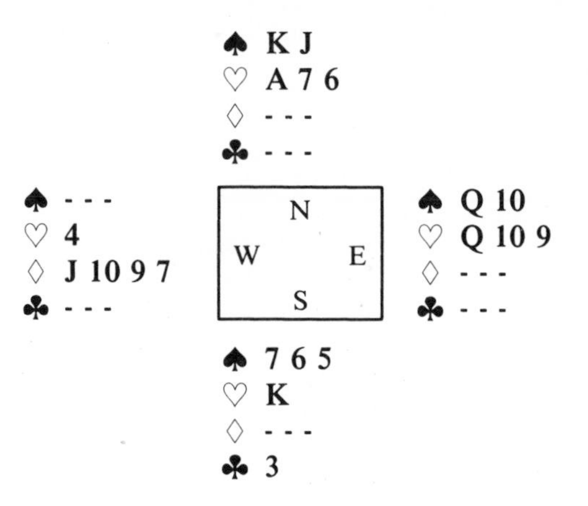

On the last trump dummy's jack of spades was discarded and East had no answer: if he let a spade go, I would play a spade to the king and a low heart, while if he discarded a heart, I would cash the king of hearts and lead a spade to dummy which would then be high.

Here is the complete hand again:

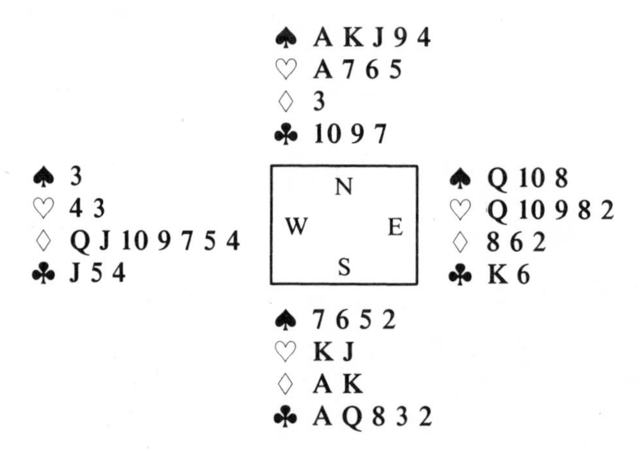

At the other table our teammates were East-West and did not interfere. North-South thus had no problem in reaching the spade slam (1♠ : 2♣, 2♡ : 3♠, 4♠ : 6♠). East led the 6 of diamonds. Declarer won the ace, cashed the ace and king of spades, finessed the queen of clubs and discarded a club on the king of diamonds.

Good Teamwork

In a teams tournament in 1974 in Marbella, Spain, both Italian pairs combined to produce a deserved pickup on this difficult slam hand:

♠ K 6 3
♡ 8 5 2
♢ A 10 7
♣ A 4 3 2

	N	
W		E
	S	

♠ A Q J 10 9 2
♡ K 4
♢ 4
♣ K Q 6 5

Both sides vulnerable. The bidding:

WEST	NORTH	EAST	SOUTH
	Pabis-Ticci		*D'Alelio*
		2♡*	Double
Pass	3♡	Pass	4NT
Pass	5♡	Pass	6♠
Pass	Pass	Pass	

*Weak two-opening

West led the 8 of clubs.

How should South plan the play?

This was the complete deal:

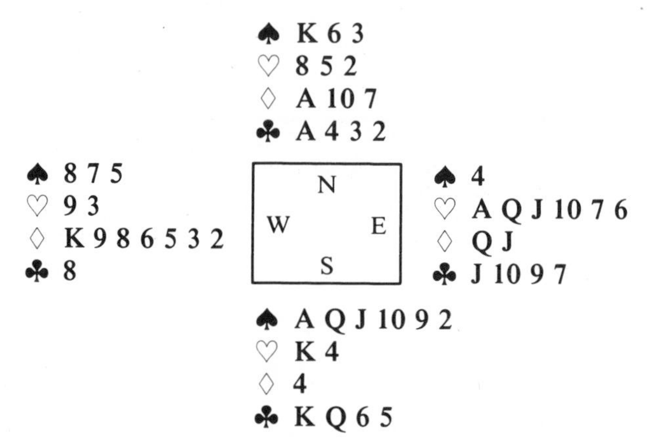

In view of East's Two Heart opening and West's failure to lead that suit, the 8 of clubs lead figured to be a singleton. Acccordingly, East started with six hearts and four clubs. With an inevitable heart loser (not two losers, for the ace of hearts was surely with East), the problem was not to lose a club as well.

D'Alelio therefore engineered the play to effect a heart-club squeeze on East. Winning the lead with the king of clubs, he ran three rounds of spades, ending in dummy, East discarding two hearts. When he led a heart from dummy, East decided to duck it (had East risen with the ace of hearts, declarer's task would have been simplified). D'Alelio won the king of hearts and cashed two more trumps to reach this ending:

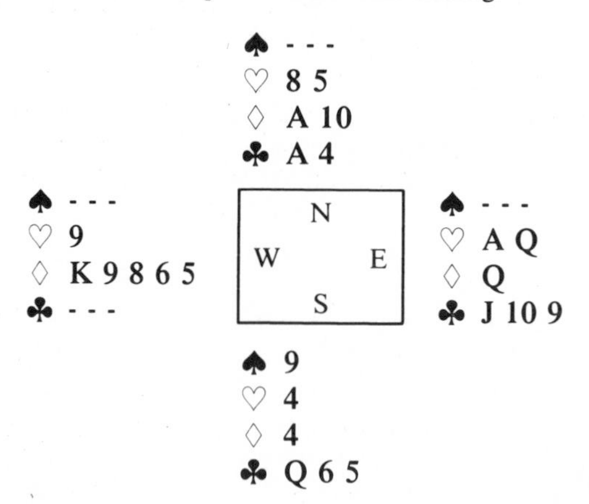

Declarer continued with a diamond to the ace and a diamond ruff. On the second round of diamonds, East was squeezed: to hold on to three clubs, he was forced to discard a heart. D'Alelio then led the 4 of hearts, thus setting up dummy's 8.

At the other table, East-West were Vivaldi and Belladonna, winners of the pairs event at that tournament. There the bidding proceeded:

WEST	NORTH	EAST	SOUTH
Belladonna		*Vivaldi*	
		2♡	3♠
Pass	5♠	Pass	6♠
Pass	Pass	Pass	

Belladonna also led the 8 of clubs and the play followed more or less the same lines. I say "more or less" because Vivaldi defended more accurately than his counterpart. This was the six-card ending at their table:

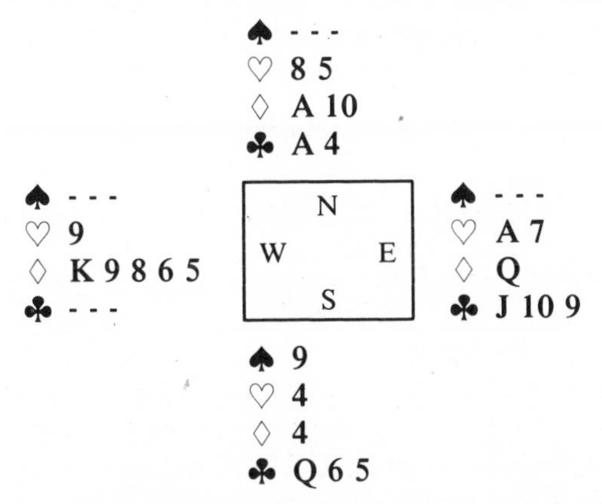

As you can see, Vivaldi foresaw the inevitable squeeze and carefully retained the 7 of hearts to afford some protection (if South had held the 9 of hearts, the slam would have been unbeatable). South now led his last spade on which West, dummy and East discarded a diamond each.

At this point declarer had to decide whether West held the 9 of hearts and East the 7 or vice versa. He opted for the 9 with East and the 7 with West and continued with a diamond to the ace (which would have squeezed East had he held the A-9 of hearts).

This enabled Vivaldi to produce a spectacular defence: on the ace of diamonds he jettisoned the ace of hearts! Declarer could have resigned himself to one down, but still hopeful that he might find the 9 of hearts with East, he continued with a heart. Belladonna won with the 9 and he was able to cash three more diamond tricks!

Had South divined the heart position, after cashing the last spade he would have had to lead the 4 of hearts, putting West on lead with the 9 (East could not afford to overtake without setting up dummy's 8). The forced diamond return would then effect the heart-club squeeze on East.

In the six-card ending, if declarer had followed the same line as D'Alelio, namely a diamond to the ace and a diamond ruff, you can be sure that on the second diamond, Vivaldi would have duly discarded the ace of hearts.

No Clouds On The Horizon

A theoretically unmakable contract may sometimes be made by virtue of an ingenious manoeuvre. Take a look at the following deal, played by Benito Garozzo in the 1975 Italian Championships:

♠ K 9 5
♡ K 6 4
◊ 5 4 3
♣ K Q 8 5

	N	
W		E
	S	

♠ A Q J 10 8 6 2
♡ A 5
◊ Q 8 6
♣ 7

East-West vulnerable. The bidding:

WEST	NORTH *Belladonna*	EAST	SOUTH *Garozzo*
Pass	Pass	Pass	1♠
Pass	2♣	Pass	4♠
Pass	Pass	Pass	

West led the king of diamonds, East playing the 2, and switched to the queen of hearts.

How should declarer plan the play?

This was the complete deal:

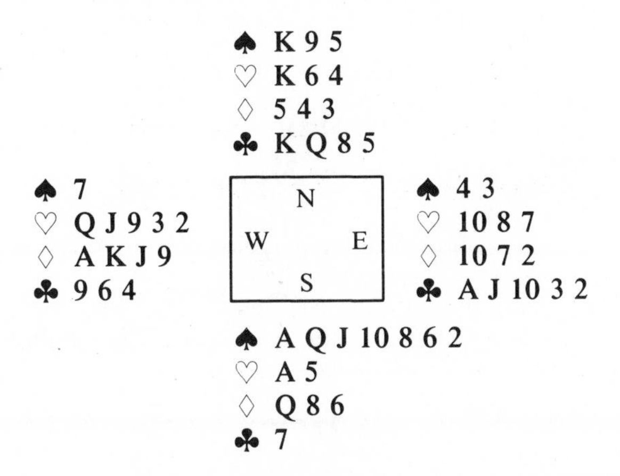

Garozzo took his chances and allowed West to hold the trick with the queen of hearts!

This was his reasoning: West had revealed the A-K of diamonds and the Q-J of hearts. He therefore could not also hold the ace of clubs, for that would give him 14 points, impossible in view of his initial pass.

Thus the ace of clubs was with East. Had Garozzo won the heart shift, drawn trumps and led a club, hoping to discard a diamond on the established club winner, East would have had no trouble in returning a diamond upon winning the ace of clubs.

In view of all this, Garozzo decided to duck the queen of hearts, hoping that West would continue the suit rather than switch to clubs. In fact, West, ignorant of the trap set for him and seeing no clouds on the horizon, continued hearts, expecting to find the ace with East.

The hand was now over. Garozzo won the ace and continued with the ace and king of spades. On the king of hearts he discarded his solitary club and the king of clubs allowed the ace to be ruffed out. The 9 of spades was the entry to dummy to allow the queen of clubs to be cashed and a diamond discarded. The defence thus came to only three tricks, two diamonds and a heart.

An Original Ending

The following deal played by Walter Avarelli in a pairs tournament produced a truly original ending:

♠ A 7 5 4
♡ J 10
◊ K J 10 5 3
♣ J 2

N
W E
S

♠ 8
♡ A K Q 9 8 5 4
◊ A 2
♣ 10 8 3

Neither side vulnerable. The bidding:

WEST	NORTH *Garozzo*	EAST	SOUTH *Avarelli*
1◊	Pass	1♠	3♡
3♠	4♡	All pass	

West led the king of spades. Ten tricks were obviously laydown but the problem at pairs is to procure the greatest number of tricks possible.

How would you have planned the play?

This was the complete deal:

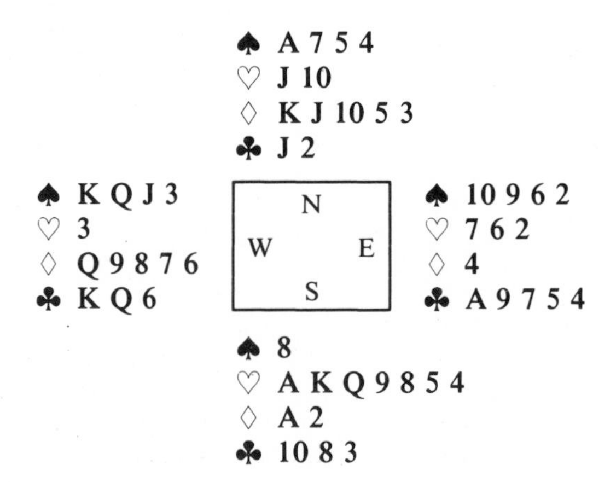

Avarelli won the ace of spades and continued with a spade ruff, a heart to the jack, a spade ruff, a heart to the ten, a spade ruff and the ace of hearts.

This was the position:

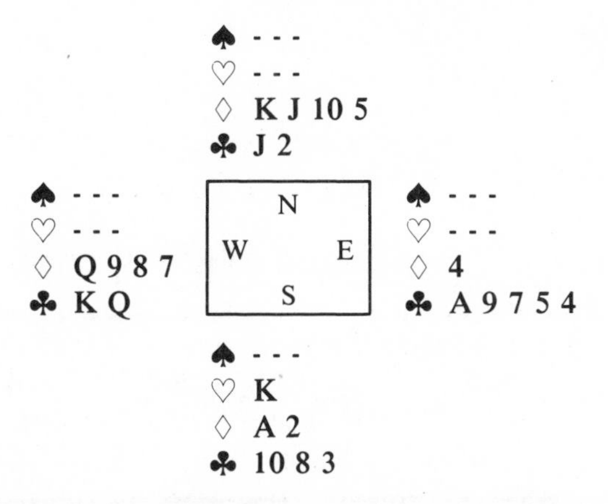

You can treat the ending as a double dummy problem:
With hearts trumps, South to play and make five tricks against any defence.

Avarelli cashed the king of hearts, discarding a club from dummy. West, forced to hold on to four diamonds, had to discard a club honour. South then played the ace of diamonds and a diamond to the jack, reaching this ending:

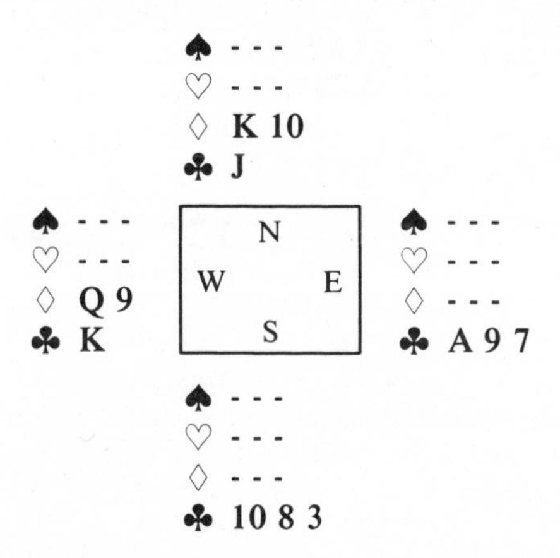

At this point 11 tricks were guaranteed but Avarelli who had by now completely reconstructed the opposition hands was still not satisfied. He was after an extra overtrick and therefore continued with the jack of clubs. If West had won this, he would be forced to concede the last two tricks to dummy's diamond tenace, while if East rose with the ace, he would have to yield up the last two tricks to declarer's club tenace.

It is worth noting that the above ending would not have been reached if declarer had not taken the preliminary step of eliminating the spades.

From Belladonna With Accuracy

Even when a contract seems routine, one should go through the motions and take the requisite precautions. This deal played by Giorgio Belladonna in the 1975 Albenga tournament is a highly instructive example:

♠ A 9 5 4
♡ A Q 10
◇ J 7 6 5
♣ 4 3

	N	
W		E
	S	

♠ K J 7 6 3
♡ 3 2
◇ A 10 9
♣ A K Q

Neither side vulnerable. The bidding:

SOUTH	NORTH
Belladonna	*Forquet*
1♠	4♠
Pass	

West led the jack of clubs. When Belladonna saw the dummy he realized that even a sledgehammer would have little chance of breaking this contract. Even so, precautions were in order so that declarer would not lose four tricks if it turned out that the missing honours all lay badly.

Firstly, the standard safety play with this trump combination had to be taken to avoid two trump losers. Had declarer started mechanically by leading a trump to the ace, this could have been disastrous if West had started with all four trumps. Belladonna therefore started by leading the king of trumps from hand (if West had shown out, he would have continued with a spade to the ace and a low spade towards the jack). Once both defenders followed, Belladonna crossed to the ace of spades, on which East discarded the 5 of hearts.

How would you have continued?

After you have made up your mind, take a look at the complete deal:

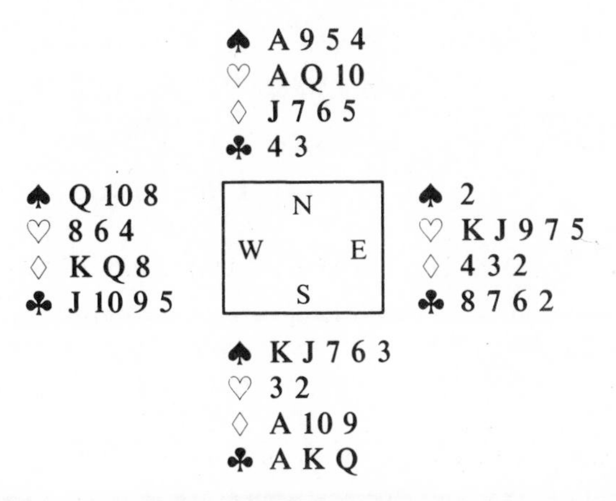

Had Belladonna made the mistake of taking a diamond finesse now, the unfavourable lie of the red honours would have led to the demise of the contract. West, after winning the queen of diamonds, would have returned a heart and the defence would have come to four tricks: one spade, one heart and two diamonds.

Belladonna of course foresaw all this and continued with the king and queen of clubs, discarding the 10 of hearts from dummy.

This was the position:

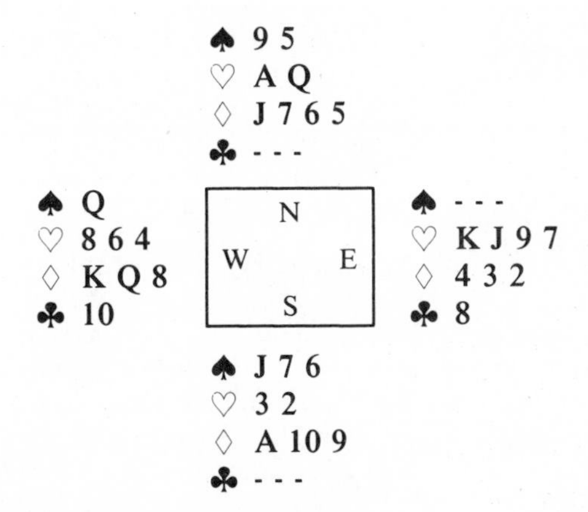

If at this point Belladonna had succumbed to the temptation of the heart finesse, East on winning the king would have returned a diamond to West's queen. West would then cash the queen of spades and exit with a heart, again leading to the defeat of the contract.

However, Belladonna renounced this finesse too and in perfect safety played off the ace and queen of hearts. East's diamond return was ducked to the queen but West could do no better than cash the queen of spades before being forced to lead into South's diamond tenace or concede a ruff-and-discard.

The Might Of The Lion

In recent years Mimmo D'Alelio's appearance in international events has become rare. His class, however, remains constant, as exemplified by this slam played by him at the 1975 Marbella Festival:

♠ A 2
♡ J 10 5
◊ A 5 4 3
♣ A J 4 2

	N	
W		E
	S	

♠ K Q J 10 9 3
♡ A 6
◊ K 6 2
♣ K 9

Neither side vulnerable. The bidding:

SOUTH *D'Alelio*	NORTH *Pabis-Ticci*
1♠	2♣
3♠	4◊
4NT	5♣
5NT	6♣
6♠	Pass

As you can see, there are 11 top tricks. The problem lies in finding the twelfth.

A club lead allows South to make sure of the contract by ducking in dummy. If East plays low the 9 wins; if East plays the queen, dummy's jack becomes high; if East plays the 10, South wins with the king and after drawing trumps, runs the 9 of clubs.

A diamond lead does not guarantee the contract but South is still well-placed. Winning in hand (lest East ruff the lead), declarer ducks a diamond after drawing trumps. If a heart is then played, South wins the ace and continues with the king of clubs, a club to the ace and a club ruff. If the queen of clubs has not appeared, declarer runs the remaining trumps, making whenever diamonds are 3-3 or West falls victim to a diamond-club squeeze or a diamond-heart squeeze. If after South ducks a diamond the defence continues diamonds, declarer falls back on the club finesse if diamonds have not split evenly.

Unfortunately for D'Alelio, however, West did not find either the club lead or the diamond lead but began with the 9 of hearts. The jack was played from dummy and East covered with the queen.

How should South plan the play?

After you have settled on your plan, consult the complete deal and see how your approach would have worked out:

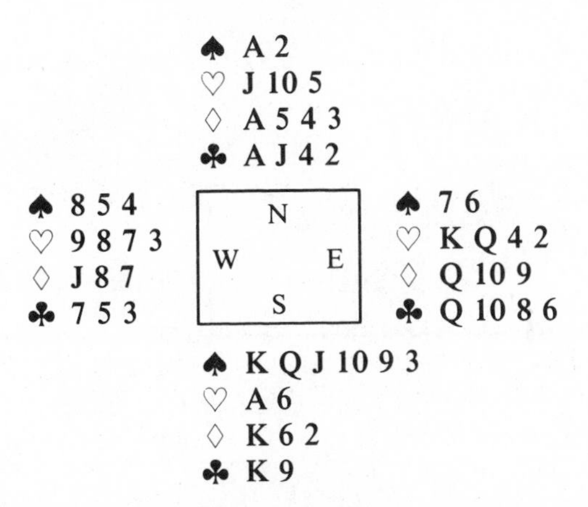

The heart lead prevented the ducking play in diamonds and so the slam seemed to hinge on developing three tricks from the club suit. Although the finesse offers the better chance than trying to drop the queen by ruffing the third round of clubs, D'Alelio opted for the latter play. If this failed there were still residual chances while if the club finesse lost, that would be the end of the hand.

Taking the queen of hearts with the ace, D'Alelio continued with the king of clubs, a club to the ace and a low club ruffed. The queen did not drop but declarer still had an ace up his sleeve. Crossing back to dummy with a spade to the ace, D'Alelio ruffed the fourth club high and then led out his trumps, coming down to this ending:

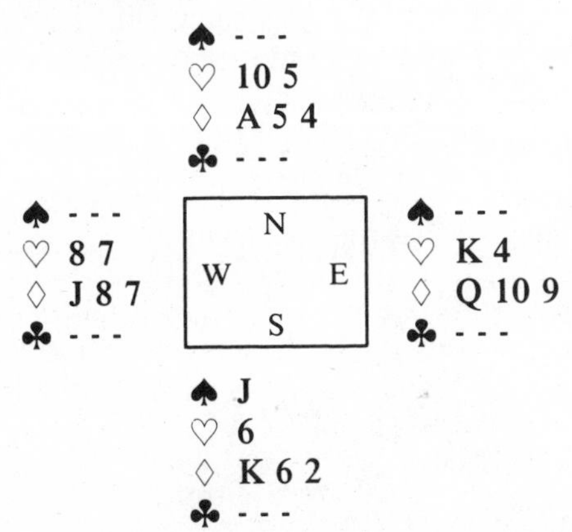

On the last spade declarer pitched a diamond from dummy and the defence was helpless. West had to let go a diamond (a heart discard would enable South to lead a heart, establishing dummy's 5) and East was no better off: if he let go a diamond, declarer's third diamond would become the slam-going trick, while if he pitched a heart, South would have been able to set up dummy's 10 of hearts by ducking a heart to East's bared king.

A Promising Debut

In 1974, in Venice, Arturo Franco made a successful debut with the Blue Team by winning the World Teams Championship. The following deal shows his technical mastery:

♠ A 7 5
♡ K 7 4
◊ K J 2
♣ A K 4 2

	N	
W		E
	S	

♠ K 4
♡ A Q J 5 3 2
◊ 4 3
♣ 7 6 5

Neither side vulnerable. The bidding:

WEST	NORTH	EAST	SOUTH
		1♠	2♡
Pass	2♠	Pass	3♡
Pass	4♣	Pass	4♡
Pass	5♡	All pass	

West led the 2 of spades.

How should declarer plan the play?

This was the complete deal:

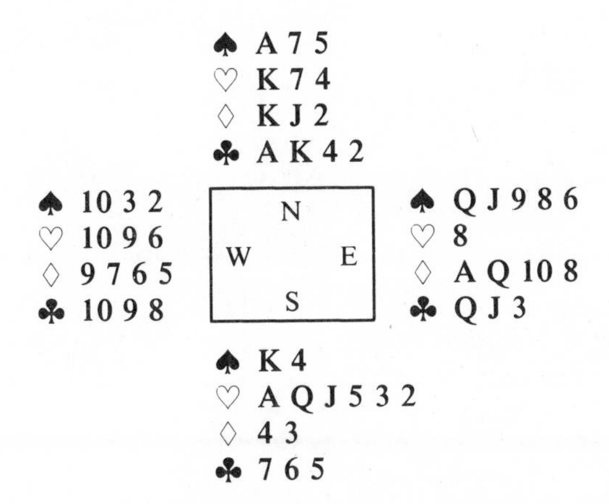

If Franco had won the lead, drawn trumps and played off three rounds of clubs, East would have been able to unblock, allowing West to win on the third round (on the first round, East would have signalled with the queen and West with the 10). The diamond switch from West would then have put paid to the contract.

Arturo foresaw this danger and allowed East's jack of spades to win trick one. East continued spades and declarer won the king, cashed the ace and queen of hearts, crossed to dummy with a club to the ace, discarded a club on the ace of spades and continued with the king of clubs and a club ruff. He returned to dummy with a heart to the king and discarded a losing diamond on the thirteenth club.

When Arturo related this play to me, I remarked to him that the famous Terence Reese had pulled off a similar coup some thirty years previously. "I wasn't even born then," was his laconic reply.

An Unexpected Complication

The following deal was played by Giorgio Belladonna in the 1975 World Teams Championship:

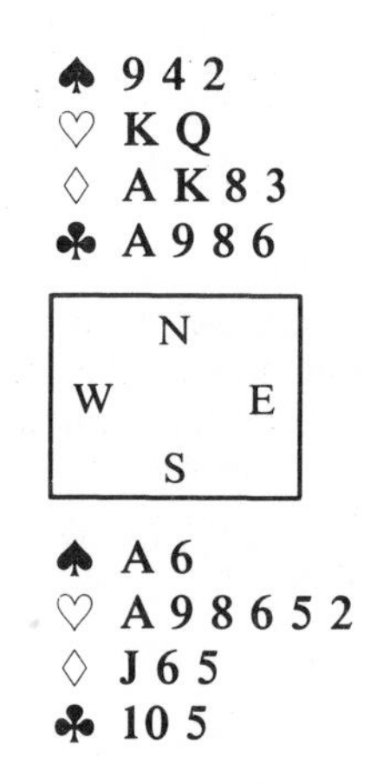

Neither side vulnerable. The bidding:

SOUTH	WEST	NORTH	EAST
Belladonna		*Garozzo*	
2♡	Pass	4♡	All pass

West led the king of clubs. With trumps 3-2, there would be no problem since the defence could come to no more than a spade, a diamond and a club. The 3-2 split generally has a 68% probability. I say "generally" because Giorgio always complains that this split does not apply to him. On his good days he is happy to find five missing trumps breaking no worse than 4-1.

Normally I would place Giorgio in that category of players whom I call "professional moaners" but on this occasion when he played the king of hearts at trick 2, East discarded a spade!

How would you have continued?

This was the complete deal:

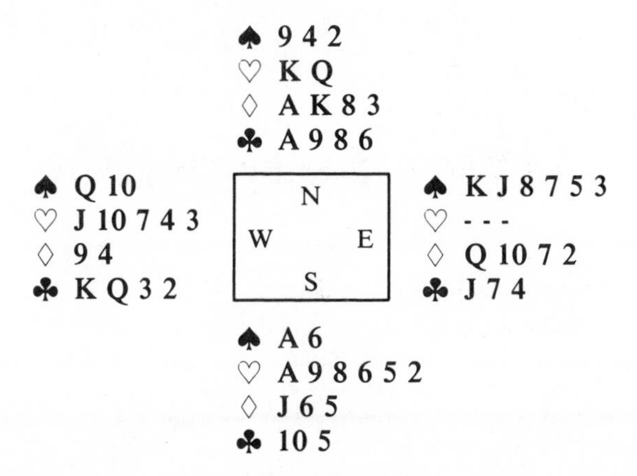

After the king of hearts had revealed the trump break, Belladonna continued with the 6 of clubs. East won with the jack and returned a spade. Taking the ace, Giorgio crossed to dummy with a heart to the queen and on the 9 of clubs he discarded his remaining spade (a loser-on-loser, but setting up the 8 of clubs in the process). Winning the diamond return with the ace, he ruffed a spade, crossed to dummy with the king of diamonds and discarded his diamond loser on the 8 of clubs.

This was the ending:

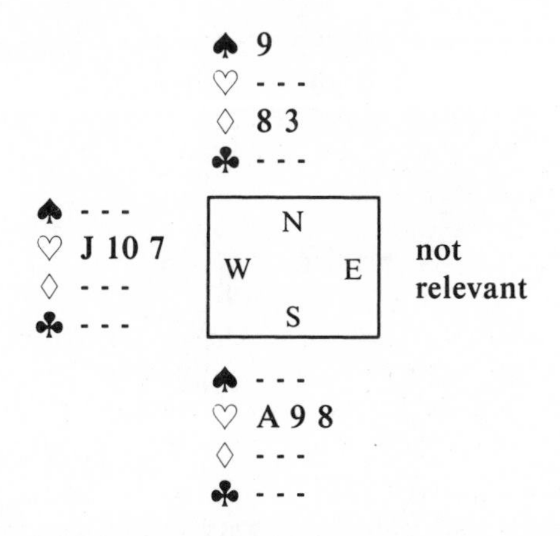

Belladonna ruffed the next lead from dummy with the 8 of hearts and West could do no better than overruff and then lead into South's trump tenace. The defence thus came to only three tricks: one heart and two clubs.

Two Vanishing Tricks

The Venice Teams Championship has become one of the "classics" of bridge in Italy. In 1975 the Lancia Alitalia Bridge Team (Avarelli, Belladonna, A. Franco, Garozzo, Sharif and Forquet) succeeded in repeating their success of the previous year in this tournament.

Benito Garozzo was, as usual, spearheading the team to victory. Here he is in action in a tough Five Diamond contract:

♠ K 5 4
♡ 7 5 3
◊ K 5 2
♣ A 8 7 6

	N	
W		E
	S	

♠ A 7 6
♡ A K 2
◊ A J 9 7 6 4
♣ 2

Both sides vulnerable. The bidding:

SOUTH	WEST	NORTH	EAST
Garozzo		*Franco*	
1♣	Pass	1NT	Pass
2◊	Pass	3◊	Pass
4♣	Pass	4◊	Pass
4♡	Pass	4♠	Pass
5♣	Pass	5◊	All pass

West led the queen of clubs.

How should declarer plan the play?

This was the complete deal:

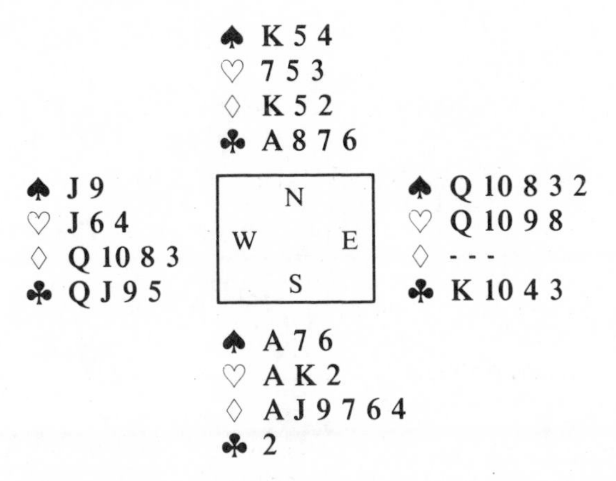

At first glance four losers appear inevitable: two diamonds, a spade and a heart. Let's see how Benito handled the play.

Garozzo took the queen of clubs lead with the ace and ruffed a club at trick 2. This move, seemingly inconsequential, proved to be critical. He continued with a diamond to the king, East discarding a spade, a club ruff, the ace and king of hearts, the ace and king of spades and a club ruff.

This was the ending:

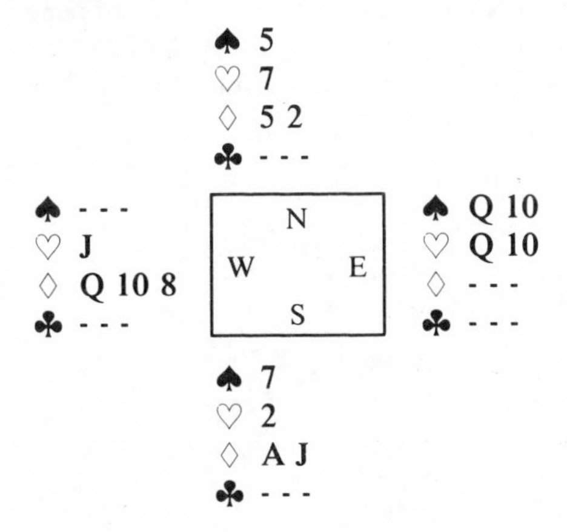

Garozzo led a heart. East won with the queen and continued the suit but declarer simply discarded a spade. West was forced to ruff and return a diamond into declarer's A-J.

It is worth noting that in the end position Garozzo picked the situation precisely. Had he exited with a spade instead of a heart, West would have been able to escape the endplay by ruffing the spade and leading the jack of hearts to East's queen.

Losing Layout

It is not easy to receive applause when one has just failed in a grand slam, yet that is precisely what happened to Benito Garozzo on this deal from the 1975 European Championship:

Both sides vulnerable. The bidding:

SOUTH *Garozzo*	NORTH *Franco*
1♣	1NT
2♣	2♡
2♠	4♣
4◊	4♡
4♠	5◊
6♣	6♡
6♠	6NT
7♣	Pass

West led the 4 of diamonds.

How should declarer plan the play?

Garozzo won dummy's ace, cashed the ace of hearts and played off three rounds of trumps, ending in dummy, East pitching the 10 of spades on the third round. Had hearts been 4-3, there would have been no further problems but when declarer played off the king and queen of hearts, West discarded the 2 of spades.

This was the position:

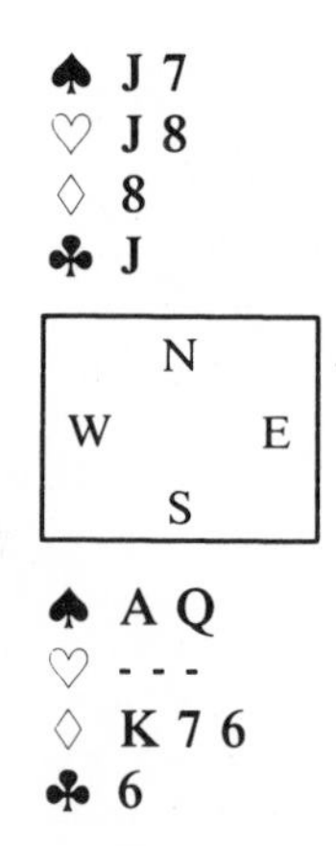

How would you have continued?

If East held the king of spades the contract could be easily made via a simple finesse, but Garozzo, suspicious of the discard of the 10 of spades, chose a different approach.

Have you spotted his line?

Garozzo cashed the jack of hearts discarding the queen of spades from hand! He was hoping to arrive at this ending:

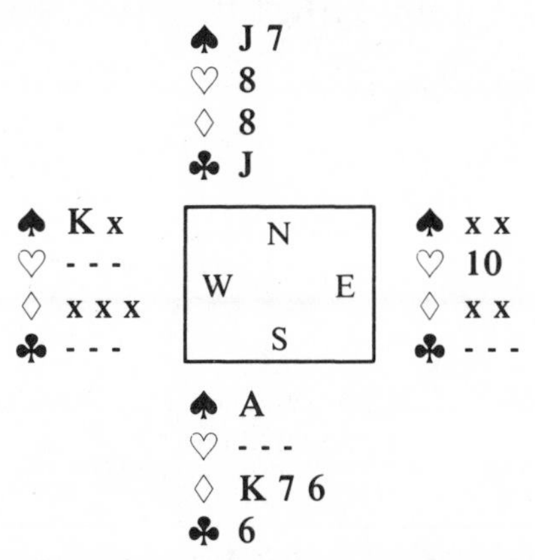

When declarer ruffed the 8 of hearts in hand, West would be caught in a spade-diamond squeeze: discarding a spade would allow South to continue with the ace of spades, establishing dummy's jack, while discarding a diamond would enable South to set up his own hand by king of diamonds and a diamond ruff.

Garozzo's plan was well-conceived as to the location of the king of spades which was indeed with West but since it was East who held the four-card diamond length, the contract could not be made. It was at this moment that the applause thundered.

This was the complete deal:

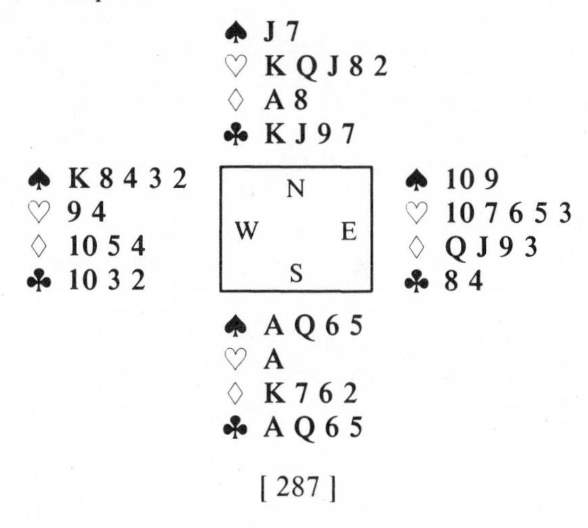

Garozzo And The Tale Of The Nine of Spades

This heart slam was played by Benito Garozzo in the Aldo Chiella Trophy in Turin, 1975:

♠ A K 10 8
♡ Q 7 6
♢ A 4
♣ A K 7 4

	N	
W		E
	S	

♠ 3 2
♡ A K 10 9 5 4
♢ 7
♣ 8 6 5 3

Neither side vulnerable. The bidding:

SOUTH	WEST	NORTH	EAST
Garozzo		*Forquet*	
2♡	Pass	2NT	Pass
3♡	Pass	6♡	All pass

The final contract is excellent, with twelve tricks laydown on a normal club break. When West led the 2 of clubs and East dropped the queen on dummy's ace, Garozzo surmised that the clubs would not be dividing normally.

How would you have continued?

This was the complete deal:

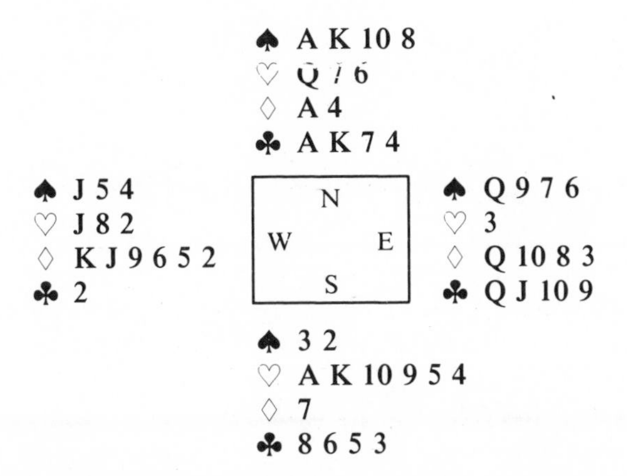

Garozzo's first thought was to finesse dummy's 8 of spades. If West held the 9 of spades and an honour, declarer would have been able to finesse first the 8 and then the 10 of spades and, all going well, discard two clubs on the spade winners.

However, this plan had to be revised, for when Garozzo started to draw trumps, East was visibly in difficulties. After following to the first round, East decided to discard diamonds on the next two rounds. Garozzo therefore decided to continue with the trumps, playing five rounds in all, to reach this ending:

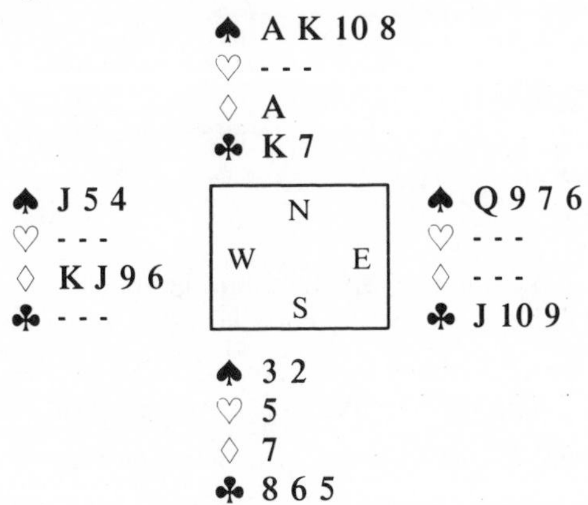

East had done his best so far but when Garozzo played a diamond to the ace, East crumbled: if he discarded a spade, South would continue with the ace of spades, king of spades and a spade ruff, while if he let go a club, South would continue with the king of clubs and another club.

The Queen Of Monte Carlo

During the 1975 Monte Carlo Teams Tournament, won by the Lancia Alitalia Bridge Team, I was partnering Omar Sharif in defending against this club slam:

♠ 7 5 4
♡ A K 9 7
◊ J 8 2
♣ 9 5 4

	N	
W		E
	S	

♠ Q J 10 9
♡ Q 8 6 4
◊ Q 7 5 3
♣ A

Neither side vulnerable. The bidding:

SOUTH	WEST	NORTH	EAST
	Sharif		*Forquet*
2♣	Pass	2♡	Pass
3♣	Pass	3♡	Pass
3♠	Pass	5♣	Pass
6♣	Pass	Pass	Pass

The Two Club opening was artificial and game-forcing, the Two Heart response showed the ace of hearts and the rest of the bidding was natural.

Omar Sharif, West, led the 10 of diamonds. Declarer ducked in dummy and won in hand with the ace. Next came the king of clubs from South.

How would you plan the defence after winning the ace of clubs?

Make a firm decision as to what you intend to play next before looking at the complete deal:

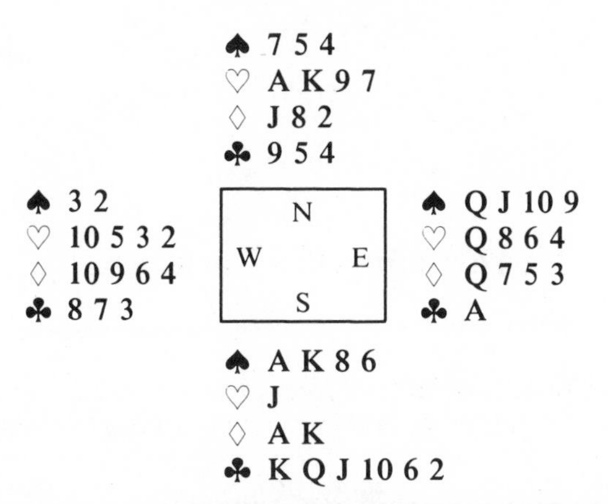

At the other table where Belladonna was faced with the same contract, the first two tricks were the same. At trick 3 East decided to switch to the queen of spades. Belladonna won the ace, cashed all the trumps and the king of diamonds and crossed to dummy via the ace of hearts.

This was the ending:

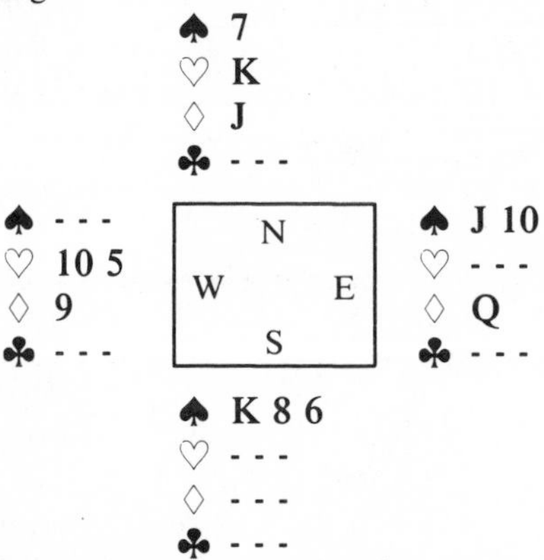

When the king of hearts was played from dummy, East was squeezed in spades and diamonds.

Foreseeing this position (it was not too hard to reconstruct South's shape), I decided to switch to hearts at trick 3 in order to cut declarer off from dummy. However, had I led a low heart, South would have been able to win in hand if, as was the case, he held the singleton jack and he would then have been able to continue with the queen of clubs and a low club to dummy's 9, using the ace-king of hearts to discard two spade losers. Consequently I selected the *queen* of hearts as the switch and not only did this sever declarer's communications with dummy, but it also pinned South's jack.

At this point the contract could no longer be made.

The King Of Bermuda

The outcome of the 1975 World Teams Championship would have been different if the king of clubs had not been with West in the following grand slam:

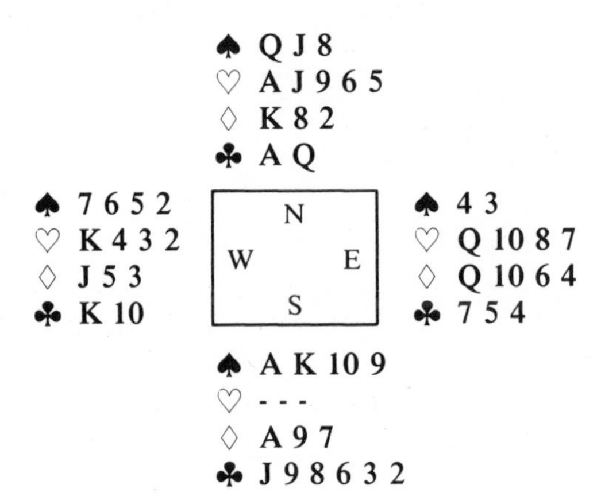

Both sides vulnerable. The bidding:

WEST	NORTH *Garozzo*	EAST	SOUTH *Belladonna*
		Pass	2♣
Pass	2◊	Pass	2♠
Pass	3♡	Pass	3NT
Pass	4♣	Pass	4◊
Pass	4NT	Pass	5◊
Pass	5♡	Double	Redouble
Pass	5♠	Pass	5NT
Pass	7♣	All pass	

The bidding of the two Italian players was indicative of the state of the match. After being 73 Imps down in the middle of the match, the 'Blue Team' still trailed by 24 Imps at the beginning of the final session. When Belladonna and Garozzo picked up the above cards a few deals from the end they believed, wrongly as it happened, that they had not yet made up the leeway and so they forced the pace in the bidding.

In the auditorium the closed circuit television allowed everyone to follow the drama. West led a heart and when Garozzo revealed dummy, Belladonna's countenance reflected first surprise and then desperation. Glumly he stared at dummy for some time and then played low, ruffing the heart in hand. He continued with a low club and when West played the 10, Belladonna called for the queen, shutting his eyes. When he reopened them and saw East's 4, he regained a little colour. He stole a glance at West whose expression told him that the grand slam was home.

When the king duly fell under the ace of clubs, everyone's reactions at the table were different. Belladonna murmured a "sorry" to the opponents, Garozzo raised his eyes to heaven, probably thanking Saint Gennaro, while West threw his cards on the table, exclaiming "Oh, my God!"

His king of clubs decided the World Championship.

Undoubtedly Giorgio was extremely lucky to find the king of clubs onside and doubleton, but West missed a golden opportunity to complicate the task facing declarer.

Suppose that on the first round of clubs West had played the king!

How would declarer then have continued?

When I asked Belladonna this very question some months after the event, Giorgio replied "I would probably still be there considering the problem."

This in fact might have been the layout:

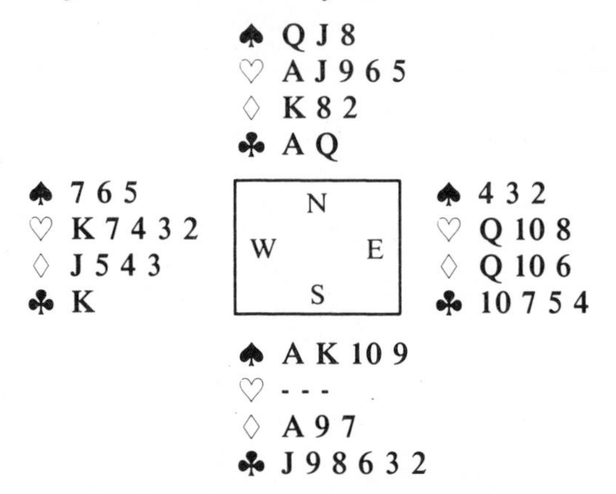

Had this been the case, declarer after winning West's king of clubs with the ace, would have been able to continue as follows: three rounds of spades, ending in dummy, the ace of hearts pitching a diamond, a heart ruff, the ace of diamonds, a diamond to the king and a heart ruff. This would have been the three-card ending:

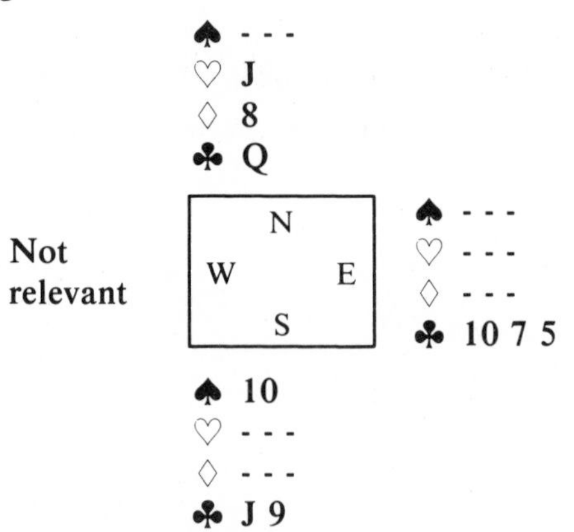

The ten of spades is ruffed in dummy, East having to underruff, and with the lead in dummy, declarer makes the last two tricks. On the actual deal, of course, this line would have failed, as East would have ruffed the third round of spades.

At the other table the Americans played in Six No-Trumps, a contract which presented no problems after the diamond lead. A heart lead would have made the success of this small slam also depend on the king of clubs lying onside doubleton.

The Hidden Snare

Many apparently simple contracts conceal their pitfalls. Take for example this contract played by Benito Garozzo in the 1974 Beirut tournament:

♠ A 5
♡ K Q J
◊ 8 7 6 5 4
♣ 8 7 6

	N	
W		E
	S	

♠ Q 6 4
♡ A 7 6 5 2
◊ K 3
♣ A K Q

Neither side vulnerable. The bidding:

WEST	NORTH	EAST	SOUTH
	Sharif		*Garozzo*
Pass	Pass	Pass	1♣
1♠	1NT	Pass	2♡
Pass	3♡	Pass	4♡
Pass	Pass	Pass	

West led the 9 of clubs.

How should declarer plan the play?

This was the complete deal:

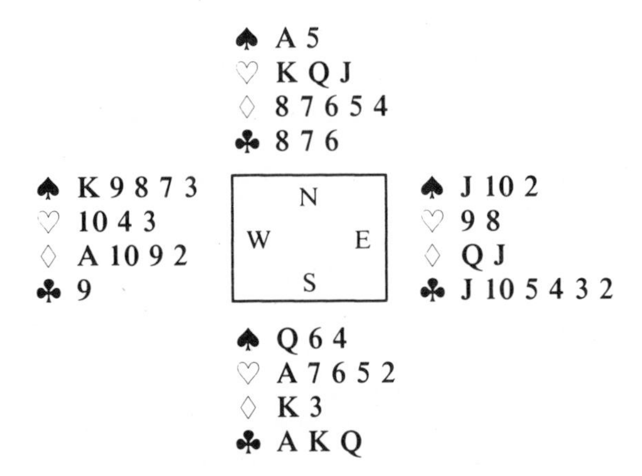

If Garozzo, after winning the lead, had played ace and another spade with the intention of ruffing a spade in dummy, this line would have failed not only if trumps happened to be 4-1, but also if West had started with a singleton or a doubleton in clubs. Suppose West had started with a doubleton club: after winning the second round of spades, West would exit with his last club. South could cash two top trumps after ruffing the spade in dummy but would be unable to return to hand without conceding a club ruff whenever West had started with three hearts.

In the light of the communication problems, Garozzo contemplated the possibility of setting up dummy. This would also entail various risks, including a 4-1 trump break, a possible overruff in diamonds and the club ruff.

Garozzo therefore embarked on a different line of play which would guarantee the contract whenever West started with the king of spades and the ace of diamonds (very likely on the bidding). He continued with the king and queen of trumps and when trumps proved to be 3-2, he overtook the jack of hearts with the ace and cashed the remaining two trumps and two clubs.

This was the position:

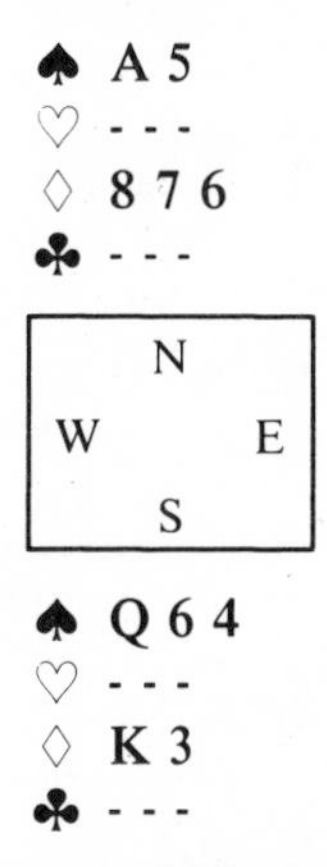

In the five-card ending West was forced to retain three spades and two diamonds (if West came down to four spades and one diamond, a diamond would endplay him; if instead West reduced to two spades and three diamonds, South would have continued with the ace of spades and a low spade, both establishing the queen and forcing West to open the diamonds; in both cases South would score an overtrick). East was likewise in difficulty: if he retained only two spades, South would have continued with the ace of spades and a spade to the queen, putting West on lead for the diamond return, while if East retained just one diamond South would have played the king of diamonds, putting West on lead for a spade return. Therefore East also came down to three spades and two diamonds:

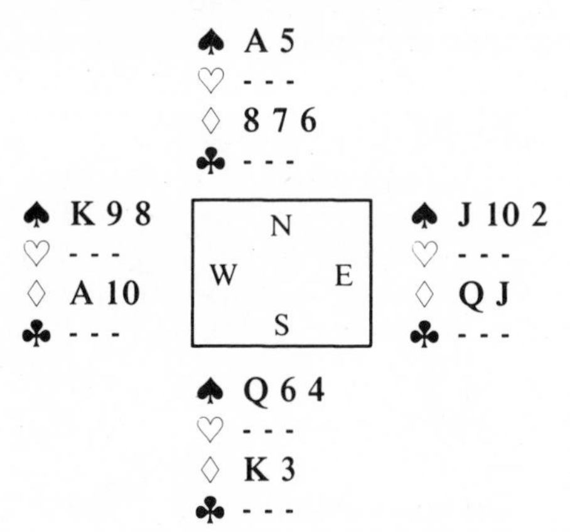

Garozzo led a low diamond in order to land an overtrick if West had come down to the bare ace of diamonds and four spades. East won the jack and returned the jack of spades. South ducked this and won with dummy's ace in order to play another diamond. West was now on lead and could not avoid giving South a spade trick.

A Finesse Without Risk

This slam arose during a friendly match played by the Blue Team:

♠ K 9 7 5
♡ 3 2
♢ A 7 6 4
♣ K 6 4

	N	
W		E
	S	

♠ A J 10 8 4
♡ A K Q
♢ K J 5
♣ A 7

Neither side vulnerable. The bidding:

SOUTH	WEST	NORTH	EAST
Forquet		*Garozzo*	
1♣	Pass	1NT	Pass
2♠	Pass	3♠	Pass
4♣	Pass	4♢	Pass
4♡	Pass	4♠	Pass
6♠	Pass	Pass	Pass

West led the queen of clubs.

How should declarer plan the play?

This was the complete deal:

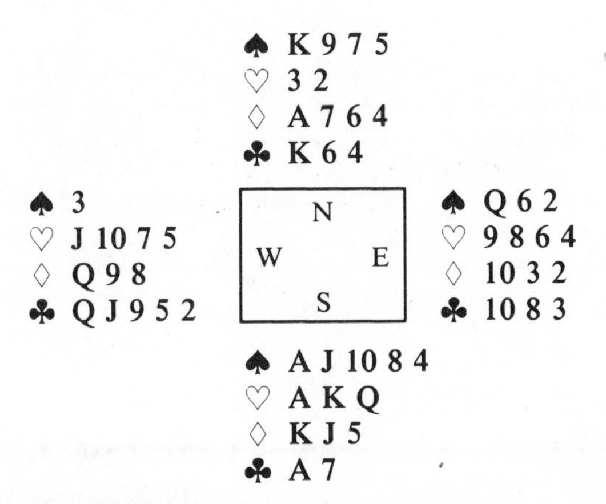

At the other table, South in the same contract won the ace of clubs and played off the two top spades. When the queen did not drop, he fell back on the diamond finesse, but when this also failed, the contract went one down.

No doubt declarer was unlucky. He would have succeeded if the queen of spades had dropped or if the queen of diamonds had been with East or even if West had held Q-x-x in spades (in that case, declarer could eliminate hearts and clubs and put West on lead with the queen of spades, forcing a diamond return or a ruff-and-discard).

At my table I took a line which gave me a few additional chances. After winning the ace of clubs, I cashed the king of spades and the three top hearts, discarding a club from dummy. Crossing to dummy with a club to the king, I led a low spade and when East played the 6, I simply took the spade finesse. In fact the finesse won but even had it lost, West would then have been forced to return a diamond or concede a ruff-and-discard.

If East had shown out on the second round of spades, naturally I would have gone up with the ace of spades and then put West on lead with the third round of spades.

Blind Faith

The following slam was played by Benito Garozzo during a tour of the United States. His partner was Katherine Wei, wife of C.C. Wei, the creator of the Precision System:

♠ J 9 5 4
♡ A K Q 5
♢ 8 5 4 3
♣ 7

N
W E
S

♠ K
♡ 6 2
♢ A Q 10
♣ A K J 10 9 8 2

Neither side vulnerable. The bidding:

SOUTH	NORTH
Garozzo	*K. Wei*
1♣	1♢
2♣	3NT
4♣	4♡
5♣	5♡
6♣	Pass

In Precision the One Club opening shows a minimum of 16 points. The One Diamond response followed by a jump in no-trumps is the 'impossible negative', showing a 4-4-4-1 shape with positive values and a singleton in partner's suit. The final contract is justified solely by Katherine Wei's blind faith in Garozzo's card play!

West led the ace of spades and continued with the 8, to the 9 and 10. After ruffing, Benito crossed to dummy with a heart and successfully finessed the jack of clubs. He ran four more rounds of clubs to which West followed with a club, two diamonds and a spade while East played two clubs and two spades.

This was the end position:

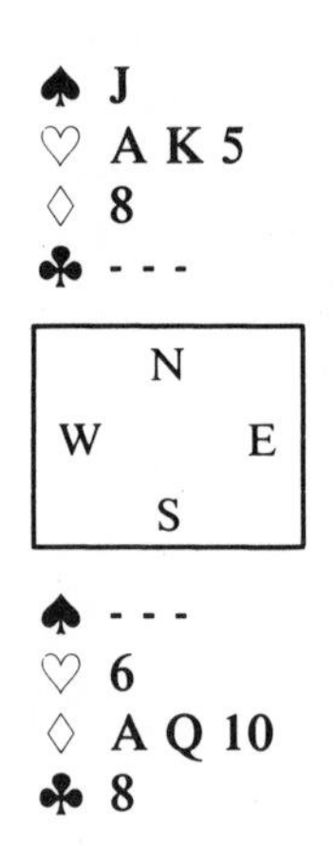

How should declarer continue?

This was the complete deal:

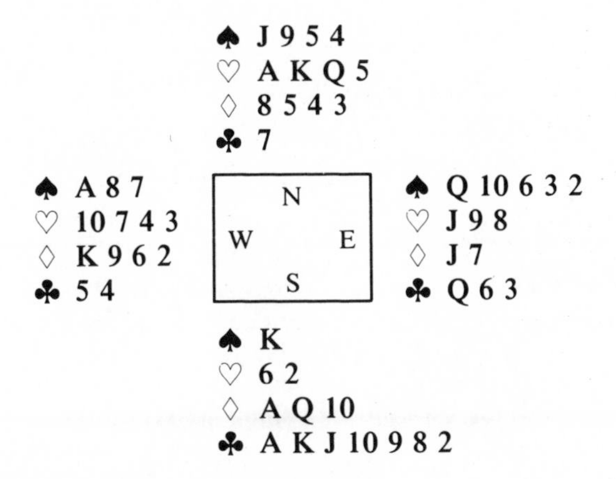

And this was the five-card ending in full:

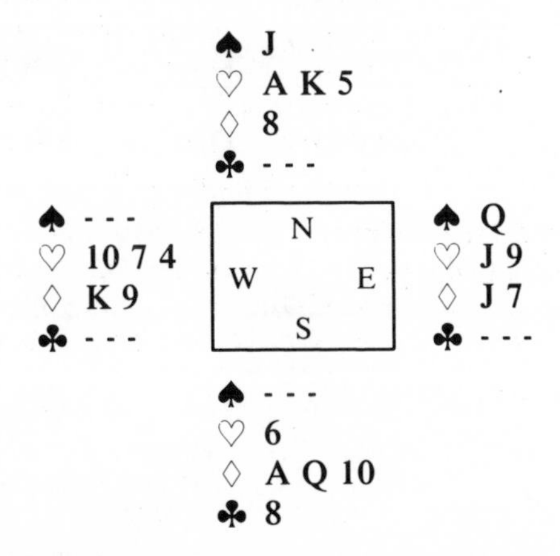

Garozzo cashed his last club and West was forced to blank his king of diamonds to keep control of the hearts. North and East discarded hearts and Garozzo continued with the two top hearts. On the last heart East was forced to discard a diamond to keep control of the spades. Both opponents had been obliged to come down to a singleton diamond so that Garozzo had no trouble cashing the ace of diamonds and dropping West's bare king.

Award For The Slam

The Charles Solomon Trophy was inaugurated in 1974 in memory of one of the most significant figures in American bridge. The trophy, awarded annually, goes to the player responsible for the best hand of the year as judged by a panel of experts. The inaugural presentation of this trophy went to Benito Garozzo for the following small slam:

North:
♠ K J 10 8
♡ J
♢ Q 10 9 6 5 4 3 2
♣ - - -

South:
♠ A 9 6 3 2
♡ A 8 3 2
♢ A 7
♣ 10 9

Neither side vulnerable. The bidding:

SOUTH *Garozzo*	WEST	NORTH *Belladonna*	EAST
1♠	Double	4♣	5♣
Double	Pass	5♡	Double
Redouble	Pass	6♠	All pass

4♣ = splinter bid: singleton or void in clubs and support for spades
The double of 5♣ = "Partner, let's defend Five Clubs rather than play Five Spades."
5♡ = first- *or* second round control in hearts
Redouble = first-round control in hearts and first- *or* second-round control in diamonds
6♠ = "As you were not too keen to play in Five Spades, try your hand at SIX!"

Thus, with a combined count of 19 points, Belladonna and Garozzo had no hesitation in using every available cue-bid, culminating in the small slam in spades.

West led the ace of clubs.

How would you have planned the play?

Benito ruffed in dummy and continued with the jack of spades, letting it run. This move proved inspired when West followed with a low spade.

How would you have continued?

This was the complete deal:

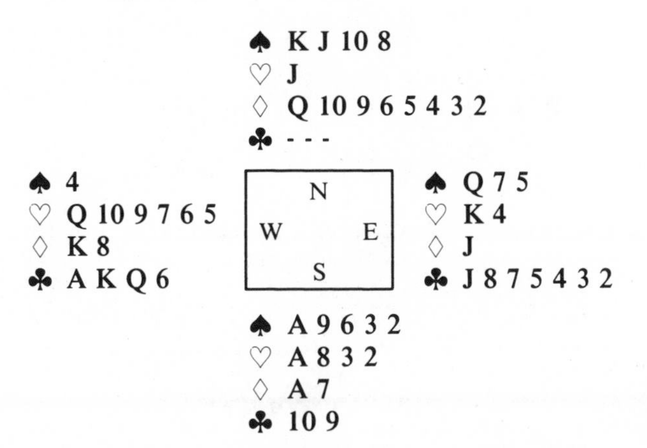

Garozzo continued with the ace of diamonds and a low diamond. West won the king of diamonds and did best by continuing clubs to shorten dummy. This was the position after the second club was ruffed in dummy:

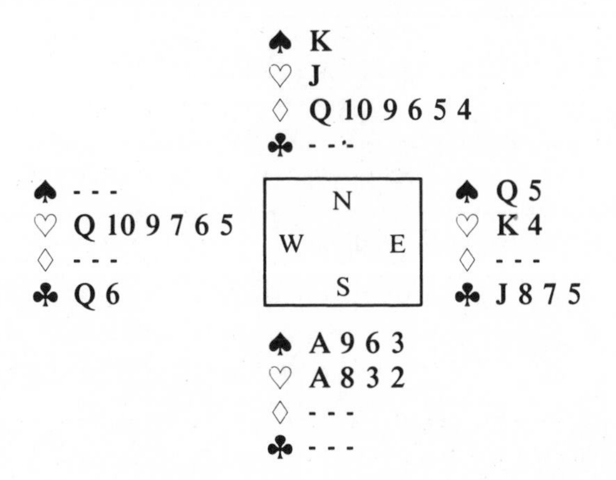

Garozzo diagnosed the singleton spade in the West hand as the basis for the take-out double and consequently, instead of cashing the king of spades which would have been the winning line if spades had been 2-2, he continued with the master diamonds from dummy.

East had no defence. Whenever he ruffed, South would overruff and cross back to dummy with a trump to the king.

Too Many Trumps

Sometimes a defender has cause for regret because he holds *too many* trumps. For example, take this Four Spade contract played by Giorgio Belladonna in a teams event in Milan in 1977:

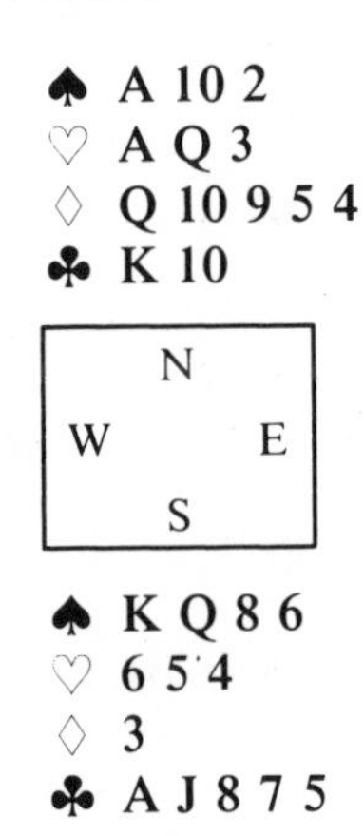

Neither side vulnerable. The bidding:

WEST	NORTH *Garozzo*	EAST	SOUTH *Belladonna*
1♢	Double	Pass	2♠
Pass	2NT	Pass	3♣
Pass	3♠	Pass	4♠
Pass	Pass	Double	All pass

West led the king of diamonds. When Garozzo tabled dummy, Belladonna regretted having missed the superior Three No-Trumps, especially as East's double heralded a bad trump break.

After studying dummy for a while, Giorgio Belladonna asked his partner, "Was your double of One Diamond for penalties?" Garozzo's reply is not printable.

At trick 2 West switched to the jack of hearts. Belladonna won with dummy's queen and East played the 9.

How would you have continued?

This was the complete deal:

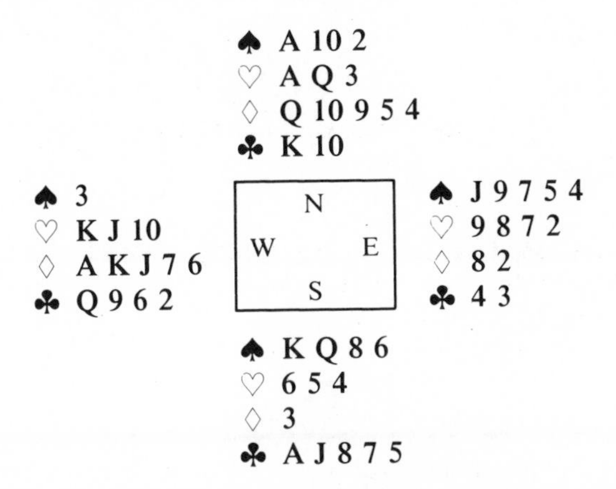

Belladonna continued swiftly with a diamond ruff, the ace of clubs, a club to the king (to prevent East discarding a club on the next round of diamonds), a diamond ruff, a heart to the ace and a diamond ruff, East discarding hearts on the last two rounds of diamonds.

This was the position:

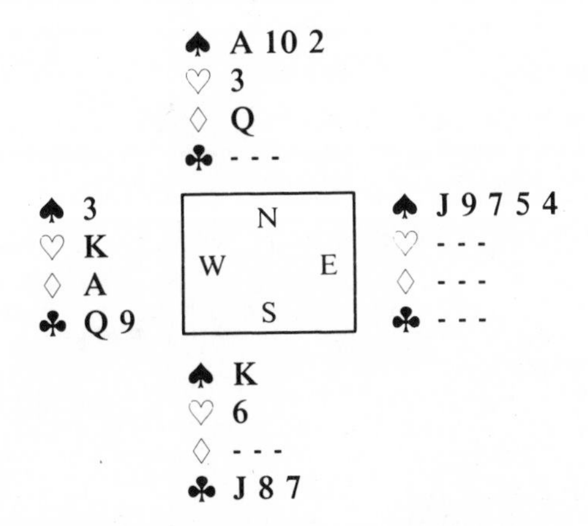

At this point Belladonna cashed the king of spades and led a club, discarding a heart from dummy. East was forced to ruff his partner's winner and lead a spade into dummy's tenace.

The contract thus succeeded by way of four spades in hand, two spades in dummy, two hearts and two clubs. East, however, could have saved the situation if on the third and fourth rounds of diamonds, he had ruffed both times instead of discarding hearts. In that case the ending would have been:

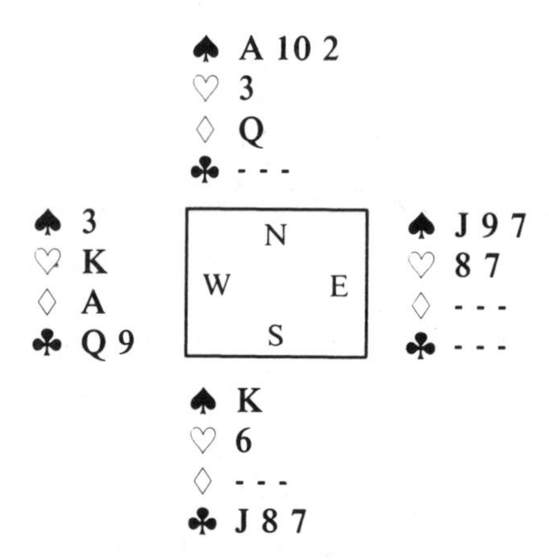

In this position South cannot come to more than two tricks. If he cashes the king of spades and leads a club discarding a heart (or a diamond) from dummy, West wins, cashes the diamond (or the heart if dummy discarded a diamond) and then leads any card. If, instead, South ruffs a club with the ace of spades and a diamond with the king of spades, East must underruff once to reduce his trump holding in order to avoid being thrown in.

Aggressive Defence

Once upon a time the 3NT opening was used for hands in the 25-26 point range. These days it is more commonly used on hands of a particular type, usually a long, solid minor, possibly with one or two side entries. Such an opening came to be called "The Gambling Three No-Trumps" particularly by the Americans because of its risky outcome.

To counteract the Gambling Three No-Trump opening, the defence has to be very aggressive, the aim being to take five tricks before declarer can get the lead and rattle off his nine.

The following deal was played in the 1974 Monte Carlo tournament:

Neither side vulnerable. The bidding:

SOUTH	WEST	NORTH	EAST
	Forquet		*Avarelli*
	Pass	Pass	Pass
3NT	Pass	Pass	Pass

Suppose you were West holding my cards:

♠ A 10 7 5 ♡ K 10 5 4 ◊ 8 ♣ Q J 10 8

What would you have led?

Suppose that, like me, you have decided to lead the ace of spades in order to win the first trick, see dummy and retain the lead. This is what you see:

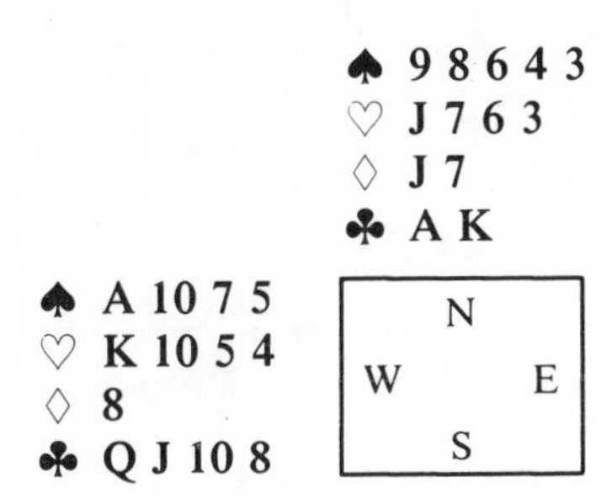

On the ace of spades, East played the 2 and South the queen.

How would you continue?

This was the complete deal:

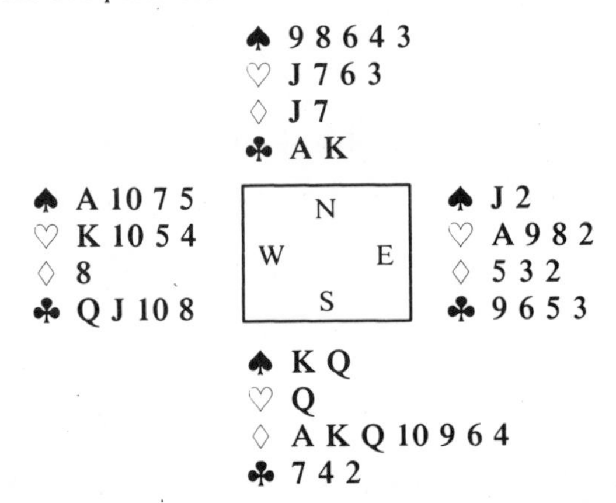

Declarer figured to have nine winners in the minors so that we would have to come to four more tricks immediately. Since this would be possible only if my partner held the ace of hearts, I laid down the king of hearts at trick 2. My partner played the apparently discouraging 2 but when South dropped the queen I had no doubts as to the significance of that 2. Naturally I continued with the 10 of hearts and the contract failed by one trick.

You have of course worked out that if Avarelli had played an encouraging 8 or 9 on my king of hearts, the contract would have been unbeatable.

The next deal was played during the 1976 Italian Championships and saw Giorgio Belladonna in operation against the Gambling Three No-Trumps:

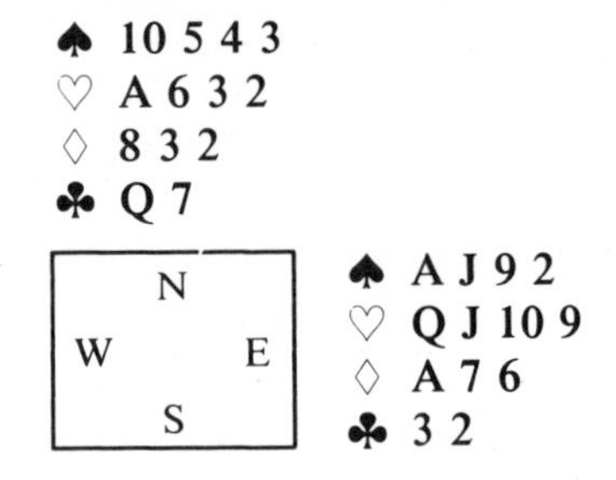

Neither side vulnerable. The bidding:

SOUTH	WEST *Garozzo*	NORTH	EAST *Belladonna*
3NT	Pass	Pass	Pass

Garozzo led the queen of diamonds.

How would you have planned the defence as East?

This was the complete deal:

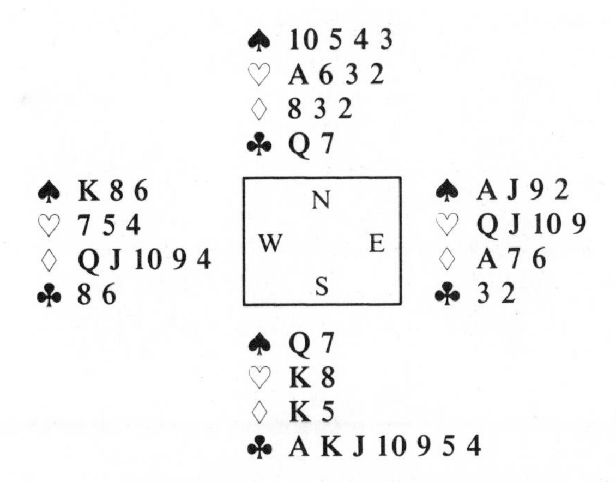

Upon winning the ace of diamonds, Belladonna realized that South would have nine tricks as soon as he obtained the lead (a heart, a diamond and no doubt seven clubs). The only chance was to take four spade tricks at once, hoping to find West with the king (or South with the singleton king).

Have you spotted the solution?

If West has the king of spades doubleton, the contract is unbeatable so that East must play for West to have at least K-x-x. If, however, East starts with a low spade, South can duck and the defence will be unable to garner more than three spade tricks. A switch to the jack of spades at trick 2 will not do either, for South will cover with the queen and when West wins the king and returns the suit, South can play dummy's 10, blocking the suit.

Belladonna came up with the answer by laying down the *ace* of spades at trick 2! He then continued with the 2 and the contract was thus easily beaten.

Note that this defence would also have been vital if South had started with the singleton king of spades, while if West had K-Q-x in spades originally, he would have had to unblock one of his honours under the ace.

Garozzo On Defence

In a teams tournament in Viareggio in 1977, Garozzo produced a spectacular defence. Here is the complete deal:

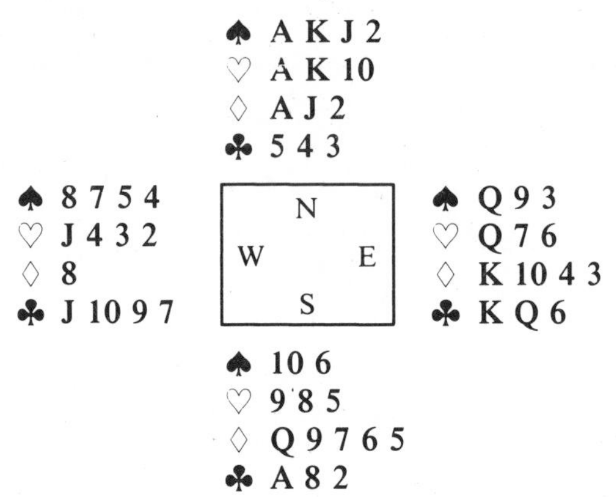

Both sides vulnerable. The bidding:

WEST *Belladonna*	NORTH	EAST *Garozzo*	SOUTH
Pass	1♣	Pass	1♢
Pass	1♠	Pass	2NT
Pass	3NT	All pass	

One Club showed at least 17 points, One Diamond was a negative, showing 0-6 points, and Two No-Trumps promised a maximum negative response.

Belladonna, West, led the jack of clubs. Garozzo overtook with the queen and continued with the king of clubs and a third club. Winning the ace South led a low diamond to West's 8 and dummy's jack. Had Garozzo won this with the king declarer would have had an easy nine tricks via two spades, two hearts, four diamonds and one club, but Benito began his brilliant defence by ducking the jack of diamonds. Declarer continued with ace and another diamond. On the second round of diamonds Belladonna was able to pitch a heart in comfort but on the third round he was in trouble and decided to let go his club winner.

Upon winning the king of diamonds Garozzo paused to reflect. The spade return could present declarer with the needed entry if South had the 10 of spades while the heart return would come to the same result if South held the jack. However, in the light of South's One Diamond response, Garozzo discounted the possibility of South holding the jack of hearts (since this in addition to South's known ace and queen would give South seven points). Accordingly Garozzo decided to switch to hearts but had he led a low heart it would have been fatal for the defence. South after winning West's jack with the king would have continued with the ace of hearts and another heart throwing Garozzo back on lead.

Therefore Garozzo came up with the winning return of the *queen* of hearts!

Winning in dummy with the ace, South continued with the jack of spades in an attempt to create an entry to hand with the 10 but Garozzo, still pursuing his precise defence, *ducked* the jack, following with the NINE! South cashed the ace of spades and Garozzo, still desperately trying to avoid the lead, unblocked the *queen!* Declarer played off the king of spades, leaving this ending:

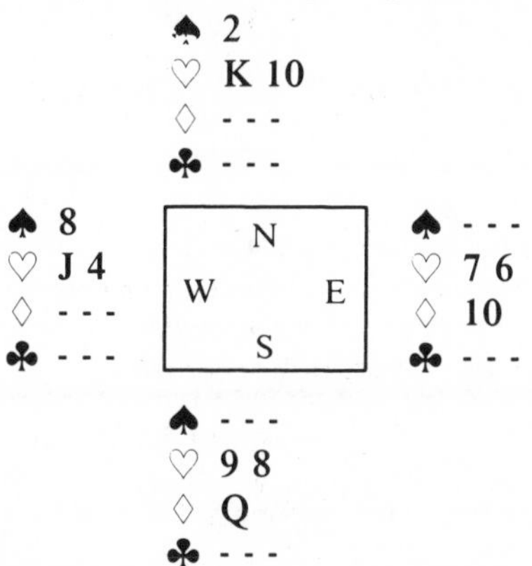

Despite all the hard work by the defence South could make his contract by leading dummy's spade and finessing on the forced heart return. However South was not certain of the end position and not unreasonably, in view of Garozzo's return of the queen of hearts, took the ending to be like this:

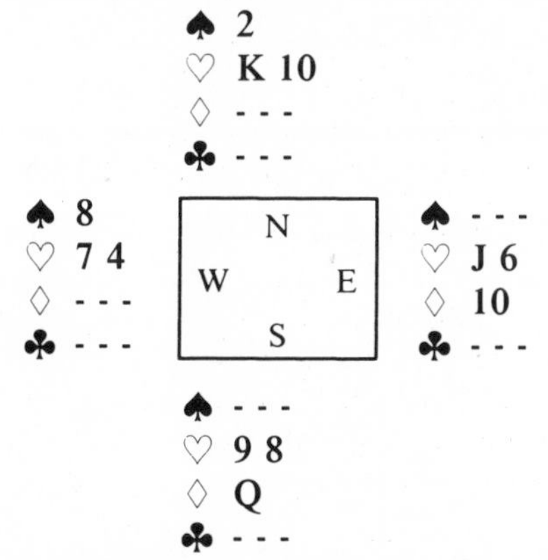

He therefore continued with the king of hearts and another heart, hoping to put East on lead as a stepping stone to his hand via the last diamond, but the actual layout doomed this move.

It is worth noting that if Belladonna had discarded a spade on the third round of diamonds, declarer would have made the contract easily. By leading the jack of spades from dummy, if East took the queen, declarer would have an entry to hand while if East ducked, dummy would make all four spade tricks. Similarly, if Belladonna had discarded a second heart his partner would not have been able to find the return of the queen of hearts without it costing a trick in that suit.

Double Your Chances

The narrow win by Belladonna and Garozzo in the pairs tournament at Porto Cervo in 1976 was due to the following deal where Benito Garozzo scored a well-deserved top, thanks to two brilliant decisions, one in the bidding and one in the play. Suppose you hold as South:

♠ A J   ♡ Q 9   ◊ A Q 9 8 7 6 3   ♣ K 10

North-South vulnerable. The bidding:

WEST	NORTH	EAST	SOUTH
Pass	Pass	1♠	2◊
2♠	3◊	Pass	3NT
4♠	Pass	Pass	?

What action would you take now?

Undoubtedly it would be prudent to double but Garozzo, in view of the vulnerability, preferred to take his chances for a better score and elected to bid Five Diamonds. West led the 2 of spades and Belladonna put down his hand:

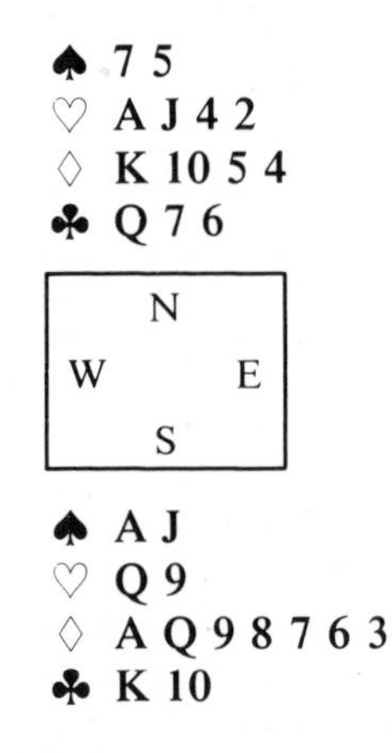

East played the king of spades on the lead.

How would you plan the play?

This was the complete hand:

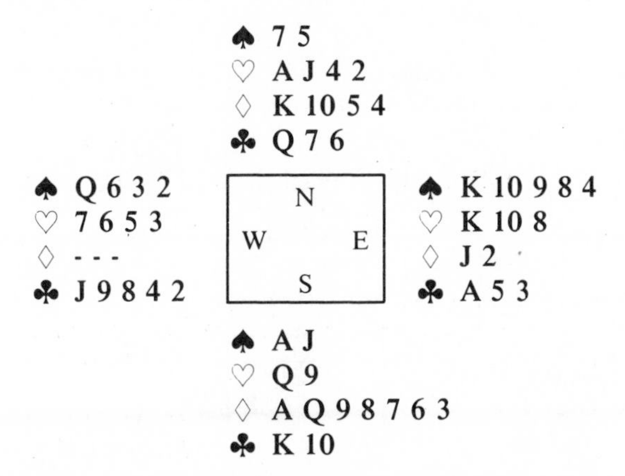

In view of East's opening bid, the heart finesse was sure to be futile. The heart loser therefore had to be eliminated some other way. One possibility was to lead a low club from dummy and finesse the 10: if East held the jack South would eventually be able to discard a heart on the queen of clubs. This play had about a 50% chance but Garozzo found a line that doubled this chance, given the almost marked position of the king of hearts and the ace of clubs.

At trick 1 declarer ducked East's king of spades, a vital move for his later plan. Winning the spade continuation, he cashed two trumps and led a low club from dummy. East had to duck and Garozzo after winning the king rattled off four more rounds of trumps, leading to this position:

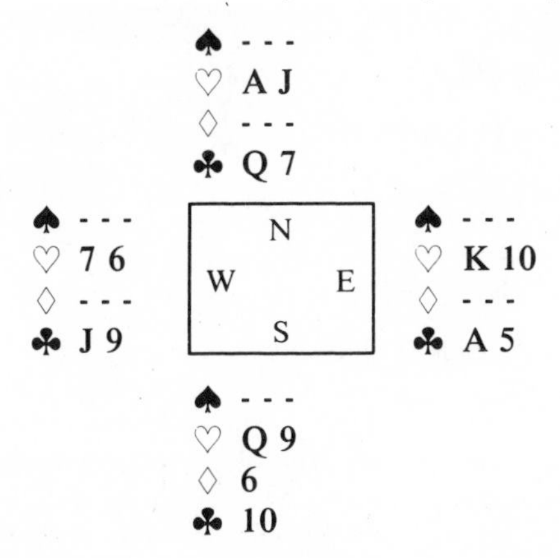

Garozzo led his last trump discarding a club from dummy. To retain the guard to the king of hearts, East discarded a club but this did not save him. At trick 12 he was thrown in with a club to his ace and forced to lead into the heart tenace.

Vivaldi's Inspiration

In the victory against Australia in the 1976 Olympiad, Antonio Vivaldi showed his technique on more than one occasion. Here he is in action as declarer in this Four Heart contract:

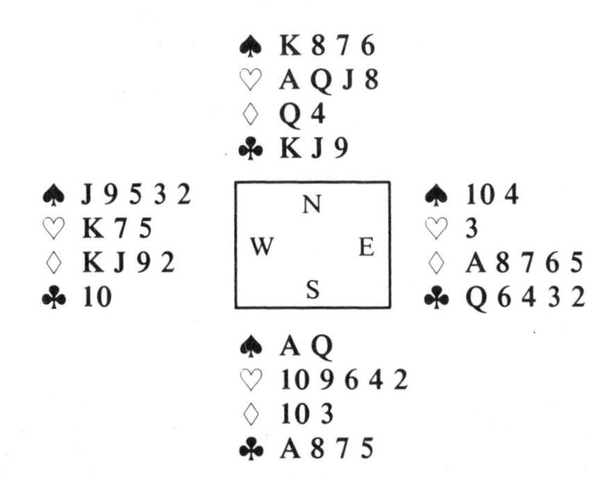

North-South vulnerable. The bidding:

WEST	NORTH *Belladonna*	EAST	SOUTH *Vivaldi*
	1♣	1◊	1♡
3◊	3♡	Pass	4♡
Pass	Pass	Pass	

West led the 10 of clubs.

How should declarer plan the play?

Obviously if South took the heart finesse after winning the lead, twelve tricks would roll in. Without being able to see all four hands, however, the heart finesse runs a grave risk for if it were to lose, the defence could take in addition to the king of hearts, two diamond tricks and a club ruff.

Accordingly, after the jack of clubs drew the queen to be captured by the ace, Vivaldi cashed the ace and queen of spades, crossed to dummy with a heart to the *ace* and discarded a diamond on the king of spades. The contract was now secure but if declarer had continued with the queen of hearts, the defence would have been able to score three tricks with the king of hearts, a diamond to the ace and a club ruff. Vivaldi brought in an overtrick by means of a simple "scissors coup", by discarding his second diamond on the fourth spade. This "loser on loser" severed the defence's communications and West's club ruff did not materialise.

On this next deal, take a look at Vivaldi's defence against 3NT:

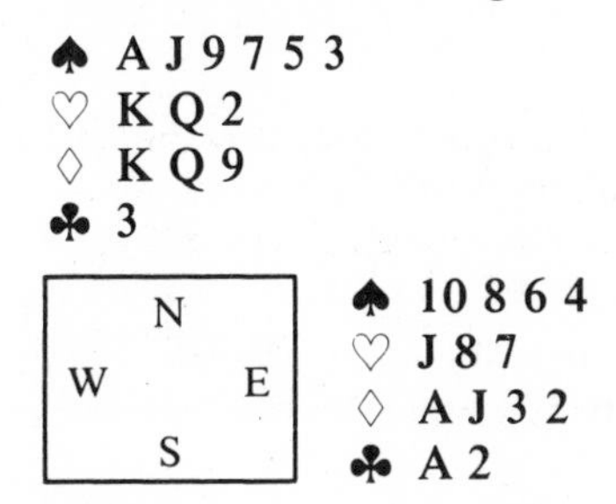

East-West vulnerable. The bidding:

WEST	NORTH	EAST	SOUTH
Belladonna		*Vivaldi*	
	1♠	Pass	2♣
Pass	2◊	Pass	2NT
Pass	3NT	All pass	

Belladonna led the 6 of hearts: two – jack – ace. Declarer continued with the queen of spades to the king and ace. Next came the jack of spades followed by a low spade, West discarding the 7 of clubs and the 5 of diamonds.

How would you plan the defence upon winning the 8 of spades?

This was the complete deal:

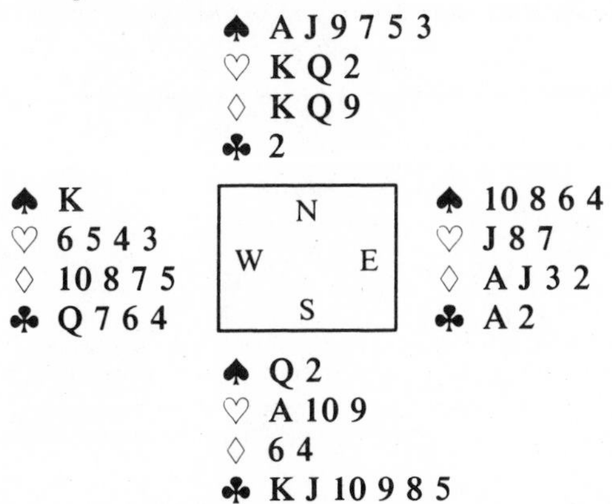

Vivaldi's defence guaranteed the defeat of the contract. After winning the third round of spades with the 8, he cashed the 10 of spades and the ace of clubs and locked declarer in dummy with a heart return. Declarer could not avoid conceding two diamond tricks at the end.

At the other table Arturo Franco was South in the same contract and West also led the 6 of hearts. The defence was less precise, however, and Franco succeeded in making the contract. If declarer leads the low spade from hand at trick 2 and not the queen, the contract will always succeed.

"You Could Have Made It!"

When his partner goes down in a contract, Benito Garozzo never fails to point out unerringly "You could have made it". These words are not always intended to be critical since Benito says exactly the same when he has hit upon the winning line of play which could be found *only double dummy.*

On this theme the following episode occurred during the qualifying rounds of the 1976 Bermuda Bowl. Playing against the Israeli team, I held as South:

♠ A K 8 2 ♡ A ◊ A 4 3 ♣ A K J 8 4

The bidding:

SOUTH *Forquet*	NORTH *Belladonna*
1♣	1♡
2♣	3♣
3◊	4◊
4♡	5♣
?	

What action would you have taken now?

Obviously I do not know your decision, but mine was Six Clubs which became the final contract. West led the queen of diamonds and when Belladonna put down dummy I realised that my decision was not exactly felicitous:

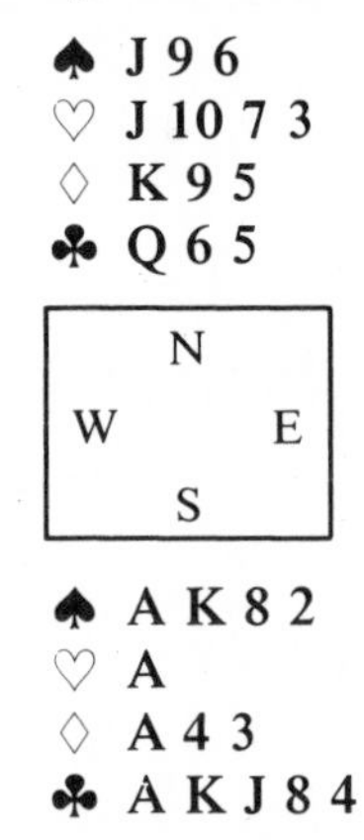

How would you have planned the play?

I won the lead with dummy's king of diamonds and led the jack of spades. East covered with the queen and I won the ace, continuing with the ace of clubs and a club to the queen. Next came the 6 of spades to my 8. When West ruffed this it was curtains.

This was the complete deal:

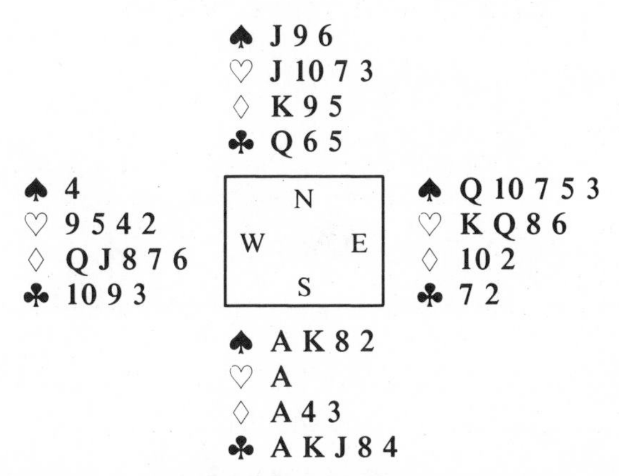

I did not regret bidding the slam, a decision that did not seem too risky, since if North could have come up with a useful queen instead of those two jacks *or* a doubleton spade *or* a doubleton diamond, the slam would have been a good contract. However, I resented West's holding three clubs for if he had started with only two, the slam would make thanks to the location of the Q-10 of spades.

These were roughly my thoughts when I recounted the slam to Garozzo at the end of the match. His comment was as swift and as punctual as usual: "You could have made it!" He immediately outlined the winning play: South wins the lead with the ace of diamonds, cashes three rounds of trumps ending in dummy, plays the jack of spades to the queen and ace, cashes another trump and the ace of hearts to reach this position:

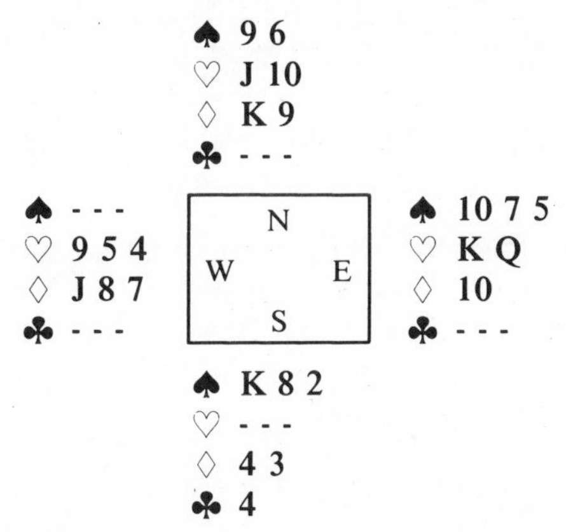

At this point South plays a diamond to the 9 and East, winning with the 10, is forced to return a heart in order not to concede a trick in spades. South ruffs and leads a diamond to the king, which squeezes East in spades and hearts. This is undoubtedly most brilliant notwithstanding it is a double dummy solution since it does presuppose a particular distribution of the remaining cards. Consequently my inner reaction was not exactly the same as my actual words, "You're right, Benito, I can make it!"

A Sacrifice Rewarded

During a tournament in the United States, Benito Garozzo playing with Omar Sharif found himself defending against this 3NT contract:

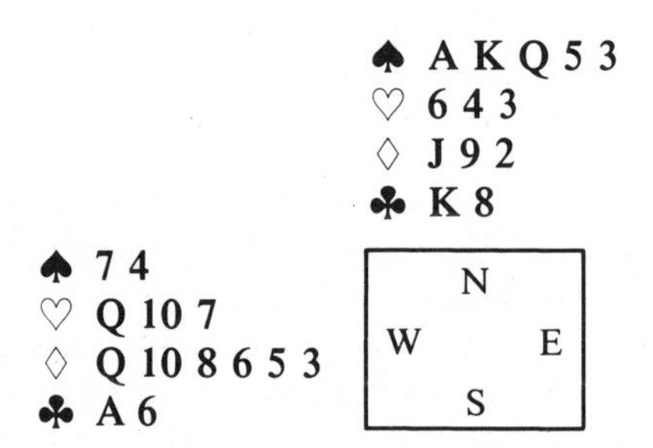

Both sides vulnerable. The bidding:

WEST	NORTH	EAST	SOUTH
Garozzo		*Sharif*	
	1♠	Pass	2♣
Pass	2♠	Pass	2NT
Pass	3NT	All pass	

Garozzo led a low diamond. Omar won with the ace and returned the 2 of hearts. Garozzo captured South's 9 with the 10 and continued with the queen of hearts which held the trick. Declarer won the third round of hearts with the ace and tabled the 2 of clubs.

What would you have done as West?

This was the complete deal:

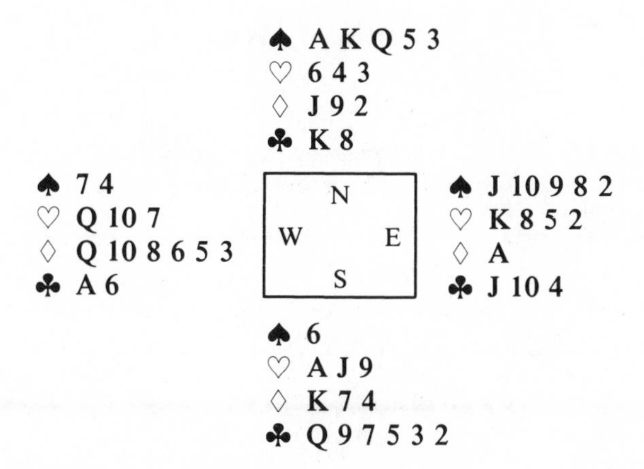

Had Garozzo ducked this, South would have made the contract. Winning with dummy's king, declarer would have led a second round of clubs, playing low from hand and setting up the whole club suit.

However, Garozzo appreciated the need to sever the communications between declarer and dummy. He rose with the ace of clubs and followed with the only card which could produce the desired result: the queen of diamonds!

This sacrifice gave declarer an extra diamond trick but prevented declarer from using the established club winners.

A Defensive Error

In choosing his line of play declarer should not overlook the possibility of a defensive error. Take for example this deal played during an exhibition match by the Blue Team:

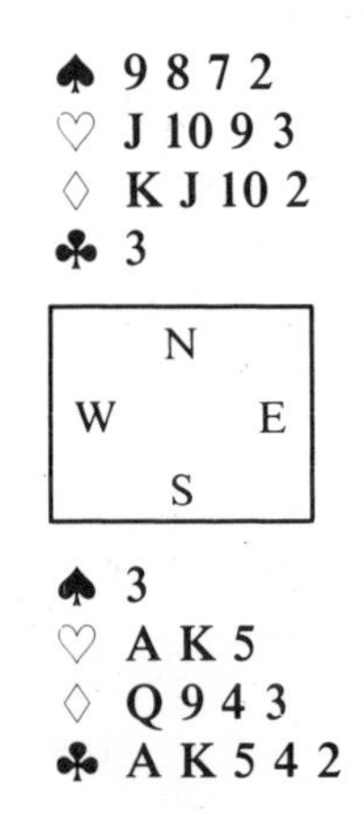

Neither side vulnerable. The bidding:

SOUTH	WEST	NORTH	EAST
Forquet		*Belladonna*	
1 ♢	Double	2 ♢	Pass
5 ♢	Pass	Pass	Pass

Playing Blue Team Club, South has an opening bid problem. As the hand does not meet the requirements for an opening of One Club (at least 17 points), the choice lies between Two Clubs and One Diamond. I chose One Diamond as I felt that the club suit lacked texture and that a Two Club opening would make it difficult to show the diamonds.

When Belladonna raised to Two Diamonds over West's double, prospects for game became excellent. A diamond raise in the Blue Team Club promises superb support since the One Diamond opening could be based on a three-card suit. Consequently I bid Five Diamonds at once and this ended the auction.

West led the ace of spades and continued with the king of spades, to which East followed with the 5 and the 4.

How would you have planned the play as South?

Do not consult the complete deal until you have planned your next move:

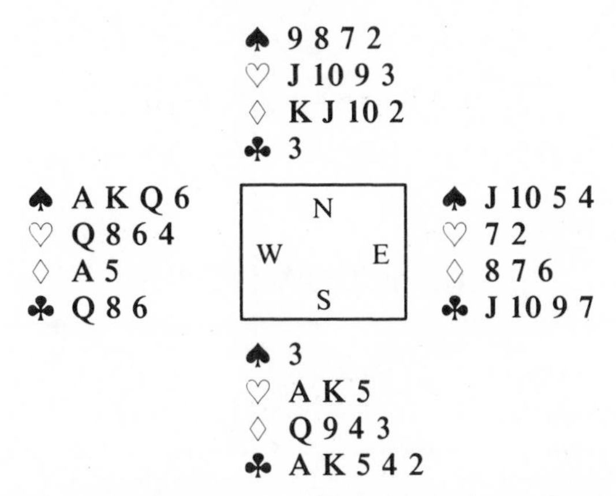

At first sight the contract seemes to hinge on the heart finesse together with a 3-3 break in that suit. If that is the case you can come to eleven tricks via three hearts, two clubs, three ruffs in hand and three in dummy.

However, after a close scrutiny of the position I spotted a line which offered a better chance, even though it might require a slight error by the defence. After ruffing the king of spades, I played the 3 of diamonds at trick 3. As I had hoped, West made the mistake of playing low, whereupon dummy's king won and so I was able to continue with a spade ruff, the ace and king of clubs (discarding a heart), a club ruff, a spade ruff, a club ruff and the ace and king of hearts. This was the end position with South on lead:

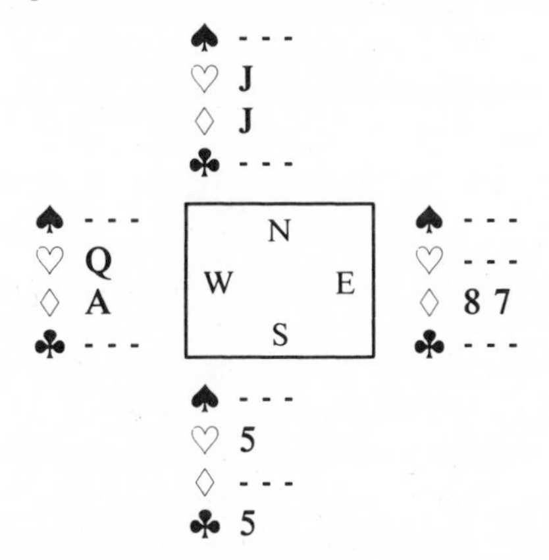

When I led my last club, West was unable to prevent me from scoring my jack of diamonds *en passant* and that was my eleventh trick.

West would have defeated the contract by taking the ace of diamonds at trick 3 and continuing with a diamond. However, if East would have held the queen of hearts three times, I would still have been able to succeed this way: win the diamond return in dummy, lead the jack of hearts letting it run if East plays low, a spade ruff, the ace and king of clubs (discarding a spade), the ace and king of hearts, a club ruff, dummy's last trump and the final heart winner.

Sojourn In Australia

Following the invitation of the Kingsgate Bridge Club of Sydney, the Lancia Bridge Team (Belladonna, Garozzo, Sharif and Forquet) toured Australia in March, 1976. In one of the matches in Sydney, Belladonna played the following slam:

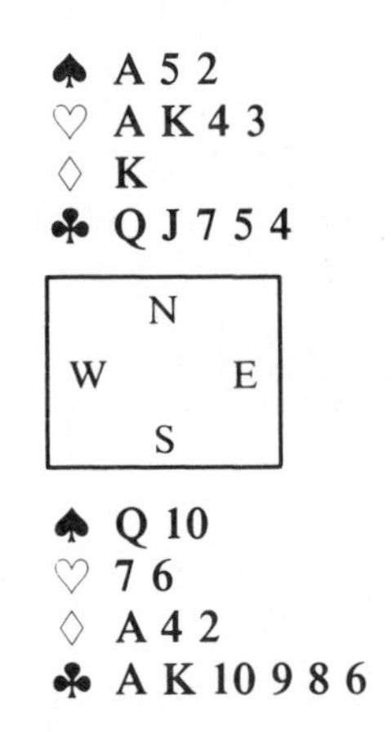

At the end of an extremely optimistic auction, Belladonna found himself faced with the task of securing the grand slam in clubs. The lead was the jack of hearts.

How would you have planned the play?

This was the complete deal:

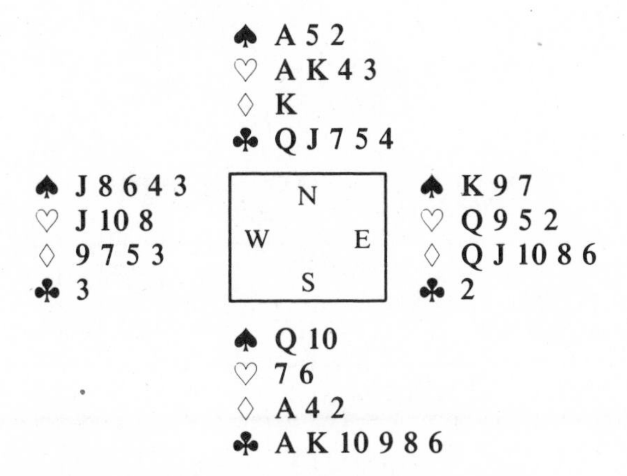

The only hope of making the contract lay in finding the king of spades and at least four hearts in the same hand.

Consequently, after winning with the ace of hearts, Belladonna organised the play to reach this ending:

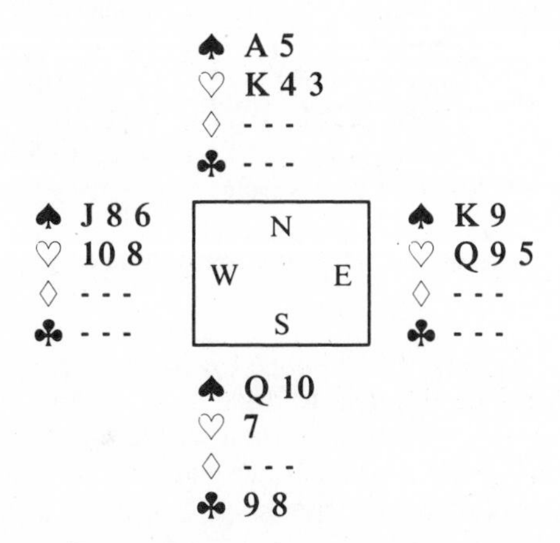

On the penultimate trump, Giorgio discarded the 5 of spades and East could not escape the squeeze. If he discarded a spade, South would have cashed the ace of spades, dropping the king and establishing the queen. If he discarded a heart, South would have followed with the king of hearts and a heart ruff, establishing dummy.

Tougher Than Expected

During the 1977 Italian Championships Benito Garozzo landed in this Four Spade contract:

♠ K 8 3 2
♡ A K 3
◊ J 4
♣ 8 7 5 4

	N	
W		E
	S	

♠ A Q J 4
♡ 9 8 2
◊ K 3 2
♣ A K 6

Neither side vulnerable. The bidding:

SOUTH	WEST	NORTH	EAST
Garozzo		*Belladonna*	
1NT	Pass	2♣*	Pass
2♠	Pass	4♠	All pass

*Enquiry for the majors

With 28 points in the combined hands and the powerful 4-4 trump fit, the spade game would normally present little difficulty. On the actual hand precise play is required to avoid losing four tricks (one heart, two diamonds and one club).

West led a low spade, East followed with the 9 and Garozzo won the ace.

How should South plan the play?

Garozzo elected to lead a low diamond towards dummy at trick 2 (perhaps it would have been more prudent to draw a second round of trumps first). His play would have allowed him to discard a heart from dummy on the king of diamonds whenever the queen of diamonds was in the West hand or the ace of diamonds was in the East hand.

Unluckily for Garozzo, East won the jack with the queen and when he continued with the 6 of diamonds, West took the king with the ace. When the 10 of diamonds was returned, Garozzo deduced the diamond division and ruffed with dummy's king of spades while East discarded a heart.

Even though the diamond honours were both badly placed, Garozzo still brought his contract home by means of an elegant manoeuvre.

How would you have continued in his position?

This was the complete deal:

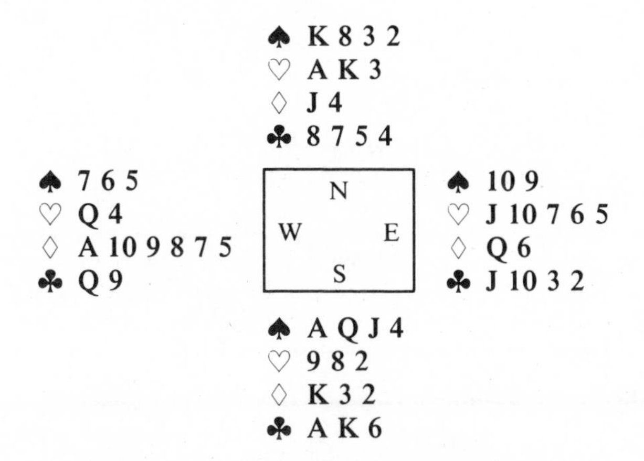

After winning with dummy's king of spades, Garozzo continued with three rounds of trumps, coming down to the following ending:

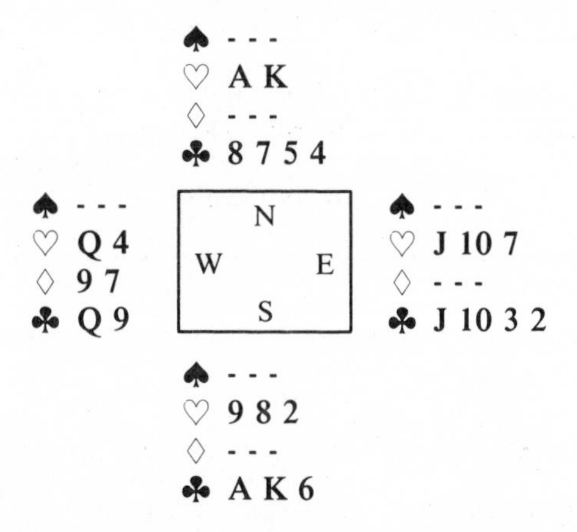

In this position East, who has yet to find a discard on the last round of spades is helpless: if he discards a club, South will run off three rounds of clubs, making dummy high; if he discards a heart, South will play off the two top hearts in dummy, setting up the third heart in hand.

The contract thus succeeded but East could have defeated the game if at trick 3 he had led a heart instead of a diamond. Then when West gains the lead with the ace of diamonds, a second round of hearts would destroy the entries needed for the squeeze.

At the other table North-South reached 3NT without ever mentioning the spades. West led a diamond and declarer had nine tricks there and then.

Teamwork

During the Intercontinental Trophy played in Rome in 1977 and won by the Inim Blue Team (Belladonna, Garozzo, Pittala, Vivaldi and Forquet, captain Cumani), Garozzo on the one hand and Belladonna on the other shared the honours on this well deserved pickup.

Here are the North-South cards:

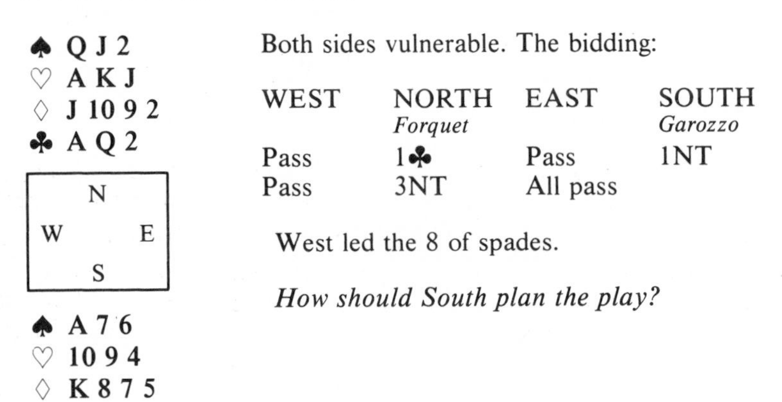

Both sides vulnerable. The bidding:

WEST	NORTH *Forquet*	EAST	SOUTH *Garozzo*
Pass	1♣	Pass	1NT
Pass	3NT	All pass	

West led the 8 of spades.

How should South plan the play?

This was the complete deal:

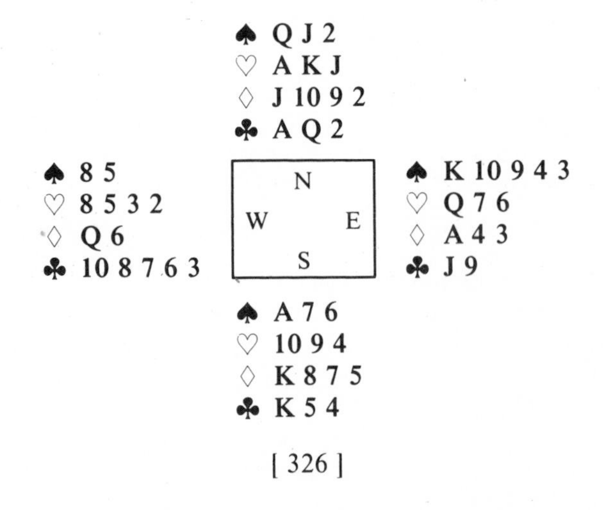

The lead of the 8 had the semblance of a doubleton and was in fact the highest spade held by West who, with little of value in his own hand, was apparently trying to hit his partner's long suit.

As a result of deliberating along these lines Garozzo decided to duck the lead both in dummy and in hand. This disrupted the defence and allowed him to establish the diamonds before the opponents could set up the spades.

West's spade continuation was won with dummy's queen (if East had covered, Garozzo after taking the ace of spades would have returned to dummy with a club to the ace) and the rest was routine: jack of diamonds losing to the queen, the heart return taken by the ace and the next diamond won by East's ace. Thus Garozzo came to nine tricks via two spades, two hearts, two diamonds and three clubs.

At the other table the bidding went:

WEST	NORTH	EAST	SOUTH
Vivaldi		*Belladonna*	
Pass	1♢	1♠	1NT
Pass	3NT	All pass	

West, Vivaldi, also led the 8 of spades but declarer mechanically played the queen from dummy. Far less mechanically, Belladonna decided to duck the queen. This move ensured the contract would be defeated.

Understanding the danger South sought some safety in leading the jack of diamonds to his king. Given that the ace of diamonds would be with East, just as surely as the king of spades, this line would have succeeded if West had started with Q-x-x in diamonds and East with only A-x, for then the second round of diamonds would have been won by East, the "safe" hand. Even if East had started with A-Q-x, South would be safe since East would be unable to attack the spade position without losing a trick thereby.

Unfortunately for declarer the queen was doubleton with West, not tripleton, and so when West won the second round of diamonds, it was no problem to find the killing spade continuation. As the spades were now set up, with declarer having only eight tricks in sight (two spades, two hearts, one diamond and three clubs), South tried the heart finesse for the ninth trick. The result was thus two down.

Of course you have already worked out that if Belladonna had covered the queen of spades with the king at trick 1, South would have been able to make the contract by letting the king win. South would then have been able to establish the diamonds before the spades became dangerous.

Defence Was Not Meant To Be Easy

Very often the approach adopted by the defence provides useful information for declarer. Take for example the following contract from the 1977 Italian Championships:

♠ A Q 7 4
♡ K 7 6
◊ J 3 2
♣ A 8 3

N
W E
S

♠ K 3
♡ A 8 5 4 3
◊ K 6 5
♣ Q 5 4

Both sides vulnerable. The bidding:

WEST	NORTH *Avarelli*	EAST	SOUTH *Forquet*
Pass	1♣	Pass	1♡
Pass	1♠	Pass	2NT
Pass	3♡	Pass	4♡
Pass	Pass	Pass	

West led the jack of clubs. I ducked in dummy and after winning with the king, East returned the 2 of clubs. Dummy's ace took the trick and when I cashed the king and ace of hearts, everybody followed. I played the third round of hearts and upon winning the queen, West played the third round of clubs taken by the queen. Your problem is to avoid losing two tricks in diamonds.

How would you proceed?

This was the complete deal:

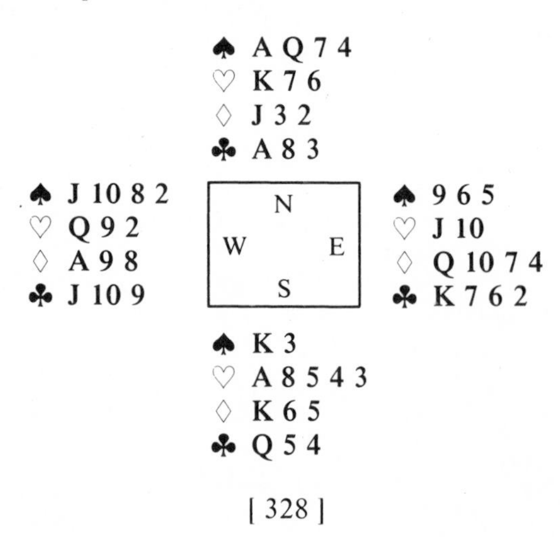

One diamond loser can be discarded on the third round of spades and then if East held the ace of diamonds, I could set up the king by leading a diamond from dummy. How likely is it, though, that East does have the ace of diamonds? The club return at trick 2 made it almost certain that East did not have the ace of diamonds for if he did, he would surely have switched to diamonds at trick 2 when he knew that I had the queen of clubs as well as the ace.

Therefore I elected to play for a spade-diamond squeeze on West and accordingly cashed another trump to arrive at this ending:

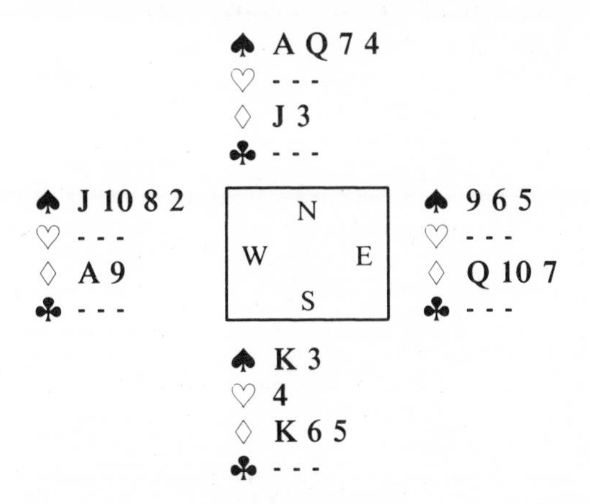

When I led my last trump West was forced to bare the ace of diamonds to preserve his four spades. I discarded a diamond from dummy and continued with a low diamond, setting up my king.

After the hand was over a kibitzer ventured that if West had returned a spade after winning the queen of hearts, this would have broken up the entries for the squeeze. This is in fact not so. I would have won the spade return in hand and still led the last two trumps. West would have been squeezed down to the bare ace of diamonds as above but I would have discarded a spade from dummy on the last trump and kept two diamonds.

Trick Or Treat?

On the following deal from the 1977 Porto Cervo Pairs Tournament an unusual ending arose. While I was endeavouring to secure my tenth trick by trumping a loser in dummy, the lie of the cards caused this plan to evaporate but in its place a squeeze arose and the outcome was an overtrick.

♠ 9 5 4
♡ A 9 2
◇ A Q J 3
♣ K Q 3

N
W E
S

♠ A J 3
♡ K Q 10 8 6
◇ 2
♣ 7 6 5 4

North-South vulnerable. The bidding:

WEST	NORTH	EAST	SOUTH
	Saladino		*Forquet*
		Pass	1♡
Pass	2◇	Double	Pass
Pass	3♣	Pass	3♡
Pass	4♡	All pass	

West led the 3 of hearts, East produced the jack and I won the king.

How would you have continued in my place?

In view of East's double of Two Diamonds, showing values in the black suits, and West's penalty pass of the double, I placed the king of diamonds with West and at trick 2 I led a low diamond to the jack which won the trick.

At this stage I could have taken a spade pitch on the ace of diamonds and all that remained was to avoid losing three tricks in clubs. As there was no urgency to take the spade pitch, I turned my attention to clubs.

Since the ace of clubs was marked with East and since the double indicated that clubs would not be 3-3, I intended to ruff the fourth round of clubs in dummy. Consequently at trick 3 I led the king of clubs. East took the ace and continued with the ten of clubs after West had dropped the jack of clubs under the ace. West ruffed the second round of clubs and switched to the 2 of spades to East's king and my ace. I cashed the ace of hearts, hoping that this would eliminate the remaining trumps but East discarded a club on this and so West still had a trump left.

How would you have continued?

This was the complete deal:

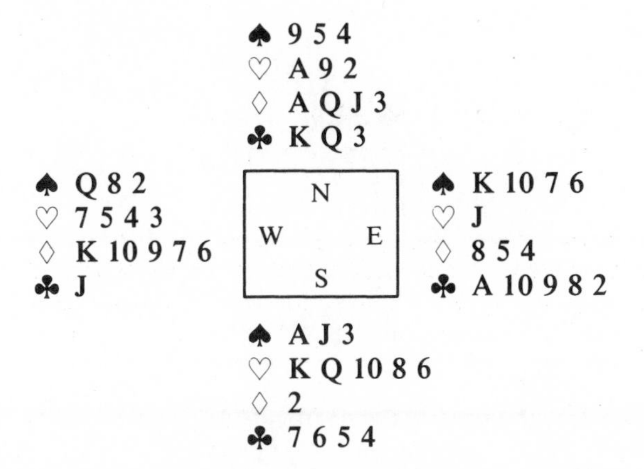

Unable to play off the queen of clubs for West would ruff this, I cashed three more rounds of trumps leading to this end-position:

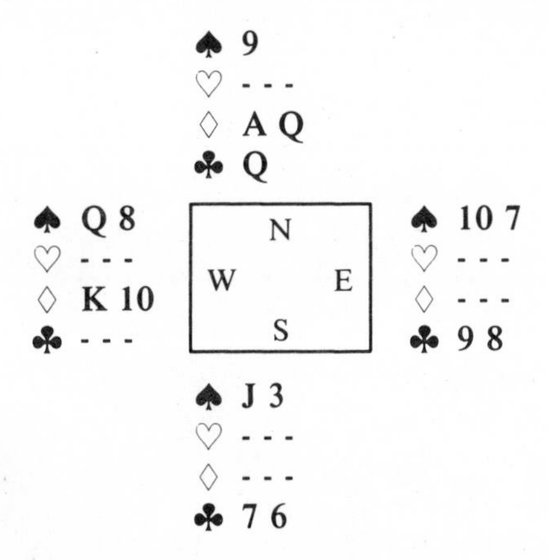

My new plan was to squeeze West when I led a club to the queen. In order to hold on to the king-doubleton in diamonds West would have to bare the queen of spades. I would then exit with a spade, forcing West to lead a diamond and allowing dummy to take the marked finesse.

Making Four Hearts would already have given us a good board but West took a view which allowed me to score an absolute top. When I led a club to the queen, West could see what was coming and to avoid the endplay West decided to discard the *queen* of spades in the hope that his partner held the jack. This was the ending:

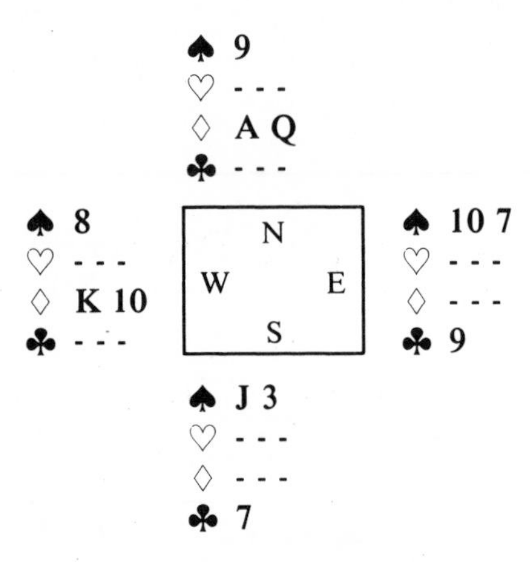

When I cashed the ace of diamonds East found himself in the vice of a spade-club squeeze. Thus the contract was made with an overtrick!

Sidestepping The Snare

In the teams tournament in Monte Carlo in 1975 which was won by the Lancia-Alitalia Bridge team, I was able to defeat this Four Spade game thanks to an expedient little stratagem:

	North	
	♠ 7 5 4 ♡ A K ♢ 8 6 4 3 ♣ Q 7 5 4	
♠ A Q 8 6 ♡ Q 10 5 4 ♢ 10 7 ♣ 8 6 3	N W E S	

Neither side vulnerable. The bidding:

SOUTH	WEST	NORTH	EAST
	Forquet		*Sharif*
1♠	Pass	1NT	Pass
2♣	Pass	3♠	Pass
4♠	Pass	Pass	Pass

I led the 4 of hearts and dummy's ace won. East playing the 9. Declarer led the 4 of spades: 3 from East - jack from declarer . . .

How would you have defended in my place?

This was the complete deal:

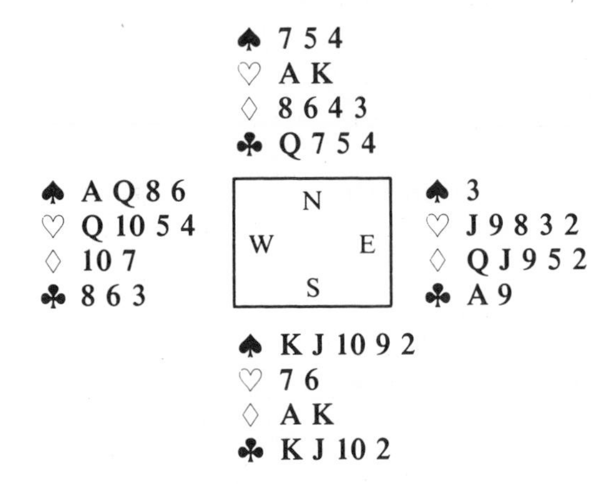

Hoping that declarer might lose trump control, I decided to let the jack of spades win.

South fell into my little trap. Confident of finding East with at least the queen of spades, he returned to dummy with a heart to the king and continued with another spade. Taking South's 10 with the queen, I cashed the ace of spades and continued with a third heart. Declarer ruffed but as he had only one trump left (as did I) and still needed to dislodge the ace of clubs, he was unable to bring in the contract.

At the other table the bidding went like this:

SOUTH *Garozzo*	WEST	NORTH *Belladonna*	EAST
1♠	Pass	2♠	Pass
3♣	Pass	4♠	All pass

Belladonna's Two Spade response despite holding only three cards in the suit was justified as they were playing 'Precision' in which the opening bid of one of a major promises at least a five-card suit.

West produced exactly the same defence as I did at trick 2 but nevertheless Benito Garozzo made his contract.

When he won trick 2 with the jack of spades, instead of returning to dummy via the king of hearts as our declarer did, Benito continued with the king of spades from hand. West took the ace and pursued the hearts, dummy's king winning the trick.

This was the position:

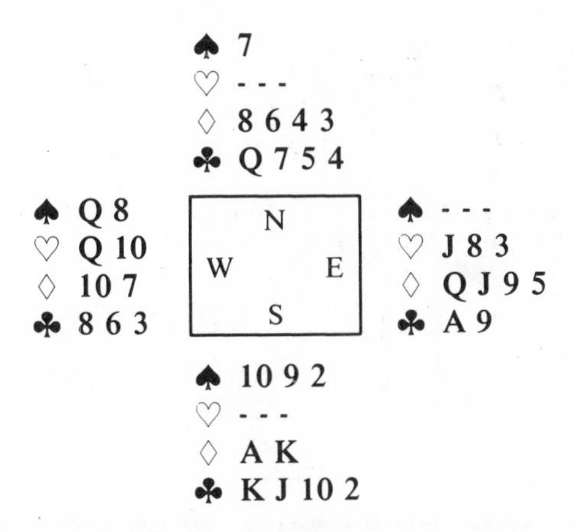

If at this point declarer had led the third round of spades, he would also have lost trump control, since after winning the queen of spades, West would have forced declarer with another heart.

However Garozzo neatly sidestepped this trap and instead of spades he played a diamond to the ace and the 2 of clubs to dummy's queen. East won with the ace but dummy's last trump protected declarer from any damage in the heart department.

The contract would have been unmakable if East had held A-x-x in clubs. In that case all that East would need to do would be to duck the queen of clubs, leaving South impaled on the horns of a Socratic dilemma: whether to die by being forced off (lead a trump next) or whether to die by letting West ruff a club (continue with clubs).

However, it is worth noting how Garozzo manoeuvred to try to induce East to make a mistake and take the ace of clubs at once even if he did have A-x-x. Instead of leading the queen of clubs from dummy, thus advertising great strength in clubs, he came to hand to lead a club up to the queen in dummy, thereby suggesting a broken holding and inducing East to win the queen mechanically with the ace. Very instructive.

Variations On A Theme By Belladonna

In a teams tournament in Venice in 1976 Giorgio Belladonna was declarer in the following Four Spade contract:

♠ A Q 10 2
♡ A K 7 5
◊ K 3
♣ 10 7 4

At both tables the bidding went as follows:

WEST	NORTH	EAST	SOUTH
Pass	Pass	Pass	1NT
Pass	2♣	Pass	2♠
Pass	4♠	All pass	

At one table West led the 9 of diamonds. East won the ace and returned the queen of diamonds, taken by the king. Declarer crossed to dummy with a club to the ace and tabled the 9 of spades, letting it run. West won the jack of spades and returned a diamond to East's jack. After ruffing this, declarer returned to dummy with a club to the king and took a second finesse in spades. The queen won the trick but the bad news was that West discarded a diamond.

This was the position:

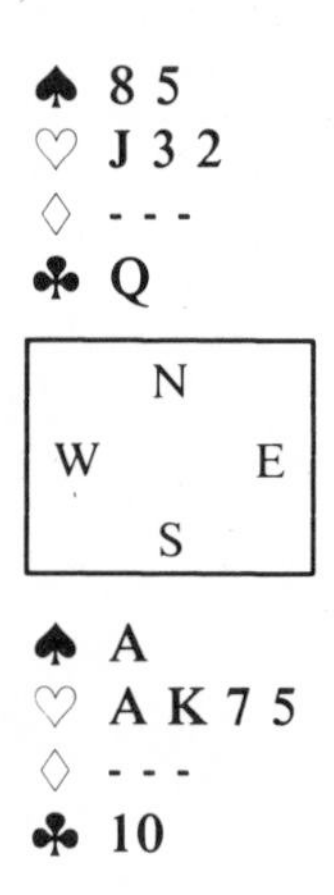

Having already lost two tricks and bound to lose a trick to the king of spades, South must try to avoid losing a trick in hearts. To this end declarer cashed the ace of spades, crossed to dummy with a club to the queen and continued with the last spade, throwing East on lead with the king. If East had only hearts left including the queen, the contract would have succeeded.

However, this was the complete deal:

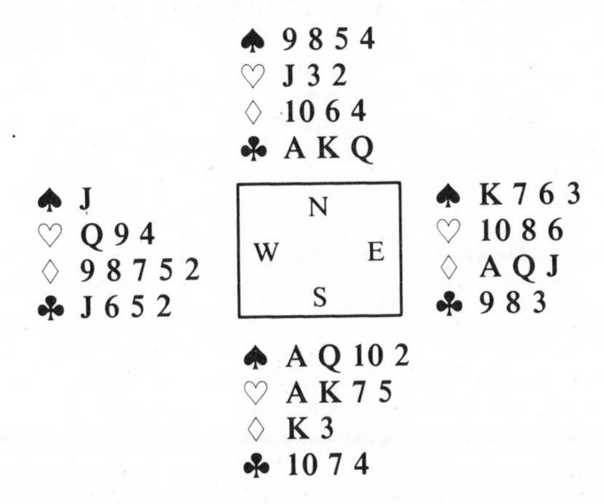

As the queen of hearts was in fact with West, the contract was defeated.

At the other table the play proceeded identically for the first three tricks. At trick 4, instead of leading the *nine* of spades from dummy, Belladonna led the *four* of spades. This apparently inconsequential choice determined the outcome of the hand.

West won the 10 of spades with the jack and continued with diamonds. Declarer ruffed, crossed to dummy with a club to the king and finessed the queen of spades, on which West discarded a diamond. At this point Belladonna could have tried to solve his problems in exactly the same way as his counterpart had, but Giorgio discounted the possibility of East holding the queen of hearts. East had already turned up with ten points and if he had started with the queen of hearts as well, he certainly would not have passed in third seat.

Have you spotted the winning play?

Belladonna cashed the queen of clubs and played three rounds of hearts to achieve this rare ending:

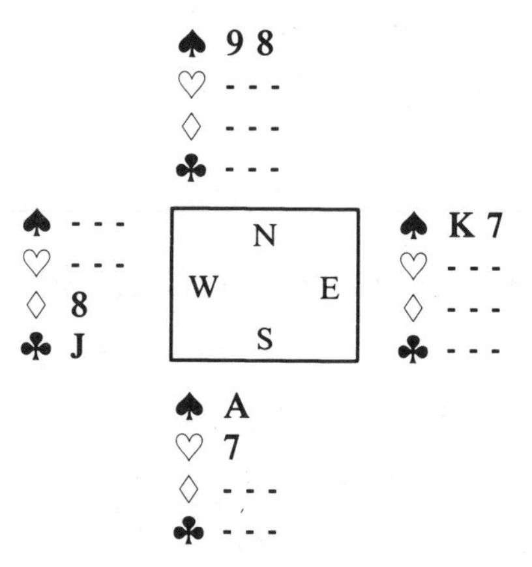

West won the queen of hearts and naturally had to lead a minor suit. It did not matter which he led, for Belladonna ruffed with the 9 of spades in dummy and East had no answer. If he overruffed with the king, South would win the ace and dummy's 8 of spades would be high, while if he underruffed with the 7, South would have simply discarded a heart.

This is a classic "smother coup" and you have no doubt satisfied yourself that the coup would not have worked if declarer had led the 9 or the 8 of spades on the first round of trumps.

Bridge Over Untroubled Waters

Following an invitation from the *Costa Armatori* the members of the Blue Team took part in the Greek bridge cruise on board the motor-vessel *Flavia* in September, 1978. In one of the tournaments Benito Garozzo and I were opponents on this deal:

♠ A K 3 2
♡ 5 4
♢ K 6 2
♣ J 7 4 3

	N	
W		E
	S	

♠ Q 10 6 5
♡ K 7
♢ Q 5 4
♣ A K 9 5

WEST	NORTH	EAST	SOUTH
Garozzo			*Forquet*
1♡	Pass	Pass	Double
Pass	2♡	Pass	2♠
Pass	3♠	Pass	4♠
Pass	Pass	Pass	

Garozzo, West, led the 8 of clubs. I played the jack from dummy and won East's queen with the ace.

How would you have planned the play as South?

With West certain to hold both red aces, the problem lies in losing no tricks in the black suits and no more than three in the red suits.

First of all, how should trumps be played? Normally with this combination it is best to play off dummy's ace and king first to cater for J-x-x-x on the right. In the given circumstances, however, this play has little merit, for if the trumps were 3-2, cashing the ace and king would lead to entry problems and if trumps were 4-1, the contract would have little hope of success in any event.

Consequently I cashed the queen of spades at trick 2 and continued with the 5 to dummy's ace, Garozzo following to this trick with the *jack.*

How would you have continued? Would you have cashed the king of spades next or would you have played on clubs first?

This was the complete deal:

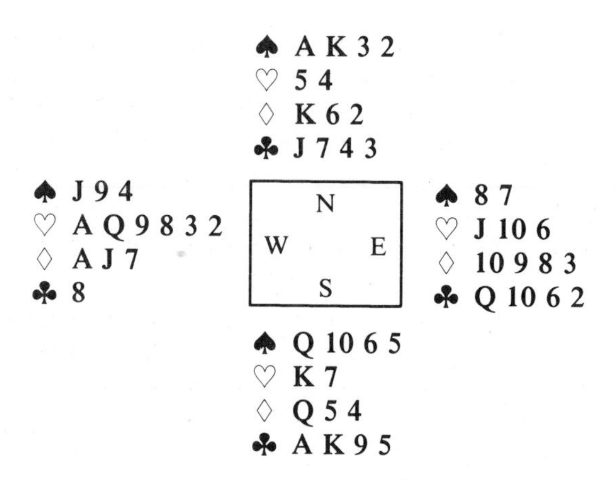

The lead of the 8 of clubs by West is indicative of a singleton or a doubleton. If it were a singleton, it would be necessary to take two more finesses in clubs to avoid losing a trick there. My initial reaction was that as the entries to dummy were limited and as Garozzo's jack of spades looked like he started with only two spades, it would be best to continue with the 7 of clubs at trick 4. After this forced East to cover with the 10, I could cross to dummy with a spade to the ace and then finesse against East's 6 of clubs.

A moment's reflection, however, made it clear that it would cost me nothing to draw the last trump before tackling the clubs. In addition, drawing the last trump would spare me the indignity of a club ruff if Benito had in fact started with three spades and had craftily dropped the jack on the second round of trumps to try to make me drop my guard.

After the king of spades I did cash the ace and saw with some satisfaction that it was indeed Garozzo who had the last trump. The 7 of clubs came next and after I had taken East's 10 with my king, this was the position:

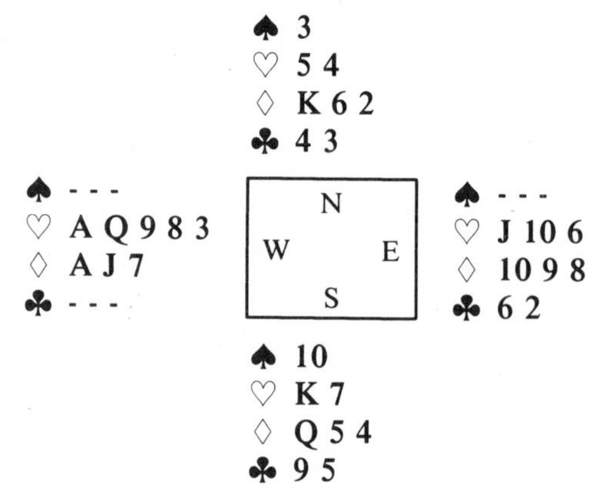

How would you have continued as declarer?

Suppose that South leads a low diamond to the king, followed by two rounds of clubs, finessing against East's 6, and then a diamond. If West has failed to jettison the jack of diamonds on the first round of that suit, he will be forced at this point to return a heart and thus provide declarer with the tenth trick.

Against Garozzo of course, the described line would certainly fail. On the other hand, if South plays a diamond to the king and two rounds of clubs and follows up with the king of hearts, West will exit with a low heart to East who can then bring the diamonds through the queen.

A better line of play but also destined to fail against expert defence is this: a diamond to the king, two rounds of clubs followed by the last trump in order to reduce West to four cards. However, West can come down to A-9 in hearts and A-7 in diamonds and will thus escape being endplayed.

What then is the winning line of play?

My continuation was the 7 of hearts. Garozzo played low but upon winning East was helpless. If he returned a heart he would have endplayed West into opening up the diamond suit or conceding a ruff-and-discard. East tried to solve the problem by leading the 10 of diamonds but I naturally let it run to dummy's king, took the club finesse and exited with the king of hearts, forcing Benito to give me my second diamond trick or the ruff-and-discard.

Had East exited with a club instead of the 10 of diamonds, I would have won in hand and continued with a diamond to the king followed by a heart to the king, coming to the same conclusion.

Being Wise After The Event

It is common knowledge that when a 4-4 major fit is held, it is preferable to play in that trump suit rather than no-trumps. Nevertheless, since the exception proves the rule, take a look at what happened to Omar Sharif and me in the 1975 Monte Carlo Teams Tournament which was won by the Lancia-Alitalia Bridge Team.

With North-South vulnerable, South picked up this collection:

♠ A K 9 8
♡ 8 5 4
♢ 10 7 3
♣ Q J 8

Omar, North, opened One Diamond which in the Blue Team Club was commonly a three-card suit in a balanced hand. I responded One Spade and Omar raised to Two Spades, promising four-card support.

Perhaps I should have passed in view of my flat shape but my ten points persuaded me to make one more try. I bid Two No-Trumps to which partner replied Three Hearts, showing high card strength in that suit and simultaneously offering a choice between Four Spades and Three No-Trumps.

Thinking I had done enough on my modest values I tried to sign off in Three Spades but Omar still had some values in reserve and continued with Three No-Trumps. As I suspected that my 4-3-3-3 shape was likely to be opposite another 4-3-3-3 shape, I decided to pass instead of converting to Four Spades.

This then had been the bidding:

WEST	NORTH *Sharif*	EAST	SOUTH *Forquet*
	1♢	Pass	1♠
Pass	2♠	Pass	2NT
Pass	3♡	Pass	3♠
Pass	3NT	All pass	

West led the 3 of clubs and Omar tabled his hand:

I viewed the dummy with mixed emotions. I regretted not having passed Two Spades but I was delighted that we had settled in Three No-Trumps and avoided Four Spades.

East won the king of clubs and returned the 9 of clubs. West played the 2, letting me hold the trick with the queen.

How would you have planned the play as declarer?

This was the complete deal:

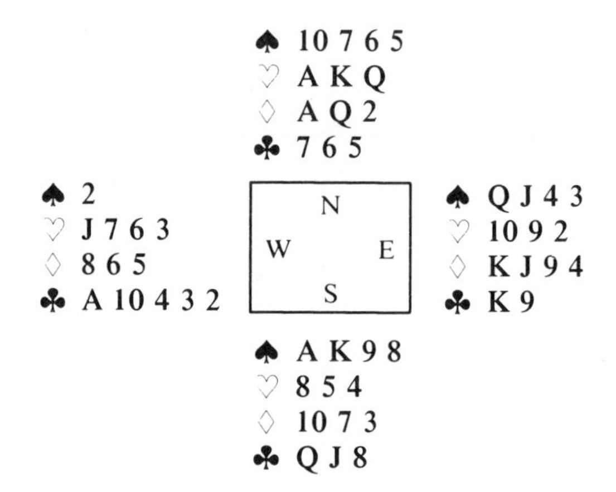

Seven tricks were available. Two more had to be found and the spade suit would have to be developed. Nevertheless before tackling the spades I thought the diamond finesse should be taken. If this finesse worked, I would need to play the spades for only *three* tricks; if it lost, I would have to try to obtain *four* tricks from the spades.

So, after being left on lead with the queen of clubs, I led a low diamond to the queen. East won the king and switched to a heart. Since I now knew that I would need four spade tricks, I had to rely on the double finesse in spades (a much better chance than playing West to hold a singleton honour). The favourable layout of the spade honours spelled success.

It is interesting to note that East would have defeated the contract *if he had played low on the queen of diamonds!* As I would then need only three spade tricks, I would have cashed the ace and king of spades in order to minimise the risk of West gaining the lead. The play would go: low spade from dummy rising with the ace when East played low, back to dummy with a heart, low spade from dummy and rising with the king when East again played low. This line prevents West obtaining the lead if East began with Q-x in spades and West with J-x-x, for if East played the queen on the first or the second round of spades, East would be allowed to hold the trick. This play is superior to the double finesse which would lose if West had started with one or two honours singleton or doubleton or J-x-x, while it would lose a makable game only if East started with Q-J-x-x. (I could cope with Q-J-x-x-x with East for this would be revealed on the first round of spades and I could then lead a low spade to dummy's 10, finessing against East's remaining honour later.)

On a close analysis of the bidding and the play as it went, one can conclude that all the clues were available for East to find this sparkling defence. Still, is it easy to find such a play at the table?

SUMMARY OF SYSTEMS USED BY THE BLUE TEAM

THE BLUE TEAM CLUB*

THE OPENING BIDS OF 1 DIAMOND, 1 HEART, 1 SPADE

These require at least four cards in the suit bid (except for 1 Diamond which is permissible on a three-card suit).

A strong two-suiter (with an upper limit of 16 high card points) is shown by bidding the weaker suit first and the stronger suit later: if the weaker suit is lower in rank, this is done by a reverse bid, while if the weaker suit is higher in rank, this is shown by a jump bid on the second round. The second bid suit is at least five cards long except when the jump bid is into clubs, where the first suit is normally a six-card suit and the clubs a four-card suit. For example:

1♡	1NT
3♣ . . .	

Opener is showing six hearts and four clubs.

RESPONSES

- Natural in principle.

With a hand worth a force to game, responder may reverse into his strong suit, bidding first a weaker suit which need not be biddable but must contain first- or second-round control.

- 2 No-Trumps or a raise of opener's suit.

These are limit bids which opener with a minimum is permitted to pass.

- Jump in a new suit.

This promises a solid or semi-solid suit at least six cards long and is forcing to game.

*The development of the bidding is too complex to cover fully in this summary. For the complete systemic treatment you should consult the original 'Blue Team Club'.

THE ONE CLUB OPENING

Conventional opening, showing at least 17 high card points, any shape

Responses with no opposition intereference

Conventional, showing the number of controls held (king = one control, ace = two controls):

1♢	=	0-2 controls, 0-5 points
1♡	=	0-2 controls, 6 points or more
1♠	=	3 controls
1NT	=	4 controls
2♣	=	5 controls
2♢	=	6 controls
2♡	=	3-5 points and a six-card heart suit with at least two honours
2♠	=	3-5 points and a six-card spade suit with at least two honours
2NT	=	7 controls or more

Notes:

1♡ is forcing to 2NT.

1♠ is forcing to game except for the one sequence: 1♣ : 1♠, 1NT : 2NT.

If after a one-level response, opener jumps to 2 No-Trumps, this shows a balanced hand of 23-24 points.

After the initial control-showing response, bidding follows natural principles.

Responses after opposition interference

(a) The interference is 1 Diamond

Responder replaces the 1 Diamond response (0-5 points) with Pass; with 6 points or more *and* two controls, responder bids 1 Heart, while with 6 points or more *and less than* two controls, responder doubles. All other responses have exactly the same meaning as though there had been no interference.

(b) The interference is 1 Heart, 1 Spade or 1 No-Trump

In these cases, the 1 Diamond response is replaced by Pass, and the 1 Heart response is replaced by Double. All other responses are given in steps, starting from the bid made by the opposition, but noting that the responses of 2 Hearts and 2 Spades count as steps only if that was the suit bid by the opposition. Otherwise they are still the natural 3-5 point bids.

(c) The interference is 2 Clubs, 2 Diamonds, 2 Hearts, 2 Spades

Here, too, 1 Diamond is replaced by Pass and 1 Heart is replaced by Double. Other actions:

2NT shows three or four controls.

Cue bid of enemy suit shows five or more controls.

Bidding any suit without a jump bid shows a six-card suit with at least two honours but less than six points.

(d) The interference is 2 No-Trumps or 3-of-a-suit

Any suit bid is natural and forcing for at least one round.

THE ONE NO-TRUMP OPENING

This shows a balanced hand with 13-17 points. If the strength is 13-15 points, opener will hold length in clubs. Where the strength is 16-17 points, any balanced shape is permissible.

Responses

Pass shows 0-8 points

2 Clubs is conventional with 8-11 points. Opener's rebids are:
- 2 Diamonds shows 13-14 points
- 2 Hearts shows 15 points (or 14 points and five clubs)
- 2 Spades shows 16-17 points
- 2 No-Trumps shows 15 points and five clubs

2 Diamonds is conventional showing 12 points or more, forcing to game. Opener rebids as follows:
- 2 Hearts shows at least four hearts, does *not* deny spades.
- 2 Spades shows at least four spades, *denies* four hearts.
- 2 No-Trumps shows 13-15 points.
- 3 Clubs shows 16-17 points, no four-card major.

2 Hearts is a sign-off.

2 Spades is a sign-off.

2 No-Trumps shows 9-10 points with no interest in the majors.

3-of-any-suit shows 6-7 points and a six-card suit headed by A-K, A-Q or K-Q.

3 No-Trumps shows 12-14 points.

4 Clubs is a transfer to 4 Hearts.

4 Diamonds is a transfer to 4 Spades.

THE TWO CLUB OPENING

This shows 12-16 points, at least five clubs and possibly a second suit.

Responses

2 Diamonds is an artificial relay, forcing for one round. Opener's rebids:
- 2 Hearts, 2 Spades and 3 Diamonds are natural, showing another suit.
- 2 No-Trumps shows a one-suiter with stoppers in two outside suits.
- 3 Clubs shows a one-suiter with a stopper in one outside suit.

2 Hearts and 2 Spades are natural, showing at least five cards in the suit bid; opener is allowed to pass.

2 No-Trumps shows controls in the other suits and is forcing.

THE TWO NO-TRUMP OPENING

This shows a balanced hand of 21-22 points.

Responses

3 Clubs requires opener to bid 3 Diamonds. If responder has a weak hand with length in diamonds, responder passes 3 Diamonds, while bids of 3 Hearts or 3 Spades show a poor hand with length in the suit bid. Opener is expected to pass 3 Hearts or 3 Spades unless an exceptional fit with responder is held.

3 Diamonds asks opener to show a major.

3 Hearts is natural and forcing.

3 Spades is natural and forcing.

THE THREE CLUB OPENING

This shows a club one-suiter with at least seven winners, of which one must be in an outside suit. Responder bids stoppers up-the-line.

THE TWO DIAMOND OPENING

This shows a three-suiter, 4-4-4-1 shape and 17-24 points.

Responses

2 Hearts is conventional and normally promises a positive response. Opener's rebid shows which singleton is held and whether the hand lies in the 17-20 range or the 21-24 range. 2 Hearts may occasionally be used on a negative response, provided, however, that responder holds at least two four-card suits.

2 Spades shows less than six points and four spades. Exceptionally one may bid 2 Spades on a three-card suit as it is intended to be a sign-off.

2 No-Trumps shows an undisclosed six-card suit headed by two honours including either the ace or the king.

3-of-a-suit shows a six-card suit headed by the ace or the king (no second honour) or by the Q-J.

SLAM BIDDING METHODS

This generally proceeds by means of multi-cuebids. Once a suit has been agreed, a player who wishes to initiate a slam try makes a cue-bid in the cheapest available suit. For example:

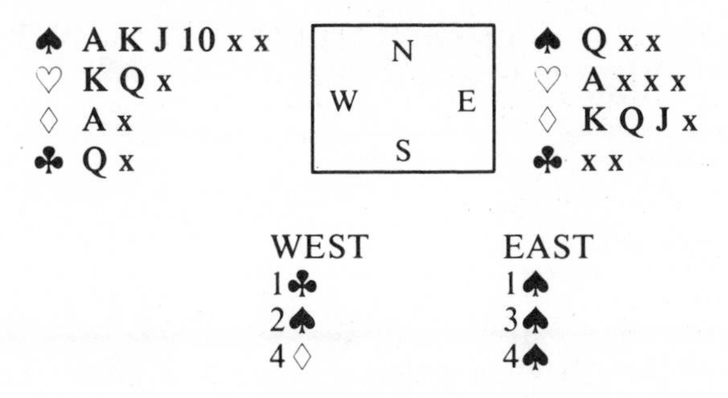

In this case East signs off in 4 Spades and does not make the 4 Heart cue-bid since he knows there are two club losers because of West's failure to cue-bid 4 Clubs. Had West held first- or second-round control in clubs, he would have cue-bid 4 Clubs, not 4 Diamonds.

Another cornerstone for slam bidding is the use of 4 No-Trumps. This bid will be Blackwood only if made as a jump bid or, in some situations, on the second round of bidding. In all other cases, 4 No-Trumps asks partner to show any extra values held or to clarify his hand as best he can.

Sometimes 4 No-Trumps is not merely an enquiry but is significant in a cue-bidding sequence. For example:

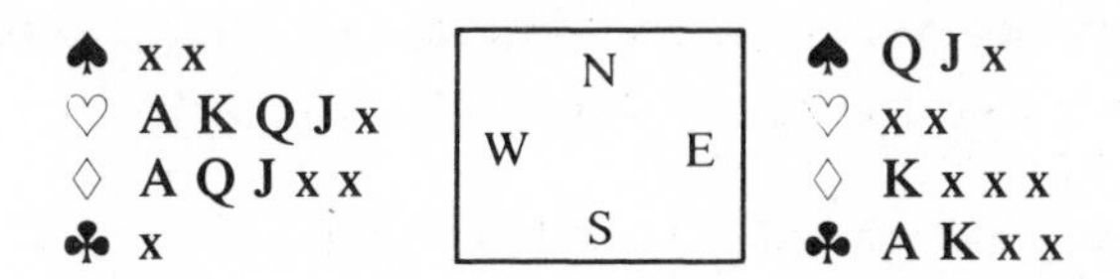

If West had held first- or second-round control in spades, he would have bid 4 Spades, not 4 No-Trumps. Thus 4 No-Trumps denied spade control and East, knowing that the partnership is off two top spades, is content to sign off in 5 Diamonds without cue-bidding 5 Clubs.

II. THE ROMAN CLUB

The Roman Club follows canape principles, i.e. bidding the shorter suit first. The second suit bid is always at least five cards long while the first is normally four but can exceptionally be a three-card suit.

OPENING WITH A BALANCED HAND

1♣ (a) 12-16 points, or
(b) 21-22 points, or
(c) 25-26 points.

1NT 17-20 points

2NT 23-24 points

Responses to the One Club opening

1♢ Artificial negative, 0-9 points.
Opener rebids as follows:
With (a): A four-card major (bidding hearts with 4-4 in the majors), else 1NT.
With (b): 2NT
With (c): 3NT

1♡/1♠ Shows a biddable suit and at least 9 points.
Opener rebids as follows:
With (a): 1♠, 1NT or a raise to the two-level with 12-14 points. Two of a new suit, not clubs, with 15-16 points.
With (b): 2NT. On the next round opener can specify the strength and the degree of support by steps (see later).

2♣/2♢ Shows a biddable suit and at least 9 points.
Opener rebids as follows:
With (a): Two of a suit with 12-14 points, 2NT with 15-16.
With (b): Jump in NT.

1NT Balanced hand of 12-15 points.
Opener rebids as follows:
With (a): Two of a major with 12-13 points. With no major to show, bid 2♢. With 14-16 points, bid 2NT.
With (b): Jump in NT.

2NT	Shows a balanced hand and at least 16 points. Opener rebids in steps: 3♢ = 12-13 points 3♡ = 14 points 3♠ = 15 points 3NT = 16 points
2♡/2♠	Shows five or more cards in the suit bid, headed by at least two of the top three honours and a minimum of 12 high card points. Opener rebids in steps: Step 1 = 12-13 points, no support for partner's suit Step 2 = 12-13 points with support Step 3 = 14-16 points without support Step 4 = 14-16 points with support

Note that in making step responses one must bypass the club step, i.e. the cheapest club bid does not count as a step and has a separate meaning.

Responses to the 1NT opening

2♣	Artificial negative. Opener is required to bid 2♢ and the next action by responder is a sign-off.
2♢	Artificial enquiry with interest in opener's major suits. Opener rebids as follows: 2♡ or 2♠ with 17-18 points and four cards in the bid major. 2NT with 17-18 points and no four-card major. 3♢ with 19-20 points and no four-card major. 3♡ or 3♠ with 19-20 points and four cards in the bid major. 3NT with 19-20 points and 4-4 in the majors.
2♡/2♠ 3♣/3♢	These are all forcing to game and show at least five cards in the bid suit. Opener specifies the hand strength and the degree of support for responder by steps in the same manner as after the 1 Club opening.
2NT/3NT	Natural, with no interest in the major suits.

Responses to the 2NT opening

3♣	Artificial, asking opener to bid four-card suits up-the-line. Indicates slam interest.
3♢	Artificial enquiry for the majors.
3♡/3♠	Natural, showing at least a five-card suit.
3NT	To play.

OPENING WITH AN UNBALANCED HAND

1♣ (a) 17-20 points with four clubs and a second suit at least five cards long. Over any response opener rebids in clubs.

(b) Artificial on any shape with no more than three losers. Over any response, opener shows this type with a jump in a new suit and responder, if the initial response was 1 ♢ or 1NT, shows the degree of support held for opener's suit with 9 steps:
Step 1 = two or three cards, jack high or worse
Step 2 = singleton or void
Step 3 = top honour singleton or doubleton
Step 4 = top honour tripleton
Step 5 = four cards, jack high or worse
Step 6 = four cards including one top honour
Step 7 = two or three cards with two top honours
Step 8 = four cards with two top honours
Step 9 = all three top honours

1♢/1♡/1♠ At least 12 points counting distribution. One- or two-suited. The suit opened is taken to be at least four cards long.

2♣ Artificial. 12-16 points and three-suited (4-4-4-1 or 5-4-4-0), but no five-card major.

2♢ 17-20 points and the same shapes as for the 2♣ opening.

2♡/2♠ 12-16 points, five or more cards in the suit bid and at least four clubs.

3♣ and higher bids are normal pre-empts.

Responses to the 1 Diamond, 1 Heart and 1 Spade openings

NEGATIVE RESPONSES (0-9 points):
Bidding the next step up, either the next higher suit or 1NT over 1 Spade.
Simple raise
Bidding game in opener's major

Opener's choice of rebids are:

Weak 12-14 points: Rebid of suit opened or an artificial rebid of 1NT showing five cards in the suit bid artificially by responder.

Ambiguous 12-16 points: Change of suit.

Strong At least 17 points: a jump rebid.

SEMI-POSITIVE RESPONSES

1NT (except after a 1♠ opening) shows a balanced hand with 12-15 points.
Simple change of suit or a jump to 2 of the negative suit (e.g. 1♡ : 2♠).

ABSOLUTELY POSITIVE RESPONSES

2NT shows a balanced hand of at least 16 points.
Jump raise of opener's suit includes two top honours and five or more trumps.
Jump-shift shows at least 12 points and a solid or semi-solid suit.

Responses to the 2 Club and 2 Diamond openings

The artificial positive response is 2NT.

Opener shows the short suit and responder then:

- With no slam ambitions, signs off in game.
- With slam ambitions, bids a suit below game, setting that suit as trumps.

In this case opener clarifies his hand by step bids, excluding as a step the next no-trumps bid which is reserved to show a void:
Step 1 = Minimum hand and weak in responder's suit
Step 2 = Minimum hand and two top honours in support of responder's suit
Step 3 = Maximum hand and weak support
Step 4 = Maximum hand and strong support

Any initial response other than 2NT is a sign-off from responder's point of view. If responder has bid opener's short suit, opener bids the next suit up (bidding 2NT over 2♠). When opener has support for responder's suit, opener passes with a minimum hand (or after a 2♢ opening, opener may take a view and bid on), or with a maximum, bids the short suit (but bids 2NT if the short suit is the next step up, as bidding the next step up would deny a fit with responder's suit).

Responding to the 2 Heart and 2 Spade openings

The artificial positive response is 2NT after which opener rebids as follows:

3♣	With 5-4-2-2 shape
3-of-opener's suit	With 6-4-2-1 shape
3NT	With 5-5-2-1 shape
3-in-a-new-suit	With 5-4-3-1 shape, the new suit being the fragment
4♣	With 5-5 shape and 3 cards in the other major
4♢	With 5-5 shape and 3 cards in Diamonds

After opener's rebid responder can sign off in game or commence an enquiry with slam ambitions.

All responses other than 2NT are natural.

SLAM METHODS

If using a cue-bid or an asking bid (via a jump), the replies are in steps:
Step 1 = No control
Step 2 = Singleton
Step 3 = King
Step 4 = Ace
Step 5 = Void
Step 6 = Ace and King

To ask for aces and kings, Roman Blackwood uses these responses:
♣ = 0 or 3
♢ = 1 or 4
♡ = 2
♠ = 2 plus a top honour in trumps

THE ARNO CLUB

The Arno Club follows canape principles. The second suit bid is always at least five cards long, while the first is normally four but can exceptionally be made on a three-card suit.

OPENING WITH A BALANCED HAND

1♣	Artificial, 12-16 points
1♢	Artificial, 17-20 points
1NT	21 points or more

Responses to the 1 Club opening

1♢	Artificial, 0-9 points, any shape. Opener rebids with a four-card major (bidding hearts if 4-4 in the majors), otherwise 1NT.
1♡/1♠	At least three cards in the suit bid and 9 or more points. Opener rebids as follows: 1♠, 1NT or a raise to the two-level on 12-14 points 2♣ as an artificial force to game on 15-16 points
2♣/2♢	At least five cards in the suit bid and 9 or more points. The suit may be just four cards long or even three, provided that responder holds 12 or more points and plans to bid a new suit on the next round (canape).
1NT	Forcing to game, showing a balanced hand of 12 or more points. Opener rebids as follows: 2-of-a-suit (preferably a major) with 12-14 points 2NT on 15-16 points
2♡/2♠	Forcing to game and showing a solid or semi-solid suit at least six cards long, 12 or more points. Opener rebids in steps: Step 1 = 12-14 points, no support for partner Step 2 = 12-14 points with support Step 3 = 15-16 points, no support Step 4 = 15-16 points with support Support must include at least one top honour in responder's suit.

Responses to the 1 Diamond opening

After any response a balanced hand is shown by a rebid in No-Trumps and subsequent bidding is developed along natural lines.

The most common auction in this area is a response of 1 Heart (artificial, 0-9 points) followed by a 1 No-Trump rebid by opener, after which responder has the following options, other than passing:

2♣ Artificial negative. Opener is required to bid 2♢, after which responder's next action is a sign-off.

2♢ Artificial, with interest in the majors. Opener rebids:
2♡ or 2♠ with four cards in the suit bid, 17-18 points
2NT with no four-card major and 17-18 points
3♢ with no four-card major and 19-20 points
3♡ or 3♠ with four cards in the suit bid, 19-20 points
3NT with both four-card majors

2♡/2♠ At least a five-card suit, game-forcing

2NT/3NT Natural, with no interest in the majors

Responses to the 1 No-Trump opening

Responder shows how many aces are held by steps:
2♣ = No ace
2♢ = One ace, and so on.

Opener rebids as follows:
2NT with 21-24 points, not forcing
2-in-a-suit with at least 25 points, game-forcing

OPENING WITH AN UNBALANCED HAND

1♣ 17-20 points with a one-suiter (six or more clubs) or with four clubs at least and a five-card or longer suit outside, with this restriction: clubs cannot be the longer suit. Opener rebids in the longer suit at a level higher than that used to show the balanced hand type.

1♢/1♡/1♠ 12-20 points, with a one-suiter, a two-suiter or a 5-4-4-0 shape containing a good five-card major. A major-suit opening promises at least four cards but 1 Diamond might be artificial as it can include these possibilities:
12-16 points and six or more clubs, or
15-16 points and a five-card or longer major

1NT	Artificial, 21 points or more, any shape
2♣	Artificial, 12-16 points, 4-4-4-1 or 5-4-4-0 (5-card minor)
2♢	Artificial, 17-20 points, same shapes as for 2♣
2♡/2♠	15-16 points with five cards in the suit bid and four clubs. As the distribution becomes more unbalanced, the high card strength requirements can be reduced.
2NT	Artificial, 12-16 points, at least 5-5 in Clubs and Diamonds
3♣/3♢	Solid six-card suit with no outside values

3♡ and higher bids are normal pre-empts.

Responses to the 1 Diamond, 1 Heart and 1 Spade openings

These are divided into "negative", "limit", "forcing for one round" and "forcing to game" responses.

NEGATIVE RESPONSES (0-9 points)

Next step up, i.e. the next higher suit or 1NT over 1♠
A simple raise = 4-9 points (but 1♢ : 2♢ = 8-9 points)
Jump to game in a major suit

Opener rebids as follows:

Weak	12-14 points: rebid of opener's suit or an artificial rebid of 1NT after a 1♠ response to 1♡ to show length in spades
Ambiguous	12-16 points: Bidding a suit lower in rank than the suit opened or rebidding the diamond suit
Medium	15-16 points: Bidding a suit higher ranking than the suit opened
Strong	17-20 points, making a jump rebid

LIMIT RESPONSES (10-11 points)

Jump raise to the three-level in a major suit

RESPONSES FORCING FOR ONE ROUND

A simple change of suit or two of the negative suit (1♡ : 2♠).

Strong rebids are shown by changing suit to a higher ranking suit or raising a higher ranking suit or any jump rebid.

Weaker rebids are shown by rebidding the first suit or changing suit to a lower ranking suit.

GAME FORCING RESPONSES (12 or more points)

1NT (except after an opening of 1 Spade) to show a balanced hand.
A jump-shift to show a solid or semi-solid suit, at least six cards long.

Responses to the 1 No-Trump opening

After having shown aces with the first response (see above), responder must do the utmost to show the most important distributional features of the hand. Later the strength can be clarified, culminating in a cuebid if appropriate.

Responses to the 2 Club and 2 Diamond openings

The artificial positive response, forcing to game, is 2NT.

Opener then shows the short suit and responder:
With no slam ambitions, signs off in game.
With slam ambitions, sets the trump suit by bidding it below game-level. Opener then makes a step rebid, excluding the No-Trump bid which is reserved to show a void:

Step 1 = Minimum strength, weak in responder's suit
Step 2 = Minimum strength, two top honours in responder's suit
Step 3 = Maximum strength and weak support
Step 4 = Maximum strength and strong support

Any response other than 2NT is intended as a signoff by responder.
If short in responder's suit, opener bids next suit up (2NT over 2♠).
With support for responder, opener passes with a minimum (or he may take a view and bid on after a 2♢ opening), but with a maximum, opener bids his short suit, bidding No-Trumps if the short suit coincides with the next suit up (as this bid would deny support for responder).

Responses to the 2 Heart and 2 Spade openings

The artificial positive response, forcing to game, is 2NT.

Opener rebids as follows:
Repeating the suit opened shows a 6-4 shape
Bidding clubs shows five-cards in that suit
Bidding the three-card suit with a 5-4-3-1 shape
Bidding 3NT with 5-4-2-2

If responder has no slam ambitions, responder signs off in game. If responder does have slam ambitions, responder supports one of the suits shown with the opening bid or bids the cheapest new suit (as a cue-bid), the distinction between these actions being based on the principle of economy.

All responses other than 2NT are natural. In particular, bidding the other major is forcing for one round.

Responses to the 2 No-Trump opening

All bids are natural. Bidding a major suit normally implies a six-card suit and is forcing for one round.

SLAM METHODS

Other than cue-bids, of which mention has already been made, Blackwood is used to ask for aces and kings. The responses are:
♣ = 0 or 3 ♢ = 1 or 4 ♡ = 2 ♠ = 2 and a void.

The jump to 5 No-Trumps is a grand slam try. Partner bids seven with two of the top three honours.

HISTORY OF THE BLUE TEAM AND THE WORLD TEAMS CHAMPIONSHIPS

Italy's first international success occurred in 1951 with victory in the European Open Teams Championship in Venice. That team consisted of Paolo Baroni, Eugenio Chiaradia, Pietro Forquet, Mario Franco, Augusto Ricci and Guglielmo Siniscalco, with Carlo Alberto Perroux as non-playing captain. In the same year this team played against the United State at Venice for the world title but was soundly defeated.

In the following years, up to 1955, Italy despite several excellent placings did not manage to win the European Championship again.

In 1956 the team that came to be known as the "Blue Team" was formed. Its members were Walter Avarelli, Giorgio Belladonna, Eugenio Chiaradia, Mimmo D'Alelio, Pietro Forquet and Guglielmo Siniscalco, with Carlo Alberto Perroux as non-playing captain.

1956
Stockholm

After a dramatic struggle against France, the Blue Team won the European Championship and with it the right to contest the 1957 World Championship.

1957
New York

Italy won the Bermuda Bowl, the World Teams Championship.

The details of the result and the line-ups were:

Italy defeated the United States by a total of 10,150 rubber bridge points.

ITALY	UNITED STATES
Walter Avarelli	Charles H. Goren
Giorgio Belladonna	Boris Koytchou
Eugenio Chiaradia	Peter Leventritt
Mimmo D'Alelio	Harold Ogust
Pietro Forquet	William Seamon
Guglielmo Siniscalco	Helen Sobel
Non-playing captain:	*Non-playing captain:*
C. Alberto Perroux	R. L. Miles, Jr.

Vienna

With exactly the same team, Italy won the European Championship and with it the right to contest the World Championship in 1958.

1958
Como

Italy won its second Bermuda Bowl, the World Teams Championship.

For the first time in the history of the World Championship, the South American zone was represented, in addition to the winners of the North American zone and the European Championship. Argentina, the United States and Italy competed in a round robin.

These are the details of the results and the line-ups:

Italy defeated the United States by 211 to 174 (old Match Points).
Italy defeated Argentina by 239 to 167.
United States defeated Argentina by 255 to 193.

ITALY	UNITED STATES	ARGENTINA
W. Avarelli	B. Jay Becker	Alberto Blousson
G. Belladonna	John R. Crawford	Carlos Cabanne*
E. Chiaradia	George Rapee	Ricardo Calvente
M. D'Alelio	Alvin Roth	Alejandro Castro*
P. Forquet	Sidney Silodor	Marcelo Lerner
G. Siniscalco	Tobias Stone	*Co-captains
Non-playing captain:	*Non-playing captain:*	
C. A. Perroux	J. G. Ripstra	

Oslo

Still with the same team, Italy won the European Championship and with it the right to contest the World Championship of 1959.

1959
New York

Italy won the Bermuda Bowl,the World Teams Championship for the third

Italy won its third Bermuda Bowl, the World Teams Championship.

These are the details of the results and the line-ups:

Italy defeated the United States by 233 to 183 (old Match Points)
Italy defeated Argentina by 218 to 178
United States defeated Argentina by 252 to 209

ITALY	UNITED STATES	ARGENTINA
W. Avarelli	Harry Fishbein	Alberto Berisso
G. Belladonna	Sam Fry jr.	Ricardo Calvente
E. Chiaradia	Leonard Harmon	Alejandro Castro
M. D'Alelio	Lee Hazen	Carlos Dibar
P. Forquet	Sidney Lazard	Arturo Jaques
G. Siniscalco	Ivar Stakgold	Egisto Rocchi
Non-playing captain:	*Non-playing captain:*	*Non-playing captain:*
C. A. Perroux	Charles J. Solomon	Luis Santa Coloma

Palermo

Italy won the European Championship and with it the right to contest the World Championship in 1961. This was because in 1960 the World Bridge Federation staged the inaugural World Teams Olympiad.

1960
Turin

The first World Teams Olympiad. Thirty-six teams participated, divided into three sections of twelve. The two leading teams from each section qualified for the final. Italy won its qualifying section but could finish no better than sixth and last in the final.

The Olympiad was won by the French team of Rene Bacherich, Gerard Bourchtoff, Claude Delmouly, Pierre Ghestem, Pierre Jais and Roger Trezel, with Robert de Nexon as non-playing captain.

The Italian team, including four Blue Team members, was Walter Avarelli, Giorgio Belladonna, Roberto Bianchi, Eugenio Chiaradia, Pietro Forquet and Giancarlo Manca.

1961
Buenos Aires

Italy won its fourth Bermuda Bowl, the World Teams Championship.

These are the details of the results and the line-ups:

Italy defeated Argentina by 422 to 283.
Italy defeated France by 370 to 261.
Italy defeated North America by 382 to 264.
North America defeated Argentina by 411 to 284.
North America defeated France by 262 to 236.
France defeated Argentina by 339 to 287.

ITALY

W. Avarelli
G. Belladonna
E. Chiaradia
M. D'Alelio
P. Forquet
B. Garozzo

Non-playing captain:
C. A. Perroux

NORTH AMERICA

John Gerber
Paul Hodge
Norman Kay
Peter Leventritt
Howard Schenken
Sidney Silodor

Non-playing captain:
Frank T. Westcott

FRANCE

Rene Bacherich
Claude Deruy
Pierre Ghestem
Jose Le Dentu
Roger Trezel

Non-playing captain:
Robert de Nexon

ARGENTINA

Jorje Bosco
Ricardo Calvente
Alejandro Castro
Hector Cramer
Carlos Dibar
Egisto Rocchi

Non-playing captain:
Carlos Cabanne

The three competing teams had become four. The qualifying formula had been changed so that the winner of the preceding Bermuda Bowl had the right to compete in the next championship to defend its title.

Thus Italy competed as the winner of the 1959 World Championship and France, second in the 1959 European Championship behind Italy, was admitted as the European zone representative.

The Blue Team also changed its composition. In place of Guglielmo Siniscalco, whose business commitments prevented him from devoting time to competitive bridge, Benito Garozzo entered the team.

At the start of this year the Blue Team declined to contest the European Championship since we had automatically qualified for the next World Championship.

1962
New York

Italy won its fifth Bermuda Bowl, the World Teams Championship.

These are the details of the results and the line-ups:

Italy defeated Argentina by 420 to 328.
Italy defeated Great Britain by 365 to 286.
Italy defeated North America by 331 to 305.
North America defeated Argentina by 400 to 242.
North America defeated Great Britain by 345 to 332.
Great Britain defeated Argentina by 318 to 311.

ITALY

W. Avarelli
G. Belladonna
E. Chiaradia
M. D'Alelio
P. Forquet
B. Garozzo

Non-playing captain:
C. A. Perroux

NORTH AMERICA

Charles Coon
Mervin Key
Lew Mathe
Eric Murray
G. Robert Nail
Ron von der Porten

Non-playing captain:
John Gerber

GREAT BRITAIN

Nico Gardener
Kenneth Konstam
Anthony Priday
Claude Rodrigue
Albert Rose
Alan Truscott

Non-playing captain:
Louis Tarlo

ARGENTINA

Luis Attaguile
Alberto Berisso
Carlos Cabanne
Ricardo Calvente
Arturo Jaques
Egisto Rocchi

Non-playing captain:
Desiderio Blum

1963
St. Vincent

Italy won its sixth Bermuda Bowl, the World Teams Championship.

These are the details of the results and the line-ups:

Italy defeated Argentina by 372 to 282.
Italy defeated France by 421 to 236.
Italy defeated North America by 313 to 294.
North America defeated France by 340 to 251.
North America defeated Argentina by 496 to 261.
France defeated Argentina by 453 to 319.

ITALY

G. Belladonna
E. Chiaradia
M. D'Alelio
P. Forquet
B. Garozzo
C. Pabis-Ticci

Non-playing captain:
C. A. Perroux

NORTH AMERICA

James Jacoby
Robert Jordan
Peter Leventritt
G. Robert Nail
Arthur Robinson
Howard Schenken

Non-playing captain:
John Gerber

FRANCE

Rene Bacherich
Gerard Desrousseaux
Pierre Ghestem
Jacques Stetten
Georges Theron
Leon Tintner

Non-playing captain:
Robert de Nexon

ARGENTINA

Luis Attaguile
Ricardo Calvente
Egisto Rocchi
Marcos Santamarina
Alfredo Saravia
Luis A. Schenone

Non-playing captain:
Guillermo Malbran

As it was impossible for Walter Avarelli to participate in the championship, Carlo Alberto Perroux replaced him with Camillo Pabis-Ticci.

1964
New York

Italy won the 2nd World Teams Olympiad.

After the qualifying rounds in which 29 teams took part, Canada, England, Italy and the United States qualified for the semi-finals.

These are the details of the results and the line-ups:

Semi-finals:
Italy defeated Great Britain by 126 to 120.
United States defeated Canada by 133 to 117.

Final:
Italy defeated United States by 158 to 112.

ITALY
W. Avarelli
G. Belladonna
M. D'Alelio
P. Forquet
B. Garozzo
C. Pabis-Ticci
Non-playing captains:
C. A. Perroux and Sergio Osella

GREAT BRITAIN
Jeremy Flint
Maurice Harrison-Gray
Kenneth Konstam
Terence Reese
Boris Schapiro
Joel Tarlo
Non-playing captain:
Sidney Lee

UNITED STATES
Robert D. Hamman
Robert Jordan
Donald P. Krauss
Victor Mitchell
Arthur G. Robinson
Samuel M. Stayman
Non-playing captain:
Frank T. Westcott

CANADA
Ralph Cohen
R. Forbes
Sam Gold
Jack Howell
Sammy R. Kehela
Eric R. Murray
Non-playing captain:
A. M. Lando

Walter Avarelli returned to the team replacing Eugenio Chiaradia who had moved to Brazil.

1965
Buenos Aires

Italy won its seventh Bermuda Bowl, the World Teams Championship.

These are the details of the results and the line-ups:

Italy defeated Argentina 325 to 237.
Italy defeated Great Britain by 354 to 233.
Italy defeated North America by 304 to 230.
North America defeated Argentina 359 to 250.
North America defeated Great Britain by forfeit.
Argentina defeated Great Britain by forfeit.

ITALY

W. Avarelli
G. Belladonna
M. D'Alelio
P. Forquet
B. Garozzo
C. Pabis-Ticci

Non-playing captains:
Sergio Osella and C. A. Perroux

NORTH AMERICA

B. Jay Becker
Ivan Erdos
Dorothy Hayden
Peter Leventritt
Kelsey Petterson
Howard Schenken

Non-playing captain:
John Gerber

GREAT BRITAIN

Terence Reese
Jeremy Flint
Maurice Harrison-Gray
Kenneth Konstam
Albert Rose
Boris Schapiro

Non-playing captain:
Ralph Swimer

ARGENTINA

Luis Attaguile
Alberto Berisso
Carlos Cabanne
Marcelo Lerner
Egisto Rocchi
Agustin Santamarina

Non-playing captain:
Eduardo Marquardt

1966
St. Vincent

Italy won its eighth Bermuda Bowl, the World Teams Championship.

A fifth competitor was added to the Bermuda Bowl Championship to represent the Asian zone and this was Thailand.

These are the details of the results and the line-ups:

Italy defeated North America by 319 to 262.
Italy defeated Holland by 326 to 198.
Italy defeated Thailand by 486 to 143.
Italy defeated Venezuela by 362 to 203.
North America defeated Holland by 477 to 243.
North America defeated Thailand by 359 to 234.
North America defeated Venezuela by 398 to 260.
Venezuela defeated Holland by 331 to 247.
Venezuela defeated Thailand by 326 to 290.
Holland defeated Thailand by 293 to 230.

ITALY

W. Avarelli
G. Belladonna
M. D'Alelio
P. Forquet
B. Garozzo
C. Pabis-Ticci

Non-playing captain:
C. A. Perroux

NORTH AMERICA

P. Feldesman
R. Hamman
S. Kehela
L. Mathe
E. Murray
I. Rubin

Non-playing captain:
J. Rosenblum

VENEZUELA

R. Benaim
D. Berah
M. Onorati
R. Rossignol
R. Straziota
F. Vernon

Non-playing captain:
J. Albert

HOLLAND

R. Blitzblum
P. Boender
H. Kreyns
L. Oudshoorn
R. De Leeuw
C. Slavenburg

Non-playing captain:
G. Kramer

THAILAND

A. Boonsupa
E. Gaan
B. Gimkiewicz
H. Istenveli
S. Nandhabiwat
T. Raengkhan (Capt.)

1967
Miami Beach

1967 saw the retirement from the bridge scene of Carlo Alberto Perroux, the mentor and captain of the Blue Team. His position was taken over in Miami by Guido Barbone.

Italy won its ninth Bermuda Bowl, the World Teams Championship.

The format of the championship was altered so that the five teams would play a qualifying round robin after which the two leading teams would play off in a final.

These are the details of the results and the line-ups:

Qualifying rounds:

1st	Italy	170 points
2nd	North America	161 points
3rd	France	132 points
4th	Thailand	73 points
5th	Venezuela	64 points

Final:

Italy defeated North America by 338 to 227.

ITALY

W. Avarelli
G. Belladonna
M. D'Alelio
P. Forquet
B. Garozzo
C. Pabis-Ticci

Non-playing captain:
Guido Barbone

NORTH AMERICA

E. Kaplan
N. Kay
S. Kehela
E. Murray
W. Root
A. Roth

Non-playing captain:
J. Rosenblum

FRANCE

J. M. Boulenger
J. Pariente
J. M. Roudinesco
J. Stetten
H. Svarc
L. Tintner

Non-playing captain:
R. Huni

THAILAND

A. Boonsupa
E. Gaan
B. Gimkiewicz
S. Nandhabiwat
K. W. Shen
C. Sitajitt

Non-playing captain:
H. Lau

VENEZUELA

R. Benaim
D. Berah (Captain)
E. Loynaz
M. Romanelli
R. Rossignol
F. Vernon

Non-playing captain:
R. Chapin

1968
Deauville

Italy won the third World Teams Olympiad.

After a qualifying round in which 33 teams took part, Canada, Holland, Italy and the United States qualified for the semi-finals.

These are the details of the results and the line-ups:

Semi-finals:
Italy defeated Canada by 171 to 120.
United States defeated Holland by 174 to 142.

Final:
Italy defeated the United States by 172 to 123.

ITALY
W. Avarelli
G. Belladonna
M. D'Alelio
P. Forquet
B. Garozzo
C. Pabis-Ticci
Non-playing captain:
A. Tracanella

UNITED STATES
R. Jordan
N. Kay
E. Kaplan
A. Robinson
W. Root
A. Roth
Non-playing captain:
J. Rosenblum

HOLLAND
J. Kokkes
H. Kreyns
M. Rebattu
M. J. Rebattu
C. Slavenburg
A. van Heusden
Non-playing captain:
C. van Calcar

CANADA
G. Charney
W. J. Crissey
C. Bruce Elliott
S. R. Kehela
E. R. Murray
P. E. Sheardown
Non-playing captain:
A. Lando

1969
Rio de Janeiro

Italy won its tenth Bermuda Bowl, the World Teams Championship.

These are the details of the results and the line-ups:

Qualifying rounds:

1. Italy	185 points
2. Taiwan	166 points
3. North America	141 points
4. France	126 points
5. Brazil	116 points

Final:

Italy defeated Taiwan by 429 to 182.

ITALY
W. Avarelli
G. Belladonna
M. D'Alelio
P. Forquet
B. Garozzo
C. Pabis-Ticci
Non-playing captain:
A. Tracanella

TAIWAN
F. Huang
P. Huang
C. S. Shen
K. W. Shen
K. Suchartkul
M. Tai
Non-playing captain:
C. C. Wei

NORTH AMERICA
W. Eisenberg
R. Goldman
R. Hamman
E. Kantar
S. Lazard
G. Rapee
Non-playing captain:
O. Jacoby

FRANCE
J. M. Boulenger
G. Desrousseaux
J. Stetten
H. Svarc
G. Theron
L. Tintner
Non-playing captain:
R. Huni

BRAZIL
P. Assumpcao
M. Branco
G. Chagas
D. Coutinho
R. Mello
A. Porto D'Ave
Non-playing captain:
P. Brum de Barros

1970
Stockholm

These are the details of the results and the line-ups:

Qualifying rounds:

1. North America	229 points
2. Taiwan	151 points
3. Brazil	136 points
4. Norway	118 points
5. Italy	105 points

Final:

North America defeated Taiwan by 308 to 167.

NORTH AMERICA

W. Eisenberg
R. Goldman
R. Hamman
J. Jacoby
M. Lawrence
R. Wolff

Non-playing captain:
O. Jacoby

TAIWAN

C. Cheng
E. Hsiao
P. Huang
H. Lin
M. F. Tai

Non-playing captain:
D. Mao

BRAZIL

P. Assumpcao
P. P. de Barros
E. Bastos
G. Chagas
O. G. de Faria
S. M. Ferreira

Non-playing captain:
E. Amaral

NORWAY

E. Hoie
T. Jensen
K. Koppang
B. Larsen
A. Strom
W. Varnas

Non-playing captain:
B. Baardsen

ITALY

G. Barbarisi
E. Cesati
B. De Ritis
V. La Galla
A. Morini
R. Tersch

Non-playing captain:
A. Tracanella

1971
Taipei

These are the details of the results and the line-ups:

Qualifying rounds:

1. Dallas "Aces"	228 points
2. France	182 points
3. Australia	154 points
4. Taiwan	118 points
5. Brazil	103 points
6. North America	98 points

Final:

The Dallas "Aces" defeated France by 243 to 182.

DALLAS "ACES"
W. Eisenberg
R. Goldman
R. Hamman
J. Jacoby
M. Lawrence
R. Wolff
Non-playing captain:
O. Jacoby

FRANCE
J. M. Boulenger
P. Jais
J. M. Roudinesco
J. L. Stoppa
H. Svarc
R. Trezel
Non-playing captain:
R. Huni

AUSTRALIA
J. Borin
N. Borin
R. Cummings
D. Howard
T. Seres
R. Smilde
Non-playing captain:
J. Rothfield

TAIWAN
C. Cheng
S. Chua
E. Hsiao
P. Huang
V. Reyes
M. F. Tai
Non-playing captain:
C. C. Wei

BRAZIL
E. Amaral
P. Assumpcao
G. Chagas
G. Cintra
A. Porto D'Ave
T. Kenedi
Non-playing captain:
A. Truscott

NORTH AMERICA
E. Kaplan
N. Kay
D. Krauss
L. Mathe
J. Swanson
D. Walsh
Non-playing captain:
L. Hazen

1972
Miami

Italy won the fourth World Teams Olympiad.

After a qualifying round in which 39 teams took part, Canada, France, Italy and the United States qualified for the semi-finals.

These are the details of the results and the line-ups:

Semi-finals:

Italy defeated France by 178 to 88.
United States defeated Canada by 203 to 85.

Final:

Italy defeated the United States by 203 to 138.

ITALY

W. Avarelli
G. Belladonna
M. D'Alelio
P. Forquet
B. Garozzo
C. Pabis-Ticci

Non-playing captain:
U. Barsoti

UNITED STATES

R. Goldman
R. Hamman
J. Jacoby
M. Lawrence
P. Soloway
R. Wolff

Non-playing captain:
L. Hazen

FRANCE

G. Bourchtoff
P. Chemla
C. Delmouly
J. Klotz
M. Lebel
D. Leclery

Non-playing captain:
R. Bacherich

CANADA

G. Charney
W. Crissey
S. Kehela
E. Murray
B. Gowdy
D. Phillips

Non-playing captain:
A. Lando

1973
Guaruja, Brazil

Italy won its eleventh Bermuda Bowl, the World Teams Championship.

These are the details of the results and the line-ups:

Qualifying rounds:

1. Dallas "Aces"	177 points
2. Italy	176 points
3. Brazil	148 points
4. North America	140 points
5. Indonesia	101 points

Final:

Italy defeated the Dallas "Aces" by 333 to 205.

ITALY

G. Belladonna
B. Bianchi
P. Forquet
G. Garabello
B. Garozzo
V. Pittala

Non-playing captain:
S. Salvetti

DALLAS "ACES"

M. Blumenthal
R. Goldman
R. Hamman
J. Jacoby
M. Lawrence
R. Wolff

Non-playing captain:
I. G. Corn, Jr.

BRAZIL

P. Assumpcao
M. Branco
P. Branco
G. Chagas
G. Cintra
C. Fonseca

Non-playing captain:
A. Porto D'Ave

NORTH AMERICA

B. J. Becker
M. Becker
A. Bernstein
J. Rubens
P. Soloway
J. Swanson

Non-playing captain:
R. Stern

INDONESIA

M. Aguw
J. A. Fransz
H. Lasut
E. Najoan
D. Sacul
F. R. Walujan

Non-playing captain:
Ch. A. Bahasuan

1974
Venice

Italy won its twelfth Bermuda Bowl, the World Teams Championship.

These are the details of the results and the line-ups:

Qualifying rounds:

1. Italy	149 points
2. North America	148 points
3. Brazil	111 points
4. Indonesia	82 points
5. France	71 points
6. New Zealand	17 points

Semi-finals:

Italy defeated Indonesia by 233 to 145.
North America defeated Brazil by 173 to 82.

Final:

Italy defeated North America by 195 to 166.

ITALY
G. Belladonna
B. Bianchi
S. De Falco
P. Forquet
A. Franco
B. Garozzo
Non-playing captain:
S. Salvetti

NORTH AMERICA
M. Blumenthal
R. Goldman
R. Hamman
S. Kehela
E. Murray
R. Wolff
Non-playing captain:
I. G. Corn, Jr.

BRAZIL
P. Assumpcao
M. Branco
P. Branco
G. Chagas
G. Cintra
C. Fonseca
Non-playing captains:
G. Vero and S. Apoteker

INDONESIA
M. Aguw
W. D. Karamoy
H. Lasut
F. E. Manoppo
M. F. Manoppo
W. A. Moniaga
Non-playing captain:
D. B. Masengi

FRANCE
J. M. Boulenger
M. Lebel
C. Mari
H. Svarc
Non-playing captain:
C. Deruy

NEW ZEALAND
S. A. Abrahams
R. J. Brightling
M. Cornell
R. P. Kerr
P. H. Marston
J. R. Wignall
Non-playing captain:
F. P. S. Lu

1975
Bermuda

Italy won its thirteenth Bermuda Bowl, the World Teams Championship.

These are the details of the results and the line-ups:

Qualifying rounds:

1. Italy	134 points
2. North America	116 points
3. France	105 points
4. Indonesia	90 points
5. Brazil	73 points

Semi-finals:

Italy defeated Indonesia by 280 to 134.
North America defeated France by 159 to 147.

Final:

Italy defeated North America by 215 to 193.

ITALY

G. Belladonna
G. Facchini
A. Franco
B. Garozzo
V. Pittala
S. Zucchelli

Non-playing captain:
S. Salvetti

NORTH AMERICA

W. Eisenberg
R. Hamman
E. Kantar
P. Soloway
J. Swanson
R. Wolff

Non-playing captain:
A. Sheinwold

FRANCE

J. M. Boulenger
M. Lebel
F. Leenhardt
C. Mari
H. Svarc
E. Vial

Non-playing captain:
R. Bacherich

INDONESIA

I. Arwin
H. Lasut
F. Manoppo
M. Manoppo
W. Moniaga
D. Sacul

Non-playing captain:
O. Wullur

BRAZIL

M. Amaral
P. Assumpcao
P. de Barros
G. Chagas
N. Ferreira
S. Ferreira

Non-playing captain:
S. Apoteker

1976
Monte Carlo (Olympiad)

45 teams participated in a complete round robin with no semi-finals or final.

These are the details of the results and the line-ups:

1. Brazil 654 points
2. Italy 648 points
3. Great Britain 646 points
4. Poland 621 points
5. Sweden 615 points
6. France 594 points

BRAZIL

P. Assumpcao
S. Barbosa
M. Branco
G. Chagas
G. Cintra
C. Fonseca

Non-playing captain:
S. Apoteker

ITALY

G. Belladonna
A. Franco
B. Garozzo
C. Mosca
S. Sbarigia
A. Vivaldi

Non-playing captain:
S. Salvetti

GREAT BRITAIN

W. Coyle
J. Flint
T. Priday
C. Rodrigue
I. Rose
R. Sheehan

Non-playing captain:
T. Reese

POLAND

J. Klukowski
M. Kudla
L. Lebioda
A. Macieszczak
A. Milde
A. Wilkosz

Non-playing captain:
M. Frenkiel

SWEDEN

S. O. Flodquist
H. Gothe
T. Gullberg
A. Morath
E. Pyk
P. O. Sundelin

Non-playing captain:
S. E. Berglund

FRANCE

J. M. Boulenger
P. Chemla
M. Lebel
D. Leclery
P. Sussel
H. Svarc

1976
Monte Carlo (Bermuda Bowl)

These are the details of the results and the line-ups:

Qualifying rounds:

1. North America	131 points
2. Italy	119 points
3. Israel	114 points
4. Brazil	109 points
5. Australia	83½ points
6. Hong Kong	32½ points

Final:
North America defeated Italy by 232 to 198.

NORTH AMERICA
W. Eisenberg
F. Hamilton
E. Paulsen
H. Ross
I. Rubin
P. Soloway
Non-playing captain:
D. Morse

ITALY
G. Belladonna
P. Forquet
A. Franco
B. Garozzo
V. Pittala
A. Vivaldi
Non-playing captain:
S. Salvetti

ISRAEL
J. Frydrich
M. Hochzeit
S. Lev
Y. Levit
P. Romik
E. Schaufel
Non-playing captain:
R. Kunin

BRAZIL
P. Assumpcao
M. Branco
P. Branco
G. Chagas
G. Cintra
C. Fonseca
Non-playing captain:
A. Porto D'Ave

AUSTRALIA
R. Cummings
D. Howard
R. Klinger
L. Longhurst
T. Seres
R. Smilde
Non-playing captain:
E. Ramshaw

HONG KONG
A. Chow
Y. L. Chung
R. S. P. Chow
T. S. Lo
L. L. Sung
D. Zen
Non-playing captain:
W. Tsing

1977
Manila

Italy did not qualify for the 1977 World Championship.

These are the details of the results and the line-ups:

Qualifying rounds:

1. Defending Champions	136.75 points
2. North American Challengers	119.75 points
3. Sweden	94.75 points
4. Argentina	91.00 points
5. Australia	79.00 points
6. Taiwan	68.75 points

Final:

The North American Challengers defeated the North American Defending Champions by 245 to 214.5.

NORTH AMERICA

W. Eisenberg
R. Hamman
E. Kantar
P. Soloway
J. Swanson
R. Wolff

Non-playing captain:
R. Stern

DEFENDING CHAMPIONS

F. Hamilton
M. Passell
E. Paulsen
H. Ross
I. Rubin
R. Von der Porten

Non-playing captain:
J. Silverman and E. Theus

SWEDEN

A. Brunzell
S. O. Flodquist
H. Gothe
J. Lindquist
A. Morath
P. O. Sundelin

Non-playing captain:
S. E. Berglund

ARGENTINA

L. Attaguile
C. Cabanne
H. Camberos
M. Monsegur
A. Santamarina
E. Scanavino

Non-playing captain:
A. Berisso

AUSTRALIA

J. Borin
R. Cummings
G. Havas
J. Lathbury
J. Lester
T. Seres

Non-playing captain:
R. Smilde

TAIWAN

C. Cheng
E. Hsiao
P. Huang
C. H. Kuo
H. Lin
M. Tai

Non-playing captain:
D. Mao

1978
New Orleans

There was no Bermuda Bowl World Teams Championship this year as the World Bridge Federation restructured the international bridge calendar so that the Bermuda Bowl would be held in odd-numbered years, the World Teams Olympiad in the Olympic Years and the World Pairs together with the Rosenblum Open Teams in the other even-numbered years. The 1978 Rosenblum Open Teams was won by the Polish team of Marian Frenkiel, Andrzej Macieszczak, Andrzej Wilkosz and Janusz Polec who defeated the Brazilian team of Gabriel Chagas, Pedro Paulo Assumpcao, Gabino Cintra, Marcelo Branco, Roberto Taunay and Sergio Barbosa by 164-80 in the final.

1979
Rio De Janeiro

These are the details of the results and the line-ups:

Qualifying rounds:

1. Italy	180 points
2. North America	176 points
3. Australia	166 points
4. Taiwan	127½ points
5. Central America	123½ points
6. Brazil	108 points

Final:
North America defeated Italy by 253 to 248.

NORTH AMERICA	ITALY	AUSTRALIA
M. Brachman	G. Belladonna	J. Borin
W. Eisenberg	D. De Falco	N. Borin
R. Goldman	A. Franco	R. Cummings
E. Kantar	B. Garozzo	A. Reiner
M. Passell	L. Lauria	R. Richman
P. Soloway	V. Pittala	T. Seres
Non-playing captain:	*Non-playing captains:*	*Non-playing captain:*
E. Theus	G. Barbone/S. Salvetti	D. Howard

TAIWAN	CENTRAL AMERICA	BRAZIL
K. Y. Chen	A. Calvo	P. Assumpcao
P. Huang	A. Dhers	J. Barbosa
C. H. Kuo	S. Hamaoui	M. Branco
S. C. Liu	J. Hand	G. Chagas
M. F. Tai	J. Maduro	G. Cintra
Y. P. Tu	F. Vernon	R. Mello
Non-playing captain:	*Non-playing captain:*	*Non-playing captain:*
A. T. Chong	J. L. Derivery	S. Barbosa

1980
Valkenburg, Netherlands

58 countries participated in the 6th World Teams Olympiad. The teams were divided into two sections of 29 teams, the top four from each section to qualify for the quarter finals. Italy was represented by Benito Garozzo, Lorenzo Lauria, Vito Pittala, Fabio Rosati, Silvio Sbarigia and Antonio Vivaldi, with Salvatore Modica as non-playing captain but failed to reach the quarter-finals. These are the details of the results and the line-ups:

GROUP A		GROUP B	
1. Denmark	419 points	1. France	428 points
2. Brazil	409 points	2. Indonesia	414 points
3. Taiwan	404 points	3. U.S.A.	409 points
4. Netherlands	392 points	4. Norway	405 points
5. Canada	389 points	5. Germany	393 points
6. Great Britain	381 points	6. Italy	373 points
7. Turkey	370 points	7. Australia	372 points
8. Sweden	359½ points	8. Ireland	361 points

Standings after the quarterfinal matches:

BRACKET I		BRACKET II	
1. United States	346 points	1. France	242 points
2. Netherlands	122 points	2. Norway	235 points
3. Denmark	120 points	3. Taiwan	233 points
4. Indonesia	114 points	4. Brazil	10 points

Final:

France defeated the United States by 131 to 111.

FRANCE	UNITED STATES
Paul Chemla	Fred Hamilton
Michel Lebel	Robert Hamman
Christian Mari	Mike Passell
Michel Perron	Ira Rubin
Philippe Soulet	Paul Soloway
Henri Svarc	Robert Wolff
Non-playing captain:	*Non-playing captain:*
Pierre Schemeil	Ira G. Corn

1981
New York

Italy did not qualify for the 1981 World Championship.
These are the details of the results and the line-ups:

Qualifying rounds:

1. United States	160$\frac{1}{2}$	5. Great Britain	142$\frac{1}{2}$
2. Pakistan	151	6. Australia	131
3. Poland	146	7. Indonesia	129
4 Argentina	145		

Semi-finals: United States defeated Poland by 178 to 119.
Pakistan defeated Argentina by 174 to 113$\frac{2}{3}$.

Final: United States defeated Pakistan by 271 to 182$\frac{1}{3}$.

UNITED STATES

R. Arnold
R. Levin
J. Meckstroth
A. E. Reinhold
E. Rodwell
J. Solodar
Non-playing captain:
T. K. Sanders

PAKISTAN

Nishat Abedi
Nisar Ahmed
Munir Ata-Ullah
Jan-e-Alam Fazli
Zia Mahmood
Masood Salim
Non-playing captain:
Sattar Cochinwala

POLAND

A. Jezioro
J. Klukowski
M. Kudla
K. Martens
A. Milde
T. Pryzbora
Non-playing captain:
M. Frenkiel

ARGENTINA

G. Alujas
L. Attaguile
H. Camberos
A. Santamarina
E. Scanavino
D. Zanalda
Non-playing captain:
G. Araujo

GREAT BRITAIN

J. Collings
P. Hackett
S. Lodge
I. Rose
R. Sheehan
T. Sowter
Non-playing captain:
G. Calderwood

AUSTRALIA

R. Cummings
W. Jacobs
P. Lavings
G. Lorentz
T. Seres
D. Smith
Non-playing captain:
D. Howard

INDONESIA

M. Aguw
W. Karamoy
H. Lasut
D. Sacul
F. Waluyan
Y. Wijaya
Non-playing captain:
J. Rimbuan

1982, Biarritz. There was no Bermuda Bowl as this was the year for the World Pairs and the Rosenblum Open Teams. The Rosenblum Open Teams was won by the French team of Albert Feigenbaum, Michel Lebel, Dominique Pilon and Philippe Soulet with Pierre Schemeil as non-playing captain, who defeated the American team of Ed Manfield, Chip Martel, Peter Pender, Hugh Ross, Lew Stansby and Kit Woolsey by 178-161 in the final.